MW01032047

The Roots of Justice

Studies in Legal History

Published by The University of North Carolina Press
in association with the American Society for Legal History

Editor Morris S. Arnold

EDITORIAL ADVISORY BOARD

John D. Cushing
Lawrence M. Friedman
Charles M. Gray
Thomas A. Green
Oscar Handlin

George L. Haskins
J. Willard Hurst
S. F. C. Milsom
Joseph H. Smith
L. Kinvin Wroth

Lawrence M. Friedman

and Robert V. Percival

The Roots of Justice

Crime and Punishment in

Alameda County, California

1870–1910

The University of North Carolina Press

Chapel Hill

© 1981 The University of North Carolina Press

All rights reserved

Manufactured in the United States of America

Library of Congress Cataloging in Publication Data

Friedman, Lawrence M   1930–
  The roots of justice.

  (Studies in legal history)
  Includes index.
    1. Criminal justice, Administration of—California—
Alameda Co.—History.   2. Alameda Co., Calif.—History.
I. Percival, Robert V., joint author. II. Title.
III. Series.
KFC1199.A4F74   345.794'6505   80-29036
ISBN 0-8078-1476-8

To Leah, Jane, Amy, and Sarah
LMF

To my parents
RVP

Contents

Tables

xii | *Tables*

Illustrations

Acknowledgments

The research on this study was supported, and generously, by LEAA Grant No. 75–N1–99–0080, and NSF Grant No. SOC 76–24217. We want to thank both these agencies for their willingness to invest funds in historical study. Final touches and last-minute research were supported by the Law and Behavioral Research Fund of Stanford Law School.

Many students helped us with the research, and we want to thank them, especially Mark Chavez, Thomas Devine, Anne Doolin, Janet Feldman, Jack Gillman, Clifford J. Halverson, Walter Lion, Carol Lombardini, Craig Nelson, Anne Packer, Donald Percival, and Lawrence Ponoroff. We also want to thank Richard Abel, Jonathan Casper, Thomas Grey, Marc Haller, Herbert Jacob, and Sheldon Messinger for their helpful suggestions, and very specially, Stanton Wheeler; also Joseph D. Flagiello, Jr., Mrs. Frances Buxton, George Sumner (Warden of San Quentin), and the following institutions: California State Archives, the Oakland Museum, Oakland Public Library, Stanford Law School Library, especially Myron Jacobstein, Iris Wildman, Joan Howland, and Kathy Shimpock, and the Office of the County Clerk of Alameda County. Mrs. Joy St.John typed draft after draft with great patience and efficiency.

A Note on the Citation of Sources

The reader will note the following conventions: sections of the California Penal Code are cited by section number only; other statutory provisions are cited more fully. Casefiles from the records of the Superior Court of Alameda County are cited with defendant's last name, case number, and the year the case was filed—for example: Jones, no. 1567, 1894.

The Roots of Justice

Chapter 1
An Introductory Word

This is a study of crime and punishment. In every organized community, there is crime and there is punishment. But each community defines crime for itself; each time and place has its own way of chasing criminals and curbing crime. Our study takes one county (Alameda), in one state (California), in a single country (the United States), at one specific period (1870–1910). This is, in other words, a case study. It is a slice of life—a single specimen, dissected and put under the microscope.

Actually, what we have here is even less than a slice of life; it is the merest sliver. Our study deals with what is, after all, one remote corner of civilization, a dot of land in the ocean of history. It is a story where the whole, we hope, is greater than the parts. This is not a study of great men and women, or of great events, or great institutions, or famous places. Hundreds of people parade across these pages, but none is a household word. History does not trumpet the names of A. L. Frick, or Clara Fallmer, or George McClellan, or Christopher Ruess, or Walter Teale. Some of these people, to be sure, were prominent in their day. We will meet a few successful judges or lawyers, some people of substance, some pillars of the church. We will also meet a few notorious villains or notorious victims. But, overwhelmingly, our cast of characters is remarkable only for its utter obscurity—men and women dredged up from the bottom of society, people tangled in the nets of the law; people who stole a purse; or smashed somebody's skull, or tried to; or broke into a store; or picked pockets; or seduced the neighbor's girl; or staggered about drunk in public; or forged a check; or gambled and whored. Most were, on the whole, abject failures: people who chronically mismanaged their lives. Others were innocent bystanders, falsely accused. Still others were warped, antisocial creatures, who preyed on their fellowmen for a living. Still others fell into the hands of the law because they were weak and misguided. Most were, in short, society's losers.

Often, their stories are interesting in themselves. But there are reasons beyond this for disturbing their dust. Crime, its management and punishment, are central tasks in *any* social order, and therefore in the United States as well. In the last generation, crime has become a major issue. The public, or some large part of it, is disgusted, worried, and fearful about crime. People want something done about crime, and the sooner the better.[1]

Crime *is* a problem; a plague on the lives of its victims, and a curse on those trapped by weakness, evil, or vice. Where crime has become a big issue, the spotlight falls on criminal justice too. This is the official, public engine for dealing with crime. Today the system is, on the whole, in confusion and disarray. In any event, hardly anybody has a good word to say about it. On the one side, it is denounced as too biased or paralyzed to do justice, a bundle of dirty rags that spreads infection instead of curing or containing it. On the other side, it is denounced as so slipshod and soft, so flabby and spineless, that offenders wriggle out of its net to prey on the innocent again. The true situation is harder to get at. One thing is clear: to reform the system, one must first understand it. That means, at the very least, some investment in research. Society is beginning, at last, to make that investment. In recent years, there has been an outpouring of studies, reports, articles, and books about crime and criminal justice —more, perhaps, than ever before.

All well and good, and much has been accomplished. But we think it essential to balance pictures of the system as it is with those that show it as it was. Every generation, in a sense, makes its own system of criminal justice. But on the whole, society cuts its products to old designs. The people are new, the events are new; but patterns, templates, and dies have a longer life. They wear out slowly, they change style slowly, they are never discarded all at once. This is not because of laziness, or inertia; it is because felt needs and social forces themselves are slowly turning wheels. The past—at least the immediate past—remains close and familiar, so that we recognize easily its forms and faces, like the photographs of our grandparents in a yellowing scrapbook.

The same but different. Similarities and differences are both important. So many theories, hypotheses, explanations, biases, clichés about crime and punishment have an *implied* historical premise. They assume that something is getting better, or getting worse. They suggest that in days gone by there was no plea bargaining, or less crime, or fewer people in jails, or more arrests. Almost never is there hard data (or even soft data) to back up these propositions. No historical

1. See *New York Times*, June 4, 1976, p. 12, col. 2; John E. Conklin, *The Impact of Crime* (New York, 1975), pp. 76–77; National Data Program for the Social Sciences, *Spring 1975, General Social Survey* (Ann Arbor, 1975), p. 98.

study can really answer tough policy questions; but the study of time past can clear away underbrush, dispel myths, offer clues to what can and ought to be done. In any case, we hope that our picture of crime and punishment in Alameda County from 1870 to 1910 carries a message to the modern world. At a number of points in this book we will make this message clear.

As we said, there is—right now—great interest in crime and criminal justice. But *historical* study of these subjects is another story. We are hardly saturated, to say the least. Out of the tons of books, articles, and monographs on American history, and the tons about criminal justice, that pour out every year, only a handful marry history and criminal justice. The history of crime and punishment (and the police) is beginning—just beginning—to blossom as a "field."[2] Some aspects of the subject do boast a larger literature. Crime sells newspapers; murder sells books; and a few great mysteries (the Lizzie Borden case is one) are rehashed time and again, in popular or scholarly books. It is also easy to fill a good-sized shelf with books about the witchcraft trials in Salem. But despite a long hunt we found *nobody* who tried to do what we did—describe one criminal justice system, in one place, more or less as a whole, from top to bottom, in as much detail as we and the reader could digest. Nobody had explored criminal justice, systematically, for our period: roughly from the Gilded Age to the eve of the First World War. Paradoxically, there are far more pages in print about crime and punishment in colonial Boston than about New York or California, or anywhere, in the age of Garfield, McKinley, or Teddy Roosevelt.

Criminal Justice: A Semidefinition

This book is about criminal justice—but what is that? Most people have a fair idea, or think they have. They know about police, trials, prisons, the electric chair. They would no doubt find it hard to *define*

2. See, for example, Michael S. Hindus, "The Contours of Crime and Justice in Massachusetts and South Carolina, 1767–1878," *Am. J. Legal Hist.* 21 (1977): 212; Eric H. Monkkonen, *The Dangerous Class: Crime and Poverty in Columbus, Ohio, 1860–1885* (Cambridge, Mass., 1975); Jack K. Williams, *Vogues in Villainy: Crime and Retribution in Ante-Bellum South Carolina* (Columbia, S.C., 1959). The rather richer literature on the colonial period goes back a generation or two—for example, Julius N. Goebel, Jr., and T. Raymond Naughton, *Law Enforcement in Colonial New York: A Study in Criminal Procedure, 1664–1776* (New York, 1944)—and continues to be productive—for example, Douglas Greenberg, *Crime and Law Enforcement in the Colony of New York, 1691–1776* (Ithaca, N.Y., 1976). A recent general survey is Samuel Walker, *Popular Justice: A History of American Criminal Justice* (New York, 1980).

the system, but they are vaguely aware of its boundaries. We will not try to set out an exact definition; but a few remarks are in order about what we mean by criminal justice, and what it does for society.

When we talk about criminal justice, we may be speaking of two important, but quite distinct processes. The first is the process of making up rules about crime and punishment—developing, labeling and defining norms, rules, and codes. In most "advanced" societies, there is some book or document, official or unofficial, that lists crimes, explains what they are, and tells how they are to be (collectively) punished. The book or document will also describe ways and means for changing, reforming, abolishing, and renewing norms and rules. During our period, the basic California law on crime was the Penal Code. This was a long, elaborate statute, passed by the state legislature in Sacramento, which set out, in rather appalling detail, a list of crimes and punishments. The code also included (and includes) a rather dense body of ancillary rules about catching and arresting criminals, and about how to deal with them once they are caught in the web.

Let us take a closer look at the Penal Code as it stood in 1909. It was a tight little book, divided into "titles," and further divided into about 1,500 separate "sections." The first section announced the official title of the book (the Penal Code of California); § 1,615, the last section, gave the County Board of Health power to cut the hair of county prisoners to a "uniform length of 1 1/2 inches." In between these two sections was packed an immense amount of matter, some of it important, some of it trivial. The Penal Code became law in 1872. But it was based on two earlier laws, the Crimes and Punishments Act and the Criminal Practice Act, both passed in 1851. These in turn were based, to some extent, on New York models, although the commissioners who put the code together used other sources too.[3] After 1872, there was no real root-and-branch change in the catalog of crimes; but at each sitting of the legislature, there was *some* tinkering with the list, some adding or subtracting here and there. For example, under § 397 of the code it was a crime to sell liquor to Indians; an act of 1897 made it also an offense to sell to a "habitual or common drunkard." The same legislature raised the age of consent to sixteen (for purposes of rape), and altered the fish and game laws, among other things.[4]

The Penal Code was not the only place where rules about criminal justice were found. Provisions about crime, police, juries, and the like

---

3. Penal Code, 1871, preface, iii, iv.

4. Laws Cal. 1897, pp. 29, 201, 347. A fairly elaborate attempt to revise parts of the Penal Code (among other laws) was enacted in 1901 (Stats. 1901, p. 117), only to be declared unconstitutional in Lewis v. Dunne, 134 Cal. 291 (1901).

were scattered through other California codes. Even the Civil Code had a few criminal provisions— § 275, for example, made it "unlawful" to "entice, counsel, or persuade" an apprentice to run away from his master. The California Constitution contained some general provisions about courts, and a Bill of Rights, which had a strong, direct bearing on procedure in criminal cases. And of course, the California courts—particularly the Supreme Court—played a role in making and unmaking rules about criminal justice. The Supreme Court heard and decided about four hundred cases a year, among them a fair number of criminal appeals. Technically speaking, the Supreme Court was entitled only to "interpret" the Penal Code, filling in minor chinks and gaps. In practice, the court made up a good deal of law. This was an important, creative—but limited—role. The court could not add a new crime to the code, or subtract an old one. It could pull and stretch at meanings, to be sure; but the code was a sheet of rubber, not a ball of clay.

Alameda County—and California—were part of a larger whole, of course; and the general law of the United States, the commands of the national Constitution, the statutes of Congress, the dictates of federal courts, ruled in Alameda County, as they did everywhere else. Federal law was vital in ways that were, perhaps, not directly felt. Standards of fair trial in the California Constitution owed a great deal to models in the federal Constitution. These standards percolated into the minds of lawyers, judges—and the public at large. The Bill of Rights, however frayed about the edges, was a living reality in the courts. Still, in many ways, the federal government was a far-off, rather shadowy ruler. Only rarely does national law penetrate our records directly; even the Constitution rings only an occasional gong. In most ways, the federal government had not yet grown into a mighty overlord. The few federal prisoners were guests in state cells. (No federal prison was built before 1891.) The federal court, sitting in San Francisco, heard only a tiny fraction of the number of cases the state courts heard. A few of these were criminal cases, some from Alameda County—in 1894, for example, the pitiful case of young Eugene Kelley, assistant postmaster at Decoto (at $5 a month), who stole $3,000 from the till.[5] In Alameda County, once in a while a

5. *Oakland Tribune*, Sept. 29, 1894, p. 5, col. 3. We made a stab at the records of the Federal District Court for the Northern District of California. These records are housed in the Federal Archive Center in San Bruno, Calif. It is difficult to find out exactly how many criminal cases in the district came up out of Alameda County; but we satisfied ourselves that there were very few—two or three a year, if that. Some matters, of course, were the exclusive province of federal courts—immigration matters, for example (which meant the Chinese to all intents and purposes). Robert B. Bell ("Turn-of-the-Century Criminal Justice: A Case Study of the Federal District Court for the

defendant invoked federal law in his defense. Edward R. Reddy, an Oakland peddler, represented a firm in Rhode Island. He was arrested for hawking goods without a city license. But Reddy argued that "foreign" drummers could not be taxed in Oakland, because of the commerce clause of the federal Constitution; and the judge dismissed the case.[6]

Alameda was also a county, and counties, under state law, had rule-making power. Alameda was in fact a "first-class" county. This had nothing to do with climate or style; it simply meant a county with more than twenty thousand people (Pol. Code, § 4006). A board of seven supervisors ran first-class counties. They managed county roads and county institutions (including the jail and the poor farm); they raised county taxes. They also had some administrative powers. They could take steps to protect "game, fish, and shellfish," or to destroy "gophers, squirrels . . . and noxious weeds" (Pol. Code, § 4046 [23]). They could also license a motley group of business people: auctioneers, people engaged "in buying or selling gold-dust," jugglers, wire or rope dancers, pawnbrokers, traveling hawkers and peddlers, and people who hired out stallions, jacks, and bulls for "the purpose of propagation" (Pol. Code, § 4045).

Still, this mélange did not amount to much; even a first-class county was a third-class lawmaker. Cities and towns were more significant makers of law. All of them—Oakland, Berkeley, Alameda, San Leandro—had important powers under their charters, and busily churned out ordinances (from time to time unchurning or changing them). As we shall see, a fair proportion of the people arrested in Alameda County were charged with breach of local ordinance. Ordinances were many, and varied. Oakland's ordinance no. 1137, which went into effect May 15, 1890, forbade any "profane or vulgar language" uttered "within the hearing of two or more persons." (This grave "misdemeanor" carried a possible fine of up to $100; if you could not pay the fine, you went to jail, to work off the fine at the rate of $2 a day.) Another ordinance struck at concealed weapons—slingshots, brass or iron knuckles, dirk or bowie knives, iron bars, or

---

Northern District of California, 1899–1901," unpublished paper, Stanford Law School, 1979) sampled the criminal work of the court for the years in question. Of 100 cases, 45 were attempts to deport Chinese. The other 55 cases were on scattered subjects: seven counterfeiting cases; seven cases of defendants who brought silk or tobacco into the country, but failed to pay duty; six cases of sale of liquor or tobacco without an IRS stamp; four post office embezzlements; four mail offenses (fraud, obscene matter); and four violations of a federal statute prescribing an eight-hour day for federal contractors. The rest were strewn about among matters ranging from mutiny aboard ship to selling liquor to an Indian.

6. *Oakland Tribune*, Aug. 30, 1894, p. 5, col. 5.

guns. There were ordinances about licenses, liquor sales, and traffic; about false alarms, defacing buildings, and keeping inflammable materials; about prostitutes and pawnbrokers, against sleeping in barns or sheds without the owner's permission, against running opium dens; and many more.

Life in Alameda County, then, was no state of nature; it was packed with rules—a dense thicket of formal norms, surrounding behavior on all sides. But norms mean nothing without the second aspect of criminal justice: the system of enforcement. Here our cast of characters is large: sheriffs, marshals, police, and bailiffs; judges, prosecutors, defense lawyers; prison wardens and guards. There was also a huge, shifting cast of amateurs and extras: men who served on juries, and—perhaps the most crucial—men, women, and children who were victims or witnesses, who started the motor of criminal justice, or who kept it running. These people worked inside a large, complex structure. Police force, court, prosecutor's office, prison, jail, were all parts of the structure. In the real world, criminal justice was and is a vast, tangled system, a network of processes, intertwined like a mass of spaghetti. It begins with detection (and prevention) of crime, and goes through many steps from arrest through trial, ending up in a system of "corrections," a cruel and faceless word for pains and penalties that includes the bleak walls of San Quentin and once included the gallows itself. The system in 1880, or 1910, complex as it was, was probably a good deal simpler than big-city justice today. But there is a striking family resemblance between the then and the now. This book will explore similarities and differences, trying to explain both stability and change.

The Functions of Criminal Justice

Scholars have sometimes disputed whether criminal justice is universal—whether very small or simple societies have it at all, whether it is absent on tiny, isolated islands like Tristan da Cunha, or among hunters and gatherers, or in Eskimo society. We cannot resolve this dispute, which is partly a matter of definition. In any event any elaborate community—and California in the nineteenth century was certainly that—cannot get along without criminal justice. California, to be sure, never tried.

But why do we have such a system? What *is* the job of criminal justice? What does it do for society? These questions seem almost foolish; we take the system for granted. Still, the functions of criminal justice are worth at least a short look.

Foucault

The first function is control of dangerous behavior. In every complex society, some behavior is considered dangerous (to members, or to society itself); society makes at least some effort to stamp out or control that behavior. No society is completely successful, of course; and some do better than others. Every society has its own way of defining what is dangerous. It is almost universal to condemn murder, rape, arson, robbery, and assault. But this statement is a bit misleading. What is murder to one society is not necessarily murder to another. Some societies allow killing in revenge, or the disposal of excess daughters. To us, both of these are illegal; that is, they are murder.

In most societies, everybody knows the standard crimes. A reader might not be able to define arson precisely. (The Penal Code describes it as "wilful and malicious burning of a building," § 447.) But he has the general idea. Murder is the "unlawful killing of a human being" (§ 187). It is only the technical details (the concept of "malice aforethought" in murder, for example) that go beyond the average citizen.

To the small group of common, general crimes, each society adds its own list of dangerous or antisocial acts. These vary from society to society. A Russian can be shot for currency speculation; in the United States that is a lawful (and lucrative) business. For medieval Mongolians it was a crime, punishable by death, to urinate into water or ashes.[7] Sedition is in many countries a serious crime; in others, carping at government is a national pastime. The definition of "dangerous" also changes with context: in wartime, a soldier may legally kill enemy soldiers, but it may be a crime to overcharge for cheese.

Each society, then, draws up a list of behaviors that threaten social order; when this is done, society hands over to criminal justice at least *some* of the job of repressing or controlling "crime." We say *some* of the job, because society cannot and does not rely on so blunt and slow a system to do the whole job. Punishment, after all, comes after the fact—after the damage is done. It has, or is supposed to have, deterrent effect; but how much? and is it enough? Police, courts, and prisons are, in a way, only auxiliaries. Social energy also goes into methods of prevention: alarm systems, streetlights, metal detectors. Most important, the basic institutions of society—family, school, church, newspapers, magazines, clubs—work hard to prevent bad behavior. All over society, people teach norms, openly or implicitly; they warn, they instruct, they cajole.

Criminal justice does more than restrain truly dangerous behavior.

---

7. For that tidbit, see Valentin A. Riasonovsky, *Fundamental Principles of Mongol Law* (Bloomington, Ind., 1965), p. 83.

Many parts of the Penal Code prohibit acts that are hardly "dangerous" in the sense of arson or murder. Every society rests (or thinks it rests) on a foundation of moral order. People honor or obey religious, moral, or customary rules.

The process of defining and expressing rules of morality goes on throughout society, and at all times; the message comes from teachers and preachers, parents and politicians. Society is full of moral pulpits. The Penal Code is not the least of these. In our period it was heavy with moral freight. The code made incest a crime, and bigamy; it was also a crime to send a minor "to any saloon, gambling house, house of prostitution or other immoral place" (§ 273a). It was a crime to live "in a state of open and notorious cohabitation and adultery" (§ 269a). Many of these norms were about sexual behavior. Free love and pansexuality were never the official line, in Western societies. Neither were drunkenness and gambling. Today, many of these transgressions are called "victimless crimes"; many are no longer treated as crimes at all. There is a strong trend, for example, to legalize (for consenting adults) sex in any form, shape, or position.

Generally speaking, people in society believe in moral norms, though not necessarily the norms in the Penal Code. There is rarely if ever only *one* moral code in a complex society. One code may be dominant or official; but there are sure to be variants or rivals. Moral codes are by no means universal. The rules are often *very* controversial; several sets may compete for moral leadership in one community. They cannot all go into the Penal Code, especially when they contradict each other. Polygamy cannot be both God's work and the devil's. Fornication cannot be both harmless fun and deadly vice. Some norms must win and some must lose.

The concept of "victimless crime" reflects this struggle for dominance. The phrase implies that these acts harm no one, and should be legalized. But this is only one way to look at these "crimes." There are plenty of people who still believe that fornication and gambling are hazardous to social health. (Even they, perhaps, see a basic difference between *these* crimes and armed robbery or murder.) The late nineteenth century was not so naive as to imagine that God might destroy America as he destroyed Sodom and Gomorrah. But many people did feel, rather deeply, that chastity and virtue were essential to a strong and durable society; that immorality and lust would rot our social timbers, sooner or later; and that criminal justice had the right—no, the duty—to take morality seriously, under the laws of God and man.

These, then, are two functions of criminal justice: *to control dangerous behavior*, and *to set out, and enforce, the moral code*. A third

function is *to keep order*. A policeman stands on a busy corner, direct-
ing traffic. The streets swarm with people, buses, taxis, private cars,
or (in our period), bicycles, horses, carriages, and streetcars. The
behaviors of walkers and riders, taken one by one, are not dangerous;
they are certainly not immoral. All together, they create a problem of
order. Without the policeman, traffic might grind to a halt. Much of
criminal justice is concerned with keeping order—with traffic, in the
literal sense, and in other more subtle ways.

The idea of "order" implies a rationing process. Some social good
is scarce; there is not enough to go around. Nobody needs traffic
rules if drivers or strollers appear only occasionally on the streets. A
law of 1909 ordered people to stop trapping or killing seals in the
Santa Barbara Channel (§ 637c). There would be no need for this law
if seals had ratty fur, and were as common as ladybugs. To tan leather
or slaughter pigs next to a row of houses is a "nuisance," and (usually) against the rules, even though tanning and slaughtering are not
dangerous or immoral; they merely smell bad. The modern state has
built a vast house of rules and regulations. Crowds of people press
against limited resources. Furry animals, clean-smelling air, and rush-
hour space on the boulevards are all scarce goods. Rules of order
decide who gets what, and when and how. Criminal justice runs part,
but only part, of the system of order. Administrative agencies, from
the Interstate Commerce Commission down to local zoning boards,
have another piece of the action. But administrative codes usually
include some threat of prosecution—at least for hard-core offenders.

Order is a complex concept, and we might want to distinguish it
from *discipline*. This is a somewhat similar concept, but it has a
distinctive nuance. Generally speaking, rules of order control behavior that is not bad in itself; it is only a danger or a nuisance if too
many people do it at once, at the wrong time, or in the wrong place.
Behavior subject to discipline is disorderly and perhaps also *slightly*
dangerous or immoral. A rule about public drunkenness, or quarreling and brawling in the streets, is perhaps best described by such a
word. *Discipline*, like order, aims to control, not suppress; it is a way
of keeping the lid on.

These terms—order, discipline, dangerous behavior, immoral behavior—have a fairly flat, neutral tone. But people have passionate
ideas about criminal justice. They may not see it simply as a neutral
servant of the general good. Some writers put heavy stress on the
way criminal justice serves people in control. They point out that
police and courts protect haves against have-nots. What, after all, is
stealing? It is taking away what another man owns—his property. If
we prevent or punish stealing, we protect the rights of property. That

means, of course, the rich: those who have something to steal. Criminal justice, then, guards the status quo. Laws against stealing are only one blatant example. The whole penal system, it is said, tilts toward the rich and powerful. It is *their* system; they benefit; the poor and the weak bear the burden.[8]

Is this a fair description? It is certainly a possible one. It depends on what lens you use to look at the system with. A change of emphasis here and there, a shift in terms and labels, and you can change, dramatically, your assessment of the system. If you stress how police and courts protect property, how they clamp down on deviants and dissenters, you can paint the system as an engine of oppression, run by an army of "pigs." You can just as easily use rosier colors: the system is a shield, working to protect respectable people against vultures and devils. It may also serve as society's angel of vengeance. There are, of course, many other points of view.

Which one is right? We have already tipped our hand: no one of these, *completely*. We mean to ask, in the following chapters, what functions did the system serve? and how shall we assess those functions? To answer these questions, we put crime and punishment in Alameda County under a magnifying glass, so to speak. Our best answer is that the system had many functions; it did all of the things we described. It kept order; it enforced discipline; it protected life and property against violent and dangerous behavior; and it upheld, more deeply than most people realized, one particular, rather narrow moral code. This, of course, should come as no surprise. After all, the functions are interrelated. Both property and authority must be maintained. Neither stands without the other.[9] What is interesting—and this we must look for—is the particular manner and mix.

And how do we judge the system? There we will have to be more cautious still. Was the system fair? Did it provide due process for the man or woman charged with crime? That depends. There is a central core of ideas about law in the United States. Phrases like "the rule of law," "due process," "trial by jury" express these beliefs and ideals. Some scholars talk about the ideals as "myths." The word is a shade too cynical. Of course, if "due process" means trial by jury, a full, fair hearing buttoned up with procedural safeguards, then "due process" was rare in felony cases in 1870, or 1910. The rule of law governed in

8. For example: "Legal order benefits the ruling class in the course of dominating the classes that are ruled. . . . The perception of criminal law as a coercive means in establishing domestic order for the ruling class is . . . basic. . . . " Richard Quinney, *Criminal Justice in America: A Critical Understanding* (Boston, 1974), pp. 18–19.
9. See Douglas Hay et al., *Albion's Fatal Tree: Crime and Society in Eighteenth-Century England* (New York, 1975), p. 25.

Alameda County; but it was stretched a bit, to say the least. In only a handful of cases did defendant make use of his rights to their full theoretical limit. These few—the show trials—served as propaganda for the system. One might even call them false advertising. They flashed an image of process on the public screen; but this was no normal image: it was special and rare. On the other hand, the blind lady of justice was *not* consistently ravished. This was America, not Hitler's Germany. Ideals were more than empty window dressing. Fairness was more than a word. When all our evidence is in, readers can decide, on their own, how far off target the system was—and why.

So much for fairness in the individual case. What about fairness—and social justice—overall? There is no doubt that criminal justice took the social system for granted—as it was, not as it might be. The law *did* protect the status quo. It took on the colors of its surrounding society. It was no better, no worse. California was no utopia; no society of gentle sharers. It was an open, somewhat raw, free-market economy—not the free market of libertarian dreamers, but an economy of people who respected businessmen and often (not always) let the market have its head. It was also a society where the people who counted were almost all white Christian men. Women, blacks, and Orientals were supposed to keep their place. The Chinese, in particular, were persecuted and despised. There was a pyramid of wealth and of power in Alameda County, and a moral pyramid as well. At the top of this pyramid were those who preached (and lived?) a conventional Christian life. On the bottom were the "depraved," the "debauched," the "beasts."

This was the world outside the courthouse and the police station. The world inside reflected the world outside—*had* to reflect it. Criminal justice was not unique in this regard; each period stamps its brand on politics, business, culture, the schools, the churches, the press—on everything, in short. The legal system is no exception; it goes hand in glove with its society; it changes as society changes. Our overall assessment is worth repeating: no better and no worse.

This, then, is one central argument of the book. The criminal justice system of Alameda County, in our period, had no single function, and cannot be summed up in a single, simple formula. A second and related point has to do with what we might call *layering*. Not only was there no single function, there was, in an important sense, no single *system*. Rather, there were a number of systems, each with its own job, its own process, its own way of looking at the world and the work. The systems were arranged one on top of another, like layers in a layer cake. At the top was the domain of the great show trials; at the bottom, the realm of the drunks in police court; in the middle, ordinary burglaries, thefts, and assaults in Superior Court.

The layering idea should not be taken too literally. The boundaries between layers were never *that* distinct. The layers melted into one another. There were, as we said, at least three. To each, we will devote a chapter or more, describing how the system worked and exploring the social function of that layer. But first we have to sketch in the background and the setting. Chapters 2 and 3 introduce us to Alameda County, to its legal institutions, and to the men and women who took part in the system.

A Note on Method

This book straddles two fields: American legal history and the study of law and society. As we dug up facts and analyzed them, our techniques were far from unique or revolutionary. But a comment or two about method is in order, for what it is worth.

First, as to history—more specifically, the history of law. There has been a good deal of fuss about quantitative methods in history. In one sense, the arguments pro and con seem rather pointless. At the most abstract level there is one overarching rule of method: use the best evidence you can find, and the best techniques you can to squeeze meaning from that evidence. For some kinds of history, this will obviously mean hard statistics. For other kinds of history, quantitative methods are impossible or absurd. Both approaches can be misused or abused.

The historian, to be sure, is likely to lack some data that modern scholars enjoy. Surveys cannot be conducted among the dead. There are often holes in historical data that cannot be filled. What is gone is gone. This is something a historian learns to live with.

For this book, we used many sources—arrest blotters, court registers, felony case files, appellate court records, prison log books, newspapers, and other scraps of data. Wherever possible, we drew samples and counted cases; sometimes we ran simple statistical tests. But at every step of the way, we also tried to get behind our figures. We read reams and reams of documents, stuck away in drawers in the courthouse basement. We could not read *all* the newspapers, but we read as many as we could, sometimes randomly, sometimes following up a lead. *Both* steps, we felt, were necessary. Without figures, we have only impressions, stories, fleeting moments, vague opinions. Numbers alone, on the other hand, are blind and mysterious: tablets written in an undeciphered script. When you put the two together, you begin to approach, however distantly, the pulse of life. The two methods fit like lock and key. For studies like this, only this double technique, we believe, can work.

So much for the historical side. Now let us turn to the general theory of law and society. There has been much debate there too about methods, values, and the truth or falsity of this or that perspective: Marxist views, pluralist views, what have you. There is no way, empirically, to resolve *basic* issues of value and method. But any study casts a shadow in some particular direction. From time to time, we will make comments of a general nature about law and society—never forgetting, of course, that our study deals with a single time, place, and subject. Our message, on the whole, is eclectic. To us, no *one* perspective seems entirely right. Perhaps this is, in part, because we tried to study a *system*, not *part* of a system. Instead of, for example, tracing the history of the jury from the Middle Ages to modern times (that is, studying a single institution) or looking at a single facet of the legal system (or criminal justice) across time and place (plea bargaining, for example), we chose to look very intensely at a *whole system* in one county. That kind of lens refracts whatever theory one started with; the very richness and complexity of evidence tilts an interpreter toward a coalition of approaches. In Alameda County, no single social theory looks true, no single method looks correct. We will say more on this score in the following pages.

A Note about Sources

Finally, we need to add a word or two about our sources. As we said, gaps in the historical record are inevitable; history deals with what is dead and gone. In the years gone by, fire, flood, earthquake, and human neglect have preyed on the records of criminal justice in California. We were lucky to find a rich lode of records in Alameda County.

One of our first discoveries was the original Oakland arrest blotters. On these, the police recorded the sex, age, race, country of birth, height, weight, literacy, residence, occupation, and complexion of every person hauled in for transgressing the law between 1872 and 1910. This kind of record is not usually preserved. An Oakland librarian with foresight personally retrieved these bulky volumes, which the police were about to discard to make room for a computer system. Except for a single year (1891), the record is intact, complete with personal notes from police, attorneys, bail bondsmen, and judges inserted inside their covers. The arrest blotters provide details about nearly 140,000 arrests, and the outcome of whatever charges they produced. We drew a random sample of 1,555 of these arrests for intensive analysis of who was arrested, why the arrests were made, and what happened to those arrested. We also paid special attention to certain mass arrests; and, for certain years, we noted how many there were of each type of offense, and how, in these years, all felony charges were disposed of.

In the Oakland Museum we found a Minute Book from the Oakland Police Court. It covered a period of fourteen months, from May 1880 through June 1881. The court handled 1,919 cases during this period, and the Minute Book told what happened in court after each arrest. From this document we recorded a good deal of information: on the nature of the charges, how long the process took, how cases were disposed of, and what sentences were handed out. Unfortunately, no other records of police or justice courts seem to have survived.

Felony trial court records begin with the establishment of the Superior Court, in 1880. There are two rich sources of information: the Register of Actions and the case files. The register lists defendant's name, the case number, and the charge, and gives the procedural history of the case, in outline. The case files hold the complaint or indictment, transcripts of proceedings in the lower courts, and many other documents. We examined the Registers of Actions to determine the number of felony prosecutions, and we drew a random sample of one-fourth of the felony cases—696 cases in all—for close analysis. For each of these cases we combed the registers and case files, skimmed through the documents, and systematically recorded information about every stage of the case. This produced a good crop of information about lower court proceedings, bail, attorneys, charges, dispositions, and sentences. The registers were sometimes poorly kept, and the files sometimes defective, but the two together usually told the story. Besides our sample, we browsed through, dug into, and pored over dozens and dozens of other files, which caught our attention for one reason or another, or which filled in some hole in the data.

We also studied the appellate process. Our primary concern was not how doctrine developed; our concern was to complete the picture of criminal justice in our county, and the life cycle of a small number of cases included appeal to a higher court. The annual reports of the California attorney general, who represented the state in all criminal appeals; the registers; and California Supreme Court records in the State Archives at Sacramento helped us reconstruct the path of all 103 criminal appeals brought from Alameda County between 1870 and 1910. Grounds for decision have not always been preserved; but we could tell who won and who lost, and we could trace what happened to defendants after the higher court made up its mind.

Losers at trial or on appeal often ended up in prison. What happened to prisoners is set down in the records of San Quentin and Folsom, filed in the State Archives in Sacramento. Prison log books, intact for our period, record sex, place of birth, age, race, offense, prior record, and sentence for each prisoner. We recorded this information for all 1,471 prisoners who went to the "big house" from Alameda County between 1870 and 1911 (we extended the outer bound of our study an extra year to take in persons prosecuted in 1910). By examining the dates on which prisoners were received and released, and the reasons for their releases, we were able to tell if sentences imposed were actually carried out. Annual reports of the wardens, governors' messages to the legislature, and governors' pardon pronouncements gave us additional information, and so did legislative investigations into prison conditions, and accounts by the prisoners themselves.

These were not the only sources we consulted. We also looked at reports of grand juries, coroners, and probation officers. Much of this information was unsystematic—bits of paper stuck in old drawers in the basement of the county court house—but these pieces and fragments were often very enlightening. And, as we said before, we made every effort to get behind the raw records, to develop a "feel" for what was happening at the time. For this, the newspapers, and especially the *Oakland Tribune*, were absolutely invaluable. Our results, we hope, allow us to reconstruct a rough picture of criminal justice in our county about a century ago—a picture fuller and more accurate than any before drawn for the nineteenth and early twentieth centuries in this country.

Chapter 2
A County and Its Crime

In the opening chapter, we introduced ourselves to the criminal justice system. This chapter will try to anchor our study a bit more firmly in time and place; we will also take a first look at the county's harvest of crime.

First, a word about the times. Most of our data fall within the period 1880–1910. The Superior Court was organized in 1880. The earlier criminal records seem to be lost, but we do have arrest records from the city of Oakland from 1872; and we have scattered facts about crime and punishment in the 1870s, largely scraped up from the newspapers. In one way or another, we deal with a period of about forty years. For California, for the United States, and for the world, these were years of enormous change. In 1870 the Civil War was a very recent memory. Federal troops still occupied the Deep South; Ulysses Grant sat in the White House. California was a baby among states, some twenty years old. The first railroad to the Pacific has just been finished. Abroad, Queen Victoria was on the throne of England, mourning her Albert. The Franco-Prussian War was about to break out. Across the Pacific, Japan was stirring; the Meiji restoration had occurred in 1867.

Between 1870 and 1910, some forty turns of the wheel, a great deal happened here and abroad. Presidents came and went: Rutherford B. Hayes, who won a disputed election; Garfield, shot down by the lunatic Guiteau, and replaced by Chester Alan Arthur; Grover Cleveland, Benjamin Harrison; McKinley, who fell to another bullet; Theodore Roosevelt; and finally William Howard Taft. Reconstruction ended; the population grew from under 40 million to over 90 million; in 1876, the telephone was patented; later, electricity began to light up the world; the Wright Brothers made their first, fluttering flight in 1903; by 1910 automobiles were no longer a novelty. This was the age of the Robber Barons, the Haymarket riots, the Pullman strike, the Interstate Commerce Commission, and the Sherman Act. It was an age of social upheaval: cities began to dominate the farms; industry expanded and exploded; crowds of immigrants from southern and eastern Europe were washed ashore. Colorado became a state in 1876, and later on so did Utah, Montana, Idaho, the Dakotas, and

Washington. Abroad, the queen got old and fat and died; her son, Edward VII, succeeded her in 1901, and held the throne for nine years. England fought the Boers; Japan and Russia battled in the far, far East. Europe explored and conquered various corners of the earth. Brahms wrote symphonies, Mark Twain published *Huckleberry Finn*, Pasteur struggled in the war against germs. In California, it was an age of population growth and uneven prosperity. The Kearneyites fulminated against the Chinese. The Southern Pacific was "the Octopus," its tentacles everywhere in political affairs. All over there was movement, growth, and change. In 1906 the very crust of the earth buckled and cracked; in the fire storm that followed, the heart of San Francisco died. And, as always, as in every society, there was crime and the punishment of crime.

Alameda County

Today, Alameda County's heart beats with a mighty pulse. The county is dense with people and vibrant with the rhythm of urban life: a tight ganglion of cars, houses, stores, factories, highways. It has an area of 840 square miles. Alameda County is only part of a sprawling mega-city, whose nerve center lies in San Francisco, across the Bay, but whose arms and legs encircle the whole of the Bay. Santa Clara and San Mateo counties are bedroom and satellite centers to the south of San Francisco; the southern anchor, San Jose, has half a million people inside its ragged boundaries. To the north of San Francisco, across the Golden Gate, lies Marin County, thickly settled along the rim of the Bay, its population falling away as we ascend the sides of the mountains, until we reach wilderness between the crests and the fog-bound shore. Alameda County lies along the eastern rim of San Francisco Bay, south of Contra Costa County; its southern tail touches Santa Clara County, at the point where the bay ends in salt flats and mud. From Oakland and other East Bay cities San Francisco is plainly visible, glittering across the water. Even on a night of fog, the towers and hills of this fabulous city rise up out of the mist. More than a million people live in Alameda County. The Bay Bridge and the BART tunnel link it to San Francisco; the San Mateo and Dumbarton bridges span the Bay to the south peninsula counties. These bridges were built long after our period. (The earliest, the Bay Bridge, opened in 1936.) In our day, connection between cities was by boat. More accurately, it was by ferry. In 1881 the Central Pacific Railroad operated nine ferry boats and carried a total of 7,032,366 passengers across the Bay.[1]

The whole area, including Alameda County, sprouted like a weed between 1870 and 1910. In 1870, about 24,000 lived in Alameda County; in 1880, nearly 60,000; in 1890, 93,874. By 1910, the population was 246,131. More than 90 percent of these lived in urban areas, that is, in cities of over 5,000. The rural townships were sparsely settled (see Table 2.1). The population was and is concentrated along the western fringe of the county—in the bayside lowlands. A short distance from the Bay there rises a series of hills that, today, are elegant home sites. Over the crest of these hills are more hills, dry and thinly populated, abandoned to grazing and ranching. Beyond them is the Central Valley.

Table 2.1. Population of Alameda County by Townships and Cities, 1870–1910

	1870	1880	1890	1900	1910
Alameda County	24,237	62,976	93,864	130,197	246,131
Township Population					
Alameda Township	1,557	5,708	11,165	16,464	23,383
Brooklyn Township	2,816	7,484	11,383	19,585	49,140
Eden Township	3,341	5,687	7,336	9,330	11,515
Murray Township	2,400	4,361	5,937	7,172	4,137*
Oakland Township	11,104	35,144	52,447	70,732	147,199
Pleasanton Township	—	—	—	—	2,883*
Washington Township	3,019	4,592	5,596	6,914	7,874
Population of Cities					
Oakland	10,500	34,555	48,682	66,960	150,174
Berkeley	—	—	5,101	13,214	40,434
Alameda	1,557	5,708	11,165	16,464	23,383
San Leandro	426	—	—	2,253	3,471
Hayward	504	1,231	1,419	1,965	2,746
Emeryville	—	—	228	1,016	2,613
Livermore	—	855	1,391	1,493	2,030
Piedmont	—	—	—	—	1,719
Pleasanton	—	—	—	1,100	1,254

*Pleasanton Township was formed from part of Murray Township in 1902.

1. Frank Clinton Merritt, *History of Alameda County, California* (Chicago, 1928), 1:119.

As counties go, Alameda was young in 1870. A mission founded in 1797, San Jose de Guadalupe, once stood in the south-central part of what is now the county. The Spanish divided the land into enormous "ranchos" in the early nineteenth century. One of the largest was the Rancho de San Antonio, granted to Luis Maria Peralta, who died in 1851. By this time, California was no longer Spanish or Mexican; it was an American state. Oakland was incorporated in 1852, on land once part of Peralta's rancho. In 1853 the legislature created Alameda County (see Figure 2.1). The first county seat was Alvarado; the next was San Leandro. Oakland became the county seat in 1873, and held onto this prize.

By then, Oakland was already the dominant city in the county. Its harbor was improved between 1874 and 1881. From 1869 on, it was the end of the transcontinental line.[2] San Francisco is a peninsula, a thumb sticking up between ocean and Bay; the Western Pacific Railroad never got past Oakland. From there, it was ferry or swim. The rapid growth of Alameda County was, in good measure, the rapid growth of Oakland. In 1870, the city had 10,500 people; in 1880, 34,555; in 1890, 48,682; in 1900, 66,960; and in 1910, 150,174—just over 60 percent of the county population, and all in all a considerable city.

But never, of course, *the* city. That prize has always gone to San Francisco, gaudy and shimmering across the bay, fabled and fabulous, hero of dozens of books, plays, movies, and songs. No one ever sang a song for Oakland, the city with no "there" there. Oakland has always been jealous of San Francisco, its fame, beauty, reputation. Oakland looks across the bay like Cinderella scrubbing floors and cleaning ashes while the dance of life goes on. But where would San Francisco be without the port, the factories, the railroad yards? There has always been a touch of sour grapes in Oakland's attitude. A brochure, published in 1905, made much of the point that Oakland was a better place to live. "Hundreds of workmen" with jobs on Oakland's waterfront once lived in San Francisco. These men brought their families to the "beautiful surroundings of Oakland." Here climate and "conditions of life" were far better than those of the "bleak promontory" where "pioneers," ignorant of "Alameda County's superior advantages," founded San Francisco.[3]

2. See Hubert Howe Bancroft, *History of California, Vol. VII, 1860–1890*, vol. 25 of *The Works of Hubert Howe Bancroft* (San Francisco, 1890), pp. 686–87.

3. *Alameda County, The Facts Concerning Its Growth and Development: Its Advantages and Possibilities* (Oakland, 1905). The San Francisco, Oakland, and San Jose Railway, the Oakland Traction Consolidated, and "the realty syndicate" joined to put out this bit of propaganda; on a similar theme, see *Oakland Herald*, May 2, 1904, p. 5, col. 2.

FIGURE 2.1
Townships and Cities of Alameda County, California, 1870–1910

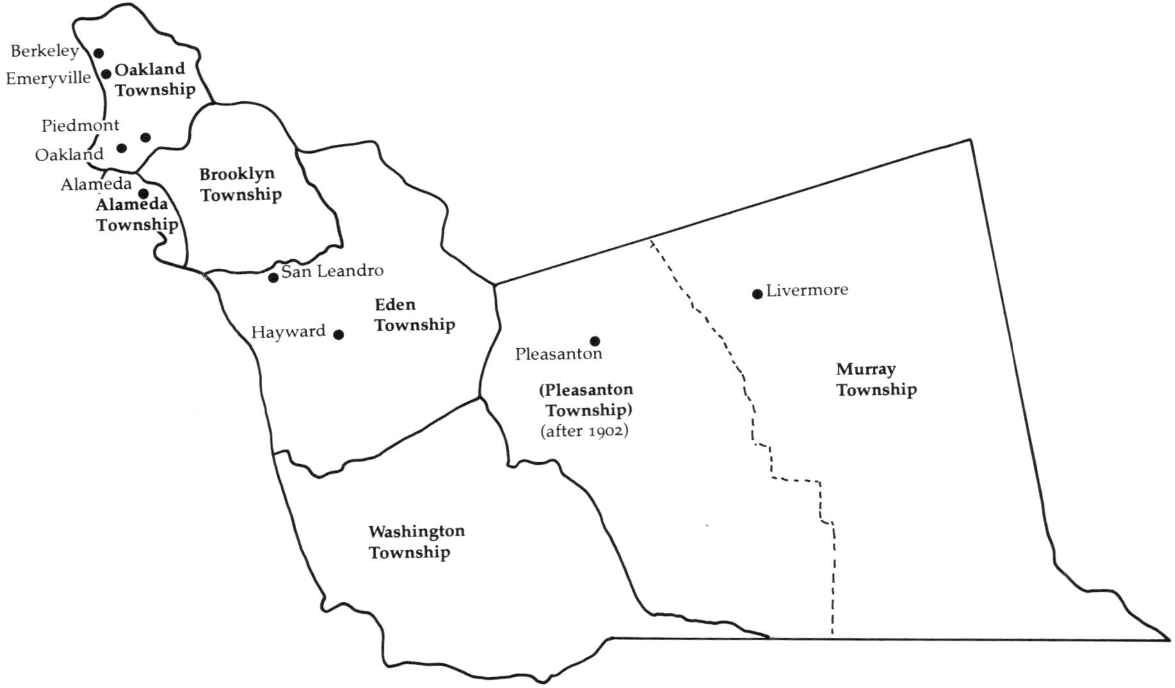

In Alameda County at least, Oakland was king. It was the seat of government, the center of finance and trade. There were seven banks in Oakland in 1895, four daily newspapers, fifty churches. The chief refinery of the Pacific Coast Borax Company, owned by F. M. Smith, the "borax king," was located in Alameda, a town just below Oakland; the refinery stood "on the shore of the bay, its white front visible for miles."[4] In Oakland, or just outside of it, were brass and iron foundries, textile mills, canneries, flour mills, brickyards. Outside the cities and towns, Alameda County was still a quiet place of ranches, farms, and orchards. Grapevines grew in the Livermore hills, thirty miles from Oakland. There were salt works in the marshes of Mount Eden.

The second city of the county, in 1910, was Berkeley, home of the state university. This was a recent sprout. The university opened for business in Oakland in 1869; in 1873, it transferred to Berkeley, then nothing but a "tiny and distant settlement," a few houses on one street "at the end of the car line"; from Berkeley to San Francisco was a long trip by "the slow bob-tail car to Oakland," or by omnibus to the ferry at West Berkeley.[5] The university grew rapidly and quickly developed sound academic traditions: as early as 1878, students came to the attention of the grand jury because of the hazing of freshmen by seniors—freshmen were tossed in blankets, shaved, painted "on their naked bodies," deluged with water, and subjected to other "abusements."[6] Berkeley grew along with the university. Just after the turn of the century, the university had become one of the country's largest, with something on the order of 3,000 students. Tuition was free, and the university could be "reached from any part of Oakland for a 5 cents fare."[7] The population of Berkeley was about 5,000 in 1890, the first year in which the census took notice of this upstart. In 1910 it was 40,000. Alameda, the third city of the county, had 23,000 people in 1910. None of the other towns in Alameda County—San Leandro, Hayward,[8] Emeryville, Livermore—was particularly large.

If we look over the population figures (Table 2.1), we see that both Oakland and the county grew by a factor of ten between 1870 and 1910. A person who left Oakland in 1870 and came back forty years later would hardly have recognized the place. These were forty years

4. *Oakland, California: A City of Great Commercial Promise, Its Industries and Environs* (Oakland, 1903); see Merritt, *History of Alameda County*, 1:229–31.

5. Merritt, *History of Alameda County*, 1:344.

6. Grand Jury Report, September Term 1878, filed Sept. 27, 1878.

7. *Oakland, California*.

8. "Hayward" has always been the official name of this town. During our period, people often referred to it, colloquially, as "Haywards."

of fantastic change—years of total transformation. The change was, no doubt, more dramatic than forty years of change in Boston, Richmond, or even Chicago. But this was a matter of degree. People everywhere lived in a shaking, pulsing world. The period begins with the horse and buggy, and ends with the automobile. It begins in a country that had barely digested its continent, barely survived its Civil War, a country still largely North European, still mostly living on the farm. By the end of the period, the United States was a world power: it had nibbled at remnants of the Spanish empire, scooped up the Hawaiian Islands, swallowed Puerto Rico and the Phillipines. It was more and more a country of cities and factories, not villages and farms. Immigration was changing the faces of its people; old values trembled and fell.

There were great events in the country and the world, and there were slow changes in the basic premises of social life. These changes were subtle, subterranean; they crept up on the man in the street day by day, until he was surprised to look back and see how the world had altered. Meanwhile, daily life went on, for every man, woman, and child: building a nest, getting bread and circuses, or just getting along. Patterns of life strike us in some ways as all too familiar; in other ways, as totally different. Ads cajoled readers to "buy a home on the instalment plan," and "stop paying rent." In 1888, however, the price for an "elegant two-story house of 8 rooms and bath," in the "aristocratic" section of Oakland, was $4,500.[9] Still, this was nine years of wages for a workman. A four-room "cottage" was $1,500. Prices were low, and so were incomes.

The pages of the county's newspapers were local windows on the larger world; but the reader also saw reflections in the tiny pools of county life. Here we find tragedies and triumphs, big and small, and all the bagatelles of social life in a California county: club meetings, shows, sermons from the pulpit, houses burned and bodies found, grief and exultation. Ringling Brothers invited people to come see "the last giraffe in the entire world."[10] Crusts of sensation were served up for breakfast, from far and near. A Canadian professor, Ezekiel Wiggins, announced that men lived on Mars, sending signals to earth.[11] A scandalous rumor right at home concerned tanners in Berkeley; it was said they used human skin ("soft as chamois" when tanned, and fetching a "big price" from men who found "ghoulish delight in morbid things").[12] Reading the papers, one is struck by

9. *Oakland Tribune*, Jan. 10, 1888, p. 1, col. 8.
10. Ibid., Aug. 17, 1901, p. 7, col. 6.
11. Ibid., Aug. 4, 1894, p. 1, col. 6.
12. Some people, apparently, were quite willing to buy "sandals, purses, book

the numbers of suicides reported. The motives (insofar as they could be guessed) were the classic ones: failure in business, poor health, blighted love. In Berkeley in 1906 an "unknown man," about thirty years old, took poison in a "lonely spot by Strawberry Creek," leaving a picture of a woman named Edith, and a suicide note in French.[13] In 1901 the body of George A. Snook was found in the bay, drowned, with his pocket full of rocks. Snook, a widower, and retired, had been in "failing health."[14] Last but not least, the papers were full of crime and criminal justice—in endless shapes and forms. It is this parade of events that forms our subject.

Crime and Crime Rates

From books, pictures, maps, and newspapers, a good deal of the flavor of life in the county comes back, a dead flower pressed in the pages of a scrapbook: a good deal, but not all. Much of course is forever lost. Some parts of life leave records and traces; others are gone with the wind.

There are gaps in what we know about criminal justice; but all in all, this system leaves vital fossils behind. Crime itself is another matter. It tends to be hidden and secret. Moreover, it is often a question of judgment whether some behavior was "crime" or not, and what to call it if it was. An incident takes place in a bar; was it a friendly shove, a minor battery, a dangerous assault? A body is found; was it accident or murder? Money is gone; was it borrowed, stolen, or lost? We are, at bottom, in the dark about crime rates in our period. There is nothing we can measure directly. Unreported crime slips out of notice forever. We have systematic information on arrests (for Oakland only). But how much do we dare infer from these records? Numbers must be handled with care. The police do not arrest every criminal; plenty of thieves and burglars go uncaught. Still, arrest rates tell us something about crime rates—and about police enforcement. For some major crimes, especially murder, newspaper accounts and coroner's reports add some facts. Out of these bits of evidence, we can draw a picture, rough but serviceable.

What conclusions can we come to from all this? In the next pages,

covers, watch cases," or, worst of all, "gloves for the living hand . . . made from the skin of the dead." *Berkeley Reporter*, Feb. 10, 1906, p. 1, col. 2.

13. Ibid., Feb. 23, 1906, p. 1, col. 6. On suicide during this period, see Frederick L. Hoffman, "Suicides and Modern Civilization," *Arena* 7 (1892–93): 680; William B. Bailey, "Suicide in the United States, 1897–1901," *Yale Rev.* 12 (May 1903): 70.

14. *Oakland Tribune*, Apr. 25, 1901, p. 1, col. 5.

we set out the data. They lead to the conclusion that serious crime (murder, armed robbery, violent rape, burglary) was on the decline in the late nineteenth century. We are not sure *why* this was the case, but it was apparently a general trend, in the United States and indeed in the Western world. If we are right, then this is an important piece of background information, against which we can measure and assess our later findings. To put it bluntly and generally, crime was not a major problem in the county between 1870 and 1910; and if anything, the problem got better, not worse.

This fact is vital. It means that society was in no real, imminent danger from serious and violent crime; it could afford to spend the energy of criminal justice on other purposes: order, discipline, upholding a moral code. We do not mean to argue that this was a golden age, a crime-free, gentle age; that would be totally wrong. But serious and violent crime did not command hysterical attention, and for good reason, we believe. It was not the problem that it is today.

Here, first, are the facts. At one time (we are told), Alameda County was a violent place. Men spilled blood in disputes over title to the ranchos near Oakland. The rule of law took its time in traveling west. San Francisco went through the turmoil of its Vigilance Committees in the 1850s; in Oakland, at this time, it was easy "to raise a mob to hang a cattle thief." Judge Lynch made some notable visits to the county.[15]

In any event, Oakland had a different image by the 1870s. Its boosters claimed it was no longer the raw, jagged edge of civilization; Oakland (and its county) had settled down. According to the city physician, there were only two homicides in the first half of the 1870s, along with thirty-six accidental deaths and eleven suicides. Oakland was quiet, almost sedate; people from San Francisco came over for Sunday picnics. The main problems were "sneak thieves" and "rowdies." In 1879 the mayor boasted that "life and property" were "unusually secure in Oakland." The only crime was "petty" crime; burglary was rare and hardly anyone was "molested in a public highway." Gas lamps had been extended into "remote parts of the city," and they helped maintain security: "Crime is committed in the darkness, its opportunities are dispelled by the light."[16]

The mayor, to be sure, was a booster. But he may have been right. Violent crime was apparently rare, and continued to be. The coroner reported only four homicides in the county in 1893; people killed each other at a very low rate, less than 0.04 per thousand—four times

15. Ibid., Dec. 4, 1875, p. 3, col. 4.
16. Ibid., Feb. 4, 1879, p. 3, col. 2.

lower than the reported rate for 1878, which was already low. According to the coroner, accidental death (0.61 per thousand) and suicide (0.25) were much greater risks in the county than murder.[17]

Arrest rates in Oakland confirm the idea of a long, deep decline in serious crime over the years. Of course, as we said, it is tricky to infer crime rates from arrest rates. Some crimes are not reported, and a great deal depends on the police. The police change policies; they get more (or less) corrupt. All of this influences arrest rates. Still, some offenses are less sensitive to policies than others. Generally speaking, the most serious crimes are the least sensitive. The police do not "drop" a murder case. They take burglary seriously, on the whole. The problem is to find and catch the murderer or burglar; if a prime suspect turns up, he is sure to be arrested. The police are much more fickle about "victimless" crimes, like gambling or drunkenness. Sometimes the police tolerate vice (or live off it); sometimes they persecute and prosecute. Sometimes they help drunks home; sometimes they lock them up. Arrest rates in themselves therefore tell very little about "true" rates of drunkenness or gambling. Arrest rates, in short, mean a good deal if we want to measure rates of serious crime; for victimless crimes and petty crimes they tell us less about foxes than about hounds.[18]

What is a "serious" crime? One useful rough line is the line between felonies and misdemeanors. Each state (and era) puts different crimes in these pigeonholes. Luckily for us, the definition in California was stable between 1870 and 1910. A felony was a crime punishable by death or "by imprisonment in the state prison" (§ 17). Murder, robbery, rape, assault with a deadly weapon, burglary, and

---

17. Ibid., Jan. 7, 1893, p. 1, col. 3, Jan. 2, 1879, p. 1, col. 4.

18. There is a rich literature on police discretion, and its influence on arrest rates. A pioneer study was Joseph Goldstein, "Police Discretion Not to Invoke the Criminal Process: Low-Visibility Decisions in the Administration of Justice," *Yale L. J.* 69 (1960): 543; see also Wayne R. LaFave, *Arrest: The Decision to Take a Suspect into Custody* (Boston, 1965). Researchers have, nonetheless, sometimes used arrest rates as indicators of crime rates; see, e.g., Theodore N. Ferdinand, "The Criminal Patterns of Boston since 1849," *Am. J. Soc.* 73 (1967): 84; Sam B. Warner, *Crime and Criminal Statistics in Boston* (Cambridge, Mass., 1934). Some studies have tried to take police discretion into account; some have not.

Of course, some leeway in police work is inevitable. First of all, criminal codes cannot possibly spell out *exactly* what is forbidden and what is allowed. There is always room for "interpretation." Secondly, police have limited resources, and a giant fistful of rules to enforce. Finally, the police have their own norms and values; they use them— and get away with it. These norms and values are not the same as those expressed in the letter of the law. Still, police have, or use, least discretion with regard to *very* serious crimes. There is strong consensus that these crimes should be punished. See Peter H. Rossi, Emily Waite, Christine E. Bose, and Richard E. Berk, "The Seriousness of Crimes: Normative Structure and Individual Differences," *Am. Soc. Rev.* 39 (1974): 224, a study of the way the public rates crimes on a scale of seriousness.

grand larceny—these were felonies. Everything not a felony was a misdemeanor.

Table 2.2 shows the number and rate of total arrests in Oakland, between 1870 and 1910, and in 1920. The general rates, as we see, were fairly stable in the 1870s, dropped, then rose to a rather high rate by 1890, dropped sharply to 1900, then rose in the 1900s. There was a huge bulge after the earthquake of 1906, when law and order became a major problem; we will discuss this matter further in Chapter 4. The rate rose again, reaching a peak in 1919. In the 1920s it fell again, to about 60 per thousand.[19] These rates, of course, include

Table 2.2. Arrest Rates in Oakland, 1870–1920

Year	Population	No. Arrests	Arrests/1000 Population
1870	11,104	702	63.2
1872	12,011	824	68.6
1875	24,840	1,800	72.5
1880	34,555	2,141	62.0
1890	48,682	4,177	85.5
1900	66,960	2,599	38.8
1910	150,174	8,495	56.6
1920	216,261	19,870	91.9

Sources: Population data from U.S. Census Bureau, except for 1872 and 1875 data, which come from special censuses of Oakland and are reported in Oakland city directories for those years. Arrest data are from Oakland police Arrest Books, except for 1920 data, which are from Walter G. Beach, *Oriental Crime in California* (Stanford, Calif., 1932), p. 30.

19. It is interesting to compare Oakland's rates with those of other cities. Arrest statistics are on hand for seventeen large cities, with populations over 100,000, for 1880. Oakland's rate—62 per 1,000—was higher than those of most of these cities (New York's was 59.3, Chicago's 56.6, Cleveland's 46.4). U.S. Bureau of the Census, *Social Statistics of Cities*, pts. 1 (1886) and 2 (1887). In its own size class (25,000 to 45,000), Oakland ranked fourth highest of twenty-seven cities. Generally speaking, southern and western cities had high arrest rates. (San Francisco arrested 90 per thousand, Sacramento 121, Stockton 145.) Big cities arrested more people, proportionately, than small cities; but regional differences were greater than differences between size categories.

In 1907, South and West still led the country in arrest rates. U.S. Bureau of the Census, *Statistics of Cities Having a Population of over 30,000: 1907* (1910), p. 14. The Pacific region (California, Oregon, Washington) arrested 115 per 1,000; the industrial North (New York, New Jersey, Pennsylvania) only 51 per 1,000. Jumping ahead to 1972, we find that the Oakland police made 39,325 arrests, a rate of 108 per 1,000. California Bureau of Criminal Statistics, *Crimes and Arrests, 1972* (1972), p. 97. Of course, most of these were arrests for petty crimes; many were traffic violations. Still, the rates (and of course the raw numbers) are considerably higher than a century ago, though differences between the 1970s and, say, 1910, are by no means striking.

*Table 2.3. Number and Rate of Arrests for Felonies
against Persons and Property in Oakland, 1875–1970*

Type of felony	1875		1880		1890	
	No. arrests	Per 1,000 population	No. arrests	Per 1,000 population	No. arrests	Per 1,000 population
Personal violence	28	1.13	42	1.21	35	0.72
Property crimes	197	7.94	152	4.39	62	1.27
Total persons & property	225	9.07	194	5.60	97	1.99

Sources: Oakland Police Department, *Annual Report of the Chief of Police*, 1875, 1880, FY 1900; Oakland Arrest Books for 1890 and 1910; Oakland Police Department, *1970 Annual Crime Survey* (1971).

all arrests, including drunkenness and gambling, rates that have no obvious relationship to how much people actually gambled or drank.

Table 2.3, on the other hand, gives the number and rate of selected felony arrests in Oakland for selected census years between 1875 and 1910 (and in 1970). The reader will immediately note a sharp drop in the rate between 1875 and 1910. The decline was particularly dramatic for property crimes—grand larceny, burglary, theft. In 1875, for example, the police arrested 197 people for these crimes—a rate of 7.94 per thousand. In 1900 there were 35 arrests for these crimes—a rate of 0.52 per thousand. Between 1900 and 1910, the rate rose; even so, the arrest rate in 1910 was less than 10 percent the rate for 1875. There was also a sharp drop in the arrest rate for felonies against the person—murder, rape, robbery, assault with a deadly weapon—between 1880 and 1910. The rate fell to less than one-third of what it had been. In 1875 over 13 percent of all arrests carried a felony charge. By 1910, however, felony arrests were down to less than 3 percent of all arrests. Over our period, catching felons took less and less police time and energy. If we leave out felonies likely to go up and down with enforcement policy—nonsupport, for example—the trend is even more pronounced. As we saw, the overall Oakland arrest rate was lower in the early 1900s than in the 1870s. Both the rate of felony arrests and their share of total arrests dropped off in a major way (see Table 2.4).[20] By way of contrast, we also show figures for 1970. What-

20. The rate of felony arrests dipped sharply between 1886 and 1900; otherwise, the decline was steady until about 1905, when the rate leveled off.

1900		1910		1970	
No. arrests	*Per 1,000 population*	*No. arrests*	*Per 1,000 population*	*No. arrests*	*Per 1,000 population*
37	0.55	53	0.35	1,538	4.25
35	0.52	117	0.78	7,665	21.20
72	1.07	170	1.13	9,203	25.45

ever their problems of accuracy, they certainly do suggest a huge, real increase in crime.

How can we explain the decline in felony arrest rates? Possibly the police simply did a poorer job. Were they overwhelmed by work? This is unlikely: the average number of arrests per policeman in Oakland rose swiftly from 1868 to 1875; after that, it wobbled back and forth inconclusively (see Table 2.5). During the 1880s and 1890s, the police force grew faster than the population, but made fewer felony arrests. Between 1900 and 1910, the arrest rate for serious crimes inched upward; the number of police per 1,000 people actually fell.

There is no reason to think that serious crime strained police resources in Oakland. Between 1875 and 1900, felony arrests per policeman in Oakland went down precipitously, from 18.8 to 1.2 annually. (Between 1900 and 1910, it rose slightly, to 1.7.) Were the police better at their jobs? Not if arrest rates are any measure: Table 2.6 shows arrests per officer, in our period; and it certainly does not support such an idea.

Did the decline in felony arrest rates occur in other parts of the county as well? We cannot be sure, for our arrest information is only from Oakland. But we can trace what happened to the rate of felony *commitments* in other areas of the county between 1880 and 1910; we know in what part of the county each case in our Superior Court sample originated. Table 2.7 presents the results. The most urbanized townships in the county, Oakland and Alameda townships, show substantial declines in the rate of felony prosecutions in each decade, while the rate in Murray Township, the most sparsely populated, in

*Table 2.4. Felony Arrests as a Percentage of
All Arrests by Oakland Police, 1875–1970*

Type of felony	1875		1880		1890	
	No. arrests	% of total	No. arrests	% of total	No. arrests	% of total
Personal violence	28	1.6	42	2.0	35	0.8
Property crimes	197	10.9	152	7.1	62	1.5
Subtotal	225	12.5	194	9.1	97	2.3
Other felonies	11	0.6	40	1.8	20	0.5
Total	236	13.1	234	10.9	117	2.8

Sources: Oakland Police Department, *Annual Report of the Chief of Police*, 1875, 1880, FY 1900; Oakland Arrest Books for 1890 and 1910.

the rural eastern expanse of the county, increased a bit. Washington Township, in the lightly populated southern area of the county, shows a sharp decline in the rate of felony prosecutions in the last decade, while moderately populated Brooklyn and Eden townships show no clear trend. No township shows a substantial increase. These figures suggest that the decline in the rate of felony prosecutions was not uniform throughout the county, although it was particularly pronounced in the most populous areas.

What are we left with? We must conclude, a bit timidly, that real crime rates probably declined in the county. Apparently, in the late nineteenth century, Oakland became less violent, more orderly. The city grew rapidly; so did its police force; so too (apparently) did law and order. Arrest rates fell. City (and county) became more "civilized." And the change was more striking precisely where crime seems most at home: that is, in the cities.

It is treacherous to compare arrest rates from city to city; no two seem to count the same way. But within the same city, changes in arrest rates may tell a fairly coherent story. There is good reason to think that Alameda County was not alone in its experience. Most authorities believe that serious crime did decline in the late nineteenth century, and that it kept on declining in the twentieth century, until, at some point, unknown forces turned the crime curve upward again.

1900		1910		1970	
No. arrests	*% of total*	*No. arrests*	*% of total*	*No. arrests*	*% of total*
37	1.2	53	0.6	1,538	2.8
35	1.2	117	1.4	7,665	13.7
72	2.4	170	2.0	9,203	16.5
4	0.1	62	0.7	3,691	6.6
76	2.5	232	2.7	12,894	23.1

Graphs of arrest rates have a similar pattern, by and large, in many different cities. Most notably, Ted Gurr and his associates found this pattern of ebb and flow in London, Stockholm, and Sydney, Australia.[21] The crime rate bottomed out some time early in this century, then rose slowly for a while in the period up to the Second World War. After that came the flood. Felony arrests in Oakland in the 1970s utterly dwarfed the rates of arrest between 1872 and 1910. Drug cases are to blame for some of this explosion. Still, when we put arrest rates for major crimes in Oakland in 1970 next to those of 1870, the results are startling. Modern rates are, on the whole, nearly three times greater than they were a century ago, and more than twenty

21. Roger Lane, "Urbanization and Criminal Violence in the 20th Century: Massachusetts as a Test Case," in *Violence in America: Historical and Comparative Perspectives*, ed. H. D. Graham and Ted R. Gurr (New York, 1969); Ted Robert Gurr, and Peter N. Grabosky, *Rogues, Rebels and Reformers: A Political History of Urban Crime and Conflict* (Beverly Hills, 1976); Ted R. Gurr, Peter N. Grabosky, and Richard C. Hula, *The Politics of Crime and Conflict: A Comparative History of Four Cities* (Beverly Hills, 1977); Peter N. Grabosky, *Sydney in Ferment: Crime, Dissent, and Official Reactions, 1788 to 1973*, (Canberra, Australia, 1977); Ferdinand, "Criminal Patterns of Boston," p. 84; Leonard V. Harrison, *Police Administration in Boston* (Cambridge, Mass., 1934), pp. 12–18. The results in Edwin H. Powell's study, "Crime as a Function of Anomie," *J. Crim. L.C. & P.S.* 57 (1966): 161 (Buffalo, 1856–1946), are also generally consistent with the results of these other studies. See also Waldo L. Cook, "Murders in Massachusetts," *J. Am. Statistical Ass'n*, n.s., no. 23, Sept. 1893, p. 357.

*Table 2.5. Number of Arrests, Number of
Police, and Arrests per Officer in Oakland, 1868–1910*

Year	No. arrests	No. police	Arrests / officer	Year	No. arrests	No. police	Arrests / officer
1868	368	6	61.3	1890	4,177	38	109.9
1869	450	7	64.3	1891	3,495	40	87.4
1870	702	11	63.8	1892	3,094	46	67.3
1871	866	10	86.6	1893	3,210	50	64.2
1872	824	12	68.7	1894	3,032	50	60.6
1873	1,079	12	89.9	1895	3,144	49	62.9
1874	1,265	10	126.5	1896	3,066	50	61.3
1875	1,800	12	150.0	1897	2,790	50	55.8
1876	2,162	15	144.1	1898	2,505	60	41.8
1877	2,989	21	142.3	1899	2,955	61	48.4
1878	2,143	23	93.2	1900	2,599	61	42.6
1879	2,063	26	79.3	1901	3,314	—	—
1880	2,141	25	85.6	1902	4,162	66	63.1
1881	2,123	27	78.6	1903	4,718	66	71.5
1882	1,940	27	71.9	1904	4,869	—	—
1883	2,200	23	95.6	1905	4,431	70	63.3
1884	2,105	27	78.0	1906	9,478	71	133.5
1885	2,639	27	97.7	1907	11,308	—	—
1886	3,082	29	106.3	1908	9,945	111	89.6
1887	2,974	33	90.1	1909	8,852	112	79.0
1888	3,312	34	97.4	1910	8,495	102	83.2
1889	3,702	32	115.7				

Sources: Oakland Police Department, *Annual Report of the Chief of Police* (1900), p. 29; Oakland city directories; Oakland Arrest Books, 1872–1910.

*Table 2.6. Number of Felony Arrests per Policeman for
Offenses against Persons and Property in Oakland, 1875–1910*

Year	No. arrests	No. police	Arrests / policeman
1875	225	12	18.8
1880	194	25	7.8
1890	97	38	2.6
1900	72	61	1.2
1910	170	102	1.7

Sources: Oakland Police Department, *Annual Report of the Chief of Police*, 1875, 1880, FY 1900; Oakland Arrest Books for 1890 and 1910; Oakland city directories.

Table 2.7. *Estimated Average Annual Rates of Felony Prosecutions in Alameda County by Township, 1880–1910*

Township	1880–1889		1890–1899		1900–1910	
	No./ year	Per 1,000 popu- lation	No./ year	Per 1,000 popu- lation	No./ year	Per 1,000 popu- lation
Alameda Township	6.6	0.78	6.3	0.46	6.9	0.34
Brooklyn Township	1.0	0.11	4.1	0.26	5.4	0.15
Eden Township	2.0	0.31	2.3	0.28	3.1	0.29
Murray Township	3.5	0.67	4.9	0.75	6.4	0.91
Oakland Township	55.0	1.25	57.6	0.93	91.4	0.81
Washington Township	4.5	0.88	5.5	0.87	3.1	0.42
Total Alameda County	72.7	0.95	80.7	0.73	116.3	0.62

Source: Calculated from estimated distribution of felony prosecutions among townships derived from sample of Superior Court case files, applied to known total number of felony prosecutions in county.

times greater than arrest rates in 1910. Since the Second World War there has been, for whatever cause, a worldwide stampede toward crime.

Attitudes toward Crime

We have argued that serious crime was probably declining in the late nineteenth century. But people living then had no way of knowing this precisely. They were completely in the dark about crime rates. All they had were impressions, and some scraps of statistics, mostly about arrests and prison populations. These figures were unreliable; and, in any case, they were feeble shadows of actual crime rates.[22]

Scholars, too, had nothing better than prison populations to go on. The figures suggested to one authority, writing in 1910, that serious crime had "increased out of proportion to the population" between

22. See Louis N. Robinson, *History and Organization of Criminal Statistics in the United States* (Montclair, N.J., 1911); President's Commission on Law Enforcement and the Administration of Justice, *Task Force Report: Crime and Its Impact—an Assessment* (Washington, D.C., 1967), p. 124. Even in more recent times, we can ask whether *national* figures are any good. See Stanton Wheeler, "Criminal Statistics: A Reformulation of the Problem," *J. Crim. L.C. & P.S.* 58 (1967): 16.

1880 and 1904; the big bulge came between 1880 and 1895.[23] Another scholar, Roland Falkner, argued years earlier that prison figures were unreliable—indeed, positively pernicious, because they raised, unjustifiably, "the spectre of increasing crime."[24] Arthur Train, a shrewd observer, thought (in 1912) that crime was decreasing; he also thought the "popular impression" was otherwise, especially during crime waves.[25]

There is little doubt that attitudes toward crime and punishment have a profound effect on the way the system works. Yet our sources fail us here completely. We know next to nothing about what people thought about criminal justice. All we have, basically, are scattered columns of print in the *Oakland Tribune* and in other county papers. These add up to very little, even if we were sure we knew who the press really spoke for. Still, the topic is so crucial that we have to take a stab at it. There is one piece of negative evidence; if crime was a dark, ever-present physical threat, we would expect to find traces of this fear in the newspapers. We find very little. Street crime haunts the cities today; the papers are full of reports of horrible, senseless crimes. The silence of the press between 1880 and 1910 speaks volumes. To be sure, the pages of the newspapers were stuffed with crime news. But fear and horror of crime are harder to find. What was reported was mostly theft, and crimes of passion. Crime was, apparently, no immediate danger, no brooding threat.

On the other hand, crime stories in the press are striking in another regard: their total lack of compassion. Once in a great while, some sympathy is expressed for people caught up in crimes of love and hate: a woman who killed her seducer, for example. But generally speaking, there is hardly any sense that members of the "criminal class" are of the same species as the *Tribune*'s reporters, or the judges, or policemen on the beat. The most that can be said is that people saw two types of criminal—those who were criminal "from accident or association," and those criminal "from congenital predisposition or degeneration." The first group were to be made "fit—if possible." The second group had to be "sequestered" for life, or snuffed out as "unfit to live."[26]

---

23. Charles A. Ellwood, "Has Crime Increased in the United States since 1880?" *J. Crim. L.* 1 (1910): 378. Ellwood was professor of sociology at the University of Missouri.

24. Roland P. Falkner, "Crime and the Census," *Annals* 9 (1897): 42, 44–45. Waldo Cook, in "Murders in Massachusetts," argued that murder in Massachusetts had decreased between 1871 and 1892.

25. Arthur Train, *Courts and Criminals* (New York, 1912), p. 214.

26. *Oakland Herald*, May 4, 1904, p. 2, col. 3. These were also the views of more scientific observers. See Edward S. Morse, "Natural Selection and Crime," *Popular Science Monthly*, August 1892, p. 433.

In general, there is no trace of "there but for the grace of God go I," no hint that these wretched, naked lives are the lives of fallen angels. The truly guilty, the "unfit," are creatures apart. The Chinese are the extreme case. Chinese criminals are always spoken of with disgust and contempt: "Mongolians," "celestials," "highbinders." The white population also gets its lumps. The serious offender is a fiend; the petty offender, a joke.

Was it always so? It was always the case that people divided criminals into two degrees: those that could be saved, and those eternally damned. And the damned were always deeply different from the savables. In colonial New England, for example, crime and sin overlapped. Most offenders were servants, and punishment was paternal in form. Convicted criminals were fined, whipped, made to sit in the stocks, held up to shame. Magistrates treated offenders like wayward children, black sheep of a single flock. Only those who sinned repeatedly showed themselves as children of the devil: these, then, were branded, cast out, or, in intractable cases, hanged. The Salem witch trials were unusually savage; here the criminals were literally devils. No odium, no punishment, could be too severe for the forces of darkness, masquerading as human beings.

Alameda County was too advanced to believe in witches and devils. Yet here too the "real" criminal belonged to a different order. Sometimes he was an outsider in the literal sense—a member of another race, or a transient, a stranger, a wanderer, a tramp. Or he might be rotten from birth—genetically weak, doomed to crime from the womb or before—or so weak in character, so debased by bad company or sex, so sozzled by opium or drink that he was past redemption.[27] He was the enemy, inside the gates. He wore a human skin, but was really an alien life form, an invader from space.

27. We will return to this point at a number of places in this study, and in the conclusion. For now, it might be enough to point to Cook's "Murders in Massachusetts." Cook found that murder was declining; but, to his puzzlement, many of Massachusetts' murders between 1872 and 1892 took place in remote rural towns that were losing population. Perhaps the "best stock of the old families" had moved away, leaving the least desirable of "the old native stock. . . . Population has dwindled and the consequent inter-marriages between relatives have perhaps caused deterioration in many families." Ibid., p. 377.

A belief that "hereditary tendencies" helped form the criminal character did not necessarily mean that the person of bad stock was absolutely fated to become a criminal. People varied greatly in the weight they assigned to blood and to environment. Richard Dugdale, for example, struck by the relationship between crime and the business cycle, felt that "commercial and industrial crises" tended to "restore the chronic conditions of savage life—war and hunger—which produce reversions toward barbaric impulse" even among "fairly civilized" races. Richard Dugdale, "Origin of Crime in Society," *Atlantic Monthly* 48 (October 1881): 452, 458. See also, in general, Ysabel Rennie, *The Search for Criminal Man: A Conceptual History of the Dangerous Offender* (Lexington, Mass., 1978).

This was a new community, growing like a weed, striving and searching; its population too was striving and new. It lacked roots, it lacked tradition. Society as a whole was short on self-confidence, perhaps. It came to value respectability inordinately, and it despised lawlessness and crime. The real threat of crime was not physical so much as moral—crime was society's underbelly, its vice, its weakness, its nightmare, its secret soul. It had to be debased and repressed. Of course, we know none of this directly. We have to infer these attitudes, from words here and there, from the *feel* of the age. The public was, as always, invisible, inarticulate. It was a chorus that never stepped on the stage, but whose breathing can be felt behind the scenes.

Chapter 3
The Skeleton of the Law

In this chapter, we will describe, in rough outline, how the criminal justice system in Alameda County was put together. We will say a few words, in a preliminary way, about the way the system worked—the people, the roles, the institutions.

Of the people, some were amateurs, plain and simple: the victims of crime, for example, and the men who sat on juries. Others made a living out of criminal justice: police, sheriffs, detectives, coroners, lawyers, and judges. Still others were more or less in between: part-time policemen, constables who had other jobs. Many lawyers, too, were on the fringes; they were civil lawyers who turned a criminal trick now and then. At the beginning of the period, the amateurs predominated—they overwhelmed the system. Slowly, but definitely, criminal justice became more professional. More and more, the hands at the helm were those of people who did nothing else but work at the practice and law of crime control. This shift from amateur to nonamateur is one of the major themes of this study. We meet it first in this chapter; we will see it later in more detail.

The Pyramid of Justice

There were three levels of courts in California, ranked in the usual pyramid form. The basic criminal court, from 1880 on, was the Superior Court. The court heard all felony cases. It replaced the old County Court, which tried criminal cases before 1880. Underneath the Superior Court were justices' courts or police courts—petty courts that heard cases of petty crime. At the top of the pyramid was the Supreme Court of California. Until 1905, this was the only true appellate court.[1] We consider appeals in Chapter 8.

Justice courts operated in townships. They handled cases of petty larceny; assault and battery;[2] breaches of the peace; "riots, routs,

1. *Some* cases did go from justice or police court to Superior Court. See the next section of this chapter.
2. But not assaults committed on a "public officer in the discharge of his duties" or "committed with such intent as to render the offense a felony."

affrays"; willful injuries to property; and misdemeanors punishable by fines of less than $500, or imprisonment of six months or less (§ 1425). A police court also had power to deal with vagrants, "lewd or disorderly persons," and violators of city ordinances (Pol. Code, §§ 4426, 4427). An endless parade of drunks, gamblers, brawlers, and noisy neighbors filed through these courts—a daily harvest of misery, grievance, disorder, and spite. We discuss these courts in Chapter 4.

The Superior Court

After 1880, all important criminal cases passed through Superior Court. The court had original jurisdiction over all felony cases in the county. "Original" means that these cases belonged, first and last, to this court: they did not start elsewhere and move up to Superior Court by way of appeal. (They were, however, *screened* elsewhere, by a grand jury or magistrate, as we shall see.)

The Superior Court also heard cases that began in petty courts. If a justice or police court slapped a fine of thirty-five dollars, or more, on a defendant, or ordered him to jail for eighteen days or more, he had the right to take his case to Superior Court. Strictly speaking, these were not true appeals; the cases were tried in Superior Court *de novo*. This means that the court did more than comb the record for "errors"; it did the whole case over again. Superior Court also heard a handful of misdemeanor cases, and some cases of habeas corpus, that is, complaints that people were illegally held (usually in jail).[3]

Table 3.1 shows the distribution of criminal work in Superior Court. Most of the cases—80 percent—were ordinary felony cases, starting in Superior Court. A tiny number were misdemeanors.[4] Rather more were appeals. The numbers of appeals fluctuated quite wildly. There were 29 in 1899, but none at all in 1907. In the whole period, 1880–1910, there were 294 appeals, or about 9.5 a year. These were a varied lot. Maria Rogers, in 1880 (no. 53), let two cows "run at large upon a

3. The court, in the days before juvenile courts, also heard petitions to commit boys and girls to state institutions—usually at the request of disgusted parents. Ard Sparman, age sixteen, was convicted in justice court of disturbing the peace. His father asked the court to send his son to the Preston School of Industry (no. 1931, 1896).

4. Under Code Civ. Proc., § 76, the Superior Courts handled misdemeanors "not otherwise provided for." Code Civ. Proc., § 115, stated that justice courts were *not* to handle cases of assault and battery of police officers, or misdemeanors punishable by fines of more than $500 or imprisonment for more than six months. There were only a few such serious misdemeanors, for example, destruction or injury to a bridge, dam, or levee, which carried a fine of up to $1,000 and a term in county jail of up to two years (§ 607). Code Civ. Proc., § 115, was repealed in 1907, but § 1425, Penal Code, enacted in 1905, contained the same provisions.

*Table 3.1. Criminal Proceedings in
Alameda County Superior Court, 1880–1910*

Year	Felony cases	Misdemeanors	Appeals	Habeas corpus
1880	112	5	17	0
1881	86	1	9	0
1882	58	3	5	0
1883	60	0	10	0
1884	62	1	13	0
1885	80	2	13	0
1886	68	2	5	0
1887	55	1	13	0
1888	71	4	4	12
1889	76	2	4	13
1890	78	0	6	24
1891	73	3	13	18
1892	95	0	16	13
1893	100	3	8	11
1894	93	1	7	15
1895	78	1	18	13
1896	71	0	15	28
1897	89	1	6	16
1898	65	0	5	14
1899	65	1	29	6
1900	75	0	11	13
1901	80	1	4	9
1902	83	1	12	7
1903	86	5	1	23
1904	85	3	8	19
1905	87	2	6	20
1906	105	0	9	24
1907	176	0	0	34
1908	166	0	9	28
1909	151	2	10	26
1910	183	2	8	13
1880–84	378	10	54	0
1885–89	350	11	39	25
1890–94	439	7	50	81
1895–99	368	4	73	77
1900–1904	409	10	36	71
1905–9	687	4	34	132

Table 3.1. (continued)

Year	Felony cases	Misdemeanors	Appeals	Habeas corpus
1880–89	728	21	93	25
1890–99	807	11	123	158
1900–1909	1,096	14	70	203
1880–94	1,167	28	143	106
1895–1909	1,464	18	143	280
1880–1910	2,814	47	294	399

public street"; this violated an Alameda ordinance. Whether out of outrage or stubbornness, she refused to accept the verdict against her, and appealed to the higher court. Mary McGladry, in 1881, was found guilty of battering her stepson with a butcher knife. This was in justice court in Eden township. The sentence—thirty dollars or thirty days in county jail—stuck in her craw; she appealed (and lost again) (no. 257). Albert Konigsberg lived in Berkeley. In 1908 he threw a wiring inspector out of his house. The inspector said that Albert called him names ("cheap fifteen dollar inspector," and "dirty son-of-a-bitch") and kicked him on the thigh. Konigsberg was fined fifty dollars. He hired a lawyer, Charles F. Craig, and took the case upstairs. He too lost again (no. 4474).[5] Most of these appeals were socially insignificant; in a few cases, the dollar stake was small, but the principle large. We will see some examples later. Habeas corpus cases were also really appeals from lower courts, whatever their technical form. They too varied greatly in number from year to year. There were six in 1899, thirty-four in 1907.[6]

The Superior Court's workload was not, by modern standards, oppressive. In the 1880s, there were as few as 55 felony prosecutions a year (1887); the average was 73. This rose to 81 in the 1890s, and 110

5. His defense was that he thought the man was an intruder; that he never kicked him; and that the inspector called him a "Jew son of a bitch."

6. Another writ, much rarer, was the writ of prohibition. This was an order issued to a lower court telling that court to stop some sort of proceeding, because the lower court was exceeding its powers. The Superior Court would issue the writ only if no other "plain, speedy, and adequate remedy" was available (Code Civ. Proc., §§ 1102, 1103). A certain Conrad Frischknecht, for example, applied for the writ in 1904 (no. 2794). His trial, in justices' court of Brooklyn Township, ended in a hung jury. He was tried again; again the jury hung. Frischknecht then tried to finish off the case, arguing that the court had done nothing for more than sixty days after the second trial. This made the case stale, and it should have been dismissed. But the trial judge claimed that Frischknecht (and his lawyer) had agreed to the delays; thus they lost their right to complain that the case was stale.

in the 1900s. If we throw in appeals, habeas writs, and misdemeanors, the yearly averages for the three decades were 87, 110, and 138 cases, respectively. There was, in short, a steady growth in case load. But the growth was slow, and it lagged behind population growth.[7] In 1974, by way of contrast, there were about 2,000 felony cases in Superior Court.

There were two ways an ordinary criminal case could reach Superior Court—information or indictment. In some states, indictment by grand jury was and is the preferred way, sometimes the only way. In these states, when a person is arrested, he goes before a magistrate. If the magistrate finds "probable cause"—that is, if he feels there is enough of a case to hold the man for trial—he sends the case on to the grand jury. The grand jury sifts the evidence, and decides whether to indict. If it does indict, the defendant faces trial.

California followed this method until 1880. But there were problems with the grand jury system: it was cumbersome, unwieldly. The trouble was that the grand jury sat only four times a year. In other words, cases were first delayed, then bunched together. This was tolerable, or unavoidable, in the days before full-time prosecutors. Full-time prosecutors saw little need for a grand jury to dig up facts and develop evidence, however; grand jury delays did not seem worth the trouble.

In 1880, California changed its law to add a different route to Superior Court.[8] As before, a person arrested on a felony charge went before a magistrate (justice of the peace or police judge). This judge conducted a *preliminary examination*. If the judge found probable cause, he "bound the defendant over" to Superior Court. There the prosecution filed a kind of complaint, called an *information*. The Superior Court, unlike a grand jury, was in continuous session (except for vacations).[9] From 1880 on, the state used both information *and* indictment. But indictment shriveled in importance. Only 8 percent

7. The number of felony "cases" in Table 3.1 is adjusted for multiple charging; it represents the number of separate felony prosecutions, rather than the raw numbers of charges.

There were no petitions for habeas corpus in registers or files for 1880–88. It seems most unlikely that there were no such petitions; they were apparently not recorded in the usual way, and all knowledge of them has vanished. This may throw work-load figures slightly off for the 1880s, but would not affect the general trend.

8. Calif. Const. 1879, Art. 1, § 8. In Hurtado v. California, 110 U.S. 516 (1884), the U.S. Supreme Court upheld the new California procedure. The technical question was whether the Fourteenth Amendment incorporated the federal requirement of indictment, and imposed it on the states. The court, over Justice Harlan's dissent, said no.

9. In 1906, for example, the court fixed June 18–August 17 as its vacation period; even so, a judge (or two) would sit, to handle the "vacation calendar," that is, urgent or interim matters. *Berkeley Reporter*, Mar. 27, 1906, p. 1, col. 3.

of the cases between 1880 and 1910 started out by way of indictment. (Indictment accounts for an even smaller number today—on the order of 1 percent.)

The Superior Court was, in theory, a single court, whose writ ran throughout the county. But Alameda County was a big, populous county. From the very first, the Superior Court had more than one judge, and the court sat in "departments." In 1880 there were two departments. Department One took over the business of the old District Court. This meant it could hear treason cases, murder or manslaughter cases, civil cases worth $300 or more, and insolvency actions. Department Two fell heir to most of the business of the old County Court. This included probate work, and the rest of the criminal cases. Department Two, then, was essentially the criminal division. In 1880, too, the court had two judges, one for each department —W. E. Greene and Addison Crane.[10]

Judge Crane has left us a description of the court at work in 1880, in the old County Courthouse at Forrest and Broadway. The court, he said, was "open" at all times "during business hours, and on judicial days." On days when there were no trials, at least one judge was "in chambers." But either judge could "make any order or transact any business in either or both departments." The court met five days a week; sometimes it also sat on Saturdays, to finish a trial already under way. Arguments and motions were heard every morning in Department One at 9:30 from September to March, and at 9:00 the rest of the year.

As the years went on, and the county grew in population, the caseload also grew. The legislature added more judges, and for each judge, the court created another department. In 1900, there were five departments and five judges (there are thirty-seven today). It is not always crystal clear how business was divided among departments, but one or two departments always handled most of the criminal business. We look at felony proceedings in more detail in Chapters 5 and 6.

The Judges

The justice of the peace and the police judge were at the bottom of the judicial pyramid. Under California law, each township had to have at

---

10. In a few cases—cases with a possible death sentence, for example—the judges sat together. They also sometimes "exchanged" departments. Statement of Superior Court Judge A. M. Crane, *Oakland Tribune*, Jan. 5, 1880, p. 3, col. 3.

least one justice of the peace. The County Board of Supervisors could, if it wished, add a second justice court, in any township that needed it (Code Civ. Proc., § 110). In 1870 every township had two (Brooklyn and Murray townships later dropped to one). Oakland township had five justices between 1890 and 1910. Cities above a certain threshold size (10,000 in 1880, 15,000 in 1891) had to have a *city* justice; cities the size of Oakland (over 20,000 population in 1880, over 34,000 population in 1891) were allowed to have two. Besides Oakland, there were eventually city justices in Berkeley and in Alameda. By special law, the legislature created a police court in Oakland, and, later, a recorder's court in Emeryville. Police judges, city justices, and recorders had the same jurisdiction as township justices, plus power to enforce local ordinances. The judges ran for office, were nearly always Republicans, and served two-year terms (after 1898, four-year terms).

Justices in the 1870s had no salaries; they made money from fees. Rural justices often complained that the pickings were poor. Oakland did away with the fee system in 1880. City justices and the police judge were to earn salaries of $2,000, and all fees would go to the city treasury. This brought Oakland a tidy profit. In 1908 the city's courts earned $70,000 from fees and fines; expenses were only $12,000. From 1906 on, township justices in Oakland, Alameda, and Brooklyn Township were paid $2,700 a year; judges in Eden, Murray, Pleasanton, and Washington townships received $900 (Pol. Code, § 4232). Township justices could keep their civil fees.

Who were the judges in these petty courts? When the fee system was in full flower, they tended to be middle-aged laymen. Asa Howard was a wheelwright, George Smith a fruit grower. Charles M. Radliff was justice of the peace for Alameda Township in 1876; he was fifty-eight years old, Scottish born, a machinist. Joseph Collingridge, a farmer in his mid-sixties, born in England, was justice of the peace for Eden Township between 1874 and 1879. Augustus Church was a wanderer, a jack-of-all-trades, who made and lost a fortune. He became a justice in Murray and Oakland townships and served until he was sixty-seven. The city justice of Oakland, on the other hand, had to be a member of the bar. Sextus Shearer, a lawyer from Massachusetts, served from 1878 to 1881 while he was in his seventies.[11]

Later justices tended to be younger. In 1880 the average age of the justices was fifty-three; in 1890 it was thirty-nine. The Oakland justices were, on the average, twenty-eight years old in 1900. Henry

---

11. A study of 164 justices in Washington Territory, 1853–89, found that their average age on starting their careers was 40.5 years. John R. Wunder, *Inferior Courts, Superior Justice: A History of the Justices of the Peace on the Northwest Frontier, 1853–1889* (Westport, Conn., 1979), p. 46.

Melvin was one of the new breed of justices. He was appointed justice for Brooklyn Township at twenty-five; he was then a law student at Hastings. (Melvin later joined the district attorney's office, became a Superior Court judge, and eventually served on the state Supreme Court.) By state law, Oakland justices could not practice law in other justice courts (Code Civ. Proc., § 103). This made the job less inviting for an established lawyer than for a young, up-and-coming lawyer. Outside Oakland, the justices had a hodgepodge of backgrounds and jobs; one was a saloonkeeper (Samuel Sandholt), one an Irish painter (Patrick C. Quinn), another a barber from the Azores (Joseph Pimental), still another a butcher from Tennessee (Robert Graham).

Like Henry Melvin in Brooklyn Township, many ambitious young lawyers served in the lower courts of Oakland. Some were destined for higher things. The job was an excellent springboard. Twelve men took office as lower court judges in Oakland between 1885 and 1910; seven of them later became judges of Superior Court: Frank Ogden, Fred Henshaw, John Allen, Fred Wood, James Quinn, Mortimer Smith, and George Samuels. Two became district attorneys (Charles Snook and John Allen); one (Emil Nusbaumer) became a deputy.

Seventeen men sat as trial court judges in the county, for felony cases, between 1870 and 1910 (see Table 3.2). After 1880, all felony cases went to Superior Court. There were fourteen judges on this court between 1880 and 1910.[12]

Of the seventeen judges, only four (Frick, Hall, Waste, and Wells) were natives of California. Two were foreign born: McKee was born in Ireland; Brown was born to American parents in Japan. Superior Court judges were elected for six-year terms. Sixteen of the seventeen were Republicans; Samuel Bell McKee, a District Court judge, an immigrant who struck it rich, was the only Democrat. A speaker told the state bar association in 1910 that a Democrat "could not break into one of the judicial positions with a jimmy."[13] Indeed, most judges

12. Five other men served as court commissioners. Under the law, any Superior Court could appoint such commissioners (Code Civ. Proc., §§ 258, 259). The commissioners, at the direction of trial judges, could conduct fact-finding hearings. They also had power to "approve bonds and undertakings." In practice, court commissioners worked mainly on surety bonds and depositions. For an example of deposition work in a robbery case—the defense lawyer was present and cross-examined the witness—see Charles Cropper et al. (1880, no. 142). The court commissioners did not play much of a role in the criminal justice system. John F. Havens (1880–82) and George Babcock (1896–1902) were men in their late sixties when they were appointed commissioners. David Connor (1889–90) later served as justice of the peace in Washington Township. Frederick E. Whitney (1883–88; 1891–95) was a teacher who graduated from law school at the age of thirty-two.

13. Oscar A. Trippet, quoted in California Bar Association, *Proceedings of First Annual Convention* (1910).

Table 3.2. Felony Trial Court Judges in Alameda County, 1870–1910

Name	Court	Term	Year born	Age when made judge	Originally elected or appointed
Samuel B. McKee	District	1865–79	1822	43	Elected
Stephen G. Nye	County	1868–78	1834	34	Appointed
R. A. Redman	County	1878–79	1830	48	Appointed
Addison M. Crane	Superior	1880–84	1815	65	Elected
William E. Greene	Superior	1880–1905	1836	43	Elected
Noble Hamilton	Superior	1882–88	1832	50	Appointed
Elkanah M. Gibson	Superior	1885–90	1842	42	Elected
John Ellsworth	Superior	1889–1913	1842	47	Elected
Fred W. Henshaw	Superior	1891–94	1858	32	Elected
Frank B. Ogden	Superior	1893–1918	1858	34	Appointed
Abraham L. Frick	Superior	1894–96	1866	28	Appointed
Samuel P. Hall	Superior	1897–1905	1854	43	Elected
Henry A. Melvin	Superior	1901–8	1865	35	Appointed
William H. Waste	Superior	1905–18	1868	36	Appointed
Thomas W. Harris	Superior	1905–50	1869	36	Appointed
Everett J. Brown	Superior	1908–21	1876	31	Appointed
William S. Wells	Superior	1909–19	1861	47	Appointed

were Republican stalwarts. They were, as far as we can tell, an energetic, ambitious lot, and mostly self-made men. (Harris, an only child of a poor family, once worked in a livery stable.) Eight judges were former prosecutors—four were district attorneys, four were assistants. Six had previous experience on the bench—three as county judges, two as Oakland police judges, and one (Wells) as Superior Court judge in Contra Costa. Greene had been a county judge in San Joaquin County. (He quit this job to manage his own lumber company.) The eight judges of 1870–90 were forty-seven years old on the average when they took office; the last nine judges were, on the average, only thirty-six. Six of the nine judges who took office *before* 1892 were elected; seven out of eight who took office *after* 1892 were appointed. Three of these latter—Ogden, Melvin, and Wells—were appointed because the court expanded; they headed new departments. Frick replaced Henshaw, who was elected to a higher court. Harris was appointed when Greene died.

Until 1880, the judges could practice law on the side, though not in their own court, or in any lower court from which their court took appeals (Code Civ. Proc., § 171). Judgeship was basically a part-time job. Stephen G. Nye took office in the late 1860s; the job, he later recalled, "hardly interfered" with his practice. By 1878, the job took up his "entire time," and his outside practice was "not worth $100 a year. In other words, the harder I worked the poorer I grew. I therefore resigned."[14] A law of 1880 set the salary of Superior Court judges at $4,000 (it was raised to $5,000 in 1905), and barred judges from practicing law in any California court.[15]

The Superior Court, of course, handled civil cases too. Between 1880 and November 1885, Judge Greene in Department Two took all the criminal cases. In November 1885, the court began a rotation system. Department Two (Judge Gibson) would hear criminal cases in January, April, July, and October; Department Three (Judge Greene) in February, May, August, and November; Department One (Judge Hamilton) in March, June, September, and December.[16] (Cases that began in one department usually stayed there, even if they ran over into other months. Transfers between departments were uncommon.) After July 1895, the court tried a new type of rotation. Criminal cases would all go to one department (Department Four until 1901, then Department Five); but each year a different judge would sit in that department. As a matter of fact, virtually all of the seventeen judges had *some* exposure to criminal cases during our period.[17]

Seven judges returned to private practice when they left the bench. Greene and Ogden died in office; Harris and Crane retired. Five went on to higher courts: Hall and Waste to the District Court of Appeals, McKee, Melvin, and Henshaw to the California Supreme Court. McKee was elected to the high court in 1879, a nominee of the Democrats and of the Workingmen's party. He was not renominated in 1886, and went back to private practice. Henshaw resigned from the Supreme Court in disgrace in 1917, under suspicion of taking a bribe in a will case. The charge was never proven positively, but a bad smell hung about the whole affair, and it tarnished his career.[18] Waste be-

14. Stephen G. Nye, "Before the Bar," *Oakland Tribune*, Dec. 19, 1891, p. 29, col. 4.

15. In 1881 the prohibition was extended; judges above the level of justice court were also not to practice law "before any department of the state or general government," or in the federal courts (Code Civ. Proc., § 171).

16. A petition for a writ of habeas corpus could be taken to any judge and at any time.

17. Under Article 6, § 7, of the California Constitution, "A Judge of any Superior Court may hold a Superior Court in any county, at a request of a Judge of the Superior Court thereof, and upon the request of the Governor it shall be his duty so to do." A visiting judge, Raker, from Modoc County, sat in Superior Court in Alameda County during part of 1894.

18. On Henshaw (1858–1929) see J. E. Johnson, *Supreme Court Justices of California, 1850–1950* (San Francisco, 1963), pp. 198–206.

came associate justice of the California Supreme Court in 1921. From 1926 to 1940, he served as chief justice.

The District Attorney and His Men

The district attorney was an elected county officer, an attorney who acted as "public prosecutor" (Pol. Code, §§ 4256, 4259). Ten men served as Alameda County district attorney between 1871 and 1910 (see Table 3.3). They were all young—none over forty when elected, none over forty-five on leaving office. They came, on the whole, from good families. John Glascock's father, William, had been a county judge, and was quite wealthy by the standards of the age. He reported assets of $160,000 to the census takers of 1870. Albert A. Moore was the nephew of Judge O'Melveny of the Los Angeles Superior Court. Colonel E. M. Gibson, who lost a leg at Gettysburg, was descended from people who came over on the Mayflower. Two of the ten were school-trained lawyers: Gibson graduated from the law department of George Washington University (1867); Everett Brown finished Hastings Law School in 1901. The rest "read law."

All had experience in private practice. Charles Snook worked for a San Francisco firm, Lowenthal and Sutter, in 1886. Everett Brown served in the law office of Congressman Victor H. Metcalf (later secretary of commerce and labor under Theodore Roosevelt). William H.

Table 3.3. Alameda County District Attorneys, 1871–1910

Name	Term	Year born	Age admitted to bar	Age became district attorney
Albert A. Moore	1871–74	1842	22	28
John R. Glascock	1875–77	1846	22	28
Henry Vrooman	1878	1844	30	34
E. M. Gibson	1878–82	1842	32*	36
Samuel P. Hall	1883–88	1854	28	29
George W. Reed	1889–92	1852	27	35
Charles E. Snook	1893–98	1863	23	30
John J. Allen	1899–1906	1863	23	36
Everett J. Brown	1907–8	1876	25	31
William H. Donahue	1908–12	1871	28	37

*Gibson was admitted to the California bar at age 32; he had been admitted to the District of Columbia bar at age 25.

Donahue went into practice with Thomas W. Harris, deputy district attorney, later judge of Superior Court.

Under state law the district attorney had to be twenty-one years old, a resident of California, eligible to vote (this excluded women), and, after 1891, a member of the bar (Pol. Code, § 4023). The district attorney was an elected official. This meant, in practice, that he was a well-connected Republican; throughout the period, the Republican party dominated county politics.

Three paths led to the district attorney's office. Four of our district attorneys worked their way up through the ranks. Henry Vrooman served as deputy district attorney under Albert Moore, and got Moore's job in 1878. Moore's brother-in-law, Samuel P. Hall, became Vrooman's deputy; after five years he was elected district attorney himself. Four of the ten—Moore, Glascock, Gibson, and Reed—came out of private practice. Charles E. Snook and John J. Allen had been justices of the peace in Oakland.

Serving as district attorney was not a full-time job in the 1870s. Case loads were light. There were four terms of court, and cases were tried in the first month of term. The district attorney practiced law on the side—civil work, so as not to conflict with his official duties. In the 1870s, he had no staff to speak of. Private lawyers sometimes helped him out in important cases. Gradually, as population grew, the job became more demanding; district attorneys had to drop most or all of their outside practice. And the staff grew to include "deputies." There were three lawyers on the staff in 1885, six in 1901, nine in 1910.[19] The deputies were usually fresh young lawyers. William H. L. Hynes was hired in 1899, six months out of Hastings. A few were more experienced. Ezra DeCoto signed on in 1907; he had practiced law for five years, and had also been Alameda County's first full-time probation officer. Emil Nusbaumer was a township justice for six years and then assistant district attorney (1889). Except for *very* important cases, deputies handled preliminary examinations. In Superior Court, they helped the district attorney in jury selection, motions, and cross-examination. They prosecuted misdemeanor cases in police court.

Deputies often had a civil practice on the side. The partnership of Snook, Frick and Church, formed in 1893, consisted of the district

19. The salary of the district attorney was $2,500 until 1897, then $4,000 [Laws Cal. 1897, p. 504, ch. 277, § 160(8)]. One chief deputy district attorney (Lin S. Church) received $2,000 per year in 1897. Assistant District Attorney Carlton W. Greene was paid $1,500; Deputy District Attorney A. A. Moore, Jr., made $1,200. There were two prosecuting attorneys, Henry A. Melvin and Abe P. Leach. Gaylord B. Ingersoll was a detective on the district attorney's staff; he earned $1,500 a year.

attorney himself and two of his assistants. In 1908, District Attorney William H. Donahue appointed young Anton A. Rodgers as a deputy. "Attorney Rodgers," said the *San Leandro Reporter*, "will also practice law and for the present will have his office at his home on Estudillo Avenue, where he will be pleased to have his friends call."[20]

The district attorney's office was, for some lawyers, a stepping-stone to success. Six deputies eventually became district attorney themselves. Ezra DeCoto got the post in 1918; he was succeeded in 1924 by Earl Warren.[21] Eleven prosecutors eventually became Superior Court judges. Colonel Gibson ran unsuccessfully for railroad commissioner and for mayor of Oakland; finally, he was elected to Superior Court. John Glascock was elected to Congress in 1878, the year he stepped down as district attorney. He was later mayor of Oakland, and president of the Alameda County Bar Association. George DeGolia, Vrooman, and Nusbaumer succeeded each other as Republican party leaders in the county. Abe P. Leach was attorney for the public administrator in 1909. James Johnson was Oakland's city attorney for more than a decade. Charles Snook became attorney for the Board of Regents of the state university in 1903. And others, of course, built solid careers as members of the bar.

Law Enforcers and Investigators

Judges and prosecutors were not the only players in the game of criminal justice. The police had a crucial and significant role. We treat them in more detail in the next chapter. The police were *city* officials. There were, in addition, county officers. One was the sheriff, whose duty was to preserve the peace. By law, the sheriff was to arrest and bring to a magistrate everyone who committed, or attempted, a "public offense." He was supposed to prevent and suppress riots, and to attend Superior Court and obey the judge's "lawful orders and directions." The sheriff also served process, and was in charge of the county jail (§ 4176). Constables were supposed to attend the justice courts in the various townships. There they had duties much like the sheriff's (§ 4314). In practice, it was the police who made arrests in the cities; the sheriff and his men served process.

The *coroner* had a minor role in the drama of crime. This ancient officer dealt only with death, or rather, dead bodies. The coroner

20. *San Leandro Reporter*, Dec. 26, 1908, p. 4, col. 3.
21. Warren described DeCoto as "not . . . particularly aggressive"; DeCoto "did little to change the status quo, although he insisted on integrity." Earl Warren, *Memoirs of Chief Justice Earl Warren* (Garden City, N.Y., 1977) p. 61.

stepped in if someone in the county was murdered, or killed himself, or died suddenly or suspiciously. The coroner's job was to look at the body—dig it up if necessary—and "inquire into the cause of the death." A coroner's *inquest* was a proceeding with a jury of nine to fifteen men. They had the grisly duty of viewing the corpse. The coroner could, if he wished, call in a doctor, or a "chemist" (to "make analysis of the stomach or the tissues of the body"). The coroner's jury heard testimony and called witnesses. It would then return a verdict, in writing, "setting forth who the person killed is, and when, where, and by what means he came to his death; and if he was killed, or his death occasioned by the act of another, by criminal means, who is guilty thereof" (§§ 1510–20).[22]

The coroner was archaic, but not obsolete. In 1905, he held 288 inquests, charging the county $10 per inquest, 25 cents for each witness subpoenaed, and mileage and miscellaneous expenses. About half the time, a doctor looked over the body. About one time out of four, there was an autopsy. (For an autopsy, the doctor charged $15; a mere inspection cost $5.) In this year the coroner subpoenaed 1,166 witnesses.[23] For the most part, the coroner worked quietly and obscurely. Sometimes, however, a horror or scandal pushed him into the limelight. In 1893 he had to examine the "gruesome relics" of a baby's body, inside a zinc-lined box.[24] This was the child of Dr. and Mrs. P. W. Poulson, of Fruitvale. Mrs. Poulson swore her baby was born alive; she hinted that her (estranged) husband killed it. But there was no proof, and the zinc box went back beneath the earth, this time for good. In 1902 a woman from Berkeley died mysteriously. Was she kicked to death, or did she die of drugs? The jury could say only that she died from "hemorrhage due to a rupture of the hepatic artery"; the cause was "unknown." The case was never solved.[25]

Citizens in the Halls of Justice: The Grand Jury

The grand jury was another ancient institution. As we noted, it lost the lion's share of its criminal work in 1880. It kept its role as a watchdog—that is, a general agency of investigation.[26] The grand

22. If the inquest pointed an accusing finger at someone, the coroner could issue a warrant for that person's arrest.
23. Expert's Report for the Grand Jury, for the Year 1905, filed July 24, 1906; Expert's Report for the Grand Jury, for the Year 1903, filed May 2, 1904. In only nine cases in 1905 was there neither an autopsy nor an inspection.
24. *Oakland Tribune*, Aug. 22, 1893, p. 3, col. 4.
25. Ibid., May 17, 1902, p. 5, col. 6, May 21, 1902, p. 2, col. 2.
26. The grand jury *was* a bit uncertain and defensive about its role. In its report of

jury was supposed to look over public contracts, sniff out official corruption, inspect jails and county buildings. Its report for December 1882, for example, criticized Oakland for allowing pools of stagnant water near the schools, analyzed the way the sheriff ran his office, complained about disgraceful conditions in the county jail, and exhorted the state to set up a "school of industry" for young offenders.

Who were the grand jurors, and how were they chosen? At the beginning of the year, the Superior Court judges estimated how many people they needed for the grand jury pool. (On January 3, 1894, they set the estimate at about 100.) Probably they picked names themselves, out of voter lists. The jurors, of course, were all men. There were two grand juries a year, each with nineteen jurors. To get these nineteen, the clerk was ordered to draw from the grand jury box "30 slips of paper containing the names of 30 persons." The sheriff and his deputies then summoned these thirty men to appear at the courthouse.[27] They served notice personally, or left the papers at their homes. The order was also posted at the courthouse. Naturally, not all thirty could typically be found. In June 1902 the sheriff was "unable to find W. T. Weitch. . . . I am informed and believe that [he] has gone to Honolulu." C. F. Acker, in September 1904, had gone on a much longer trip: the deputy sheriff could not find him at all, and was "reliably informed that he is dead." Others had medical excuses. Robert W. Edwards, chosen in 1896, got a letter of excuse from his doctor: Edwards had Bright's disease, was "confined to . . . the bed most of the time," and "had to use an instrument each time he empties his bladder." H. A. Pleitner, chosen in 1910, claimed bronchitis as his excuse. His doctor wrote that he had had "two attacks of pneumonia," and had to be "extremely careful."[28]

The sheriff usually managed to bag between twenty-five and twenty-seven men out of the thirty. The nineteen jurors were chosen,

---

Mar. 24, 1897, the jury referred to a "common practice" of speaking "slightingly of Grand Juries and their usefulness. . . . [I]n our opinion the money invested in Grand Juries . . . is well spent. The fact that a Grand Jury is in existence is to a certain extent a restraint upon crime, and it is public notice to all citizens who have grievances that they can come before such juries with their complaints at any time and they will be investigated."

27. See, for example, Dept. No. 2, In the Matter of Grand Juries, order dated Oct. 1, 1883 (Superior Court files). Our material on grand juries is drawn from scattered, unindexed papers in various file drawers in the Alameda County Courthouse.

28. Apparently some who should have excused themselves did not. A man named Held served on a grand jury in 1895, which indicted Myron Whidden on Sept. 11, 1895, for forgery, embezzlement, and falsifying public records. Whidden's attorneys argued successfully that Held was insane at the time of the indictment, and the indictment was quashed. Held died in October 1895; Whidden was reindicted, but a jury acquitted him.

apparently by lot, from this group. Because some produced medical or other excuses at *this* point, the judges sometimes found themselves with fewer than nineteen men. In spring 1895, for example, only eighteen survived the process, one juror short. The court issued an order to the sheriff, at 10:00 A.M., to "forthwith summon one good lawful man." The sheriff lost no time. He served an order on Daniel Stuart at 11:50 A.M. Where he found Stuart, and how, is not recorded.

After the grand jury was sworn in, the judge read the "charge" to the panel. This was a statement telling the panel what its duties were, and listing any "public offenses likely to come before the grand jury" (§ 905). The files still contain the texts of a few of these charges, though none earlier than 1894. The surviving texts are rather cut-and-dried. The judge would give a short lecture on the law of felonies, but then admit that the panel would "have but little to do" with such crimes. The other procedure (information) was "complete and just." Still, "certain classes of offense" belonged "peculiarly" to the grand jury. As Judge Ellsworth told the grand jury in December 1903, the grand jury would examine crimes where "the public press, or public rumor" spread the story about, but no one individual knew or cared enough "to lodge a complaint." District attorneys and magistrates did not act without a complaining witness. The grand jury (in theory) could. Grand jury power also extended to "cases of willful or corrupt misconduct in office."[29]

In fact, the few indictments handed down by grand juries did often include cases of official corruption. The grand jury also sometimes stepped in when the district attorney, for whatever reason, refused to make the first move on his own. In 1906 a young (and pregnant) woman, Isabel Davis, accused a state senator, M. W. Simpson, of seduction. The district attorney turned a deaf ear, and she tried the grand jury next. It duly returned an indictment.

Citizens in the Halls of Justice: The Trial Jury

The grand jury was shrinking in importance during the period. So, too, was the petit jury (the ordinary trial jury), as we shall see in later chapters. Still, this body played a far more important role in criminal justice than the grand jury did.

California law defined the jury as a body of men "returned from the citizens of a particular district, . . . sworn to try and determine,

29. Judge Ellsworth also told the grand jury that their room had been "transformed into a courtroom" for one of the judges. "There is, therefore, at present no regular room for you to hold your meetings in." They had to be satisfied with temporary use of a courtroom.

by verdict, a question of fact" (Code Civ. Proc., § 193). In cases of serious crime, the jury decided if a defendant was innocent or guilty. It was the voice of the people, but of course not all of the people. For one thing, all jurors were men. They also had to be citizens, twenty-one years old, residents of California for at least one year, and residents of the county for at least ninety days. They had to have "ordinary intelligence," and understand English. A convicted felon could not serve, nor anyone who was "decrepit." Jurors had to be property owners, "assessed on the last assessment-roll of the County" (Code Civ. Proc., § 198). A long list of people were exempt from jury duty: judges; lawyers; politicians; ministers; teachers; doctors; druggists; officials of almshouses, hospitals, asylums, and jails; express agents; mail carriers; telephone and telegraph workers; railroad engineers, brakemen, motormen, and conductors (Code Civ. Proc., § 200). A juror was excused if he had already done a turn that year. And of course he was excused if jury duty threatened his health or his property (Code Civ. Proc., § 201).

Jurymen were picked the same way grand jurymen were. In January the Superior Court would estimate how many jurors it would need in the pool for the year. (The judges in 1906 guessed that they would need 300 names.) Here too the judges apparently chose the names themselves, perhaps out of voter lists. In 1906 the five Superior Court judges divided the county into "five equal parts"; each judge took the district he knew best, and "selected and put in the trial jury box the names of 60 trial jurors."[30] The county clerk copied the names onto little pieces of paper, folded them, and put them in a box. The statute went so far as to tell the clerk to "shake the box . . . so as to mix the slips of paper . . . as well as possible" (Code Civ. Proc., § 219). Again, the sheriff had the job of summoning the jurors. Jurors were paid two dollars a day and fifteen cents a mile for travel from house to court and back.[31]

Unlike grand jurors, a petty juror had to face still another hurdle before he could serve: a possible "challenge" by lawyers on one side or the other. We will look at challenges, and the work of the jury, in Chapter 5.

---

30. *Berkeley Reporter*, Jan. 26, 1906, p. 3, col. 3.
31. The rules of residence were the same for jurors in justice and police courts, but selection procedures were less elaborate. Jurors were notified "orally" and told "the time and place at which their attendance is required" (Code Civ. Proc., § 231). For more details on selection of justice and police court jurors see "Trials in the Police Court" in Chap. 4, below.

Lawyers and Judges

In the drama of criminal process, lawyers were indispensable players. The judges of Superior Court were lawyers, and lawyers represented both sides in most of the cases. In some countries, the three roles—defense lawyer, prosecutor, judge—are quite distinct. It may be impossible or difficult to cross from one to the other; each has its own separate career line, its customs and traditions. The United States is otherwise. Judges, prosecutors, and defense attorneys come from the same social bag; they are members of a single occupation. Of course a sitting judge of Superior Court could not practice law, but all judges began their careers as ordinary lawyers, and sometimes they ended up that way as well. Some judges, too, were former prosecutors. A. L. Frick[32] occupied all three roles. Frick, son of a Sonoma County rancher, graduated from Hastings in 1888. In 1891 he became a deputy district attorney. In December 1894 he was appointed to Superior Court; he was only twenty-eight years old. After two years on the bench, he went back into private practice.

The United States is a country of lawyers; it has more lawyers per thousand people than any other country—about half a million lawyers in all. The sheer number of lawyers was growing rapidly in the late nineteenth century. It was not a hard profession to get into; and it was a known and attractive way up the ladder of success. Between 1870 and 1900, the general population grew by 97 percent; the number of lawyers, according to the census, grew much faster. In 1870 there were 40,000 lawyers in the country, 1.06 per 1,000 people; in 1900 there were 114,460, 1.51 per 1,000. California did even better; it was blessed (or cursed?) with a rich supply of lawyers—nearly twice as many, in proportion, as in the country as a whole. Between 1870 and 1900, California's population grew by 165 percent; but the legal profession nearly tripled. There were 1,115 lawyers in the state in 1870, or 1.99 per 1,000; there were 4,278 in 1900, or 2.88 per 1,000. Young lawyers seemed to think that success came quicker and easier in the West. We hear about "enormous numbers of fellows" heading west in the 1890s—lawyers on the train, at the depot, in the hotel, at table, "jostling you on the sidewalk . . . and when you board the train again to go further on to look for better pasture, some of them will go with you."[33] California, of course, was the end of the line: there were no further pastures, better or worse.

32. The initials stood for Abraham Lincoln, but that must have sounded too pompous for Frick. He consistently avoided using his full name.

33. *Law Student's Helper* 1 (1893): 144, 164.

California lawyers, as one might expect, were not spread evenly throughout the state. They clustered in urban areas, where the business was. In Alameda County, this meant, essentially, Oakland. Thanks to raw census returns for 1870 and 1880, we can be a bit more precise: Oakland, Brooklyn, and Alameda townships had most of the population, and most of the lawyers. Of 58 lawyers in 1870, 39 lived in Oakland Township; of 171 in 1880, 115 lived in Oakland Township. Rural Washington Township had only two.[34]

It is not easy to get an exact count of the lawyers who worked in the county. The census figures may be misleading. They are higher than figures one gets from Oakland city directories. These listed 51 lawyers in 1880, for example—less than half what the census suggests—94 for 1896, and 215 for 1910. Martindale's *American Law Directory of 1909* listed 287 lawyers in Alameda County: 234 in Oakland, another 10 in Alameda, 31 in Berkeley, 2 in Fruitvale, 5 in Hayward, 3 in Livermore, and 2 in San Leandro. Directories, of course, probably understate the number of lawyers; the bottom sediment of the bar did not list itself or get itself listed. California attorney's directories for 1895 and 1897 give still other figures that do not jibe: 141 and 145 for the county, 115 and 117 for the city of Oakland.[35] Still, despite the confusion, it seems that something over a hundred lawyers worked in the county around 1890; and the number was growing faster than population. No doubt there was intense competition for business. In 1890 the national rate of unemployment for lawyers was 1.8 percent; the California rate was 2.1 percent. In 1900 it was 2 percent nationally, 2.7 percent in California, and 3.8 percent in Oakland.

After 1900, the growth rate of lawyers slowed down. This much is clear; how much is hard to say. The Census Bureau made matters difficult by changing its way of counting lawyers. Before 1910, the census lumped together abstractors, notaries, magistrates, justices, and lawyers. In 1910 the Census Bureau strained abstractors and notaries out of this soup. The 1910 census counted 114,704 lawyers in the country. The old basis would have given 122,139. The new way of counting was especially hard on women; their numbers dropped from 1,343 to 558—a sign of how few women were "real" lawyers. Still, the number of lawyers per 1,000 apparently did drop between 1900 and 1910 in the country as a whole, and in California, too (to 2.06). Oakland was a special case. The San Francisco earthquake drove

34. Census data, taken literally, suggest that Oakland had more lawyers, proportionately, than San Francisco. In 1900 there were 273 lawyers in Oakland (4.08 per 1,000); in San Francisco, there were 1,215 lawyers (3.54 per 1,000). But some "Oakland" lawyers probably commuted to San Francisco.
35. *California Attorney's Directory* (C. W. Palm, 1895 and 1897).

lawyers to Oakland, along with other refugees. A. F. St. Sure, for example, quit the attorney general's office in San Francisco and moved to Oakland to set up a practice. Still, Oakland's population grew so fast—it jumped by 124 percent—that the numbers of lawyers per 1,000 could hardly keep pace.

The Path to the Bar

When a young man of the nineteenth century set his mind on becoming a lawyer, few barriers stood in his way. In California, all he needed was twenty-one years of life, "good moral character," and "the necessary qualifications of learning and ability" (Code Civ. Proc., § 275). As to these last, California was one of the looser states. Along with sixteen others, California prescribed no minimum period of law study. It was one of only two states without a written bar examination in 1908. And law school was the exception, not the rule.[36] A fledgling lawyer "read law" (under the wing, more or less, of some practicing lawyer), took an oral exam, and then hung out his shingle (or went to work for an established lawyer). Fred Fry, for example, arrived in Oakland on September 30, 1885. He read Blackstone in his spare time. Young Fred met Melvin Chapman, who invited him to study in Chapman's office library. Two years later, Fry was admitted to the bar.[37] Asa Mendenhall, a California native, worked as a stagecoach driver for three years. Then he read law under his sister's husband, G. W. Langan, while working as a traveling salesman.[38] Edgar Trefethen was a stenographer for a law firm in Oakland and absorbed his law in that way.[39]

But law school was getting more popular. Some California lawyers came to the state out of eastern law schools. William Chickering was a Harvard graduate of 1875. The first law school in California was Hastings, founded in 1878 as part of the state university. Stanford's law school dates from 1893; Boalt Hall, in Berkeley, from 1902; Southern California's school from 1904. The state gave these schools the so-called diploma privilege. This means the state admitted their graduates to the bar with no exam at all.[40] There were other law schools,

36. H. L. Wilgus, "Legal Education in the United States," *Mich. L. Rev.* 6 (1908): 647.
37. Oscar T. Schuck, ed., *History of the Bench and Bar of California* (Los Angeles, 1901), p. 838.
38. Joseph E. Baker, ed., *History of Alameda County, California* (Chicago, 1914), 2: 28.
39. Ibid., p. 572.
40. Code Civ. Proc., § 280b, enacted in 1907. Under the statute, however, the chief justice had the power to order examinations.

not attached to universities. San Francisco's YMCA had a law school from 1901. The Kent Law School, founded in San Francisco in 1891, moved to Oakland after the earthquake. One could also study by mail; the Sprague Correspondence School of Law, in Detroit, had 1,472 students in 1893; 70 of them lived in California.[41]

A young hopeful who "read law," or who went to a school without the diploma privilege, had to appear before the Supreme Court for examination. The court held six terms a year: two in San Francisco, two in Los Angeles, and two in Sacramento. The first day of a regular court term was examination day. The applicant had to show a certificate signed by two lawyers (each with at least four years' practice), setting out where the applicant had studied, for how long, and what books he had read. The lawyers also had to certify that *they* had examined him, and found him fit to practice (Rule I, California Supreme Court, adopted April 13, 1889). The application fee was a stiff ten dollars. The justices added their own questions—on Blackstone and Kent, on such books as Story's *Equity Jurisprudence*, or Parsons' treatise on contracts, and on the California Code of Civil Procedure. In 1892 they added to their list the Civil Code and the two constitutions, federal and state.

There was no great pressure to keep the multitudes out. California drew lawyers like a magnet; but lawyers from other states were admitted simply by showing a license and "satisfactory evidence of good moral character" (Code Civ. Proc., § 279).[42] The bar exam itself was hardly harrowing. On January 12, 1874, fifteen young men appeared. On January 13, the Supreme Court admitted twelve of the fifteen. If we can believe a story from 1893, the process was fairly slapdash. The chief justice asked one man a single question: "Is the Legal Tender Act constitutional?" This man said yes. The next applicant was a "deputy sheriff with legal aspirations." The chief asked the same question. This time the answer was no. "We will admit you both," said the chief; "anybody who can answer offhand a question like that ought to practice law in this country."[43]

41. On the YMCA school, see Wilgus, "Legal Education"; on the Kent school, see *Alameda Daily Argus*, Jan. 16, 1908, p. 6, col. 2; on the Sprague school, see *Law Student's Helper* 1 (1893): 143.

42. See Henry J. Stevens, "Admission and Disbarment of Attorneys at Law," in California Bar Association, *Proceedings of First Annual Convention* (1910), p. 33.

43. *Law Student's Helper* 1 (1893): 265. In 1905 the bar exam burden was transferred to the new District Court of Appeal. See Corinne Gilb, "The State Bar Movement in California" (master's thesis, University of California, Berkeley, 1951), p. 5.

Who Were the Lawyers?

Between 1870 and 1910, the lawyers of Alameda County were almost all white males, born in the United States. Indeed, under a law of 1851, the practice of law was specifically restricted to "white males of 21 years." The law was changed in 1878 to allow "any citizen or . . . resident to practice law."[44] As late as 1910, the census could find only thirty-seven women lawyers in California; only four of these were in Oakland. Not a single woman served as defense lawyer in any felony case in our sample. The first woman lawyer in the state, Clara Foltz, was hired as co-counsel for a criminal appeal in 1899; but the defendant, William H. Allen, died in county jail before the appeal was heard. Mrs. Foltz was a minister's daughter, a widow, with five children. She was admitted to the bar in San Jose in 1878, and had a lively career, despite male opposition and grumbling. The Oakland directory in 1907 lists a Mrs. C. E. Shirland, with an office on San Pablo Avenue. She disappeared from the directory by 1910.

The bar was also lily white—there was one black lawyer in Oakland in 1900[45]—and overwhelmingly native born. ("Native born" did not mean born in California. In fact, in 1870, J. C. Alvarado was the only lawyer in the county actually born in California.) Of the lawyers practicing in 1870, 88 percent were born in the United States; the figure was 84 percent in 1880. The rest were almost to a man from Canada or the British Isles.[46] In those years, the lawyers were mostly migrants from the East, who learned their trade back home. They were somewhat on the oldish side; their average age was 41.4, and their median age was 44.8. The census noted only one law student in the county in 1870. This figure rose to twenty-six in 1880. By 1900, nearly two-thirds of the attorneys in the county were under forty-five. The growth of the bar slowed down between 1900 and 1910; and the average lawyer aged a bit. The typical lawyer was married and had two to three children. In 1870 and 1880, about half listed servants at their homes.

---

44. Laws Cal. 1851, ch. 4, § 1; Code Civ. Proc., § 275, as amended Apr. 1, 1878.

45. In 1910 the county had one black and one Oriental attorney. Lawrence Yeates Sledge, a black attorney, was admitted to the bar of Washington State in 1897; he began practicing law in Oakland in 1908.

46. Raw census returns for Alameda County, 1870 and 1880 censuses. (The 1890 raw returns were destroyed by fire; later returns were not available to us.) The only lawyers *not* from the United States, Canada, or the British Isles, in 1870 or 1880, were three New Zealanders, a Prussian, a Dutchman, and a native of India—6 out of 144 lawyers. Most foreign-born lawyers were naturalized citizens. A resident alien who had filed his declaration of intention to become a citizen was also entitled to practice law in California.

Making a Living

Between 1870 and 1910—as today—some lawyers made money hand over fist; others scratched out a meager living. In 1870, according to the census, the average net worth of lawyers was about $22,000—a considerable sum for the day. But a few spectacular successes inflated this average. Half the lawyers in Alameda County were worth $5,250 or less in 1870.

A young lawyer, without connections, had to struggle for his toe-hold in the world. Most lawyers probably started out with debt collection cases or suits in the justice courts. Criminal cases provided a few extra crumbs. Unless he had family money, a new lawyer could hardly afford to set up an office. After all, as one writer pointed out, he could not "live in a tub while . . . waiting for business. He must appear prosperous and successful, and create confidence and esteem in the breast of his wily client." This meant a decent room in a decent building, at $25 to $30 a month; furnishings, even the "most meagre," cost about $150, not to mention about $100 worth of books. Could a young lawyer get a leg up by starting out with a law firm? It was not easy, at the beginning of the period. There were no firms to speak of in Alameda County. Even two-man partnerships were rare. The 1880 records listed *no* lawyers practicing in partnership. In 1910, according to city directories, there were forty-three—hardly an overwhelming number.

A few lawyers doubled as collection agencies; the Oakland Directory listed, for example, a "Dean Law and Collection Agency" in 1907. Some lawyers went into the real estate business. Some earned money as notaries public. A fortunate few got work with corporations, notably railroads. We hear of a lawyer who in 1871 was getting rich working for the Central Pacific Railroad Company, "with a salary of $1,000 per month, and a good practice besides."[47] But for many lawyers, professional life was a rat race, with very little cheese at the end. It was easy to get into the profession, but hard to get rich, and easy to drop out. Some men barely hung on; they had to scramble for work on the margin of legality and even lower in public esteem. These were the "shysters" and "pettifoggers." A few lawyers fell so

47. Letter of J. B. Crockett to Oscar L. Shafter, Mar. 1, 1871, reprinted in *Life, Diary, and Letters of Oscar L. Shafter*, ed. Flora M. Loughead (San Francisco, 1915), p. 231. A two-man firm in San Jose (Santa Clara County) had a net income of almost $13,000 in 1870, but only $7,800 in 1871. Their billings were (apparently) about $4.50 an hour. Rent ran about $150 a year; coal and gas cost another $60. Richard T. Williams, "Settling In: The Courts of San Jose, 1870" (unpublished paper, Stanford Law Library, 1971).

far from grace that they ended up in our sample of defendants. David Mitchell was accused of statutory rape; J. S. Delancey and Charles E. Kinard were charged with embezzlement.[48]

No one cared officially about these lost souls, one way or the other. "The bar" was hardly an entity. There was no permanent state bar association before 1909, only county and city groups.[49] In any event, bar associations made no attempt to be catholic; they were quite frankly clubs for the better class of lawyer. In Oakland, any member of the Committee on Examinations and Admissions could blackball a prospect. When the California Bar Association was formed in 1909, most of the lawyers in Alameda County were outside looking in. Only seven Oakland attorneys made the grade in 1910.[50]

The Criminal Bar

In general, there were three kinds of lawyers in the criminal bar. First there were young lawyers, fledglings trying out their wings. They took misdemeanor cases, or defended the poor on appointment from the court, hoping to build reputations and work their way up. Second, a handful of distinguished, experienced lawyers defended people willing and able to pay. Last, and lowest, were the police court lawyers, who squeezed out a living by hanging around lower courts buttonholing defendants. Many lawyers never touched a criminal case. Others, who were not specialists in criminal justice, took on a case now and then. Our sample of one-quarter of the felony cases turned up the names of 250 different lawyers. Most appeared in only a few cases, or only one. A few came in from outside (mostly from San Francisco).

Carol H. Abbott, appointed to defend Joseph Sauza in 1892, was a good example of the young lawyer type. Abbott had finished at Has-

---

48. On lawyers charged with mishandling estates, see *Oakland Tribune*, May 22, 1890, p. 5, col. 2 (John H. Wall); ibid., June 10, 1891, p. 2, col. 3 (H. A. Powell); *Alameda Daily Argus*, Jan. 28, 1908, p. 1, col. 3 (Frederick A. Berlin).

49. The first bar association in the state was formed in San Francisco in 1872. Later, a group of lawyers got together in the offices of Montgomery and Martin, in Oakland, and organized an Alameda County Bar Association. C. W. Taylor and Theodor H. Chapin, *Bench and Bar of Alameda County* (Angwin, Calif., 1953), p. 11. In 1889 an attempt was made to form a statewide bar organization; two Oakland lawyers, A. A. Moore and William R. Davis, were active in this effort. This bar association fell apart in two years. New efforts in 1901 also failed; a firm, lasting California Bar Association did not come about until 1909.

50. They were M. C. Chapman, William H. Donahue (the district attorney), R. M. Fitzgerald, A. L. Frick, George W. Reed, George Samuels, and Charles E. Snook. California Bar Association, *Proceedings of First Annual Convention* (1910), p. 131.

tings Law School one year before. His client, Sauza, pleaded guilty to grand larceny, and got two years in prison. Young lawyers rarely won acquittals. Probably they did little more than tell their man to plead guilty. Of course, some of these cases were hopeless to begin with. But there was perhaps a point to the charge that lawyers sometimes railroaded defendants. The lawyer, "desiring to walk before he can creep," used "the cheap notoriety of the petty criminal trial" as a "stepping stone"; the prisoner's life and liberty were "the plaything of inexperienced amateurs."[51]

Of course, young lawyers were not all incompetent and careless. After all, even the best criminal lawyers once were beginners. Melvin Chapman was one of the best. He came to the law rather late: he was a real estate agent, admitted to the bar in 1884, at the age of thirty-four. He went into partnership with Roscoe Havens. Chapman sometimes helped other (court-appointed) lawyers in criminal cases. In September 1886, he teamed with M. H. Crocker to defend Nathan Sutton, a man accused of first-degree murder. Crocker was a veteran of some twenty-three murder trials; he was also, alas, a veteran of the bottle. Chapman carried the whole load, because Crocker was never sober enough to try the case. (Sutton's defense was insanity, but he went to the gallows.) In 1887, Chapman became a state legislator; from 1889 to 1891, he was mayor of Oakland. He was unusually successful in his criminal work. About two-thirds of his clients got off: either the charges were dismissed, or a jury acquitted the defendant. Whether this was because of Chapman's talents, or an aura of celebrity that impressed the jury, or whether he had some "pull" is impossible to tell.

Men who had done a turn as district attorney, or worked in that office, were among the most successful criminal lawyers. Lin S. Church, deputy district attorney (1889–99), went into partnership with Charles Snook, the retiring district attorney. Albert A. Moore served two terms as district attorney, and then went back into private practice in 1875. A prominent man like Moore got to handle big cases. When the auditor of Alameda County, Myron A. Whidden, was accused of forgery, embezzlement, and falsifying public records, Moore was in his corner (1885).[52]

Moore was one of the handful of lawyers who dominated criminal

51. *Yale L. J.* 1 (1892): 218.
52. Moore's clients usually won. A few pleaded guilty—for example, Maro P. Kay, a deputy county clerk, accused of forgery in 1883. In 1897, Moore moved his practice to San Francisco, and became a railroad lawyer. He also worked for the defense in the great San Francisco graft cases, which grew out of the chicanery of Boss Abe Ruef and Mayor Schmitz. See Walton Bean, *Boss Ruef's San Francisco* (Berkeley, 1952).

practice in Superior Court. Melvin Chapman appeared in over 4.3 percent of the cases sampled—more than any other lawyer. In the 1890s, Chapman took six percent of the cases. A. L. Frick handled over 3 percent of the cases. F. J. Brearty, Colonel Thomas F. Garrity, and Lin Church were also frequently in court. The men listed in Table 3.4 were *the* criminal bar.

At the other end of the spectrum was the police court or justice court lawyer, the lawyer who dealt in petty crimes. This was the lowest form of lawyer in the public eye. The *Yale Law Journal* called him a "legal shark, a kind of tolerated legal vermin, devoid alike of honesty, learning and industry."[53] These lawyers depended on high volume at low margins. They "buttonhole[d] every petty offender and assure[d] him . . . that his only hope [was] to secure their services." Their fees—five or ten dollars for petty larceny, twenty-five dollars for burglary, or "as much more as can be squeezed from the client"—were usually paid "at once and in advance." "Jewelry, pawn tickets, anything is taken rather than nothing." But in the end these lawyers made a miserable living, learned "low ideas of life," moved "in a bad atmosphere," and became the same low life form as their clients.[54] The petty courts were, in this view, a swamp that corrupted everyone, lawyer and client alike. In the next chapter we take a closer look at this swamp.

Conclusion

This brief stroll through the halls of justice has introduced the chief role players in our drama: lawyers, judges, and laymen. The forty years of the study were years of considerable change—much of it, as we suggested, in one particular direction: professionalization, for want of a better word. Lay justice, in general, lost influence and power. The grand jury, a body of laymen, was stripped of a major function. The gainers were full-time men, judges and lawyers. *Within* the profession, there was a similar trend—away from apprenticeship toward university training; away from part-time toward full-time prosecutors. In succeeding chapters we will see more evidence of this shift.

The focus of this study is on the process of criminal justice; we are interested, of course, in lawyers, but they share the stage with defendants, victims, witnesses, judges, policemen, jailers, and others.

53. *Yale L. J.* 1 (1892): 218.
54. *Law Student's Helper* 1 (1893): 40.

Table 3.4. Attorneys Most Frequently Appearing for
the Defense in Alameda County Felony Cases, 1880–1910

1880–89		1890–99		1900–1910	
Name	% of cases	Name	% of cases	Name	% of cases
F. J. Brearty	7.2	Thomas F. Garrity	10.0	A. L. Frick	6.0
Albert A. Moore	6.7	Melvin C. Chapman	6.0	Lin S. Church	5.0
Melvin C. Chapman	5.6	F. J. Brearty	4.0	Burton J. Wyman	3.8
Welles Whitmore	5.0	W. F. Aram	4.0	W. H. O'Brien	2.8
R. M. Fitzgerald	5.0	Hugh S. Aldrich	3.5	George J. McDonough	2.8
Fred E. Whitney	3.3	Edward J. Rodgers	3.0	Melvin C. Chapman	2.5
E. M. Gibson	2.8	William J. Donovan	2.5	Tom Bradley	2.5
George W. Lewis	2.8	F. W. Sawyer	2.5	Philip M. Walsh	2.5
C. S. Colvin	2.2			John L. McVey	2.5
				Edward E. Gehring	2.2

Source: Sample of Superior Court casefiles, 1880–1910.

It is a point worth making that lawyers did not stand out from the crowd, in certain ways. The lawyers of Alameda County were not drawn from the ranks of an elite, nor did they form an elite, except for a very few at the top of the ladder. Nothing in Alameda County remotely resembled the English bar. The judges, too, were of an American type; they were also not drawn from an elite, nor did they form one. They were members of the solid middle class. The lines between judges and lawyers, between lawyers and laymen, between *all* role players, were relatively fluid. America, as a society, was relatively open and mobile. We say "relatively," because success was, after all, a club for white males. But compared to England and Europe, slots in criminal justice were not reserved for men of gentle birth; they were jobs for young men on the make, regardless of background. Criminal justice in Alameda County, from a continental perspective, was rough, raw, even vulgar. We will see more of this trait in chapters to come.

Chapter 4
Petty Crime, Police, and
the Basement of Justice

In the last chapter we drew a quick sketch of the criminal justice system in Alameda County. In this chapter we describe the bottom or base of the system. Most people were arrested for minor offenses. It was also the case that most people who appeared in court were arrested for minor offenses; they were rather ordinary people, somewhat more foolish, perhaps, than most, or more hot-tempered, or more unlucky. They dealt with the police, with justice or police courts, with some lesser civil servants. For many of them, a brush with the law was no great turning point in their lives; it left no permanent warp—no more than an arrest for speeding would today. Yet when we lump all their experiences together, what happened to people's lives in these dingy precincts had great importance in society.

Each layer of criminal justice had its major and minor actors. At the bottom of the system, the police played a starring role. Most of our hard information about the police comes from Oakland. Other cities had police—Berkeley, San Leandro, Alameda.[1] But Oakland had the largest and most significant force. Also, by a lucky chance, the raw arrest records of the Oakland police have escaped destruction for our period, and we can learn a great deal from these.

In this chapter, we talk about police work in Alameda County and then add what data we have (alas, rather skimpy) about the work of the lowest courts—justice courts and police courts—as they handled minor crimes. (Superior Court and serious crimes will be treated in the next two chapters.)

Information on the police and on the petty courts is a mosaic made up of tiny details: entries in arrest books, scraps of paper, short paragraphs buried on inside pages of the newspapers. What do we learn when we are through?

1. See Nathan Douthet, "August Vollmer, Berkeley's First Chief of Police, and the Emergence of Police Professionalism," *Cal. Hist. Q.* 54 (1975): 101; on Vollmer's career, see also Gene E. Carte and Elaine H. Carte, *Police Reform in the United States: The Era of August Vollmer, 1905–1932* (Berkeley, 1975); for a glimpse of the Berkeley Police force, see *Berkeley Reporter*, Jan. 2, 1906, p. 7, col. 1.

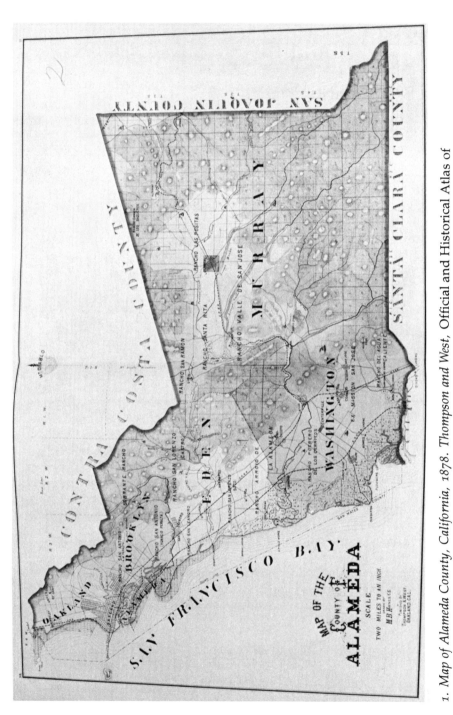

1. *Map of Alameda County, California, 1878. Thompson and West, Official and Historical Atlas of Alameda County, California. Courtesy of the Map Division of the Library of Congress.*

2. *Alameda County Courthouse, Washington Square, Oakland, circa 1875.
Opened in 1875, this courthouse was the home of the Superior Court and
its predecessor, the County Court, and the place where the county's felony
cases were tried.*
Photo courtesy of the Oakland Museum History Department.

3. *Oakland, California, Looking West from City Hall, 1879.*
Photo courtesy of the Oakland Museum History Department.

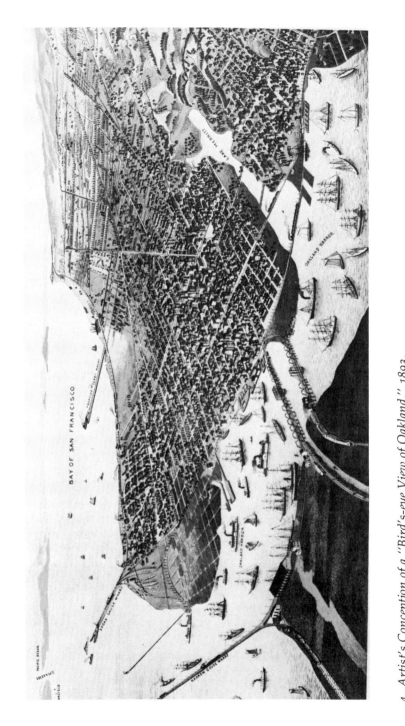

4. Artist's Conception of a "Bird's-eye View of Oakland," 1893.
Photo courtesy of Oakland History Room, Oakland Public Library.

5. *City Hall, home of the Oakland Police Court, at 14th and Broadway, Oakland, 1910.*
Photo courtesy of the Oakland Museum History Department.

6. *Oakland Police Chief William F. Fletcher and Staff in Front of Oakland City Jail, located in the basement of City Hall, Oakland, circa 1898.*
Photo courtesy of the Oakland History Room, Oakland Public Library.

7. *Oakland Police Rifle Team, November 27, 1899.*
Photo courtesy of the Oakland Museum History Department.

8. Oakland Police Force with Mayor Anson Barstow (fourth from left), circa 1902.
Photo courtesy of the Oakland History Room, Oakland Public Library.

9. Oakland Police Department's First Car, a 1909 Pope Hartford, with Police Chief Adelbert Wilson seated on the far right, circa 1909.
Photo courtesy of the Oakland Museum History Department.

First, we learn that here too the system slowly became more professional. Perhaps "professional" is not quite the right word. At any rate, police work became more self-consciously a skill and an occupation. At the beginning of the period, almost anybody could be a policeman; and sometimes it seems as if just about anybody was. By the end of the period, the police were on the brink of civil service status. The forces recruited a bit more cautiously; in Berkeley a famous police chief, August Vollmer, had already brought higher standards to the job. Police forces were starting to specialize; as early as 1870, Oakland had detectives on its force.

Second, the primary role of the police—by no means their only role—was *order*. They were, above all else, disciplinarians; they were concerned with peace and decorum in public places. Most arrests were for drunkenness, brawling, public hell-raising, or for private disputes that burst into public notice. The police represented not so much middle-class morality as middle-class self-discipline. The discipline was imposed not only on "criminals," but on ordinary people who stepped out of line—primarily working-class adults, almost all of them men.

Third, the police represented (as always) community sentiment; they were neither better nor worse than the average citizen. They were prejudiced against the Chinese, they despised "tramps," they tolerated gambling. They twisted formal law, sometimes unconsciously, in accordance with everyday values, ideas, and sentiments. The police were not legalistic. Vollmer himself spanked a juvenile who committed a minor offense. Nothing in the law gave him the right to hit a child. But no one protested. People in Alameda County were not as rights-conscious as they are today. The system tempered formal law with what it thought was common sense.

This leads to a fourth point: the people who were arrested strike us as even more powerless than they would be today. Admittedly, this is only an impression, based on feelings and shadows. Some defendants were outsiders and deviants. Some were hanging on to respectability by their fingertips. Some had done something a little wrong, and were scared and ashamed. They had no ACLU, no public defenders, no spokesmen; and not the remotest chance of protest or rebellion. Authority was tightly structured; and the network of norms was almost impregnable.

In this chapter, we deal in some instance with fairly large numbers. This is itself rather interesting. Most arrests were for quite small offenses. Proceedings were humdrum, even routine, but important in the aggregate. Police work resembled a kind of huge trawling operation, a fishing with great nets for minnows in the sea. We can ask, To what purpose? for what social end? Unconsciously, society (it seems) saw some vital purpose in police and police court action. In a complex, industrial society, the basic work force has to follow the rules, has to behave, generally speaking. Order and discipline have to prevail, at least in public. The flesh, Lord knows, is weak; violations are frequent; but if people are promptly and efficiently controlled, harassed, or mildly punished, their behavior will stay within limits of tolerance. Those fined, jailed, or warned will learn a lesson; norms will be impressed on the entire class. The class, by and large, is the working class; and the norms are those of their respectable betters. Whether people actually learned their lessons we cannot tell; but we suspect that the main point and message of this part of criminal justice was education and thereby control.

The Oakland Police: Manpower and Resources

Oakland had a police force from the 1850s on. In 1872 the force consisted of ten or eleven men, together with four "special" policemen, paid for by businessmen and property owners. A police captain was in charge, and there were two detectives on the staff.[2] These detectives—crime fighters and investigators—made $125 a month in 1894. This was $25 a month more than simple patrolmen; and the detectives' job also freed them from the "ceaseless monotony" of tramping a beat.[3] The police wore uniforms—blue coat with brass buttons, dark pants, and a black hat. A star was pinned to the outside of the coat.

Between 1870 and 1910, Oakland's population grew from about 10,000 to over 150,000; naturally, the police force grew too—from 11 policemen to 109. But (see Table 4.1) the force did not grow relative to population. In 1910, Oakland had 109 police, or 0.73 for every 1,000 people—about the same as in 1880.[4] At first, the city council con-

2. Frank Clinton Merritt, *History of Alameda County, California* (Chicago, 1928), pp. 282–83.

3. *Oakland Tribune*, Sept. 11, 1894, p. 3, col. 1.

4. In 1972 there were more than 2.5 Oakland police per 1,000 people. California Bureau of Criminal Statistics, *Crimes and Arrests, 1972* (1972), p. 97. In 1906, Berkeley had 12 policemen for a population of about 30,000 which Chief Vollmer understandably felt inadequate. *Berkeley Reporter*, Apr. 2, 1906, p. 8, col. 3.

Compared to larger, older cities, Oakland was not very heavily policed (see Table 4.2). Among twenty-eight cities in its size category in 1880, Oakland ranked twentieth in police per 1,000 people. But it ranked fifth in dollars spent on police for a city of its size. U.S. Bureau of the Census, *Social Statistics of Cities* (1886). Some differences may be due to quirks of accounting or reporting, of course.

In 1905 the largest cities again were by far the most policed: cities over 300,000

Table 4.1. *Number of Police per Thousand People in Oakland, 1870–1910*

Year	No. police	Population	Police/ 1,000 people
1870	11	10,500	1.05
1880	25	34,555	0.72
1890	38	48,682	0.78
1900	61	66,960	0.91
1910	109	150,175	0.73

Sources: Oakland Police Department, *Annual Report of the Chief of Police* (1900), p. 29; U.S. Bureau of the Census; *Husted's Oakland City Directory* (1910).

trolled appointments to the department. Later a Board of Police and Fire Commissioners took over. The whole process was intensely political. Patrolmen were hired and fired for political reasons. The police captain (after 1899 he was called "chief") rose and fell with political tides. A captain or chief rarely lasted through an election year. Between 1877 and 1889, the office changed hands eight times; overall, between 1872 and 1910, there were fourteen changes.

The men appointed to the police force were apparently not always of top quality. Indeed, they were hardly qualified at all. Civil service rules did not apply to police until 1911. Anybody, it seemed, could be a policeman. In 1906, Berkeley agreed to give Chief Vollmer three more patrolmen; the trustees appointed, on Vollmer's recommendation, three "well known Berkeleyans": a former collector for the water company, an assistant station agent at Berkeley, and a third man who had "had experience as a special watchman."[5] At least these men were, presumably, respectable. This was not always the case in Oakland. Here the city council had to suspend a policeman in 1883, because he had been charged (in Contra Costa County) with assault with a deadly weapon. At the same council meeting, there were charges that Officer Pratt was too old for the job and "physically

population averaged 1.9 police per 1,000; cities between 100,000 and 300,000 population averaged 1.3; those between 50,000 and 100,000 (Oakland's size class), 1.2; and those with population under 50,000, 1.1. We do not know Oakland's 1905 population exactly; but Oakland had far fewer than 1 policeman for each 1,000 residents. It thus lagged behind the national average of 1.6 police per 1,000; it also lagged behind the average for its size class. U.S. Bureau of the Census, *Statistics of Cities Having a Population of over 30,000: 1905* (1907), p. 81.

5. *Berkeley Reporter*, Jan. 23, 1906, p. 1, col. 4.

Table 4.2. Number of Police and Police per Thousand People in the Ten Largest U.S. Cities, 1880

City	Population	No. police	Police/ 1,000 people
New York	1,206,299	2,532	2.10
Philadelphia	847,170	1,321	1.56
Brooklyn	566,663	633	1.12
Chicago	503,185	487	0.97
Boston	362,839	697	1.92
St. Louis	350,518	489	1.40
Baltimore	323,313	600	1.86
Cincinnati	255,139	343	1.34
San Francisco	233,959	394	1.68
New Orleans	216,090	276	1.28

Source: U.S. Bureau of the Census, *Social Statistics of Cities* (1886), pts. 1 and 2.

disqualified"; that James Quinlan, another policeman, had been convicted of liquor violations and drunkenness; and that still another, D. J. Murphy, had trouble with drink. A councilman claimed that "notorious law breakers" and "incompetent men" were on the force; but the motion to fire the three officers named failed by one vote. They stayed on the force.[6]

The police, then, were full-time workers; but they were not yet fully "professional"—not always even honest. In general, police in American cities were a sorry mess during the period. A flock of investigations (the most famous was the Lexow Committee in New York) turned up a mare's nest of dirt and corruption. One wonders whether police did not *make* crime on balance, just as one wonders whether doctors with leeches and nostrums did not kill more patients than they cured.[7] The Oakland police, we know, often winked at

6. *Oakland Tribune*, Sept. 4, 1883, p. 3, col. 2.

7. See, in general, Robert Fogelson, *Big-City Police* (Cambridge, Mass., 1978). For a more modern look at the Oakland police, see Jerome H. Skolnick, *Justice without Trial: Law Enforcement in Democratic Society* (New York, 1966). This is a pathbreaking study of an urban police force; the city is called "Westville," but it is obvious that behind this fig leaf is Oakland.

The literature on police history is large and growing. Noteworthy are Roger Lane, *Policing the City: Boston, 1822–1885* (Cambridge, Mass., 1967); James F. Richardson, *The New York Police: Colonial Times to 1901* (New York, 1970); James F. Richardson, *Urban Police in the United States* (Port Washington, N.Y., 1974); Wilbur R. Miller, *Cops and Bobbies: Police Authority in New York and London, 1830–1870* (Chicago, 1977).

vice, gambling, prostitution. We found no hard evidence of deeper or wider corruption. Whether Oakland was cleaner than other cities or whether its secret sins were deeply buried is impossible for us to tell.

The Work of the Police: Crime Fighting

The first job of the police, many people would say, is fighting crime— protecting bodies and goods from the "dangerous classes." But police do *not* spend most of their time battling robbers, burglars, and murderers. In Oakland, police work was mostly other, more mundane tasks: breaking up fights, handling drunks, enforcing traffic rules, catching runaways.

Table 4.3 analyzes arrests in Oakland between 1872 and 1910 by the *functions* these arrests were to serve. The tables uses four general categories, derived in the main from James Q. Wilson.[8] The first category consists of serious crimes (*felonies*): murder, rape, robbery, assault with a deadly weapon, burglary, grand larceny, arson. The second is *order maintenance*; included here are drunkenness, disturbing the peace, fighting, disorderly conduct, vagrancy, minor assault and battery. The third category is *law enforcement*. This includes "morals" arrests: gambling, prostitution, seduction. It also includes what we will call *regulatory arrests*—arrests for failure to obtain business licenses, for selling tainted chickens, and the like. Here, too, are traffic offenses—bicycle and auto crimes—and such minor property crimes as petty larceny. Finally, the police sometimes made arrests where no crime was committed at all—arrests of runaway children, or of people in a mental fog. We call these *service* arrests.

Table 4.3 is based on a random sample of 1,500 Oakland arrests between 1872 and 1910. It suggests a number of things about police work. First, order maintenance accounts for *most* arrests made by the Oakland police between 1872 and 1910. Arrest figures, of course, do not capture the flavor of a policeman's day (or night) very accurately. Still, order maintenance must have loomed large in the policeman's work life. Here we find nearly two-thirds of all the arrests. Law enforcement accounted for another quarter or so, arrests for serious crimes about 6 percent, and service arrests the rest (3 percent).

Table 4.3 shows some interesting trends. Refugees poured into Oakland when the great earthquake and fire ravaged San Francisco in April 1906. Arrests for drunkenness jumped dramatically in absolute numbers, and from 42 percent to 66 percent of all arrests. Arrests for

8. James Q. Wilson, *Varieties of Police Behavior* (Cambridge, Mass., 1968), pp. 16–17.

Table 4.3. Percentage Distribution of Oakland Arrests by Functional Offense Categories, 1872–1910

Type of offense	1872–80	1881–90	1892–1900	1901–
Felonies	10%	9%	7%	3%
Order maintenance	60%	66%	63%	63%
Drunkenness	33%	42%	41%	42%
Other public order	16%	16%	17%	15%
Minor v. persons	11%	8%	5%	6%
Law enforcement	26%	21%	27%	32%
Morals	1%	4%	2%	4%
Regulatory ordinances	15%	11%	18%	24%
Minor v. property	10%	6%	7%	4%
Service	4%	4%	3%	2%
N	313	282	264	215

Source: Sample of entries in Oakland Arrest Books for 1872–1910 (1891 missing).

ordinance violations *fell* just as dramatically—from 24 percent to 2 percent of arrests. Clearly, the police shifted gears to meet the crisis. They virtually gave up on license laws and other regulations and put their muscle into keeping the lid on the city.

But this was an interlude. The next years were more "normal." One trend is sharp and clear: arrests for moral charges (mostly gambling) rose steadily. From 1872 to 1880, they were almost nonexistent; they never came to as much as 5 percent before 1905. The spectacular rise in later years was largely due to gambling raids. Gambling accounted for less than 3 percent of arrests between 1896 and 1900, but over 25 percent in 1909–10. Regulatory arrests were notable for extreme instability, rising and falling more erratically than the other categories. We shall speak later about why these eruptions occurred.

Order and Discipline

Keeping order and discipline was a prime job of the Oakland police (and of police in other cities)[9] in the late nineteenth century—perhaps the central job (see Table 4.4). In every year between 1872 and 1910,

9. See Richardson, *Urban Police*.

	06	1907–8	1909–10	Entire period
	%	2%	4%	6%
	%	68%	58%	64%
	%	48%	41%	42%
	%	16%	14%	16%
	%	4%	3%	6%
	%	27%	36%	27%
	%	14%	25%	7%
	%	8%	8%	14%
	7%	5%	3%	6%
	)%	3%	2%	3%
	5	212	174	1555

public order dominated the arrest books. Drunkenness was at all times the single most common grounds for arrest. Hundreds and hundreds of men (and women) were arrested for drunkenness, for disturbing the peace, fighting, and general hell-raising. The police made some (but many fewer) arrests for vagrancy and begging. An arrest for assault and battery usually followed a citizen complaint. For some reason, these arrests fell off as time went on. Table 4.4 also shows, by way of comparison, Oakland's arrest rates for the same offenses in 1970. Compared to 1900–1910, Oakland had become more disorderly, more heavily policed, or both.

Behind the raw figures, of course, lay life's reality, with all its daily woes, most of them depressingly similar. But then, as now, not every drunk was arrested; not everybody who made a rumpus in the streets was hauled in. Most of the time, it probably took something extra to arouse the police to make an arrest. This might be sheer quantity or scale. George McClellan was arrested on January 27, 1881, on three charges: "Drunk, malicious mischief, and drunk and disorderly." It took "the united efforts of two officers to bring him in."[10] Mose All-bach, released from jail one Saturday morning in 1898, went on a binge and made a "public display"; the police had to bring him back

10. *Oakland Tribune*, Jan. 27, 1881, p. 3, col. 2, Jan. 25, 1898, p. 3, col. 5.

Table 4.4. Number and Rate of Arrests for
Public Order Offenses in Oakland, 1875–1970

Type of offense	1875		1880		1887	
	No. arrests	Per 1,000 people	No. arrests	Per 1,000 people	No. arrests	Per 1,000 people
Drunkenness	837	33.8	545	15.8	1,355	30.5
Disturbing peace	83	3.3	162	4.7	200	4.5
Fighting & other	57	2.3	85	2.4	106	2.4
Vagrancy & begging	21	0.8	7	0.2	13	0.3
Assaults & battery	104	4.2	219	6.3	174	3.9
Total	1,102	44.4	1,018	29.5	1,848	41.6

Sources: The figures in the first four columns are from *Annual Reports of the Chief of Police*, Oakland (1900 figures are for fiscal 1900). The 1910 figures are derived from entries in the Arrest Books. The 1970 figures are official Oakland arrest statistics.

to "his favorite cell in the City Prison." The police were most likely to act when disorder was *public*, that is, on the streets. They were more tolerant of disorder indoors, or in certain sanctuaries, like saloons. Here they intervened only when someone blew the whistle. We hear of one extreme case in 1881: a great Saturday row in the Pioneer Beer Saloon. The "hurling around of humans" got so fierce that it "threatened the mirrors and cups in Mr. Hallahan's barbershop next door." Still, the police stayed out; the doors of the saloon were closed, and no one called the police, "although there were two on the opposite corner at the same time."[11]

Most arrests for drunkenness took place at night—especially between midnight and 1:00 A.M. The seven-hour period between 7:00 P.M. and 2:00 A.M. accounted for more than half of these arrests. Nearly 70 percent of the arrests between midnight and 2:00 A.M. were

11. Ibid., Jan. 25, 1881, p. 3, col. 4. In 1898 a police officer was charged with "unofficerlike conduct and failure to perform his duty" for turning his back "when arrests should have been made." He "stood in the doorway of a saloon and watched a son floor his father with a chair, yet the officer offered no interference." Ibid., Jan. 20, 1898, p. 3, col. 1.

	1900		1910		1970
No. arrests	*Per 1,000 people*	*No. arrests*	*Per 1,000 people*	*No. arrests*	*Per 1,000 people*
1,336	19.9	3,060	20.4	12,421	34.3
158	2.4	256	1.7	1,023	2.8
84	1.2	98	0.7	1,375	3.8
122	1.8	153	1.0	0	0.0
121	1.8	228	1.5	1,685	4.7
1,821	27.2	3,795	25.3	16,504	45.6

arrests for drunkenness. Disorderly conduct, fighting, and malicious mischief were also nighttime problems. More than half of these arrests occurred between 4:00 P.M. and midnight. These facts suggest that most drunks were not chronic winos or skid-row bums; they were ordinary citizens, workingmen out on the town. Brawlers, disturbers of the peace, came from the same social class.

On April 18, 1906, the great San Francisco earthquake turned that city into a blazing ruin. In Oakland, a rooming house collapsed, crushing five people to death. But on the whole, the East Bay got off lightly. Berkeley was almost untouched. Thousands of refugees fled to Alameda County, mostly by boat. The district attorney closed the Oakland saloons and imposed a 6:00 P.M. curfew.[12] In Berkeley, Marshal Vollmer arrested 68 "thugs," rats who left the sinking ship across the Bay. Somewhat surprisingly, the Oakland police arrested fewer people in the two weeks *after* the earthquake (121) than in the two weeks before it (160). And Oakland remained fairly orderly—at

12. Ibid., Apr. 19, 1906, p. 8, col. 2; Merritt, *History of Alameda*, p. 294.

first.[13] Arrests rose sharply only after the curfew ended, and the saloons reopened for business (May 1). In the first two weeks of May, the police made 555 arrests, over 80 percent of them for drunkenness.

Vagrancy, like drunkenness, covered a multitude of sins. Vagrancy, begging, and "suspicion" were charges used to clear the streets of undesirables. If the police made life miserable enough, these undesirables might decide to move on to greener pastures. The actual arrest rate for vagrancy was low in Oakland (see Table 4.4), and varied a good deal between 1872 and 1910. The figures are not as transparent as they seem. Prostitutes were sometimes arrested as "vagrants." In 1888, we read, police were trying to break up a "gang of young hoodlums." The method was to arrest gang members for vagrancy and other minor offenses, "so as to keep them in jail."[14] Vagrancy was a weapon in the off-and-on war against "tramps." In 1893, Chief Schaefer told his men to "stop every suspicious character . . . after a reasonable hour. Tell him who you are and if he cannot give an account of himself, bring him in."[15] In Berkeley, in 1906, the police arrested "three suspicious-looking men," begging on Durant Avenue. They were locked up for the night and then told to get out of town.[16]

Most vagrancy arrests were made in winter: in 1900 half of the year's arrests took place in January.[17] California's mild winters attracted drifters. Any outsider who looked or acted strange ran a certain risk of arrest. "Two very natty young men" were arrested for

13. Merritt, *History of Alameda*, p. 294. Martial law was declared in San Francisco and the National Guard was called out. Hundreds of drunks roamed the streets of San Francisco, but the police did not try to arrest anybody, except in cases of really murderous assaults. Citizens were forced, at gunpoint, to help fight fires; there were orders to shoot any looters. The police and the National Guard were at loggerheads over how to police the city. The police wanted to avoid deadly force; the Guard was more bellicose. Some prisoners were transferred from San Francisco to San Jose for safekeeping. Twenty-five prisoners from San Francisco were sent to Oakland on Apr. 27; they returned on May 3. *Oakland Tribune*, Apr. 19, 1906, p. 1, col. 5; Oakland Arrest Book, 1906.

14. *Oakland Tribune*, Mar. 13, 1888, p. 1, col. 5.

15. Ibid., Jan. 5, 1893, p. 3, col. 2. Sometimes the "tramps" left the city only to become a headache for the county. In 1885, for example, 53.7 percent of all arrests by the county sheriff were for vagrancy. Ibid., Jan. 5, 1886, p. 2, col. 3. "In the districts away from police protection," the *Tribune* reported in 1881, "one tramp rings at the front door of a house while another knocks at the kitchen portal. As the master of the house is generally away, the mistress is so frightened by the manner and often intimidating language of the nomadic scoundrels that she gives them what food they demand, in many cases completely exhausting the household supply." Ibid., Jan. 11, 1881, p. 3, col. 4, Jan. 27, 1892, p. 1, col. 6. In 1893 the county sheriff organized five posses of ten persons each, to make nighttime raids on tramps. Ibid., Aug. 11, 1893, p. 3, col. 5.

16. *Berkeley Reporter*, May 18, 1906, p. 8, col. 2.

17. Oakland Police Department, *Annual Report of the Chief of Police* (1900), pp. 16, 23.

vagrancy in 1892; their flashy appearance made police think they were burglars.[18] An "opium fiend" was jailed for vagrancy in 1890, "in order to be cured of the opium habit."[19] And in 1894 a "pitiable wreck," Charles Marcellus, was arrested for vagrancy, another victim of opium.[20] In 1902 the police picked up an interracial couple on a vagrancy charge. The man, who was black, was acquitted; the woman forfeited bail, and a bench warrant was issued to arrest her.[21]

The figures, then, do not tell the whole story; newspaper accounts are suggestive only. Order arrests were usually, one supposes, non-controversial. But as the police patrolled the streets looking for va-grants, brawlers, and drunks, they were also patrolling the moral and social edges of society, trawling for deviance, enforcing standard norms of good bourgeois conduct. This they did, no doubt, quite unconsciously. Some aspects of police work cut more explicitly into the core of community politics, and had, perhaps, a more sinister note. Historians, generally speaking, connect the rise of the police with an increased demand for "order" from the well-to-do.[22] The police are a kind of civil army. They suppress urban riots; they main-tain the discipline that an organized urban work force must have. This is, on the whole, a rather necessary if disagreeable job; but it is not hard to cross the line into oppression. Indeed, some writers point an accusing finger at the police. They are the army of the ruling class, against labor, against strikers, against the poor.[23]

A slight change in how one describes the police, a change in word-ing or emphasis, can put them in a very different light. "Law and order" is good or bad, depending on point of view. The police *did* keep order; and no society can get along without this. But *whose* order did they keep? Clearly, it was the order of those with something to lose, something to protect. The police helped those who sat in the

---

18. *Oakland Tribune*, July 8, 1892, p. 3, col. 2.

19. According to the *Tribune*, the opium fiend "contracted the habit of smoking opium from companions, and after he had become used to the drug he had to smoke three pipes a day. This he found expensive, as it cost him 25 cents a pipe, besides a fee to the proprietor of the opium joint, so he took to morphine, for 15 cents' worth of morphine is as good as 50 cents' worth of opium, besides being much pleasanter. He says that the suffering after being deprived of the drug is terrible." *Oakland Tribune*, Jan. 15, 1890, p. 3, col. 2.

20. Ibid., Aug. 17, 1894, p. 2, col. 3.

21. Ibid., May 31, 1902, p. 3, col. 3.

22. See Allan Silver, "The Demand for Order in Civil Society: A Review of Some Themes in the History of Urban Crime, Police, and Riot," in *The Police: Six Sociological Essays*, ed. David J. Bordua (New York, 1967).

23. See Sidney L. Harring and Lorraine M. McMillin, "Buffalo Police, 1872–1900: Labor Unrest, Political Power and the Creation of the Police Institute," *Crime and Social Justice*, Fall–Winter 1975, p. 5.

cushioned seats of society. They rose no higher, ethically, than society as a whole. If society was unjust, so were they.

Did the police serve as strikebreakers, scabs, scourges of the workingman? Our data are too dry and mute to answer the question. There are scattered hints in the newspapers. It is a bit ominous to read that the police arrested striking iron-molders in 1890; the charge was vagrancy. Still, these cases were thrown out of court, and the police were told to be more cautious in making such arrests.[24] During the great railway strikes of 1894, the police had their hands full. They guarded railroad property, arrested the disorderly, kept commerce flowing. There were forty men, plus "specials," to handle a seething city.[25] Whether the police simply enforced the law or stepped across an invisible line into strikebreaking is hard to tell from our materials.

People in Alameda County no doubt felt that they lived in a free country. But standards of free speech (and freedom of assembly) change over time. In 1908 the police arrested a laborer, Alfred Roberts, who made a speech "along anarchistic lines." Roberts had "cast odium" on the city government of Oakland. His language was "so violent and fiery that he was ordered down from a box on which he had been standing . . . and taken to jail." The police had been told, said the *Alameda Argus,* to keep an eye on people "known to be connected with anarchistic organizations," and to arrest "all who attempt to preach their belief in public places."[26]

Law and Order: The Role of the Citizen

Private disputes reached the criminal justice system only if one or both parties blew the whistle. If nobody complained, nothing happened. The police often went away empty-handed, even when the neighbors or one party called them in. In 1883 the police were summoned when a "wife-beating scrape" threw a neighborhood into an uproar; the woman was screaming out, "Oh my God! my God! I am killed." But when the police came, she refused to file a complaint.[27] In

24. *Oakland Tribune*, May 17, 1890, p. 3, col. 4.
25. Statement of Chief of Police Schaffer, *Oakland Tribune*, July 18, 1894, p. 5, col. 6. The mayor called on all "law abiding citizens . . . to aid and assist the police," and directed the chief "to call for assistance upon citizens, the sheriff or military" if need be. Ibid., July 19, 1894, p. 2, col. 3.
26. *Alameda Argus*, Mar. 10, 1908, p. 5, col. 6. A German laborer, Carl Muller, out of work and pining for his native land, turned himself in to the local police; he insisted he was an anarchist, and demanded to be deported. Ibid., Mar. 26, 1908, p. 8, col. 3. So much for the First Amendment.
27. *Oakland Tribune*, Aug. 29, 1883, p. 3, col. 2.

March 1903, W. A. Weir, who ran the Brunswick Hotel, tried to shoot his stepdaughter, along with her alleged lover, one of his boarders. A policeman came, but Mrs. Weir got rid of him. "The old man was excited," she said, and hustled Weir off to bed. There were no arrests.[28] The police sometimes turned matters over to some other agency. In 1894 a "shocking" situation came to light in Oakland, in a little house near the Sixteenth Street depot. Husband and wife were drunk and fighting; on a tiny bed, in a room filled with rubbish and dirt, lay a young boy "dying of consumption. . . . His face was dirty and his head covered with flies." Neighbors called the police, who referred the matter to the Humane Society.[29]

There is no hell quite like family hell. Wife-beating and child abuse cropped up with dismal regularity among the countless cases of battery, assault, vile language, and breach of peace that reached court. Family squabbles, wrecked homes, feuds between neighbors were the daily bread of police and police court. Annie Craven, in 1876, was arrested on a charge of "malicious mischief," for letting her water run onto a neighbor's property.[30] The battle between a Mrs. Atwater and a Mrs. Clark was one of many instances in 1890; they lived next door, but were hardly good neighbors. Mrs. Clark insulted Mrs. Atwater's children (said Mrs. Atwater); and Mr. Clark often lurched home drunk, "greatly disturbing the [Atwaters'] peace of mind." Mrs. Clark, for her part, complained of Mrs. Atwater's virulent tongue, her "loud and tumultuous noise," her "offensive conduct."[31] In Berkeley, in 1906, a warrant had to be issued for a "well-known young businessman" who beat his wife and "in a fit of anger dragged her about by the hair."[32] Sometimes, in family cases, cooler heads prevailed, blood and marriage proved thicker than water, and the complainant backed off: Mrs. M. Reichert, in 1891, had her husband "arrested for disturbing her peace," but she declined to prosecute, and the case was dismissed.[33] Other cases went further. In Oakland, Mrs. Catherine Palmer was arrested on her husband's complaint. The charge was battery; the victim, her own son. The evidence "showed that she had beaten her son for not going to school." She claimed that her husband "did not want the boy to be educated." The court convicted her. In another case in 1902, Spencer Handy, "a tough looking youth," was brought in to court because he set up "such a howl Saturday when

28. *San Francisco Call*, Mar. 21, 1903, p. 9, col. 1.
29. *Oakland Tribune*, July 19, 1894, p. 6, col. 1.
30. *Oakland Daily Transcript*, Apr. 12, 1876, p. 3, col. 3.
31. *Oakland Tribune*, May 14, 1890, p. 3, col. 5.
32. *Berkeley Reporter*, Feb. 27, 1906, p. 1, col. 3.
33. *Oakland Tribune*, June 8, 1891, p. 3, col. 3.

his grandmother . . . wanted him to put on overalls instead of his best clothes to work in the Union Iron Works" that the neighbors "complained and he was arrested for disturbing the peace." The judge gave him a lecture and said that "if he ever came before him again he would send him to the reform school." Grandmother Handy thanked the judge, but the boy (if the *Tribune* can be trusted) muttered "Damn the Judge" under his breath as he left.[34]

The police often had to step in to stop a brawl. Sometimes they made peace without an arrest. In June 1891, Mrs. Annie Hules of Park Avenue called in the police; her drunken husband had locked her and her baby out of the house. He "opened the door when he saw the uniform of the officers."[35] People called the police when matters got out of hand and they could not cope. Or the loser in a fight would call the police, perhaps for revenge. This last point is suggested by the timing of arrests for assault and battery. Half were made between 9:00 A.M. and 5:00 P.M., the greatest concentration—nearly a fourth—between 9:00 A.M. and noon. These are unlikely hours for a fight. Many of these must have been "morning after" complaints.[36]

In 1880 the rate of arrest for assault and battery was 6.3 per 1,000; by 1910 it was 1.5 per 1,000. Does this mean fewer brawls, fewer arrests—or merely fewer complaints? As Table 4.4 shows, the rate in 1970 had risen to 4.7. Today it is easy to file a complaint; the police give the victim a printed form to fill out. Assaults may be more common now than at the turn of the century. The rate of arrest for drunkenness also reached a high point long after our period: It was around 20 per 1,000 in the early 1950s and climbed to over 45 in 1965, partly because the department decided to crack down on public drunks.[37] Vagrancy arrests have disappeared, however. For one thing, they pose constitutional problems.[38] Not much can be said about "true" rates of drunkenness, vagrancy, or assault. These crimes are highly sensitive to changes in law, and to policies and tactics of police.

---

34. Ibid., May 14, 1890, p. 3, col. 4, May 26, 1902, p. 3, col. 3.
35. Ibid., June 11, 1891, p. 3, col. 1.
36. Once in a while, each of two brawlers entered a complaint against the other. For an example, see *Oakland Daily Telegraph*, Nov. 20, 1868, p. 2, col. 2; the judge fined both men.
37. Wilson, *Varieties of Police Behavior*, pp. 125, 123.
38. See, e.g., Papachristou v. City of Jacksonville, 405 U.S. 156 (1972).

Morals, Thefts, and Regulatory Crimes

Table 4.5 shows the arrest rate for gambling, regulatory offenses, and minor property offenses in selected years. Gambling cut a considerable figure for 1910; otherwise, regulatory violations (breaches of ordinances on health, transportation, and commerce) were more common. The offenses in the table have rates of arrest that rise and fall with tides of policy and fashion.

MORALS

Gambling arrests before 1906 were sporadic. Between 1906 and 1910 the police mounted a sustained campaign against gambling. This crackdown and certain regulatory offenses were closely tied to the "problem" of the Oakland Chinese. In the 1870s and 1880s, prejudice was virulent and almost official. The Chinese, said Mayor Andrus in 1879, were "in every way undesirable"; every legal method, direct or indirect, should be used to "discourage" them.[39] No doubt he echoed the sentiments of most of the city's whites. Ordinances were passed specifically to "get" the Chinese. Forty-six Chinese were arrested for "fishing with a small mesh net" in three separate incidents in April and May 1877. Thirteen Chinese were arrested for visiting an opium den in December 1881. Thirty-three were hauled in during the same month for maintaining a nuisance. In four separate raids, between 4:00 and 5:00 A.M., sixty-two Chinese were arrested for "sleeping in a room with less than 500 cubic feet of air per person." Forty-three Chinese were arrested in February 1886 for "violating the laundry ordinance."[40]

Gambling, of course, was not confined to the Chinese. But Chinese

39. The mayor wanted to regulate the location of laundries and washhouses; he proposed making laundry licenses depend on the consent of people in the neighborhood. He also wanted to cut the hair of city prisoners, and enforce the "pure air" ordinance more vigorously. Annual Message of Mayor W. R. Andrus, Jan. 30, 1879, quoted in *Oakland Tribune*, Feb. 4, 1879, p. 3, col. 2.

On the treatment of minorities in California in general, see Robert F. Heizer and Alan J. Almquist, *The Other Californians: Prejudice and Discrimination under Spain, Mexico, and the United States to 1920* (Berkeley, 1971).

40. The Japanese were less numerous, and less controversial; but there was a flurry of excitement in Alameda in 1908, when Assistant District Attorney Hynes suggested radical changes in the unsanitary and indecent "Japanese bathing places," where the "sexes intermingle [and] go through their queer ablutions . . . minus even the proverbial fig leaf." *Alameda Argus*, Feb. 28, 1908, p. 1, col. 2. Elinor Stoy, writing in 1907, accused the Japanese of selling their girls to the Chinese as slaves. In Oakland, she said, a "hideous vice-culture" flourishes "almost under the eaves of the Court House." Elinor H. Stoy, "Chinatown and the Curse That Makes It a Plague-Spot in the Nation," *Arena* 38 (Oct. 1907): 360, 363.

Table 4.5. Number and Rate of Arrests for
Law Enforcement Purposes in Oakland, 1875–1910

	1875		1880	
Type of offense	No. arrests	Per 1,000 people	No. arrests	Per 1,000 people
Gambling	9	0.4	14	0.4
Other morals	8	0.3	6	0.2
Regulatory ordinances	242	9.7	339	9.8
Petty larceny	76	3.1	125	3.6
Other minor property	15	0.6	57	1.6
Total	350	14.1	541	15.7

Sources: Same as for Table 4.4.

gambling evoked more condemnation. (The police judge in 1892 argued that "white men" sold lottery tickets at prices of 25 cents to $1; at this stiff price, only adults could buy. The buyers were men who had already lost their morals. The Chinese, though, sold nickel and dime tickets; they corrupted the young.)[41] Chinatown in Oakland, like Chinatowns in other cities, was a vice quarter, a place of gambling, prostitution, opium addiction. Chinatown was exotic, poor, and unsavory; before 1900, few Chinese women lived in the United States; there was little in the way of regular family life. Americans found Chinese food disgusting; "chop suey" had not yet become popular; Chinatown lived off laundries and sin.[42]

The gambling problem, generally speaking, bubbled to the surface every once in a while, and then died down. A police captain boasted in 1876 how clean Oakland was: there was no gambling at night, no faro banks, and none of the open, bare-faced gambling found in San Francisco and the rest of the state.[43] Even if this report was true, the cozy situation did not last. In 1881 the *Oakland Daily Times* charged that large numbers of "tan games" were running, sometimes "with the knowledge . . . of the police force." The *Times* printed addresses of the games.[44] In 1887 an Oakland police judge complained that the

41. *Oakland Tribune*, Jan. 28, 1892, p. 3, col. 3.
42. Ivan Light, "From Vice District to Tourist Attraction: The Moral Career of American Chinatowns, 1880–1940," *Pacific Hist. Rev.* 43 (1974): 367; Stoy, "Chinatown," p. 361: "Chop Suey. . . . It is a Chinese dish made of chicken, mushrooms and—I dare not even guess what else."
43. *Annual Report of the Captain of Police*, reprinted in *Oakland Tribune*, Jan. 3, 1876, p. 2, col. 4.
44. *Oakland Daily Times*, July 29, 1881, p. 3, col. 5.

1887		1900		1910	
No. arrests	Per 1,000 people	No. arrests	Per 1,000 people	No. arrests	Per 1,000 people
11	0.2	41	0.6	2,028	13.5
6	0.1	35	0.5	109	0.7
471	10.6	671	10.0	1,309	8.7
169	3.8	109	1.6	274	1.8
13	0.3	23	0.3	109	0.7
670	15.0	879	13.1	3,829	25.5

gambling laws were dead letters.[45] A new police captain took office in
1888 and told his men to

> note all places, rooms, saloons, cigar stores, lottery agencies,
> tan games, or any place where gambling is carried on by means
> of cards, dice, or any device for gambling purposes, and arrest
> each and every person engaged in gambling. I want every officer
> of the Police Department to give this close attention and to use
> every means practicable to find out where any game of chance is
> carried on. . . . Report all such cases to the captain and I will
> send a detail of officers to assist you at any time, day or night.
> Arrest all sellers of lottery tickets white men or women same
> as Chinese, with no exceptions.[46]

Brave words; but gambling continued, and so did payoffs. An officer had to resign in 1893, accused of taking bribes from "Chinese
lottery dealers."[47] In the same year, an irate citizen wrote to the
Tribune: "For official information I will say that at 460 and 462 Sixth
Street, 471 Eighth Street, 419 Tenth Street, and in many other places
these slant-eyed heathens can be found in any hour engaged in their
outlawed business."[48] Another excited citizen, in 1891, denounced
the "cunning Mongolians" who ran the games, and were somehow
immune to the law. Everybody knew where these games were. They

45. *Oakland Tribune*, Feb. 4, 1887, p. 3, col. 2.
46. Ibid., Apr. 16, 1888, p. 2, col. 3.
47. Ibid., Jan. 14, 1893, p. 3, col. 3. A certain Quong Fook was arrested in 1891 for
trying to bribe the police. Ibid., June 25, 1891, p. 3, col. 3.
48. Ibid., Aug. 3, 1893, p. 3, col. 3.

were "well guarded and barricaded," but "easy of access" to insiders. Strange to say, the games were never "pulled."[49]

These outcries, and irate editorials, were a sign that at least *some* people were alarmed over gambling. In 1887 the Society for the Prevention of Vice carried out a private raid of its own.[50] Effort after effort failed; still, the movement against vice gathered momentum underground. In 1906, apparently sensing public outrage, the police at last began a serious drive to get rid of gambling in Oakland—or at least a drive to show the public its police force cared. The detective force was strengthened from four to ten in 1910.[51] On 163 separate occasions between 1906 and 1910, the police made gambling raids; they arrested 4,159 people (see Table 4.6). The climax of the crack-

Table 4.6. Arrests of Ten or More Persons and Gambling Raids in Oakland, 1872–1910

Period	Arrests of ten or more	No. involving gambling	No. arrested in gambling raids
1872–75	2	1	16
1876–80	6	2	79
1881–85	26	6	153
1886–90	18	3	84
1892–95	5	0	0
1896–1900	8	4	63
1901–5	10	1	13
1906	19	17	481
1907	36	34	1,054
1908	43	38	1,073
1909	40	40	822
1910	35	33	729

Source: Oakland Arrest Books, 1872–1910.

49. Ibid., Jan. 7, 1891, p. 2, col. 4, p. 3, col. 5. Perhaps the good burghers did not know how hard it was to "pull" a "joint." Gambling halls sometimes had lookouts to warn of raids. The police tried disguises and sneak attacks; sometimes they broke down the doors with axes. In one case a detective, disguised as a tramp, shoved a long pole into an open doorway. In this way, he kept the lookouts from closing a massive door. Ibid., Mar. 23, 1888, p. 5, col. 4. In 1906, Marshall Vollmer and his men raided a Chinese gambling den in Berkeley, and caught fourteen Chinese playing fan-tan. Vollmer and his men first reconnoitered in their stocking feet, then broke in through a heavy door with an axe. *Berkeley Reporter*, June 18, 1906, p. 1, col. 2.

50. In 1887, for example, the secretary of this group rounded up a couple of lottery ticket dealers and had them arrested. The police did not take kindly to this kind of interference. *Oakland Tribune*, Feb. 4, 1887, p. 3, col. 2.

51. *Husted's Oakland City Directory* (1910), p. 35. From 1879 until 1894 there were two detectives on the Oakland police force; from 1894 on there were four.

down came in 1908. More than 10 percent of all arrests made in Oakland in 1908 (1,073) were gambling arrests.

Our arrest figures come from Oakland. But spasms of virtue occurred throughout the county. In the city of Alameda, for example, the Civic League hired private detectives to snoop around for evidence of gambling, bookie joints, and illegal sales of liquor. Arrests, trials, and scandals erupted in 1908, in an attempt to clean up such cesspools of vice as Zingg's Cigar Store—places that threatened to make Alameda a "feeding ground for vampires."[52] In Berkeley, Chief Vollmer sent two policemen with sledgehammers to smash in "the barricaded door" of another evil cigar store; they arrested three "prominent citizens," engrossed in "the great American game of 'draw poker'" (February 1906).[53]

Such crusades were controversial. In the city of Alameda, gambling flourished unashamed in the years before the crusade of 1908. It was live and let live, as far as the police were concerned. Not until the good Reverend MacFarlane, guiding light of the Civic League, roused himself to action did things start moving and shaking. The reverend accused the police of winking at vice. Poker players came and went at all hours of the night. The patrolmen on the beat watched, yet did nothing. The "trustful" chief of police "doubtless thought it was a prayer meeting they had been holding," and that "the rattle of the chips was the taking up of a collection for the poor, the blind and the deaf."[54] But police nonchalance had backing in high places: when the crackdown began, local businessmen spoke out, but against MacFarlane, not the gamblers. The reverend, they said, gained "notoriety for himself" while ruining the reputation of their "fair city."

As this account suggests, some person, group, or incident lay behind each epidemic of law enforcement. But crusades against gambling were not isolated, random events. They were part of a larger movement, the war against vice, a war carried out on many fronts. The battles began in the late nineteenth century and continued well into the twentieth. They brought in laws against drugs, liquor, and obscene books, not to mention the Mann Act and crackdowns on prostitution in the period around the First World War. There was also a national drive against gambling. Betting on the horses was under attack, for example, from 1890 on. In California, the race tracks were regularly denounced by the virtuous. There was a track at Emeryville, just north of Oakland; Oakland enacted ordinances in the 1890s to

52. *Alameda Argus*, Jan. 28, 1908, p. 1, col. 1, p. 5, col. 1, and many stories in subsequent months.
53. *Berkeley Reporter*, Feb. 17, 1900, p. 1, col. 7; see also Mar. 8, 1900, p. 1, col. 3.
54. *Alameda Argus*, Jan. 30, 1908, p. 5, col. 3.

forbid wagering "contest(s) between men or horses."[55] In 1903–4 the
county grand jury called the racetrack at Emeryville "the very hotbed
and source of crime. The county stinks with this evil."[56] The Penal
Code had forbidden gambling games since the 1870s (§ 330); but in
1909 the legislation added another section, specifically aimed at horse-
race betting (§ 337a).[57] In 1909 even Nevada, of all places, outlawed
gambling.[58]

The nineteenth century had been willing, on the whole, to tolerate
vice—so long as it kept in its place. For example, everybody talked
about prostitution; nobody, including the police, did much about it in
Alameda County. Arrests were rare.[59] In 1883 two constables raided
Jennie Turner's "bagnio." But they were looking for opium fiends;
prostitution was not the issue—and Jennie felt safe enough, and
indignant enough, to call the police and complain! Prostitutes were
usually charged with vagrancy, not prostitution. Women arrested on
this charge were probably streetwalkers, not the women who worked
in Jennie Turner's bagnio. Enforcement of vice laws was, to say the
least, uneven. Almost surely, some police took protection money. But
generally speaking there was a kind of rough accommodation between vice and vice enforcement—a compromise, if you will. The
police aimed to control, not suppress. Discreet vice, vice that "knew
its place," vice that accepted a label of sinfulness, that did not openly
attack official morality—such vice was tolerated. True, in 1908, the
district attorney, Everett Brown, complained about "dens of vice" on
Fifth Street. But this was partly because the "tenderloin" was "in the
wrong place," too near the County Courthouse.[60] And by this date,
the Victorian compromise was crumbling, as we shall see. A ground-
swell of outrage, like the outrage against liquor and gambling, built

55. See ord. no. 1910, approved June 2, 1898; two antilottery ordinances were nos.
1604 and 1605, both approved Apr. 23, 1894.
56. Grand Jury Report filed June 23, 1904, p. 2. The grand jury recommended state
laws to curb this evil.
57. See Henry Chafetz, *Play the Devil: A History of Gambling in the United States from
1492 to 1955* (New York, 1960), pp. 375–87.
58. Laws Nev. 1909, ch. 210.
59. See "An Old Story: A Man Robbed in a House of Ill Fame," *Oakland Tribune*,
May 7, 1890, p. 3, col. 4. Out of 1,676 cases prosecuted in the police court between
June 1, 1880 and May 31, 1881, there were only three in which the offense was
explicitly connected with prostitution (two for keeping a house of ill fame, one for
being in a house of ill fame). Rough Minutes of the Oakland Police Court, 1880–81. In
1887 and 1888 there were raids on brothels; the women arrested in the raids were
charged with vagrancy. Generally speaking, the police did not bother much with
prostitution.
60. *Alameda Argus*, Jan. 6, 1908, p. 8, col. 2.

up a huge head of steam. As far as red-light districts were concerned, it would break through the surface just after the end of our period.

Drug offenses were also closely bound up with the Chinese "problem." Drug sale or use was not illegal in any way at the beginning of the period. In 1881, however, the state adopted § 307 of the Penal Code, which created a brand-new misdemeanor: operating an opium den (a "place where opium . . . is sold or given away, to be smoked at such place"). It was also a misdemeanor to "visit" or "resort" to "any such place for the purpose of smoking opium." In the same year, Oakland passed an ordinance of its own "to Suppress Opium Dens and Prevent Immorality."[61] In 1890, Oakland went a big step further and enacted an ordinance to "Prevent the Abuse of Opium and Other Drugs." No druggist was to give out drugs without a doctor's prescription; and doctors were not to prescribe drugs except for the "purpose of curing or alleviating disease." The ordinance also applied to morphine and cocaine.[62]

As far as drug use was concerned, Californians probably considered the Chinese hopeless. But opium was a habit that spread to whites as well. In 1883 a "posse" of Constable Teague's deputies raided an "opium joint" on San Pablo Avenue; six "opium fiends" were "hitting the pipe." The six—who were not Chinese—were arrested; two Chinese were also picked up, for "smoking opium on 7th Street."[63] A week later, Charles Sullivan, "a man weighing about 200 pounds," was arrested in an "opium joint," and fined ten dollars.[64] Some opium arrests, as we have seen, were concealed under other headings, for example, vagrancy. Drug use was not socially approved (despite Sherlock Holmes), but mere addiction was not against the law. Illegal or no, the habit wrecked lives. A mother and son (also named Sullivan), both "morphine fiends," were arrested on a charge of battery in 1894. According to the *Tribune*, young Eugene's eyes had the "glare of semi-madness" as he begged for "dope." His "pallid lips" spit out "great flecks of foam"; his ravaged face spoke "an awful sermon" against the habit. His mother too was a picture of "loathesome degradation," "a grinning death's head"; she could barely hold

61. Ord. no. 879, 1881. In the case of In re Sic, 73 Cal. 149, 14 Pac. 405 (1887), the Supreme Court of California struck down an opium den ordinance of the city of Stockton, partly on the grounds that it conflicted with § 307; in case of conflict, state law must prevail. As far as we know, the Oakland ordinance was not challenged.

62. Ord. no. 1214, 1890. The ordinance was probably influenced by a San Francisco ordinance, no. 2085, adopted the year before (1889).

63. *Oakland Tribune*, July 2, 1883, p. 3, col. 2.

64. Ibid., July 9, 1883, p. 3, col. 2.

her head up as she "gibbered and raved" in the courtroom.[65] But though morphine use had brought them down to the lower depths, its use was no crime in itself.

There were occasional arrests for minor moral charges. Officer Kennedy, in July 1881, arrested "two young boys" for "vulgar language to young girls."[66] William T. Johns got ten dollars or five days for "vulgar language" in 1883.[67] Foul language was a common charge across the Bay in San Francisco; 971 people were arrested in the year ending June 30, 1881, for "lewd, bawdy, obscene, profane, provoking" language—about 4.25 percent of all arrests.[68] Alameda County produced fewer arrests on this charge. Still, in Berkeley, in 1906, there were plans for a local branch of the Anti-Profanity Society of the World. The aim was to "eradicate the vice of profanity."[69] (Profanity, as always, managed to survive.) Four boys "swimming a la Adam" were arrested in Alameda in 1908. The escapade cost them two dollars each. And the police also bagged four teen-agers for violating "the ordinance prohibiting minors smoking cigarettes."[70]

Sunday closing laws, in the 1880s, were a friction point between business and morality. Scores of merchants were arrested in 1882. They demanded jury trials, and their cases clogged the police courts, to the point where no more arrests could be made. God-fearing members of the Home Protection Society wanted even more arrests. Eventually, the California Supreme Court settled the matter—in a way. The court upheld the Sunday laws. But local authorities dropped the pending prosecutions. They explained, somewhat lamely, that violators might not have known that the laws were valid. The Sunday closing law was repealed in 1883.[71]

TRAFFIC AND REGULATORY ARRESTS

Traffic was a problem even before the motor car. An Oakland ordinance of 1891 set a speed limit for horses—nine miles an hour. In

65. Ibid., July 24, 1894, p. 5, col. 4. The mother was convicted of vagrancy, the son of battery and vagrancy. Ibid., July 25, 1894, p. 5, col. 5.

66. Ibid., July 29, 1888, p. 3, col. 1.

67. Ibid., Sept. 5, 1883, p. 3, col. 6.

68. Chief of Police Report, in *San Francisco Mun. Rpts. F/Y 1880–1881*, p. 379. Ten years later, in *San Francisco Mun. Rpts. F/Y 1890–1891*, p. 202, the number had dropped to 421 arrests, less than 2 percent of the total.

69. *Berkeley Reporter*, Feb. 1, 1906, p. 1, col. 1.

70. *Alameda Argus*, Apr. 13, 1908, p. 2, col. 8. The smokers got a lecture in court and were sent home.

71. Ex parte Koser, 60 Cal. 177 (1882); on the dismissal of the pending cases, see *Oakland Tribune*, Mar. 21, 1882, p. 3, col. 3.

1897 eight miles an hour was the speed limit set for bicycles.[72] There were occasional bicycle crackdowns: during one week in August 1899, Oakland arrested seventy-one riders, nearly two-thirds of that week's arrests. In 1902, "officers in citizen's clothing" mounted themselves on wheels, the better to chase down bicycle speeders; the result was "a sprinting match, ending at the city jail."[73] Jack London, the novelist, was arrested in 1904 for riding a bike in the dark without lights; he forfeited two dollars' bail.[74]

By the beginning of the new century, the automobile had definitely arrived, bringing with it a flock of new petty offenses. T. Boland, of Fruitvale, "ran afoul of a policeman" in 1904 "for not tooting his automobile horn when rounding corners." He had to pay "the usual fine of three dollars."[75] Some unknown genius had already invented the speed trap. San Leandro in 1908 and 1909 had mastered the art and the practice. The city marshall, Geisenhofer, was "well known from Oakland to San Jose" as a deadly enemy of Sunday speeders. He arrested William B. Henshaw, president of the Union Savings Bank of Oakland, and even Superior Court Judge Ogden, who was traveling "with a party of Knight Templars from Sacramento," showing off "the beautiful surroundings." (The banker paid a fine; the judge did not.) On one Sunday, the marshall collected $115. The "merry war" between "automobilists" and San Leandro police was notorious; drivers were "liable to be pinched even when going at a snail's pace"; smart drivers gave the town a wide berth.[76] Only the well-to-do, of course, owned cars; this was one example of law enforcement that fell more heavily on the wealthier classes.

Regulatory arrests amounted to a substantial share of arrests—about 10 percent. Oakland required a license to do business in the city, and this ordinance produced a fine crop of arrests.[77] Other measures also made their mark. A "swill driver" was arrested in 1893 in Oakland, for "hauling swill in a leaky wagon, thereby endangering the clean-

72. Ord. no. 1367, 1891; Ord. no. 1829, 1897.
73. *Oakland Tribune*, May 5, 1902, p. 3, col. 2.
74. *Oakland Herald*, Aug. 7, 1904, p. 1, col. 2.
75. Ibid., May 25, 1904, p. 5, col. 3.
76. *San Leandro Reporter*, Dec. 26, 1908, p. 1, col. 3, Mar. 20, 1909, p. 1, col. 3, Aug. 28, 1909, p. 1, col. 6.
77. The license ordinance was a money-maker. In 1872 the city issued 403 licenses, and earned under $10,000. By 1879 there were more than 1,100 licenses, and revenue was over $45,000, more than one-tenth of the municipal budget. In 1905 license fees came to more than $150,000, again over one-tenth of the city's revenues. *Bishop's Oakland Directory*, 1874–80, p. 14 (1879); *Husted's Oakland Directory* (1906). Around one-tenth of the regulatory arrests between 1872 and 1910 were for violations of license ordinances.

liness and health of the city."[78] Another "scavenger," arrested in 1904, was put on trial for "dumping in places not authorized." In Pleasanton (1895), the town marshal enforced "in earnest" ordinance no. 4, that "no stock shall be allowed to run in the streets of Pleasanton."[79] The health officer of Berkeley, in 1906, charged five butchers and poultry dealers with selling poultry improperly plucked.[80] Steve Pasquale, who peddled ice cream and "hokey-pokey," was arrested in 1908 for selling adulterated goods. The city chemist tested Pasquale's wares, and found them wanting in butterfat; they also contained coloring matter "in violation of the pure food ordinance." Pasquale was fined fifty dollars, as an example to other malefactors.[81] Eight days later, a merchant was arrested "for violating the ordinance prohibiting sidewalk signs."[82]

Fish and game laws also produced arrests. The mayor of Alameda got in trouble in January 1908 for shooting out of season in the marshes of San Mateo; another citizen had to pay twenty dollars for shooting larks on Bay Farm Island.[83] Joseph Ruggiero, in 1909, shot a jack rabbit without a license in the hills behind San Leandro.[84] In the same year, a group of fishermen made the mistake of offering a "fine speckled specimen" of trout to a hungry stranger. The stranger was a deputy fish warden, and their kindness cost them twenty-five dollars in forfeited bail. L. S. Stafford was arrested in San Leandro for catching a trout less than five inches long; the fish, he said, was really seven inches long, but shrank when "exposed to the sun and heat." This fish story was too much for the judge to swallow. Stafford hastily left the courtroom—to consult his lawyer, he said. He never came back, and forfeited his bail.[85]

Ordinances on the sale of liquor were a persistent source of arrests and political heat. These were complex, controversial ordinances. Oakland's ordinance of 1895 (no. 1093) can be taken as typical. The ordinance made it illegal to run an unlicensed "saloon, bar, store, dram shop, tippling place, stand or any place where . . . liquors or wines are sold." Proprietors had to be "of good moral character"; and to get a license one needed the approval of neighbors—signatures of

78. *Oakland Citizen*, Dec. 27, 1893, p. 1, col. 1.

79. *Oakland Herald*, May 24, 1904, p. 3, col. 4; *Pleasanton Times*, Jan. 12, 1895, p. 3; col. 2.

80. *Berkeley Reporter*, Mar. 12, 1906, p. 1, col. 5.

81. *Alameda Argus*, Apr. 16, 1908, p. 8, col. 7.

82. *Berkeley Reporter*, Mar. 20, 1908, p. 1, col. 2.

83. *Alameda Argus*, Jan. 13, 1908, p. 8, col. 5, Jan. 9, 1908, p. 1, col. 1, Jan. 27, 1908, p. 1, col. 2.

84. *San Leandro Reporter*, Oct. 2, 1909, p. 4, col. 5. The judge dismissed the charge. He felt that rabbits were "pests" and could be shot without a license at will.

85. Ibid., Mar. 20, 1909, p. 4, col. 4, Apr. 10, 1909, p. 1, col. 3.

at least five residents of Oakland who owned real estate within one block from the front entrance of the place where liquor would be sold. No liquor could be sold to minors, of course; and the license could be taken away if any of the rules were broken, if liquor was sold off hours, or if the place became "disorderly or disruptable [*sic*]." Despite the five-signature rule, neighbors often objected to a license. And in every city and town, there were plenty of arrests for rule breaking. Henry Millard, a Fruitvale saloonkeeper, was accused of selling liquor after midnight (1909). He fought the case, but a jury convicted him.[86] In Berkeley, in 1906, the police raided a "speakeasy." A plainclothes-man had gone in advance and gathered his evidence—a bottle of beer falsely labeled "root beer." The raid was part of a move to get rid of "notorious and pernicious 'joints'" that flourished "within a stone's throw of the university."[87] John Hartz, a saloon keeper, was arrested in 1891 for selling liquor to a minor; he got off with a warning in police court. His offense was a "very common one about town—that of selling beer to a child who came with a can."[88]

MINOR PROPERTY CRIMES

Usually, it was a citizen complaint that touched off arrests for petty larceny. Occasionally, a policeman, guard, or watchman caught a thief in the act. A night watchman, John Salvador, nabbed a twelve-year-old boy in San Leandro, in 1909, stealing canned fruit from a cannery.[89] Victims did not usually witness the crime. Accordingly, catching thieves was often a job for detectives.[90] Arrests for petty larceny were mostly daytime arrests (see Table 4.7), probably follow-ing someone's complaint and a certain amount of detective work. Oakland detectives (the newspapers sometimes called them "thief takers") kept a "rogue's gallery." In 1888 the police took 122 mug shots; over 90 percent of these photos were of thieves.[91]

86. Ibid., May 15, 1909, p. 3, col. 4.
87. *Berkeley Reporter*, Mar. 9, 1906, p. 1, col., Mar. 30, 1906, p. 1, col. 1.
88. *Oakland Tribune*, June 5, 1891, p. 2, col. 3.
89. *San Leandro Reporter*, Oct. 9, 1909, p. 3, col. 3.
90. If a victim suspected someone specific, the police might use a search warrant. The *Tribune* reported in 1893 that "Constable Page yesterday served the search warrant sworn to by Mrs. Wells, to obtain some household property, alleged to have been stolen from her . . . by Mrs. Downer and her daughter. . . . A complete search was made of the premises, but none of the missing goods were found. Mrs. Downer and her daughter say that Mrs. Wells' age and infirmities are such as to render her irresponsible for what she says and does, yet they feel keenly the disgrace she has brought upon them by her charges of theft. . . ." *Oakland Tribune*, Aug. 4, 1893, p. 3, col. 3.
91. *Oakland Tribune*, Jan. 7, 1889, p. 8, col. 2.

Table 4.7. Percentages of Total Arrests for Each Offense Class in Oakland by Time of Day, 1872–1910

Time of Day	Drunkenness	Morals	Public order	Minor v. persons
8 A.M.–6 P.M.	32%	38%	47%	58%
6 P.M.–2 A.M.	60%	54%	46%	38%
2 A.M.–8 A.M.	8%	8%	7%	5%
N	656	107	247	100

Source: Sample of entries in Oakland Arrest Books, 1872–1910.

The arrest rate for petty larceny in Oakland was significantly lower after 1900 than in the 1870s and 1880s (1.8 per 1,000 in 1910, compared to 3.8 per 1,000 in 1887—see Table 4.5). In 1875 citizens reported the theft of $28,610 worth of property; in 1900 the figure was less than half that amount ($12,871.70).[92] Was there less thievery in Oakland? Or were people less willing to report it (or the police less able to cope)? The size of Oakland's detective force was not a factor; the number of detectives per 1,000 population in our period did not correlate at all with the arrest rate for petty larceny ($r = 0.148$). The police *may* have become a bit more efficient in recovering stolen property. In 1875 they claimed that they recovered $14,842, just over half of the amount reported stolen; in 1900 they said they recovered about 68 percent.[93] But there is no way of knowing if these figures can be trusted; police are as willing as the next folks to exaggerate how good they are. And there is no reason to assume that the police became less willing and able to prosecute. Very likely the lower rate of arrest reflected reality: less theft.

But not forever. In 1975 the Oakland police arrested 3,933 people for petty theft—11.2 per 1,000 population. This was about six times the rate in 1910. The police now encourage prosecution. The population mix in the city is also different, because much of the middle class has fled to the suburbs. Still, it is hard to resist the idea that sheer lawlessness has grown to colossal size.

92. Ibid., Jan. 3, 1876, p. 3, col. 4; Oakland Police Department, *Annual Report of the Chief of Police* (1900), p. 35.
93. Ibid.

Regul. ordinance	Minor v. property	Total arrests
66%	67%	47%
22%	27%	44%
11%	6%	9%
208	98	1,555

The Service Role of Police

Policemen have always done work not strictly part of law and order. Even today, despite dozens of government agencies for this or that social need, the police still play a service role. Everybody knows the police; not everybody knows the agencies.[94] The police are on call twenty-four hours a day; the agencies are not. And when a problem crops up with no agency of its own, who can you call but the police? So when a ghost appeared in an empty house in Oakland, in 1894, shrieking, groaning, clanking its chains, and throwing the neighborhood "into a state of violent excitement," it was the police that had to be called to get rid of the ghost.[95]

The Oakland police also ran a kind of welfare program. They gave shelter, and sometimes food, to the homeless. The city prison served as a sort of "free lodging house." There were "sleeping apartments, bunks and blankets" (similar to those provided "for the crews of clipper ships"); any one "minus the means to pay for a bed can apply at police headquarters, register . . . and obtain a bunk." This was in 1875; the police gave shelter that year to 1,045 persons. It was hardly luxury, and for some it was the end of the line: an "aged tramp," in

94. Wilson, *Varieties of Police Behavior*, pp. 107–8. See Elaine Cumming, Ian M. Cumming, and Laura Edell, "The Policeman as Philosopher, Guide and Friend," *Social Problems* 12 (1965): 1276; Paul H. Embross and Patricia French, "Social Service and the Police," *Hospital & Community Psychiatry* 23 (1972): 61–63; Richard J. Lundman, "Domestic Police-Citizen Encounters," *J. Police Sci. & Admin.* 22 (1974): 22; Arthur Niederhoffer, *Behind the Shield: The Police in Urban Society* (New York, 1969), p. 75; E. L. Barrett, Jr., "Criminal Justice: The Problem of Mass Production," in *The Courts, the Public and the Law Explosion*, ed. H. W. Jones (Englewood Cliffs, N.J., 1965), p. 95; Richardson, *Urban Police*, pp. 175–78.

95. *Oakland Tribune*, July 25, 1894, p. 6, col. 1.

1883, in an alcoholic stupor, came to the jail begging for shelter and then hanged himself in the "lodgers' cell" a half hour later.[96] In 1886 there were 3,394 lodgers, in 1887, 2,694; in 1900, 1,070.[97] Most lodgers came knocking on the doors in winter.[98] Eighteen ninety-three was a year of misery and unemployment; in December a winter storm "caused an influx of sleepers to the city prison. Forty-eight men of different classes and characteristics . . . were given cots and pallets in the prison corridor."[99]

The line between service and law enforcement was not always clear; both roles involved the police with broken, downtrodden men. For some people, to be arrested for drunkenness or lodged in jail as a homeless drifter was much the same. A certain John Kelly was a frequent inmate of city prison. He worked there as a gardener. On a cold winter day, in 1888, Kelly stopped an officer and asked to be taken in for drunkenness. He was indeed drunk, and the officer was willing. No patrol wagon was needed; Kelly went to jail by himself.[100]

Oakland police also had the unlovely job of clearing the streets of dead animals—2,514 dogs, horses, goats, cows, and cats in 1900. The patrol wagon picked up injured people, too. In the early years, the wagon took them to police headquarters; later, it took the injured to a receiving hospital.[101] The police supervised city prisoners who worked on the chain gang, repairing streets and sewers. Patrolmen were supposed to keep "a vigilant watch for fires"; in the 1870s they were also expected to help put out fires.[102]

They also picked up runaway children, and scooped up people who wandered about in a mental fog. Sometimes they arrested the runaways or the delirious: Charles Nordstrom, a Swede, was arrested in 1894. His "wild and uncouth gestures" raised a "suspicion of insanity." Or they made arrests on call: Nathaniel Lenoir, a bookkeeper, fresh from the asylum, "began to break the furniture in his house." The family, alarmed, sent for the police.[103] Hence, there were always *some* service arrests—108 in 1875 and 152 in 1910 (about 4 percent and

96. Ibid., Jan. 3, 1876, p. 3, col. 5, Aug. 21, 1883, p. 3, col. 5.
97. Ibid., Jan. 5, 1888, p. 1, col. 1; Oakland Police Department, *Annual Report of the Chief of Police* (1900), p. 30.
98. In fiscal year 1900, for example, the six months from October through March accounted for two-thirds of all lodgers who stayed in city prison. Oakland Police Department, *Annual Report of the Chief of Police* (1900), p. 30.
99. *Oakland Citizen*, Dec. 21, 1893, p. 5, col. 3. The Alameda city jail also supplied "blankets for the use of free lodgers." *Alameda Argus*, Dec. 28, 1893, p. 3, col. 2.
100. *Oakland Tribune*, Jan. 24, 1888, p. 3, col. 7.
101. Oakland Police Department, *Annual Report of the Chief of Police* (1900), p. 36.
102. *Oakland Tribune*, Apr. 10, 1877, p . 3, col. 2.
103. *Oakland Citizen*, Mar. 6, 1894, p. 4, col. 1, Mar. 10, 1894, p. 3, col. 4.

1 percent of all arrests, respectively). The decline was only a decline in *formal* arrests. In 1900 police returned 241 runaway children to their parents, but they made only 49 arrests.[104]

The police also tried to find out who owned recovered property. The *Tribune* reported in 1876, for example, that three stolen chickens "captured with Captain Charles Davis" were still at city prison, "awaiting the call of their owners."[105] And, of course, the police served warrants and subpoenas: 459 warrants and 2,996 subpoenas in 1900 alone.[106]

Who Was Arrested?

In nineteenth-century Oakland, what did respectable people think of those who broke society's laws? It is no surprise that they looked down on such people. They were misfits; and were mostly strangers, foreigners—outsiders, in one sense or another. One strong prevailing image was that of the "dangerous class"—tramps or drifters, Chinese gamblers, "fiends" crazed with opium, hoodlums from San Francisco (that Sodom across the Bay), young ruffians and toughs, moral degenerates.[107]

But if an artist drew a sketch of the *typical* person arrested in Oakland between 1872 and 1910, the picture might contain a few surprises. It would show a white male, thirty-two years old, 5 feet 7 inches tall, weighing 150 pounds, working as a laborer. Moreover, the man would be American born, a resident of Oakland, and with some education. Most people arrested, in other words, were not young thugs, or outsiders, or tramps.[108]

Of course, this does not tell us what "criminals" were really like. Not all criminals were caught; and most people arrested were not criminals at all, only people who disturbed the peace in one way or another. Still, the picture tells us a great deal about those who felt the

---

104. Oakland Police Department, *Annual Report of the Chief of Police* (1900), pp. 36, 23.
105. *Oakland Tribune*, Mar. 2, 1876, p. 3, col. 3.
106. Oakland Police Department, *Annual Report of the Chief of Police* (1900), p. 30.
107. The expression "dangerous classes" comes from Charles Loring Brace's book *The Dangerous Classes of New York and Twenty Years' Work among Them* (New York, 1880). The book describes Brace's experiences with youth gangs.
108. The person described in the text as "statistically typical" has the mean values of continuous variables and the modal values of noncontinuous variables. Although *most* people arrested in Oakland were not "young thugs, or outsiders, or tramps," these groups were overrepresented—arrested in numbers quite disproportionate to their share of the population.

(more or less) heavy hand of the law; the contrast with the 1970s is striking, as we shall see.

Insiders and Outsiders: Residence and Nationality

From the beginning, Oakland "society" saw crime as a threat from outside—from strangers, intruders, riffraff streaming across the Bay from San Francisco. The Oakland directory for 1872 stated that the "avenues of approach to the city" were "carefully guarded." The police even "inspected" trains that entered or left. On Sunday droves of picnickers came over from San Francisco by ferry, and extra police were put on. In 1875 the *Tribune* was a bit leery about the plan to put police in uniform; plainclothesmen (out-of-towners would not recognize them) could catch more "evil-doers" from across the Bay.[109] Luckily, there were only three ways to reach Oakland from San Francisco, the

> creek route and the ferries at the end of the Long Wharf
> and at Berkeley. This renders the problem of how to keep track of
> who visits us from across the bay very easy of solution. The
> police readily become familiar with Oakland faces and learn to
> note the difference between the face of a hoodlum and that of a
> respectable citizen, so that it would be really impossible for any
> dangerous number of San Francisco roughs to enter Oakland
> without their presence being instantly telegraphed from the
> ferries to police headquarters.[110]

This was probably always a fantasy; or perhaps population growth overwhelmed this happy state. In any event, between 1872 and 1910, only 10 percent of the people arrested were residents of San Francisco; more than three-quarters lived in Alameda County (73 percent in Oakland, 3 percent in the rest of the county); only one out of nine was a "drifter," in the sense of someone without permanent residence.[111] These percentages, however, did vary over time. In the 1870s, San Francisco accounted for more arrests—about one-fifth; less than two-thirds were locals. "Drifters" in the late 1890s accounted for one-fifth of the arrests, but the figure dropped to 2

109. *Langley's Directory of the City of Oakland* (1872), p. 17; *Oakland Tribune*, Dec. 7, 1875, p. 3, col. 4.

110. *Oakland Tribune*, July 31, 1877, p. 2, col. 1.

111. Only 1.6 percent were residents of other parts of California; 0.6 percent were from the rest of the United States; 0.1 percent were residents of foreign countries (Sample of 1,555 entries in Oakland Arrest Books).

percent in 1910. After the great earthquake in 1906, quite under-standably, more San Franciscans were arrested than before. By 1907 the situation was back to normal.

Crimes against the person, overwhelmingly, began at home. Resi-dents of Oakland accounted for more than 90 percent of all such arrests, both felonies and misdemeanors. But only 51 percent of the people arrested for felonies against property, and 68 percent of those arrested for property misdemeanors, were from Oakland. These re-sults should not surprise us. The victim of a beating was more likely to know the name of his attacker. Thieves, especially serious thieves, like to work where no one knows their names. And perhaps a person was less likely to call the police if he caught his neighbor (or his neighbor's boy) in an act of petty theft.

Oakland did have visitors, and some were arrested when they became drunk and rowdy, or broke local law. Visitors were probably not looking for the more advanced grades of vice; San Francisco had enough of that for all tastes. Of the people arrested on morals charges, 92 percent were locals. (Most of these were gambling arrests.) Arrests for ordinance violation, drunkenness, and public disorder fell more heavily on the man from out of town (from a quarter to a third of these arrests). And outsiders (mainly runaways) figured heavily in service arrests.

Foreigners and Minorities

Most people arrested between 1872 and 1910 were native-born Ameri-cans—55 percent. On the other hand, the native-born were at all times *more* than 55 percent of the population—59 percent at the be-ginning of the period, 73 percent at the end. The foreign-born were disproportionately arrested.[112]

Who were these "foreigners" in trouble? Eighteen percent of them were Irish, though the Irish were never more than 11 percent of the population. In the 1870s, the Irish were arrested at more than three

112. Before 1890 the census reported race, but not nationality, for people living in Oakland. We can reckon arrest rates in 1880 for the Chinese, but not for other ethnic groups. But we could estimate the arrest rate for native-born Americans by using the 1880 *Annual Report of the Chief of Police*, and census data from Alameda County, which record the numbers of native- and foreign-born. We have to assume, of course, that the proportion of native-born Americans who lived in Oakland was about the same as the proportion in the county as a whole. For 1900 we can calculate arrest rates in a similar way. About 63 percent of the people arrested in the City of Alameda in the last half of 1907, according to local police report, were natives of the United States. *Alameda Argus,* Jan. 13, 1908, p. 8, col. 5.

times their "proper" rate. Patterns of Chinese arrests were a more complex affair. The Chinese lived in the heart of Oakland, in a tightly segregated "Chinatown." White Oakland hated the Chinese; they were treated, at best, as second-class citizens, at worst as little better than animals. The frenzy against the Chinese was at its height in the 1870s and the 1880s.[113] The Chinese suffered from high arrest rates, but these rates ebbed and flowed considerably. From the mid-1870s until the mid-1890s, Chinese were disproportionately arrested—in 1880, for example, at a rate about three times greater than that for native-born Americans. By 1900 the discrepancy had all but vanished. After 1906, however, gambling raids pushed the Chinese arrest rate to its all-time high, more than 500 per thousand. The small black population was also disproportionately arrested. In 1910, for example, blacks made up 2 percent of Oakland's population, but supplied 7 percent of the arrests.

It is interesting to see what groups were arrested and for what offenses (see Table 4.8). About 40 percent of arrests of Americans, and 63 percent of Irish arrests, were for drunkenness. The Chinese were almost never arrested for drunkenness, and only rarely for public order offenses. Perhaps the Chinese were not given to carousing; or perhaps the police were indifferent to what went on in Chinatown, except when it spilled over into the rest of the city. Our evidence is not conclusive. Chinatown was not left completely to its own devices; it was a regular police beat, patrolled by an officer or two.[114] Still, we pick up hints that the police sometimes ignored disturbances in Chinatown. In 1876, we read, there was "a small riot" in the quarter. Some "saddle-colored descendants of Confucius" used their knives "quite freely." Yet no arrests were made.[115]

Probably the police were quicker to move in when the victim was white, or the offense took place outside Chinatown. Certainly there was no hesitation to arrest Chinese thieves; in 1894 two "Chinese shoplifters" were caught stealing silk handkerchiefs from a dry goods store in Alameda.[116] Regulatory and morals ordinances were another story, too. They accounted for over 85 percent of all Chinese arrests. This is hardly surprising; some ordinances were passed specifically to harass the Chinese; others were used against Chinese only. This was

113. On the treatment of the Chinese, see Heizer and Almquist, *The Other Californians*, chap. 7.
114. *Oakland Tribune*, Apr. 16, 1888, p. 2, col. 3, Jan. 5, 1893, p. 3, col. 3, Apr. 10, 1889, p. 1, col. 8.
115. Ibid., Mar. 15, 1876, p. 3, col. 1.
116. Ibid., Aug. 10, 1894, p. 6, col. 1. The shoplifters were strangers, caught after a search of Chinatown.

notably true in the 1870s and 1880s. In 1875, a certain Ah Sam was arrested for peddling without a license: "His vegetables are lying on the floor of the Police Court office, while businessmen throughout the city are going ahead as usual, very few of whom have taken out a license according to the ordinance which this poor Chinaman is charged with violating."[117] The same year, the *Tribune* noted sardonically that "Ah Dong has been arrested on suspicion of being a Chinaman."[118] In 1887 a police officer set out to arrest Wing Hop, who ran an unlicensed laundry. Wing Hop was not at home, so the officer arrested another man "at random," and booked him as Wing Hop, "on the theory that there is little difference in the appearance of Chinamen."[119] These tales from the press make it clear enough that bigotry colored the behavior of at least some policemen. Arrest rates, no doubt, reflect these prejudices, though it is impossible to say how much. As for other nationalities, we do not know how to interpret departures from the mean: were these foreigners greater sinners than most, or greater victims, or both?

Women and the Police

Crime—or at least criminal justice—was decidedly a man's job. Nine out of ten arrests in Oakland between 1872 and 1910 were arrests of men.[120] In 1887, for example, the arrest rate for men in Oakland was

117. Ibid., Jan. 9, 1875, p. 3, col. 3. A discriminatory ordinance—of San Francisco's—led to one of the most notable Supreme Court cases of the late nineteenth century. This was Yick Wo v. Hopkins, 118 U.S. 356 (1886). The ordinance outlawed laundries, except in brick or stone buildings, without city permission. Whites routinely got permission; Chinese were just as routinely denied. This, said the Court, was unconstitutional behavior.

118. *Oakland Tribune*, Jan. 5, 1875, p. 3, col. 3.

119. Ibid., Feb. 17, 1887, p. 3, col. 5. Later that evening, the real Wing Hop was arrested; but the false Wing Hop was let out of jail only after other Chinese protested to the captain of police.

120. Oakland arrest records did not record sex, but we can tell sex from the first name, except for the Chinese. The Romanized spelling of Chinese names does not show sex unambiguously. But nearly all Chinese in late nineteenth-century Oakland were men. According to the 1900 census, 96 percent of the 1,146 Chinese, Japanese, and Indians in the county were men. We have read Alameda County newspapers rather intensively (though selectively) for the period 1872–1910, and have seen only one mention of the arrest of a Chinese woman, Ah Hoe, "a notorious Chinese woman," a known "crook," arrested as a vagrant in 1893. *Oakland Citizen*, Dec. 22, 1893, p. 3, col. 1. (In 1890 one Chinese woman was reported in the Alameda County jail.) We therefore coded Chinese names as male. Even if a few of the Chinese arrested were women, the numbers would be so small that they would not affect the calculations.

If we excluded *all* Chinese from the calculations, men would still make up 87.7 percent of those arrested. Men outnumbered women in early Oakland (they were 60

*Table 4.8. Percentage Distribution of Arrests of
Persons of Selected Nationalities in Oakland, 1872–1910*

Nationality	Felonies v. persons	Felonies v. property	Drunkenness	Public order	Minor v. persons
U.S.	2%	4%	40%	17%	7%
Irish	1	2	63	17	5
Chinese	1	5	0	5	2
All	1	4	42	16	6

Source: Sample of entries in Oakland Arrest Books, 1872–1910.

over 120 per 1,000; but the rate for women was less than 12 per 1,000. In 1900 the arrest rate was 87 per 1,000 for men, for women only 5 per 1,000.[121] These differences are so great that they *must* reflect behavior. Women broke fewer laws, created fewer disturbances, than men.

This was true in every class of offense, and most especially for felonies and morals charges. Women gave men a somewhat better run for their money in drunkenness and public disorder. The figures (see Table 4.9) are a bit surprising. One might guess that women would "do best" in violating ordinances (traffic offenses, for example) and in property offenses (shoplifting), not in the street-corner brawls and drunkenness. Perhaps these arrest patterns run as they do precisely because of social expectations. Women were not supposed to fight, or get publicly drunk. *Haywards Weekly Journal* (1878), telling about a drunken woman, who was "deposited in the calaboose" to "recover from the potations," expressed this attitude quite vividly: "Great God to imagine a woman—a being who, as an image of an angel should be everything pure, and gentle, and beautiful—to . . . bring herself to a position lower than a brute and more disgusting. Drunkenness is bad enough in men, but when women worship at the shrine of Bacchus, words fail to express the horror and abhorrence that mankind feel toward them."[122] Perhaps for this reason police were more likely to arrest a drunken or disorderly woman than a man. Some women *were* notorious drunks, brawlers, or neighbor-

---

percent of the population in 1870); but the gap narrowed as more women moved west, and family life became more normal. In 1890 males were only slightly in the lead in population—51 percent.

121. *Oakland Tribune*, Jan. 5, 1888, p. 1, col. 1; Oakland Police Department, *Annual Report of the Chief of Police* (1900).

122. *Haywards Weekly Journal*, Aug. 17, 1878, p. 3, col. 3.

Regul. ordin.	Morals	Minor v. property	Service	Total	N
16%	4%	8%	4%	100%	855
5	0	6	3	100	280
20	62	4	1	100	93
15	7	7	3	100	1,532

hood troublemakers. After a "hair pulling match," in 1906, Mary Andrade accused Mary Cardoza of trying to "brain her with a kettle"; this led to an arrest for battery.[123] The poor showing of women in morals offenses has to be taken with a slight grain of salt. It was the habit in Oakland to charge prostitutes with vagrancy (a public order offense), instead of a morals charge. Yet women would still score highest in public order offenses, even if we shifted all their vagrancy arrests into "morals."

Recent figures for Oakland suggest that women are beginning to catch up in arrests; they made up 15 percent of arrests in 1970, 18 percent in 1979. Some of the increase may reflect changes in police behavior; but some of it surely means that women are breaking more laws.

Who Was Arrested? The Young and the Old

In our period, the householder who read the newspapers might well feel that wayward youth was a serious problem in the county. And there were some very young boys (and girls) who got in trouble. Albert Ward was arrested for stealing a horse in 1893; according to the *Oakland Citizen*, he was "the youngest horse thief working . . . ten years old and weighs about 35 pounds after dinner."[124] In 1903, a girl of 11, Isabella McGuire, was described as a tramp and kleptomaniac.[125] But in Oakland's harvest of arrests, the *median* age was 32.

123. *Berkeley Reporter*, Sept. 5, 1906, p. 3, col. 3.
124. *Oakland Citizen*, Dec. 28, 1893, p. 1, col. 4.
125. *Oakland Herald*, Aug. 5, 1903, p. 2, col. 2.

Table 4.9. Percentage Distribution of Arrests by Sex for Each Offense Class in Oakland, 1872–1910

Sex	Felonies v. persons	Felonies v. property	Drunkenness	Public order	Minor v. persons
Male	94%	97%	87%	79%	89%
Female	6%	13%	13%	21%	11%
N	17	60	555	196	80

Table 4.10 shows arrest rates by age group in 1900 and 1970. The median age in the 1970s was significantly younger—in 1979, it was 27, according to the Oakland Police Department's *Annual Crime Survey*. Oakland's age distribution has changed its shape a bit; but this does not begin to account for the drop in the age of people picked up by police. In 1970, 20–29-year-olds had the highest arrest rate; 15–19-year-olds came in second. In 1900, people in their 30s and 40s made up the bulk of those arrested. *Rates* have increased for every age group but most notably among the young. Have patterns of behavior changed? Or is it the police who have changed? Is it possible that the police were easier on juveniles in 1900—that they might warn and threaten instead of making arrests?

Tables 4.11 and 4.12 shed a little light on this question. Between 1872 and 1910, young people were most likely to be arrested for property crimes and for breach of ordinances. The median age of people arrested for minor property crimes was 27; for felonies against property, 28; for ordinance violations, 29. Median ages for drunks and moral offenders were much higher—38 and 39, respectively. People under 30 accounted for 62 percent of the minor property arrests, 67 percent of arrests for felonies against property, 50 percent of arrests for felonies against the person, and 55 percent of arrests for ordinance violations; but only 26 percent of the drunkenness arrests and 34 percent of arrests for moral offenses. Quirks of police practice and police prejudice may explain some of these age differences, perhaps, but surely not all. We know that the police often handled young offenders informally—even a spanking or two is recorded—but on the whole, the drunken reprobate was no callow youth, and the old greybeard was not up to breaking and entering.

In recent years rates of serious crime in Oakland have climbed dramatically. The police put great effort into felony arrests and (up to recently, at least) drug charges; disorder and petty crime must take a

Regul. ordin.	Morals	Minor v. property	Service	Total
95%	98%	92%	84%	89%
5%	2%	8%	16%	11%
173	127	91	44	1,343

back seat. Felonies and drug offenses seem to be young peoples' crimes. In 1975, as in 1872–1910, most drunks were over 30. But drunkenness and other public disorders account for a smaller share of today's arrests. Hence, changes in juvenile crime rates *and* shifts in police practice both combined to reduce the median age of people arrested in Oakland.

Who Was Arrested? Workers and Nonworkers

Thousands of names appear in the pages of the Oakland arrest books. Not much is recorded about them; but we do know what they did for a living. They were, in the main, blue-collar workers. A fair number were jobless. Housewives and students were dramatically under-represented. So were professionals (doctors, lawyers, teachers, clergymen), people in trade (merchants, bankers, and salesmen), and clerks, bookkeepers, and agents—in short, white-collar workers (see Table 4.13).

Again, we do not know positively why the workingman was arrested so disproportionately. Did he transgress more, or was he simply more harassed? We can hazard some guesses. Class status probably made a difference for some offenses (such as drunkenness). Police were perhaps more likely to send home a "respectable" or "middle-class" drunk; the man in workers' clothes or rags was more likely to be clapped in jail for the night. The arrested population was a diverse group, not a single, clear-cut "dangerous class." Most arrests were order and discipline arrests, not arrests for high crime. They were arrests to show that the norms of "respectable" people were alive and well, and working—that society meant business. These rules of social behavior hammered down on the head of the laborer who drank his pint (or two, or three), and let off too much steam.

Table 4.10. Arrest Rates by Age Group in Oakland, 1900–1970

Age (years)	1900			1970		
	No. arrests	Population	Arrests/1000 population	No. arrests	Population	Arrests/1000 population
10–14	105	5,825	18	3,076	27,882	110
15–19	288	6,153	47	8,771	28,355	309
20–29	747	12,475	60	20,853	64,156	325
30–39	775	10,451	74	9,129	36,593	250
40 & over	1,079	20,205	53	13,991	149,874	93

Sources: Oakland Police Department, *Annual Report of the Chief of Police* (1900), p. 26; U.S. Bureau of the Census, *1900 Census of Population—Part 2* (1901–2), p. 139; Oakland Police Department, *1970 Annual Crime Survey* (1971); U.S. Bureau of the Census, *1970 Census of Population* (1972).

Table 4.11. Mean Age of Persons Arrested in Oakland, 1872–1910

Type of offense	Mean age of arrestees (years)
Felonies (N = 92)	29
Felonies v. persons	31
Felonies v. property	28
Order maintenance arrests	36
Drunkenness (N = 656)	39
Public order (N = 247)	32
Minor crimes v. persons (N = 100)	33
Law enforcement arrests	30
Regulatory ordinances (N = 208)	29
Morals (N = 107)	38
Minor crimes v. property (N = 98)	27
Service (N = 47)	23

Source: Sample of entries in Oakland Arrest Books, 1872–1910.

The heavy stress on order meant a heavy load of disciplinary arrests, and the victims were ordinary workers.

Was there anything special about *these* workers? Were they different in any systematic way from others who stayed out of trouble? There is no easy way to tell. But we think they were, disproportionately, the unattached: single men, living in boarding houses, not married men with families; drifters and casual laborers, not steady workers; people who did not hold their jobs or their liquor well. This was, in a way, the exact target group of the bottom layer of criminal justice. It was discipline for those who lacked the whalebone and starch of family and church, for the potential (or actual) black sheep, who needed the rod of criminal justice to keep them in line.

Rough Justice in the Police Court

Arrest was, of course, only the first link in a chain. After arrest, the next stop was the police station. Here, at headquarters, the police released some prisoners and diverted some to other agencies. Some were let go on condition that they leave town immediately. Three drunks in Berkeley, in 1906, tried to steal a milk wagon; they were "escorted out of town" by the police.[126] Everyone else ended up in

126. *Berkeley Reporter*, May 19, 1906, p. 8, col. 5.

Table 4.12. Distribution of Arrests for Each
Offense Class in Oakland by Age Group, 1872–1910

Age group	Felonies v. persons	Felonies v. property	Drunkenness	Public order	Minor v. persons
10–19	15%	26%	2%	14%	11%
20–29	35	41	24	37	32
30–39	30	14	29	25	27
40–49	20	10	25	11	23
50–59	0	7	13	8	5
60 & over	0	2	7	5	2
Total	100	100	100	100	100

Source: Sample of entries in Oakland Arrest Books, 1872–1910.

Table 4.13. Occupations of Persons Arrested in Oakland, 1892–1910

Type of occupation	% of total Oakland arrests, 1892–1910	% of Oakland population over 10 years of age in occupation 1900	1910
Working population			
over 10 years old	79.9	48.1	53.3
Manufacturing	40.4	17.0	17.1
Domestic service	11.5	7.6	7.8
Trade	8.5	7.2	9.9
Transportation	7.3	4.1	6.7
Clerical	5.5	5.3	5.2
Agricultural	2.1	1.1	1.3
Public Service	1.7	1.0	0.9
Professions	1.7	4.5	4.0
Mining	0.8	0.5	0.5
Nonworking population			
over 10 years old	20.1	51.9	46.7
Unemployed	15.0	—	—
Housewives	2.8	—	—
Students	2.3	—	—

Sources: Sample of entries in Oakland Arrest Books, 1892–1910; U.S. Bureau of the Census.

Regul. rdin.	Morals	Minor v. property	Service	All offenses	N
25%	2%	34%	63%	13%	199
30	32	28	9	29	448
26	19	22	12	25	395
14	27	11	12	19	300
4	15	2	2	9	137
2	5	3	2	5	78
100	100	100	100	100	

% of total arrests of employed persons, 1892–1910	% of employed population in occupation	
	1900	1910
100	100	100
50.6	35.1	32.1
14.4	15.8	14.6
10.6	15.0	18.6
9.2	8.6	12.6
6.9	11.0	9.8
2.6	2.2	2.4
2.1	2.1	1.7
2.1	9.3	7.5
1.1	1.1	2.1
—	—	—
—	—	—
—	—	—
—	—	—

city jail. Here the prisoner stayed, until he came before a magistrate. In Oakland, this meant the judge of the police court.[127]

The arrest records of 1872–1910 allow us to follow the fate of people charged with misdemeanors. Because the records of the court itself are lost, the arrest information also gives us our best systematic source on *types* of case handled in police court. Table 4.15 shows that one offense dominated—in numbers, that is—the work of police court. That was drunkenness. Drunkenness accounted for 45 percent of the arrests; because almost none of these cases were dismissed, drunkenness made up an even greater proportion of the work of police court —probably nearly half. Public order offenses contributed another 15 percent or so, regulatory matters about the same, minor offenses against the person and morals offenses about 7.5 percent each, and minor offenses against property about 6 percent.[128]

127. The court, established in 1866, had exclusive jurisdiction over petty larceny, assault and battery, breaches of the peace, vagrancy, violations of city ordinances, and all other misdemeanors that carried a penalty of $500 or less, or six months in jail or less. The voters elected their police judge, for a two-year term.
Historical study of lower criminal courts was very sparse until the crime reports begin, around 1920. See R. Pound and F. Frankfurter, eds., *Criminal Justice in Cleveland: Reports of the Cleveland Foundation Survey of the Administration of Justice in Cleveland, Ohio* (Cleveland, 1922), p. 234; National Commission on Law Observance and Enforcement, *Report on Criminal Procedure* (Washington, D.C., 1931), p. 6; President's Commission on Law Enforcement and the Administration of Justice, *Task Force Report: The Courts* (Washington, D.C., 1967), p. 29; John Robertson, ed., *Rough Justice: Perspectives on Lower Criminal Courts* (Boston, 1974). A recent study of justices of the peace is John R. Wunder, *Inferior Courts, Superior Justice: A History of the Justices of the Peace on the Northwest Frontier, 1853–1889* (Westport, Conn., 1979).
In Oakland, before 1890, the police court had exclusive jurisdiction over all misdemeanor cases. In 1890 the Supreme Court of California held that the city justice court also had jurisdiction over such cases. In re Ah You, 83 Cal. 339 (1890). At all times between 1872 and 1910, both courts, the police court and the city justice court, had power to conduct preliminary examinations in felony cases.
128. Records do survive for the justice's court in San Jose Township (Santa Clara County) for the year 1887 (see Table 4.14). This offers at least some basis for comparison, although the court heard no drunkenness cases. Of the 365 cases, charges were dismissed in 93; another 100 dropped out, or bail was forfeited, or the records are incomplete. Of the defendants, 25 were bound over to Superior Court; 146 were prosecuted in justice court; 53 pleaded guilty; and 17 changed pleas from not guilty to guilty. Of the 76 who were tried, 27 were acquitted.

Table 4.14. Cases Heard in Justice Court in San Jose Township, 1887

Type of offense	No. cases	% of total	Type of offense	No. cases	% of total
Battery	72	19.7	Burglary	10	2.7
Disturbing the peace	64	17.5	Malicious mischief	10	2.7
Vagrancy	49	13.4	Prostitution & related offenses	10	2.7
Petty larceny	27	7.4	Unknown	21	5.8
Assault cases	20	5.5	Other	67	18.4
Grand larceny	15	4.1	Total	365	99.9

Source: Docket Book of the San Jose Township Justice Court, Santa Clara County.

The overwhelming majority of people accused of misdemeanors were prosecuted—over 90 percent (see Table 4.15). Of the others, 5.3 percent were simply released, 3.2 percent were returned to parents or institutions, and 0.8 percent were delivered to other law enforcement agencies. Once in a while a justice of the peace actually acted as a peacemaker. Emma Pacheco, deserted by her husband, John, swore out a complaint for nonsupport in San Leandro. The justice told Emma and John to forget their squabbles. Husband and wife agreed to live "happy together hereafter"; the case was dismissed.[129]

In some cities today, arrest is used to harass drunks, vagrants, and prostitutes. We hear of the "revolving door"[130]—people arrested again and again, but never prosecuted. This precise practice was not to be found in Oakland a century ago. A bare 1 percent of the drunks were released without charges. In service arrests, to be sure, release was the natural outcome; runaway children, for example, were sent home to mother and dad. Otherwise, the rule was to prosecute. Minor property charges were more often dropped than other offenses. This happened when, for example, complaining victims or creditors got their goods or money back, and lost their zeal for prosecuting. The case against the defendant then evaporated. Even here, charges were dropped less than one-fifth of the time.

When a man or woman came before the magistrate, the judge reviewed the charge and decided whether to set bail (and if so, how much). Occasionally, the judge simply let the prisoner go. He could also release the prisoner "on recognizance"—a personal promise to appear in court. Prisoners were supposed to be brought to police court for prompt arraignment. Usually they were. Between May 1880 and June 1881, 1,919 individuals were prosecuted in the police court; of these, nearly all were arraigned on the day of arrest, or the next day at the latest. The longest delay was eight days.[131] In petty cases, the defendant might plead guilty on the spot, and be sentenced immediately. This ended the case. Otherwise, the judge set a date for the case to be heard. If the prisoner pleaded not guilty, he could insist

---

129. *San Leandro Reporter*, Mar. 6, 1909, p. 1, col. 6.

130. Over 90 percent of all drunkenness cases in Chicago were dismissed, according to Raymond T. Nimmer, *Two Million Unnecessary Arrests* (Chicago, 1971), p. 43. A Boston report claimed that 63 percent of those arrested in the city for drunkenness were released without prosecution. Boston Lawyers Committee for Civil Rights under Law, *The Quality of Justice in the Lower Criminal Courts of Metropolitan Boston* (Boston, 1970), p. 20.

131. Ordinance violators averaged less than one day between arrest and arraignment; this was true also for cases of drunkenness, and of minor crimes against persons and property. For morals charges, the journey to police court was a bit slower; the delay was, on the average, a day and a half.

Table 4.15. Percentages of Misdemeanor Arrests
Disposed of without Prosecution by Oakland Police, 1872–1910

Disposition	Drunkenness	Public order	Minor v. persons	Regul. ordin.
N	656	247	100	208
% released without charges	1	11	4	2
% sent to parents or institutions	0	5	0	1
% sent to other jurisdictions	0	0	1	1
% not prosecuted by Oakland P.D.	1	16	5	4

Source: Sample of entries in Oakland Arrest Books, 1872–1910.

on a jury trial in police court. This happened surprisingly often, even in petty cases. If convicted, and sentenced to a fine over thirty-five dollars, or more than seventeen days in jail, the loser could appeal to Superior Court. Here the case would be tried *de novo*—that is, all over again.

The police court tried minor cases (misdemeanors) itself. But if the prisoner was accused of a felony, he had to undergo a "preliminary examination." This took place before a magistrate, either the police judge himself or one of the justices of the city's justice court, who otherwise mostly handled civil cases. At the preliminary hearing, the judge heard the evidence and decided whether to let the man go, reduce the charge to a misdemeanor, or, if the evidence was damning enough, "bind him over" for trial in Superior Court.[132] Sometimes the felony charge dropped to a misdemeanor because of a deal. A bicycle thief, Henry Hosford, was arrested in 1894 and charged with grand larceny. "In consideration of his pleading guilty to petty larceny," the felony charge was abandoned; Hosford was sentenced to six months in jail.[133] If the judge bound the prisoner over to be tried on a felony charge, the defendant was handed over to the sheriff.

132. Or, before 1880, to the grand jury for possible indictment and trial in the County Court or District Court.
133. *Oakland Tribune*, Aug. 10, 1894, p. 2, col. 2.

Morals	*Minor v. property*	*Service*	*All misdem. arrests*
107	98	47	1,463
3	19	28	5
0	1	59	3
1	2	11	1
4	22	100	9

Unless the prisoner made bail, he would sit in county jail, waiting for his case to ripen. We take up what later happened—the felony trials themselves—in the next few chapters.

BAIL AND RECOGNIZANCE

When the case was a minor one, the judge usually let the accused go free on recognizance. For some offenses, the court used bail as an easy way to extract a fine. This was the practice in gambling cases, for example; the court would fix bail, and the defendant would "forfeit," much as is done today with traffic tickets. The court fixed bail in about 38 percent of the cases in our sample. In most of these cases, bail was forfeited.

Bail was also, of course, a device for making sure that the accused showed up for his trial. It was the judge who set bail; but he generally discussed it with police and prosecutors. Sometimes we found little notes about bail, to or from police judge, city attorney, or police, wedged in the inside flaps of arrest blotters, written on the backs of envelopes, business cards, campaign posters, arrest forms, blank checks, and other scraps of paper. The judge took into account how serious the crime was, whether the accused was dangerous, how likely it was that he would come to court of his own free will, whether he worked, what his family situation was, and so on. Usually, the judge did what the prosecutor recommended.[134] In general, "respectable" people were more likely to be released without bail, or on reduced bail.

Table 4.16 shows average bail for various offenses, and the percentage of cases in which the court set bail. Bail was very frequent in gambling and regulatory cases; it was, as we said, really a kind of fine in such cases. In 1891 the *Tribune* reported a practice of fixing bail at $150 in lottery cases, and a complaint that Chinese gamblers looked on this bail "as a sort of licensing arrangement."[135] In felony cases, more substantial bond—$1,000 and up—was common. Bail in felony cases will be discussed in Chapter 5.

JUDGMENT IN THE POLICE COURT

The Oakland Police court was not a place where the ritual and majesty of law hung heavy in the air. The court often did its business in a hurry and with little fuss. Drunks and minor offenders went through quickly. Almost all of them pleaded guilty, or forfeited bail, or were

Table 4.16. Amount of Bail and Percentages of Cases Requiring Bail in Oakland, 1872–1910

Type of offense	Mean bail set ($)	% of cases in which bail required	N
Gambling	21	92	62
Bicycle ordinance	3	92	49
Selling lottery tickets	99	83	24
License ordinance violations	17	77	22
Disturbing the peace	23	57	61
Battery	41	52	89
Vagrancy	27	27	55
Drunkenness	21	23	635
Petty larceny	43	15	73

Source: Sample of entries in Oakland Arrest Books, 1872–1910.

134. In one case in 1892, for example, the police judge sent the following note to a police official: "If you think $20 for forfeiture enough—you can let her go on that amount, but if she has been arrested before, don't let her go on less than $25.00." In another case, the judge wrote, "If you say there is nothing in the case, why not let him go on his own recog until tomorrow."
Sometimes the city attorney asked for high bail, because the police wanted to hold the defendant to testify in some other case.
135. *Oakland Tribune*, July 23, 1891, p. 3, col. 3. The *Tribune* went on to say that there were lotteries "all over town," and the district attorney was "painfully aware that the $150 system is not a preventive one." Bail went up to $250.

convicted after a flimsy hearing. In this sense, there *was* a certain degree of "assembly-line justice."[136]

Other cases got more elaborate treatment. The court took some disputes rather seriously. Usually, procedures were informal. People told their stories; the judge listened; then he did justice as he saw it. In these cases, the court had something of the flavor of a neighborhood or people's court. In a few cases, police or justice court became a "real" courtroom—lawyers on both sides, jury trial, and more elaborate process. Sometimes the occasion hardly seemed to deserve the fuss: one suspects anger, obstinacy, or spite. In a few cases, the defendant had a bigger issue up his sleeve—fighting the legality of a city ordinance, for example. In 1894 an insurance man, Thomas Agnew, hired Emil Nusbaumer and battled (successfully) to prove that his business was exempt from the license ordinance.[137] But these cases were relatively rare.

POLICE COURT: RESULTS

Most defendants did not leave police court vindicated. Between 1872 and 1910, the court dismissed charges in 15 percent of its cases; a mere 1 percent were acquitted. About 61 percent of the misdemeanor defendants were convicted; another 23 percent forfeited bail.

There were quite distinct patterns of outcome for different types of cases (see Table 4.17). For minor property offenses, and for minor offenses against the person, dismissal rates were relatively high. Many of these were cases dropped because a complaining witness never showed up, or refused to testify. Sometimes the judge dropped a case out of pity, or because further punishment seemed pointless. In Berkeley, in 1906, the judge took pity on a black man, Joseph Jacobs. Jacobs was an alcoholic; in this instance he had drunk "half a bottle of alcohol in his eagerness for liquor." The judge thought the week already spent sitting in jail was punishment enough.[138] About one out of five ordinance violators won dismissal or acquittal. More than one-fourth forfeited bail. People brought in on private complaints, in other words, were more likely to "win," in police court, than those brought in by police.

136. For the term, see Herbert L. Packer, *The Limits of the Criminal Sanction* (Stanford, 1968), pp. 292–93. Maureen Mileski's study of a lower criminal court, published in 1971, found that 72 percent of the cases were disposed of in one minute or less. See Maureen Mileski, "Courtroom Encounters: An Observation of a Lower Criminal Court," *Law & Soc. Rev.* 5 (1971): 473, 479.

137. *Oakland Tribune*, Aug. 22, 1894, p. 2, col. 3.

138. *Berkeley Reporter*, Jan. 16, 1906, p. 5, col. 2.

Table 4.17. Disposition of Cases Prosecuted in Oakland Police Court, 1872–1910

Disposition	Drunkenness	Public order	Minor v. persons	Regul. ordin.
N	648	206	95	198
% dismissed	3	30	44	18
% who forfeited bail	19	16	7	28
% convicted or pleaded guilty	78	50	43	53
% of acquittals	0	3	7	1
Total (%)	100	100	100	100

Source: Sample of entries in Oakland Arrest Books, 1872–1920.

Dismissals became more common toward the end of the period, but only for certain offenses. In fiscal 1900, the police court of Oakland dismissed 57 percent of the battery cases, 34 percent of the cases of petty larceny, 62 percent of the cases of disturbing the peace. Yet of 1,336 arrests for drunkenness, only 7—less than 1 percent—were dismissed. Out of 427 arrests under bicycle ordinances, only 4 dismissals followed; and not a single one of the arrests of 95 people who violated the hitching ordinance (requiring horses to be securely hitched), or the 41 who illegally "slept out" was dismissed.[139]

TRIALS IN THE POLICE COURT

"Trials," as we noted, were not the rule in police court; in fiscal 1881, for example, over 70 percent of all cases were disposed of without trial (see Table 4.18). Drunkenness led to trial in only 4 percent of its cases. The *Tribune* in 1883 described a typical drunkenness "case":

> "James Lynch," remarked Clerk Bortree this morning in the Police Court.
> "Yes, sir," responded that individual from the prisoner's dock.
> "You are charged with being drunk."
> "Yes, sir."

139. Oakland Police Department, *Annual Report of the Chief of Police* (1900).

Morals	*Minor v.* *property*	*All* *misdemeanors*
103	76	1,325
10	38	15
83	8	23
7	52	61
0	2	1
100	100	100

"What is your plea, guilty or not guilty?"
"It ain't very likely that I'd be here if I wasn't guilty," answered the prisoner.
"Sentence tomorrow morning," remarked the Court.
"Kerrect, yer Honor; but I'd like to state in palliation of my heinous crime, yer Honor, that I am a stranger in this yer town."
"Perhaps you are, James," replied his Honor, "and you are pursuing a very excellent course to become very well acquainted in this community."[140]

Once in a while, the defendant in a routine matter—a drunkenness charge, a bicycle case—pleaded not guilty, for one reason or another. A bench trial usually followed. The court made short work of these. One such "trial" was reported, in 1874: "The administering of the oath in [the] 'presence of Almighty God' in a case of . . . an ordinary drunk always appeared to us as the biggest joke on the Lord out of jail. The court or Clerk generally runs down the gamut to so-help-you-God in a whisper, or else goes plumb asleep."[141] The "trial" was little more than a swearing match, between a policeman and the defendant. Almost always, the policeman won. Here is an example from 1895:

140. *Oakland Tribune*, Oct. 3, 1883, p. 3, col. 7.
141. Ibid., June 16, 1874, p. 3, col. 3.

Table 4.18. Percentages of Police Court Cases Brought to Trial in Oakland, Fiscal Year 1881 (N = 1,991)

	Drunkenness	Public order	Minor v. persons	Regul ordin
% tried	4	50	56	29
Bench trial	4	46	53	2
Jury trial	0	4	3	
% not tried	96	50	44	71
Guilty pleas	71	21	11	4
Other	25	30	34	2

Source: Oakland Police Court, Minute Books, 1880–81.

"I don't think I was drunk, your Honor," said Gus Harland this morning.
"Not drunk?" said the court.
"Not very drunk."
"How drunk?"
"Well—I could see the moon."
"It was raining hard Sunday night when I arrested that man," said the officer.
"Six dollars or three days. Next."[142]

The rare defendant who hired a lawyer did not do much better. The *Tribune* reported one sad case in 1895:

Plain ordinary drunks will probably not employ attorneys to defend them in the Police Court hereafter. It does not pay. This morning E. C. Ward and Tom Gallagher were in the dock charged with that offense. Attorney Hugh Aldrich made an eloquent plea for Ward. He was a hard-working citizen, never in a court in his life and barring a few extra glasses that night, a model young man.

"I saw the men last night," said the court, "just before they were arrested. They were disgracefully drunk. Six dollars or three days." There was an all-around laugh at this as the sentence on the first occasion is generally suspended.[143]

Dry figures from the records confirm these impressions from the newspapers. In fiscal 1881, for example, a drunk spent, on the av-

142. Ibid., Oct. 23, 1895, p. 3, col. 3.
143. Ibid., Oct. 18, 1895, p. 3, col. 1.

Morals	Minor v. property	All misdemeanors
51	44	30
49	41	28
2	3	2
49	55	70
32	31	42
17	24	28

erage, only a fifth of a day between his first court appearance and final disposition of his case (see Table 4.19). The court cleared its docket as quickly as it could. One fine morning in 1883, the police court docket had twenty cases, and they were "disposed of in ten minutes—two cases per minute, the fastest on record." But this record apparently lasted only a year, until 1884: "Judge Allen broke a record this morning. At 9 o'clock the court met. At 9:06 the thirteen cases on the docket had been disposed of and one minute after the Judge was on a car bound for Haywards."[144]

In some cases, the police court was a bit more "adjudicative"; often these were cases growing out of private complaints (petty larceny, disturbing the peace, minor assaults and batteries). Many of these, as we said, were dropped before trial, when tempers cooled. But not all. The court could not force prosecution, but it had *some* power. Mrs. A. McCann, in 1879, complained about "beastly treatment" from her husband. When she changed her mind about prosecuting, the judge, annoyed, fined her ten dollars as a defaulting witness.[145] Judges and prosecutors did not like these on-again, off-again cases of quarrels among relatives or neighbors. They were essentially private matters, and court officials felt "used." Once in a while they voiced their displeasure. In 1892 a landlord charged his boarder, E. S. Hodges, with "attempting to defraud" him on his board bill. Assistant City Attorney Church reported "that the matter had been compromised." The case was dropped, but Church complained that these "compromises" tended to turn the police court into "a collection agency."

144. Ibid., Oct. 15, 1883, p. 3, col. 4, Sept. 17, 1884, p. 3, col. 1.
145. Ibid., June 7, 1879, p. 3, col. 3.

Table 4.19. *Mean Time between Defendant's First Court Appearance and Final Case Disposition in Oakland Police Court, Fiscal Year 1881 (N = 1,991)*

Type of offense	Mean number of days
Morals	6.3
Minor crimes v. persons	3.8
Public order	3.4
Regulatory ordinances	2.9
Minor crimes v. property	2.7
Drunkenness	0.2

Source: 100% sample of Oakland Police Court Minute Books, 1880–81.

Judge and prosecutor agreed not to allow these dismissals, except to "subserve" the "cause of justice."[146] But the practice went on.

Defendants charged with drunkenness pleaded guilty far more often than defendants charged with minor crimes against persons and property. About half of those prosecutions went to trial. But here too "trial" meant, overwhelmingly, quick rough work by the judge. No doubt, the judge tried to ferret out the truth, when he could, and do folk-justice. At least he listened to both sides of the story. The atmosphere was informal. In 1877, Andrew Hansen, charged with stealing $220 "from the bed of a friend, at an oyster house at the foot of Webster Street," went on trial before Judge Jayne. Andrew pleaded not guilty. The complaining witness "testified positively that the amount stolen was $220. Hansen, interrupting, charged the witness with perjury, saying that the witness could not have possessed the $220, for he (Hansen) only found $140." At this, "The Court and everybody else smiled broadly."[147] Sometimes the trial was a bit more elaborate, and witnesses were sworn. In 1880,

> Mrs. J. Tarel, arrested . . . on a charge of battery, was arraigned, pleaded not guilty, and the case was placed on trial. It involved a neighborhood quarrel, . . . wherein the accused was charged with striking some children with a stick. A number of witnesses were placed upon the stand, among whom were several boys and girls of tender age. Upon the case being submitted, his

146. Ibid., July 13, 1892, p. 3, col. 2.
147. Ibid., Apr. 10, 1877, p. 3, col. 3.

Honor found the only provocation to have been that a small boy
blew smoke from a paper, but tobaccoless cigarette, into the face
of the accused, she being a large woman, and that thereupon a
battery was committed. The accused was found guilty, (but) in
view of the possibility of provocation, the fine was placed
at $10.[148]

In another case of petty larceny, for the theft of some chickens, "the
chickens were in court and recognized (their owner) with gleeful
clucking as they were handed to him for identification."[149]

The police court did take "the law" into account, though the law
wore everyday clothes, so to speak. In 1891 two boys were on trial for
stealing cherries; the prosecution finished its case, and the bailiff
casually remarked, "Why, you did not prove any venue." The judge
said, "That is so," and dismissed the case, annoying the city attorney.
One fine day in 1882, the city attorney had to break off in the midst of
voir dire, to smash a mouse with a law book. "Men rose from their
seats, voices were heard in the lobby, laughter resounded immod-
erately, and there was confusion in [the] courtroom until the [city]
attorney announced that the mouse was dead, and resumed his
examination of the juror."[150]

In rare cases, the accused—a well-heeled gambler, or a liquor
dealer prosecuted for some transgression—defended himself vigorously, using every weapon in the legal armory. In 1891 the court
suddenly jacked up bail in lottery cases to $250; some defendants
chose to fight rather than forfeit this much money. They hired well-
known lawyers, and paid fees as high as $100. Apparently, the money
was well spent: a number of defendants were acquitted.[151]

Persistent defendants had a real chance of winning, for one reason
or another. The *Tribune* complained in 1879 that it was "next to impossible" to convict Chinese gamblers. Witnesses would not testify;
they were afraid that some "highbinder" might cut their throats. In
1890 it was lottery dealers who could not be convicted, according to
the *Tribune*. The average jury consisted of men "who 'play the lottery' themselves." Still later, around the turn of the century, the city

148. Ibid., Aug. 7, 1880, p. 3, col. 4.
149. Ibid., June 10, 1891, p. 3, col. 3.
150. Ibid., June 12, 1891, p. 3, col. 3, Mar. 28, 1882, p. 3, col. 3. Not all cases, of
course, received routine treatment. In 1877, for example, the police judge personally
inspected hay in a defendant's barn loft. A city ordinance controlled the amount of hay
that could be stored in a single place. The judge dismissed the charges. Ibid., Oct. 15,
1877, p. 3, col. 2.
151. Ibid., June 23, 1891, p. 3, col. 3.

attorney of Oakland agreed that gambling trials always ended in acquittal; it was "impossible" to get a conviction.[152]

These references, of course, are to *trials*. Win or lose, trial by jury was time-consuming and expensive, even for the little cases in police court. In 1890 the *Tribune* griped about the "pernicious" jury system in police court. In Justice Henshaw's court, the calendar was "almost choked with cases set for trial"; there were 104 cases to be heard, a four-month backlog.[153] By way of contrast, a nonjury case took only 1.4 days, on the average, between arraignment and final disposition. And even the simplest jury trial cost more than the city could recoup in fines. According to a report in 1879, the cost of an ordinary license case came to $81.25; since the usual fine was $10, the city lost $71.25 on the deal (see Table 4.20).[154]

No wonder authorities took steps to discourage jury trials. The city attorney in 1895 suggested that bail should be raised for any defendant who insisted on a jury trial; "if people want jury trials for trivial cases," he said, "they should be kept in prison until they are tried."[155] In 1895 the police judge tried for a while a simple tactic: he

Table 4.20. *Cost to Oakland of a License Case, 1879*

Item	Cost ($)
Arrest of defendant, including pay of policeman	3.00
Four or five trips made by the license collector	2.50
Police judge salary one and a half days	7.50
Police court clerk's labor	5.00
Prosecuting attorney	10.00
Subpoenas, stationery, etc.	1.00
Twelve jurymen, three hours lost	9.00
Twelve jurymen, eight hours lost	36.00
Time of mayor as witness, three hours	.25
Time of three other witnesses	6.00
Total	81.25
Received (as fine)	10.00
(Loss)	71.25

Source: *Oakland Tribune*, May 8, 1879, p. 1, col. 2.

152. Ibid., May 11, 1879, p. 3, col. 3, May 13, 1890, p. 3, col. 4, Mar. 21, 1900, p. 3, col. 7.
153. Ibid., Feb. 19, 1890, p. 3, col. 3.
154. The figures are, to be sure, a bit exaggerated. The out-of-pocket costs to the city were far less—more on the order of $30.00. This is still, of course, a sizable loss.
155. Ibid., Oct. 21, 1895, p. 3, col. 2.

refused requests for jury trials. Strictly speaking, this was illegal; state law gave defendants a right to trial by jury, even for misdemeanors, for all charges except vagrancy.[156] In 1908 a jury in Judge Tappan's court could not agree on a verdict, and he raked them over the coals. The case, he said, would be decided by a judge in "two shakes of a lamb's tail"; it was "as simple as ABC." To spend days on such a case was "tommy rot"; no wonder people called trial by jury a "farce."[157] Judges from time to time tried shortcuts. In one lottery case, in 1891, the police court used a one-man jury. (Defense and prosecution agreed to this novel arrangement.) The "jury" found the defendant guilty.[158] Of twenty-eight jury trials in police court in fiscal 1881, eighteen used twelve-man juries; the rest used fewer men.[159]

How were jurors selected? The records are a little obscure on this point. All jurors, of course, were men. Clearly, they were chosen with less system and care than jurors in Superior Court. And when challenges depleted the regular stock, almost any way to collar recruits seemed allowable. In Alameda, in 1908, the *Argus* reported that a deputy constable stood outside the First Methodist Church and "nabbed" several prospects "as they came out of the house of worship." He ignored regular churchgoers (apparently he knew who they were), taking only the "semi-occasionals." This was for a special case, the trial of a liquor dealer for selling liquor without a county license; the regular panel of jurors had already been exhausted.[160] Generally speaking, jurors in Alameda were (according to the *Argus*) "picked up" off the streets by the police. This, apparently, gave police a certain amount of power to influence outcomes: in these temperance struggles, the policeman could "choose jurymen from the church element," or, if they wished, "from the opposite element." The temperance conflict induced the city to move to a new system, based on tax rolls, which could not be manipulated.[161]

In an Oakland case of 1909 (involving gambling), the policeman who gathered the jury had been told to "summon good men, men on the assessment roll." As a result, he reported that "nearly every person I have summoned in this case is engaged in business" (no. 4552).

156. Ibid., Oct. 16, 1895, p. 3, col. 7.
157. *Alameda Argus*, Apr. 22, 1908, p. 1, col. 8, p. 5, col. 5.
158. *Oakland Tribune*, Jan. 13, 1891, p. 3, col. 3.
159. In 1902 a city justice joined forces with the police judge. The justice heard drunkenness and battery cases, and ran preliminary examinations, in chambers. Meanwhile, the police judge took charge of jury trials in the main courtroom. *Oakland Tribune*, May 2, 1902, p. 3, col. 5.
160. *Alameda Argus*, Jan. 13, 1908, p. 1, col. 6.
161. Ibid., May 14, 1908, p. 8, col. 7.

But this too was exceptional. The *Tribune* in 1894 described the more normal process, a bit humorously, as follows:

> If anybody thinks it an easy and pleasant duty to get the police court jury together, he had better take Officer Phillips' job for a day and try it. It will not take him many minutes to get undeceived. A petty jury must frequently be supplied on short notice. Phillips is instructed by the police judge to summon one; and provided with authority of a general nature, he sallies forth from the city hall to execute his unenviable mission.
>
> A fruitful enlistment ground is the Free Library. Unless the institution has already been scoured for jurymen during some other part of the day, perchance the officer directs his footsteps thither. If there is anyone in the room who has been previously introduced to Phillips he suddenly remembers an unfulfilled engagement elsewhere and through the aid of sundry erratic flank movements behind first this and then that newspaper file-holder the door is reached, and he bolts through it for liberty.
>
> Phillips in a very pleasant way books as many loungers as he can subpoena for jury service before the room is emptied and then he promenades Broadway or Washington. Any citizen who does not seem to be overburdened with work is good material for a police court jury, and Phillips takes him in. All kinds of excuses are offered, and it is amazing how inventive the minds of some men in this line suddenly become; but it is "no go"—down goes the name of the protestant into Phillips' small book and off goes Phillips, smiling in search of some other shining mark.
>
> "I am sorry to disappoint you" is the remark which sometimes puts a stop to his volubility, "but you see I am a member of the humane society of Alameda County, and am exempt from jury duty." . . . Here is a man coming up the street. He is evidently a visitor and has no special duty requiring his attention for the nonce. Phillips sees him five blocks off, spots him for jury work and makes a B-line toward him.
>
> Ah, how do you do, he asks, as if he had known him for an age. Let me see, what is your name, . . . There's a little case to be heard in the police court at ——— o'clock, and you are wanted to try it. It will only take a few minutes. Consider yourself summoned. Yes, let me see—the name? . . . "But Phillips," remonstrated a real estate dealer who suddenly ran up against the officer, "I served on a jury yesterday and . . . "
>
> "Is that so, well, I'm sorry but Judge Allen wants a jury right away. It won't take more than a few minutes, and you are hereby

summoned to be in the police court at —— o'clock to try the case of the People v. John Doe. Goodbye." And off the indefatigable bluecoat rushes for another victim. . . . No pound master ever created more consternation among the owners of untagged dogs running at large than Officer Phillips does when his brown straw hat, which everybody knows half a mile off—is seen sailing at a brisk rate along Broadway, for the vagaries of its movements indicate that the bluecoat is gathering in a petty jury for the police court.[162]

SENTENCING PATTERNS

In police court, in most cases, a convicted defendant faced a simple choice: pay a fine or go to jail. A day in jail was "worth" two dollars in fines. In the 1872–1910 sample, this choice faced 60 percent of those convicted. Another 6 percent were sent straight to jail; 3 percent were simply fined. In about 31 percent of the cases, the judge suspended sentence. Sometimes the judge attached conditions. In Alameda, in 1908, Fred Stanton, a one-armed Peeping Tom, was found guilty; but the judge suspended sentence on the understanding that Stanton would forthwith "get out of town."

Sentencing patterns varied over the years. In fiscal 1881, for example, suspended sentences were not common (they were given to less than 2 percent of those convicted); the pay-or-jail choice faced 91 percent, 5 percent were sent to jail outright, 2 percent were fined. Suspended sentences were, in general, uncommon before 1890 (less than 2 percent). After 1890, they became more popular; by 1910 the judge suspended most sentences. It is not easy to say exactly why this change occurred.

Sentences varied, naturally enough, with type of offense (see Table 4.21). John Coria, an "inhuman childbeater," got six months in city jail in 1894.[163] Drunkenness and ordinance violations, the most routine cases, got the lightest sentences, on the average. For most of the period, the court used a standard formula in drunkenness cases: a $6 fine or three days in jail for the first (punished) conviction, $10 or five days for the second, $50 or twenty-five days for the third, $80 or forty days for the fourth. Drunkenness, in other words, could become an expensive habit. In other cases, too, there were standard sentences— $2, for example, in bicycle cases. In gambling cases, fines of $100 were

162. *Oakland Tribune*, Sept. 21, 1894, p. 3, col. 1.
163. *Oakland Tribune*, Aug. 10, 1894, p. 2, col. 2.

Table 4.21. Average Fines and Jail Sentences Imposed by Oakland Police Court, 1880–1881

Type of Offense	Mean fine	Mean days in jail
Minor crimes v. property	$27	37
Morals	20	30
Minor crimes v. persons	8	7
Public order	9	9
Regulatory ordinances	8	5
Drunkenness	7	4

Source: Oakland Police Court, Minute Books, 1880–81.

not uncommon. When possible, the court collected fines on the spot. In one case in 1875, a woman was fined $25 for battery:

> Moll went down to the bottom of her pocket, pulled out fifty half dollars, and as Captain Rand swept in the coin with his left hand, he employed his right in conveying each individual four bit piece to his mouth to test them and determine whether they were silver, nickel, or pewter. When he got down to the thirty-ninth he dislocated his front tooth. Then the eleven remaining bits were tested in a similar manner by the Judge and his gentlemanly clerk. They all passed muster.[164]

But at least during the 1880s, most defendants who had to choose between jail or fine went to jail. They had no money and had to sit out their fines in cells. Between 1879 and 1887, the court actually collected only between 23 percent and 43 percent of the fines and costs imposed. In 1885, for example, the court imposed fines and costs of $30,298.00, for an average of $13.85, and collected 30.6 percent, or $9,256.50.[165] Not surprisingly, the higher the fine, the less likely it was that the defendant could dig down and pay. Sometimes, halfway through a jail sentence, a prisoner bought his freedom, begging or borrowing from family or friends. The police court Cash Book reported 60 such cases in 1880; in 253 cases, fines were paid in full. Unfortunately, we have no way of telling how many people chose jail or fine in the later part of our period. Undoubtedly, a great deal depended on social class. "Tramps" had no real choice. Jail was, perhaps, more horrifying to the middle class. Mayor Andrus in 1879 complained that most of the people on the chain gang (jailhouse

164. *Oakland Tribune*, Oct. 21, 1875, p. 3, col. 2.
165. Oakland Police Court, Cash Book (1878–87).

crews who worked in the streets) were Chinese. The Chinese never paid fines, he said; "imprisonment does not disgrace them with their own class." The mayor wanted to cut off their queues instead. This would embarrass them so, he thought, that "most of them would pay their fines and not be maintained at the city's expense."[166] The mayor, of course, had no idea whether this was so or not. Empathy with people who were "different" was not a strong point of the nineteenth century.

A Summary Word

Police and justice courts handled "petty" crimes. But they were surprisingly complex institutions. They played many roles, some half-consciously. Over the period, population grew, technology advanced, and the county urbanized; justice and police courts, and the police too, had more and more business to contend with. They never lost completely the flavor of informality and folk-justice. But by 1910 the rawness of the early days was gone.

The petty courts *and* the police were vital parts of the system of order and discipline. They were an outpost of law, in a definite area of social space: the working class of Alameda County. They were stationed, that is, to deal with the lower rungs of the social ladder. The men and women arrested came mainly from this part of social space. Others came from further down—tramps and ne'er-do-wells, outsiders, habitual drunks, drug addicts, "hardened criminals." Only a few came from higher up—businessmen charged with license violations and, toward the end of the period, "automobilists" caught in the web of the traffic laws.

These were exceptions. Overwhelmingly, the job of this layer was discipline: order in public places, order imposed on the laborer. The police swept the streets day and night, gathering up these fish in their nets. It was society's way of demonstrating that the rules of order were not just pieces of paper; they were flesh-and-blood reality: a man in blue, with a star on his chest and a nightstick; a judge; and a cell in the lockup. This went beyond the symbolic: the traffic rules of life were meant to be taken seriously. Yet punishments as such were not very serious. The fish once caught were left to thrash about a bit,

166. Annual Message of Mayor W. R. Andrus, Jan. 30, 1879, quoted in *Oakland Tribune*, Feb. 4, 1879, p. 3, col. 2. San Francisco had such an ordinance, on cutting prisoners' queues. It was struck down by Justice Stephen Field, in Ho Ah Kow v. Nunan, 12 Fed. Cas. 252 (No. 6546) (C.C.C. Cal. 1879).

to gasp and gulp for air, but they were then thrown back in the sea with a lesson learned.

This job was borne by police, and by their adjunct courts, in part for want of agencies to do the work more precisely. The police were jacks-of-all-trades. They were the social agency of last resort. They were called in to stop fights, end wife-beating—even to drive out a ghost. Except for the rich, there was no place else to go in time of crisis or need. And it was the police who picked up stray boys and dogs, who lodged the homeless and took the befuddled under their wing.

The system of order required, as we said, rough justice—quick, informal, mild. Police and justice court, together with the police, were part of a single whole. And the experience of the typical defendant was a single process: drunkenness on Saturday night, arrest, hours of nausea and shame in the lockup, sheepish appearance before the judge, a small fine, a lecture, discharge. Each separate incident was, in itself, unbearably banal. To the person itself it was, of course, more significant. And the *aggregate* of these pitiful arrests made up a system of order that was vital, in some obscure way, to the larger society. Order and discipline were vital. And without the patrol, how could discipline survive? At least so society might think.

In some measure, too, society sat up and took notice. The detail in this chapter comes mostly from newspapers. The press gave daily coverage to the work of the petty courts. They reported everything: the driest proceedings in a perfunctory way, and side stories on anything amusing or disgusting or significant. In a curious way the bottom of the system of criminal justice was like the top: it interested people. In this way, its moral message, such as it was, got through to the wider public. More than one message was probably transmitted. People learned the rules of public order; they learned that some people violated them, that society rapped these people on the knuckles. The good solid burgher, reading his paper, was not often one of the violators. He felt above it all; and the message was delivered with a sneer. What we said elsewhere about another California county, San Benito, is also true here. To read the papers is like watching a kind of Punch and Judy show. The better folks, the successful folks, sit and stare, while puppets from another social world carouse, quarrel, and beat each other. At the end they are dragged off to judgment, and the audience howls.[167]

---

167. Lawrence M. Friedman, "San Benito 1890: Legal Snapshot of a County," *Stan. L. Rev.* 27 (1975): 687, 700.

Chapter 5
The Processing of Felonies

We have already briefly described the life cycle of a felony case. Felony charges could begin either with a grand jury indictment or, much more commonly, with an "information" filed after a person was "bound over" at a "preliminary examination." This chapter examines in more detail what happened between arrest and the filing of felony charges, and how felony charges were handled in trial court.

Types of Crime

The process began, of course, when a crime was discovered, and a suspect taken into custody. A "crime" was an act so defined by the Penal Code. This code was a sizable catalog of crimes. Dozens of acts were listed as offenses against the state. Most sections of the code changed very little from 1872 (when the code was adopted) to 1910, especially those parts of the code that defined basic, familiar crimes. The legislature added many new crimes to the books over the years; but these were rarely important. Most crimes in the bulky list of evil deeds were in fact quite inert; they never affected the work of Superior Court. The code made it a felony, for example, to try to "intercept" an inheritance, by fraudulently passing off some baby as an heir (§ 156). It was a felony to "willfully and maliciously sink or set adrift any vessel of ten gross tons and upwards, the property of another" (§ 608c). These were terrible crimes, to be sure; but they were rarely if ever committed, and they had nothing to do with the work life of police, prosecutors, or courts in Alameda County. A small number of crimes—two dozen, perhaps—accounted for all but a handful of the charges brought in Superior Court.

Nobody knows, of course, all of the crimes actually committed in Alameda County. We do know which ones were prosecuted. We have collapsed the various crimes into five categories: crimes against the person, crimes against property, morals offenses, crimes against public order, and regulatory offenses. Table 5.1 shows, in rough outline, the types of felony prosecutions that reached Superior Court between 1880 and 1910. Property offenses were easily the most common. Be-

135

Table 5.1. Felonies Charged in Superior Court Sample and Estimated Number of Actual Prosecutions, 1880–1910

	1880–89		1890–99	
Type of offense	% charged	No. prosecuted	% charged	No. prosecuted
Crimes v. persons	28.9	210	32.8	265
Crimes v. property	64.4	469	53.5	432
Morals	0	0	6.6	53
Public order	6.7	48	7.1	57
N		180		198

tween 1880 and 1910, crimes against the person accounted for about 28 percent of the cases; crimes against property, 62 percent; morals offenses and crimes against public order, about 5 percent each. The only regulatory offenses reaching Superior Court during this period were misdemeanor indictments or misdemeanor appeals from the petty courts.

CRIMES AGAINST THE PERSON

Crimes against the person include murder, manslaughter, serious assault, robbery, rape, and kidnapping. What they have in common is violence, or the threat of violence. Simple assaults were misdemeanors, handled by the dozens in police and justice courts. Assaults with a deadly weapon and assaults with intent to kill were felonies, and were the commonest crimes against the person in Superior Court —nearly half of all crimes in this category. Here we find a longshoreman wielding an axe (Gustave Anderson, no. 1405, 1893), and dozens of attacks with knives and guns. In one case, in 1907, the defendant, playing poker in a club room, was thrown out after a fight; he came back, threw a rock, and was arrested for assault with a deadly weapon (John Loy, no. 4112). The deadly weapon was a rock, too, in an 1881 case: Michael Clark, riding on a stage, threw a rock at Ah Hing and injured his nose (no. 243). In another case, Frank Mana hit John Neino with a glass, during a barroom brawl (no. 4051, 1907). Some of the assaults seem hardly serious enough to warrant trial in Superior Court. Ah Gow, a ranch cook, supposedly threatened a ranch hand with a knife; the man had stormed into the kitchen and grabbed some bread (no. 1403, 1893). Other cases *were* quite violent: Timothy O'Keefe slashed his ex-wife with a razor, in 1910, and came within an inch of killing her (no. 4884).

1900–1910		1880–1910	
% charged	No. prosecuted	% charged	No. prosecuted
25.4	325	28.4	799
65.4	836	61.8	1,739
7.6	97	5.3	149
1.6	20	4.5	127
	315		693

Homicide was not particularly common in Alameda County. There were about fifteen informations and indictments for murder between 1880 and 1885; there were seven in the year 1910. Overall, murder cases made up about 4 percent of our Superior Court sample. Murder was often a family affair. (This is still true.) Edward Donnelly was accused of killing his wife, Mary; if her nurse, Laura Goss, is to be believed, Edward tied Mary to a bed and "used" her "like a beast" for over four hours; she died as a consequence. The jury convicted him of second-degree murder (no. 16, 1880).[1] Arthur Brook was accused of murdering his father in 1883 (no. 375). Erland H. Soderberg, a pile driver, killed his old mother in a drunken fit in 1906; he was sentenced to prison for life (no. 4408). There were also a number of crimes of passion. Robert Curtin, a dry goods clerk, killed John Titus for "paying too much attention to Mrs. Curtin." The jury convicted him.[2] Edward Schroeder shot a dentist, Alfred Lefebvre. Alfred's attentions to his wife, he felt, went far beyond her molars. A jury let him go (no. 112, 1880).

Other murders exploded out of brawls. Lee Ah Wing, a Chinese cucumber picker, killed another picker on a ranch in San Leandro. A domino game and a small debt (less than a dollar) touched off the argument (no. 460, 1883). James Cassidy quarreled with William Galvin, in a saloon. They went outside; Cassidy hit Galvin in the head with a watering bucket; Galvin died (no. 639, 1883). Other murders occurred during burglaries: Louis Matheny stood trial for killing a policeman, shot interrupting a break-in at an Oakland saloon (no. 1426, 1893). A labor dispute apparently touched off one trial for murder.

1. Another alleged wife-killer, Hugh Cull (no. 634, 1885), was found not guilty. The main witness was the defendant's seven-year-old daughter; in Superior Court, on defense motion, the judge excluded her testimony.
2. *Alameda Argus*, May 14, 1908, p. 1, col. 8.

Benjamin Lichtenstein shot John Phelan in 1888. Both men were journeymen tailors. Lichtenstein worked at home, and for less money than Phelan and his unionized tailors. This led to drinking, quarreling, and finally death. Lichtenstein was acquitted (no. 860, 1888). Organized violence appears very rarely in the records, but when Wong Lung was convicted of murder in 1908, the crime was blamed on a war between "two big rival Chinese tongs [gangs]."[3] Murder was the queen of crimes, then as now—rare, lurid, horrifying. Most murder cases were notorious crimes; if they came to trial, they were reported in the press in great detail. We meet a few of these cases again in Chapter 7.

Kidnapping was another crime against the person, and a most serious one. But it was rare indeed in Superior Court. Our sample failed to turn up a single case. We pick up tales of kidnapping from the newspapers; but the charges were, apparently, groundless and in any event never followed up. The *Berkeley Reporter* announced (1906), somewhat hysterically, that Willie Sylva, a boy of sixteen, living in San Leandro, had been kidnapped. A band of Italians and Puerto Ricans had smuggled him onto a steamer; Willie was bound for a life of "slavery" in the Alaska canneries. But the boat was already out to sea, and police were helpless. The paper muttered darkly about "organized gangs," stealing boys for the canneries. A fifteen-year-old (it was said) had been locked overnight in a dingy room in Chinatown, then taken to a steamer. He was rescued by his mother, who swore out a warrant charging him with vagrancy.[4] To our jaundiced eyes, these cases smack more of runaway boys than kidnapping. The press had a tendency to sniff out horrid plots, especially when the "plotters" were foreigners. A month after the cannery story, the *Reporter* discovered another kidnapping. Chinese had stolen away a "golden haired" little girl, three years old. The mother was an earthquake refugee; the "kidnappers" took the little tyke to a "Chinese den at Suisun." So said the screaming headlines. Then the story dropped out of the paper completely. This too was probably nothing more than the usual case of a lost child, blown up by rumors to colossal proportions.[5]

Robbery, according to the code, was violent theft—a "felonious

3. Ibid., Apr. 20, 1908, p. 4, col. 3.

4. *Berkeley Reporter*, Apr. 17, 1906, p. 4, col. 3. The *Oakland Tribune* reported, Apr. 17, 1901, p. 3, col. 6, that Leo Block, an eleven-year-old schoolboy, disappeared "as mysteriously as if the earth had opened up and swallowed him." Neighbors felt that the boy had been kidnapped. The boy lived with his father, who was separated from his mother. One neighbor said she had seen "a strange Jewish woman" about before the boy disappeared.

5. *Berkeley Reporter*, Apr. 26, 1906, p. 1, col. 3.

taking" of property from a person, against the person's will, and with "force or fear" (§ 211). A holdup is the classic form of robbery. Robbery cases were rather rare in the files of Superior Court; they made up between 4 and 5 percent of the cases in our sample. And the facts sometimes hardly seemed to justify the strong words of the code. The complaint in the case of Ernest Holloway (no. 2705, 1903), for example, seemed very grave: that he "by means of force and violence feloniously, unlawfully, and willfully" did "steal, take and carry away from the person of . . . Ben Damerell . . . personal property." But the "personal property" turned out to be ten cents, three lead pencils, one memorandum book, and a box of matches. And Ben Damerell was thirteen years old. The incident took place on July 10, 1903. Ernest and a bunch of boys, including a certain Skinny Wright, jumped Ben. A boy named Frank Rhodes grabbed Ben's fingers and pinched them behind him. Holloway put his hand in Ben's pocket, and took out the "personal property." Granted, this was not nice behavior, but did it merit the heavy artillery of a felony trial?

Another case, from 1890, also scores low on the scale of "force and fear." Fred Johnson was accused of robbing Daniel Sullivan of "a great sum of money." The great sum was ninety cents. It was Sullivan's change, after he bought beer in an Oakland saloon. Johnson met Sullivan in the saloon; then they went to an empty house. Here are the victim's words: "There were two or three fellows in there. It was dark, there was no light. . . . All at once I felt his hand in my pocket, there was another man in front of me, and he took that 90 cents. He says, 'he hasn't any more. He ain't got but 90 cents,' and he took the 90 cents and a two-bladed knife I had paid two bits for" (no. 1058).

An even more troublesome crime "against the person" was rape. Rape was unlawful sexual intercourse, usually with force. It was defined as "sexual intercourse" with "a female not the wife of the perpetrator," where the woman resists, or gives way because of threats or drugs, or where she could not consent because she was underage, unconscious, or of "unsound mind" (§ 261). Rape can certainly be violent; but most cases of "rape" in the sample, on closer inspection, were hardly violent at all. Most were cases of sex with girls who were willing (more or less), but were too young to consent. This is so-called statutory rape (now termed "unlawful intercourse" in California). The age of consent was ten years old in California until 1889; then it was raised to fourteen; in 1897 it was raised to sixteen and in 1913 to eighteen—a remarkable change we will discuss in later chapters. A single section in the code covered all types of rape, violent or not. The punishment for all types, until 1931, was (in theory) the same. In some cases, it is not easy to tell from the files how much force was exerted on the victim. Frank Sweeney, in 1897, went on trial for raping a thirteen-year-old (no. 2070). According to her, she was on the way home from a store in West Berkeley, where she bought some lemons. It was about seven or eight at night. She met Frank Sweeney; he pushed her up against the fence, and had his way against her will.[6] Because she was thirteen, it was rape, whether violent or not.

Few cases, in fact, were unmistakably violent. Forceful rape may or may not have been common; if it was, it was rarely caught or prosecuted. In cases that *were* prosecuted, the defendant was sometimes as much a victim as the woman. Andrew Di Santos (no. 1729, 1895) was black; he lived next door to Jennie Petranick. Jennie was fifteen; she and Di Santos made love. He went to Jennie's mother and asked for permission to marry the girl. He admitted he had already "used" her, with a promise to marry her. To the mother these words were "as if anybody draw a knife on my heart. . . . I don't want her to marry any black people." What followed was not wedding bells, but arrest on a charge of rape. The complaint said Jennie was raped while unconscious; this charge fell apart, and the mother then shifted to the theory that the act was rape because Jennie was "weak-minded." This was plainly a trumped-up charge; but Di Santos was bound over to Superior Court, and freed only after a long and painful ordeal.

CRIMES AGAINST PROPERTY

Burglary, theft, forgery, and arson were the main crimes against property. Burglary and theft were the most common felonies of all—at least the most commonly prosecuted. If we could call any case "typical," it might be Charles Pauli's; the charge was breaking into D. W. Hatch's store in Oakland, in 1907, and stealing a sack of potatoes (no. 4211). Overall, nearly 30 percent of the cases in our sample were burglary cases; larceny cases made up nearly 20 percent of the sample. No other crimes were so common.

Basically, burglary was breaking into a house or store to rob it. It was defined as the crime of entering a building ("any house, room, apartment, tenement, shop, warehouse, store, mill, barn, stable, outhouse . . . tent, vessel, or railroad car") with the intention of committing "grand or petty larceny or any felony" (§ 459). First-degree burglary was burglary "committed in the nighttime"; daytime burglary

---

6. On January 20, 1898, the information was dismissed on motion of the district attorney; the reason does not appear in the records.

was second degree. First-degree burglary carried a heavier penalty (§§ 460–61).

Undoubtedly *some* defendants, in the hundreds of burglary cases, were persistent or even professional thieves. But there were also many rank amateurs, most of them hopeless bunglers. S. Johnson was a "cleanup" man for a shopkeeper. He hid in the store until after closing time, then helped himself to some cash, "small change and bogus coins" from a cash box, an old overcoat, and a revolver. He pleaded guilty, explaining, "I was drunk" (no. 2433, 1901). He got six years at Folsom. Even some repeaters were small potatoes. George Dunbar, who had prior convictions for petty larceny and robbery, broke into a room in a boardinghouse and stole a watch. Alas, the victim was a light sleeper. He woke up and chased after Dunbar, who dropped the watch. Dunbar pleaded guilty. His sentence was twenty-five years in San Quentin (no. 2733, 1901). Years and years in prison were often the price for piddling hauls: an overcoat and some fruit in one case, two pairs of pants in another, two leather purses in a third.

Larceny was "grand" if the thief took goods worth more than $50, or took them from somebody's person, or if the thief stole a horse, cow, or mule (§ 487). There are dozens of examples: Henry Hudson was accused of taking "a chestnut sorrel horse of the value of $150," plus a $10 saddle and a $5 bridle (no. 4091, 1907); W. H. Adams took opera glasses and a sealskin coat (no. 2463, 1901). Grand larceny could be the theft of money: John Ulrich was accused in 1890 of taking $1,000 from Mrs. Minnie Friedman, who stood on a platform waiting for a train (no. 1142). Grace Jones, fresh out of jail, and needing some money, rented a room for 50 cents in a lodging house, and brought in Louis Gee. He took off his clothes, and hung his pants on the wall. At about 1:00 A.M. (Gee testified), "She go out to take a pee and said she would be back in a few minutes, and she took my money" (no. 4449, 1908). Petty larceny was a misdemeanor; but a second offense became a felony. Thus, H. E. Rogers (also known as William Smith) was tried for a felony in Superior Court, even though all he stole was $4 in change from a box at LeProtti's saloon. He had been convicted once before. His sentence was two years in prison (no. 4098, 1907).

Arson was not a common charge; there was probably, on the average, less than a case a year in Superior Court. Arson for filthy lucre was *very* rare. There was an example in 1910: Israel Liever, William Schoenfeld, and Arthur Nagel were accused of burning a building to collect insurance (no. 4866).[7] In most other cases, it was anger or lust

7. George Beardon, age thirty-seven, started a fire in a closet of a house in Berkeley. He said the owner offered him $1,000 to burn the house down (no. 4737, 1910).

for revenge that lit the fires (or so it was charged). Ignacio Rozensky was a neighbor of Johanna Fink. She had him arrested for disturbing the peace; he vowed to get even. Strange kerosene fires burned her shed. But Rozensky was acquitted (no. 1482, 1893). Emeline Sweetser, estranged wife of Emery Sweetser, moved out and threatened to "burn him." The old house burned; Emery was dragged out in his bedclothes. Emeline went to trial, twice; but the prosecution gave up after two hung juries (no. 4880, 1910). In all the cases, even the commercial ones, the defendants were amateurs.

Forgery and embezzlement were more common crimes in Superior Court. Forgery, practically speaking, meant bad checks. A typical defendant was Harry Williams, ruined (he said) by the great earthquake and fire of 1906; his "forgery" was a rubber check, for $393, drawn on a Berkeley bank.[8] For other defendants, the charge was "passing fictitious checks." Punishment could be quite severe. Otis Bunnell, a thirty-one-year-old cook, wrote a bad check for $27 while drunk. This was his first offense, but the judge gave him two years in prison—and no probation (no. 4826, 1910). "Embezzlement" calls to mind the taking of money; but Albert Schultz "embezzled" a bay mare, buggy, plow, and groceries from his boss, in 1895 (no. 1683). Not all embezzlers were employees; Charles Robinson, an attorney, stood trial in 1887 for taking $77.33 that belonged to a client. He ran his own defense, and the jury acquitted him (no. 780). William Mc-Kowen was secretary to the Board of Regents of the University of California. He embezzled some money, a gift from Phoebe Hearst to the Department of Anthropology (no. 2769, 1904). He pleaded guilty, and was sentenced to a long term in San Quentin. Another "standard" embezzler was James Dodds, treasurer of Oakland from 1877 to 1883, who dipped his hands into the till.[9]

Receiving stolen property was another property crime, but not a common one. What is interesting is that defendants in the scattered cases were rarely professional "fences." William Graff, age seventeen, stole a diamond ring; he gave it to his older brother George, nineteen, to dispose of. (George gave it to a pawnbroker for forty-five dollars, paying the money to his brother Bill) (no. 3030, 1906.)[10] Another defendant, Bercovich, was a secondhand dealer. He bought thirty pounds of copper wiring from a fourteen-year-old boy. There was nothing to show that Bercovich *knew* the wire was stolen, and a jury acquitted him (no. 2127, 1898). On the whole, we get a familiar impression from the files about these defendants: luckless amateurs.

8. *Berkeley Reporter*, May 23, 1906, p. 8, col. 4.
9. See *Oakland Tribune*, Aug. 16, 1883, p. 3, col. 1.
10. *Berkeley Reporter*, Apr. 8, 1906, p. 1, col. 6.

Embezzlement and passing bad checks are usually considered "white-collar" crimes. Some defendants were men of good background, come down in the world. A poignant example was Jack Martin (no. 4605, 1909). Martin had been born in New York City in 1866. He earned a medical degree from the University of Ottawa in 1889, practiced medicine in Montreal, entered the "prize ring," practiced medicine again, served in the Spanish American War in Puerto Rico, came to San Francisco in 1900, and ran a saloon. Meanwhile he married and had two small children. The earthquake destroyed his building, killed the two children, and crippled his wife. She died, an invalid with a broken spine. Martin had been in Oakland during the earthquake: "I got across in the tug, naturally made for my place of residence. The children could not be found. My wife had been taken out. . . . " After that catastrophe, he drifted into bad company. He went to New York and then came back. He was arrested while trying to palm off a check for $110, in payment for some furniture, and claiming to be a certain Dr. Curtis.

Judge Waste had little sympathy for Martin. True, he had lived through a gruesome ordeal; true, he had pleaded guilty. But passing a bad check was a terrific "commercial" offense. It "menaces our business, the bulk of which . . . is carried on by checks, notes and other papers. If the faith in credit of the community is destroyed . . . our commercial fabric must fall." Martin had been "in distress"; but, said the judge, there were many men "who would have gone down in their pockets and given you what money you needed." The wages of Martin's sin was five years in San Quentin.

MORALS OFFENSES

This category is not easy to define. It includes many acts that today we call "victimless" crimes—violations of the official moral code. The term "victimless" crime was not used in our period. It is a modern phrase, and the idea is modern, too. It suggests that the offenses are not serious, that no one is hurt. But the general public in 1880, or 1910, probably did not see things that way. Morals offenses include sex in various forms and shapes, along with other types of forbidden fruit: drug addiction, gambling, prostitution. Such crimes are victimless when one cannot tell the victim from the criminal. More practically, these are acts without complaining witnesses. This is especially true when the parties are that notorious pair, two consenting adults. And Juan Cordiel's "victim," in a case from 1880, could hardly tell

144 | *The Roots of Justice*

her tale; he was accused of "the infamous crime against nature, committed with . . . a she goat."[11]

Since the victim does not step forward, how do these cases get to court? The main answer is that they do *not* get to court. The police bring in a few caught fish; jealous third parties blow the whistle on others. In any event, morals offenses were not common in Superior Court. Drunkenness cases, and almost all gambling cases, went to justice or police court. There were some exceptions; we found several prosecutions in 1910 for "poolselling or bookmaking," a crime defined as taking bets on a "trial or contest of skill, speed or power of endurance, of man or beast" (§ 337a).[12]

Sex cases were uncommon in Superior Court, but uncommonly interesting. G. P. Bray, in 1904 (no. 2808) was charged with "seduction." This meant sex with "an unmarried female of previous chaste character . . . under promise of marriage." The accuser was Lillian Woolf, a seventeen-year-old girl, who found herself in "a family way." Bray brought strong proof that Lillian's chastity was *very* previous; his brother, Arthur, among others, had spent the night with her. In 1906, Louise Cabral, nineteen, charged Steven Simons, twenty, with seduction. Young Steven sat in county jail. The two families had a heart-to-heart talk in the jailhouse. If Steven married Louise, she could not testify against him; and the case would be dead. Steven decided that marriage was not such a bad idea after all.[13] Isabel Davis, a telephone girl, created a sensation in 1906; she accused a state senator, M. W. Simpson, of seduction. The case jostled for public attention with the trial of Henry Logan; Logan, a deacon, Sunday school teacher, and pillar of the First Free Baptist Church, eloped with Ethel Cook, a girl of sixteen.[14]

Incest was another crime rare in the files of Superior Court. Paul Holewich, in 1892, was accused of sleeping with his "natural daughter"; he was acquitted (no. 1390). In the same month, a girl of fifteen said that her father, James Piemantel, had chloroformed her and had done dirty deeds while she lay unconscious. He denied the charge. The information was dismissed in Superior Court (no. 1392, 1892). *Adultery* (it had to be "open and notorious") was also rare in Superior Court, however common in the wicked world. A luckless pair, Malissa Fritas and Nelson H. Tower, charged in 1883, were the only

11. Juan Cordiel (no. 155, 1880). For this offense, the sentence was eight years in prison.
12. A violation of § 337a could be treated as either a felony or a misdemeanor.
13. *Berkeley Reporter*, Jan. 16, 1906, p. 4, col. 4.
14. On the Davis-Simpson affair, see ibid., Mar. 8, 1906, p. 8, col. 1, and the weeks before and after; on Logan-Cook, see ibid., June 5, 1906, p. 8, col. 2.

examples we found (nos. 417, 418).[15] The outraged husband, Manuel Fritas, pressed the case. He ran a boarding house in San Rafael. San Rafael was too dull for Malissa's tastes. She ran off to the tinsel and glitter of San Francisco, where she became a prostitute. Nelson had been a lodger in the boardinghouse. He took Malissa from her life of multiple sin in San Francisco to a life of single sin in Alameda. They were open and notorious enough to satisfy the statute; but in its own way, their love was chaste. (She swore: "Since I met defendant, no other man has known me carnally.") Manuel might have been grateful, but he felt the urge for revenge. In the end, Nelson Tower was sentenced to two months in county jail. Malissa went free.

Cases of incest or seduction, of course, were not really victimless. Malissa's husband, too, thought of himself as a victim. Even less victimless were two other crimes: bigamy and nonsupport. Bigamy was not a common charge, but there were scattered examples. Nonsupport (§ 270) was a misdemeanor until 1909. In that year the code was amended, and the law became stiffer. Now a parent who "wilfully" failed to furnish "necessary food, clothing, shelter, or medical attendance for his child" could be sentenced up to two years in prison, or fined up to $1,000, or both (Laws Cal., 1909, p. 258). The first man in the county sent to prison for nonsupport was Narciso Sylvestrie, a fruit peddler and hop picker. His wife had died, leaving four children between six and twelve years old. Judge Brown called him "selfish and inhuman," and gave him the maximum sentence (no. 4731, 1910).[16]

Sex sold newspapers; but newspaper language at the turn of the century was veiled and prudish by the standards of today. The press spoke of "atrocious crimes," "vile acts," and the like; they never called a spade a spade. On the other hand, they had no scruples about names and addresses; what victims gained through veiled language, they lost through publicity. Shame and notoriety surely made some people shy about prosecuting. Here are three examples of re-

15. A few other cases or potential cases were noted in the press; see, for example, *Oakland Tribune*, Sept. 10, 1883, p. 3, col. 4, on the arrest of "ex-Senator William Sharon . . . on a charge of adultery committed with Miss Gertrude Dietz."

16. The rare but colorful cases of criminal libel can be mentioned here, for want of a better place. A hotelkeeper in Berkeley complained, in 1889, that a newspaperman libeled him, calling his hotel a whorehouse. The defendant was acquitted (McCarty, no. 1005). Colonel Jack Lynch was accused, in 1905, of "unlawfully, wickedly and maliciously" libeling E. L. Blackman. Lynch published a scurrilous article in the *Fruitvale News*, in which he said that Blackman drank booze until he couldn't see straight, that his drinking partner was a woman "whose husband keeps a notorious dive," that Blackman helped this man get a license and "run a disorderly house in Fruitvale," that he "assaulted many a poor Portuguese while under the influence of 'booze,'" and that his wife had to stay away from the "infuriated madman" for three days (no. 3009).

porting, drawn from one month of the *Oakland Tribune* (May 1902). In one case, we read that J. D. Vandine, a "mining man," had been arrested. He enticed two little girls, daughters of a tailor and a paper-hanger, into a barn; there he committed "atrocious crimes." A police officer swore out a complaint for battery: "A stronger charge would have been placed against the scoundrel, but the children's parents fear the notoriety connected with it." (The *Tribune* published the names and addresses of everyone connected with the case.) In the second case, a girl of seventeen went on a drinking spree in Oakland; she was raped by a bartender. Neither she nor her mother was willing "to place a complaint against the fellow, fearing the notoriety it would cause." (The *Tribune* filled the vacuum, in its own way, by tattling the girl's name and address.) In the third case, the *Tribune* told about a "fiendish outrage"; a "Chinese brute" maltreated "a little school girl" of thirteen. The charge here too was aggravated assault, though if the *Tribune* can be believed, the true crime was at least (or at most?) statutory rape. The defendant ("the Mongol charged with the atro-cious crime") was a clam-digger. The girl had been out getting fire-wood. The Chinese, with promises of easy firewood, enticed her to a "secluded spot in the marsh . . . committed the crime, exercising great brutality, and then fled." He repeated the "crime" a few days later; but this time a sailboat was nearby, and its captain "observed the suspicious actions of the pair . . . through a marine glass." He rowed hastily to shore, in pursuit of the "heathen fiend," who ran away. The captain followed the girl home, and told her mother. The mother, at first, was "unwilling on account of the notoriety to notify the police," but in the end she filed the complaint.[17]

CRIMES AGAINST PUBLIC ORDER

This is a rather miscellaneous category; it includes weapons viola-tions, bribery, perjury, election fraud, escape, resisting an officer, riots, threats, and traffic offenses. Bicycles, buggies, and early auto-mobiles did not make much of a mark on Superior Court before 1910. They contributed mightily, as we saw, to the work of the petty courts, but it was not until the 1920s that traffic prosecutions—drunk driving, chiefly—exploded in Superior Court, accounting for as many as 15 percent of the cases. The whole category of public order crimes was less than 5 percent of the caseload of Superior Court during our period. The "crimes" were not rare, perhaps, but prosecutions were.

17. *Oakland Tribune*, May 26, 1902, p. 1, col. 4, May 27, 1902, p. 2, col. 2, May 28, 1902, p. 4, col. 2, May 16, 1902, p. 1, col. 4.

Illegal voting was probably rather common; few people were caught or charged. Dan Hartigan was one of these few. He was indicted in 1893; he voted in Livermore, in a local election, even though (it was charged) he had lived in his precinct less than thirty days (no. 1455). Bribery, too, was probably far more common in life than in Superior Court. A Chinese man was accused in 1906 of offering five-dollar gold pieces to a policeman, in exchange for immunity for some gambling games. He was acquitted (no. 4040).

Perjury cases were slightly more common. John Canty's was a typical case. Asa D. Hatch sued the Southern Pacific, in April 1893, claiming an injury. Canty, a hack driver, testified at the trial; the grand jury thought he had lied (no. 1454). Charles Heil was another who was accused of perjury; he swore out a false complaint (it was said) charging Lewis Ferrier with embezzling jewelry (no. 130, 1880). An unusual case of perjury came up in 1893. George McCarthe applied for a marriage license, and told the clerk that his bride, Mary Catherine White, was nineteen. In fact, she was sixteen. A jury acquitted him of the charge (no. 1442).

Escape or jail break was another crime against public order. Occasionally this offense appeared in a slight disguise. Frank Dunne was a prisoner in Oakland's city jail, serving time for petty larceny. He was made an "acting cook"; this gave him the "freedom of the cooking room," and access to knives and implements. On December 16, 1901, he was found sawing his way through the iron grating. Because he had not actually escaped, the information charged him with a different violation: that he "did wrongfully, wilfully, intentionally and feloniously injure the city prison of the city of Oakland . . . by . . . sawing, pulling down and breaking a certain iron bar forming part of an iron grating belonging to . . . a public prison for the confinement of prisoners." Dunne's impatience cost him dearly. Even though he pleaded guilty, the judge gave him five years at Folsom penitentiary (no. 2534).[18]

REGULATORY OFFENSES

Statistically speaking, regulatory offenses never made much of a mark in Superior Court. Most of these were misdemeanors and went to the petty courts. There were a few examples of misdemeanor *indictments*, which could be tried in Superior Court. Leopold Palmtag and John Booker were indicted for maintaining a public nuisance, in 1888; they

18. Charles Werner (no. 121, 1880) was also accused of injuring a public jail by sawing two iron window bars.

owned a brewery in Hayward and produced, along with beer, "slops, filthy water and refuse matter . . . offensive gases, stinks and smells" (nos. 826, 827). Another indictment in 1888 complained of the "pest house" for smallpox run by P. S. Schultheis (no. 282). Lee Sing was charged in 1902 with maintaining a public nuisance in Pleasanton ("a certain Cess-pool filled with dirty water . . . injurious to health and . . . the comfortable enjoyment of life and property by the . . . neighborhood") (no. 2460). In 1910 four cases were tried under § 636, which made it an offense to use certain nets, such as the "Chinese shrimp or bag net." These were the only regulatory offenses tried in Superior Court that entire year.

As we saw, the enforcement of regulatory offenses fell mostly on police and justice courts. The few cases in Superior Court were, in the main, appeals from these petty courts. Most were violations of local ordinances. Some few of the appeals were test cases. Others were instances of stubborn or tenacious defendants. Hanora Bently, of Berkeley, was one of the tenacious sort. A Berkeley ordinance required landlords to connect their house drains to the public sewers. Mrs. Bently owned a house at 2114 Sixth Street, Berkeley. She violated the ordinance, was fined fifty dollars, and stubbornly appealed (no. 2549, 1902). Another regulatory appeal was brought by a doctor in Alameda, J. M. Selfridge (no. 2486, 1901). Dr. Selfridge treated Irene Pattiani for diphtheria, but did not report the case to local authorities. The Recorder's Court of Alameda fined Selfridge twenty-five dollars and he appealed, perhaps for the sake of professional honor.

TYPES OF CRIME: A BRIEF SUMMING UP

What can we conclude from this survey of felony cases? One striking point is how few surprises we find in the *types* of crime. There were indeed quirks and oddities tucked away in corners of the penal code, but the Superior Court handled in the main only familiar crimes: burglary, robbery, larceny, felonious assault, forgery, rape.

The problem lurking in the records was a rather different one. It was the problem of applying the norms. Who was caught in the web and why? Were criminals people who really deserved that label? We will return to this problem again; for now we note that the labels attached to crimes often seem to be radically misleading, even when they are technically correct. We reported some examples when we spoke of robbery. Robbery implies force; most of us do not think it "force" to rummage through somebody's pockets, even if technically it is. The rape cases were equally troubling. Larceny cases presented fewer problems of definition; but it was disturbing to see how a "prior" for petty larceny turned a second petty act into a felony. It was very serious to steal twice, no matter how trivial the second theft: a dollar or two could bring years in prison. Those in the system who decide what to call a piece of behavior wield real power. (This fact also renders crime statistics even shakier than otherwise.) Of course, a jury could acquit a person overcharged for crime; and many such cases were dismissed along the way. But before this happened, a defendant might have already suffered greatly; the process, as a recent book reminds us, is itself a punishment, and a severe one at that.[19]

Another point is the dominance of stealing: taking someone else's goods. The most common accusations were accusations of theft. If we aggregate larceny, burglary, embezzlement, and forgery, we account for most of the cases in the register. Protecting private property was what felony justice was mainly about. Property crimes were more than two to one ahead of their nearest competitor, crimes against the person. Morals crimes, regulatory crimes, and public order crimes lagged very far behind.

These proportions were quite standard for the period; when we dipped into records of other California counties, we found very similar ratios. The proportions have altered somewhat over the years, however. In 1977 the Superior Courts of California disposed of 33,146 adult felony cases. The three big property crimes (burglary, theft, and motor vehicle theft) amounted to 42 percent of the total. The four big crimes of personal violence (homicide, forcible rape, robbery, and assault) came to about 30 percent. Drug offenses contributed another 19 percent—a category that did not exist, practically speaking, during our period.[20] It is interesting to note that, in 1977, property crimes were a bit more apt to be filtered out than crimes of violence. There were 93,924 felony arrests for property crimes, 42 percent of the total; but only 55,538 arrests for crimes against persons, or 25 percent. In other words, a lower percentage of violent crimes fell by the wayside before reaching Superior Court.[21] Certainly, we take stealing less seriously than murder. But it does seem clear that our period took stealing quite seriously, and the system punished those it caught with some severity.

Yet it is worth mentioning that criminal justice in our period was probably *less* fixated on stealing than had been true in the past. We

19. Malcolm Feeley, *The Process Is the Punishment: Handling Cases in a Lower Criminal Court* (New York, 1979).
20. California Bureau of Criminal Statistics, *Crime and Delinquency in California, 1977* (1978), pt. 2, p. 8.
21. Ibid., pt 1, p. 19. Drug offenses came to 46,889, or 20.8 percent of the total; sex law violations, to 1.5 percent.

have also studied certain English criminal records, notably a sample of nineteenth-century cases from the Central Criminal Courts in London. At the end of the century, the breakdown in types of case looks much like the one in Alameda County.[22] The earlier part of the century was strikingly different. Here stealing was absolutely, utterly dominant. Indeed, in 1840, one crime—larceny—accounted for 79 percent of all the court cases; and if we add other property crimes, like embezzling, the total is an astounding 96 percent; less than 3 percent of the cases were cases of violent crime. Apparently, over the course of the century, other types of crime began to demand and get a share of attention in England. Property crimes remained the most important, but they gave up what was once a virtual monopoly. It is, of course, theoretically possible that actual crime rates shifted. But this would require us to swallow a whopping assumption: that felonies of violence and immorality did not occur in any numbers in 1840. This, needless to say, would be absurd.

In Alameda County, then, we get a picture of a system concerned mostly with property crimes, but probably less so than criminal justice systems generally in the early nineteenth century.[23] It was also a system somewhat concerned with morals and sex. Crimes against morality did not make much of a splash statistically, but more were tried as time went on, and almost certainly more than in urban counties in 1800 or 1850. We return to this theme later on.

Who Were the Defendants?

We do not have systematic data about the age, race, income, or social class of defendants; raw case files sometimes give this information, sometimes not. We learn a bit from the newspapers,[24] and something more (for Oakland only) from the arrest records. On the whole, we do not know as much as we would like.

We have the first names of all our defendants, so we can at least tell

22. For 1900: 54.3 percent property crimes, 31 percent crimes against the person. Morals crimes were high, however: 13.8 percent. Less than 1 percent were public order offenses.

23. Replacing, perhaps, a still earlier obsession with crimes of morality. See chap. 10, n. 12. It is unfortunate that we have so little data on courts in the early years of the nineteenth century in the United States. Our assumptions might possibly not hold for frontier areas; see David J. Bodenhamer, "Law and Disorder on the Early Frontier: Marion County, Indiana, 1823–1850," *Western Hist. Q.* 10 (July 1979): 323.

24. The newspapers usually identified defendants by race. The *Alameda Argus*, for example, referred to Alice Collins, tried for robbery in 1908, as a "negress" who robbed "a Chinaman" of ten dollars. *Alameda Argus*, Mar. 31, 1908, p. 1, col. 3.

women from men.[25] Basically, defendants were men—overwhelmingly so. No more than 4 to 6 percent of the defendants were women. Women defendants show up in such small numbers in our sample that it is hard to say much about the crimes they were charged with. Women apparently did not go in for burglary: women burglars were very, very rare. We meet an occasional woman charged with homicide —Bessie Vencelaw, for example, who shot her husband in 1905 (accidentally, she said; she was acquitted) (no. 2984). Josephine Toddman was charged with false imprisonment: she locked another woman in a room on her ranch in 1885 (no. 606). Soledad Aldares was accused of assaulting a certain Diego with a deadly weapon, "to wit, a large knife" (no. 161, 1880). A few women appealed from convictions in the petty courts. One of these was Rose Alameda; the police court had sentenced her to six months in jail, on a vagrancy charge (probably a euphemism for prostitution) (no. 2886, 1904). On the whole, there are so few women defendants that we *must* conclude that women committed fewer serious crimes than men. No bias could be powerful enough to explain our lopsided figures.[26]

Virtually every defendant was an actual *person*. Under the Penal Code, a corporation was capable of committing crime (§ 1390–97); but few were ever prosecuted. We found only two examples. In one, the defendant was the Oakland Water Company (no. 1690, 1895). The Oakland City Council ordered the company to disgorge its list of ratepayers, tell how much they paid, and give certain other facts and figures. The corporation refused. In Superior Court, the company waived a jury, offered no defense, and asked for a speedy trial. The court found the company guilty and imposed a fifty-dollar fine.

The second was a case in 1909 against Goldberg, Bowen and Company, grocers of Oakland. This was an appeal from a justice court, in the city of Alameda. Alameda did not allow the sale of liquor inside town without a license. On May 26, 1908, a certain Mrs. E. Ehrenpfort, who lived in Alameda, gave an order for groceries to John O'Hara, who worked for Goldberg, Bowen and Company. It was a list of no great particular interest (a tin of sardines at 25 cents, one bar of "Tanglefoot Fly Paper" at 35 cents, soap, cheese, clothespins); but it included a quart of claret. The store delivered the goods to Mrs. Ehrenpfort and, of course, had no Alameda license. The company waived trial by jury. The justice convicted them of this rather technical

25. Except for the Chinese, and these were almost always men. See n. 120 to Chap. 4, above.
26. In Placer County, Calif., in the gold country, a sample of 100 felony cases between 1880 and 1910 turned up only three women. (Information provided by Mark Chavez, Stanford Law School.)

offense, and fined the company $250. Goldberg, Bowen appealed, but the judgment was affirmed (no. 4557, 1909).

We know very little about the social status of defendants. Generally, as far as one can tell, it was fairly low. But there was a scattering among the felony defendants of people with money, respectability, or position. Sometimes the fall from grace was peculiarly poignant. James Dodds, for example, had once been treasurer of Oakland. His weakness was Mexican mining stocks; to maintain this habit, he dipped his hands into the till. When the truth came out, in 1883, he swallowed poison; but that too failed. Sick and depressed, he lay in bed in a back room of his house; the city attorney came to see him. Only then could he summon up nerve to tell his wife, who knew nothing of his crime. When he said, "I'll have to go to San Quentin, Mama," she screamed: "You can't go." But in the end he went.[27]

Embezzlement was, on the whole, a crime of amateurs, and white-collar amateurs at that. Burglars were more of a mixed lot. Some were professional: they burglarized for a living. We hear, too, about gangs of burglars or "marauders" at various times and places. Other burglars, if not full-time criminals, were regulars: August F. Voss of Berkeley, for one, arrested in 1906, operated "very successfully," robbing freight cars for two years. Voss was a carpenter by trade, but claimed he could not earn "an honest living" because he was missing one leg; his Fruitvale home was filled with "loot," including "sewing machines, a set of antlers, a chiffonier, cases of elegantly bound books, boxes of dry goods, and quantities of groceries."[28] Still other burglars were rank amateurs. In some ways, David Riddell, convicted in 1909, fairly represents the type (we hesitate to call him "typical"). Riddell was forty-five years old, a boilermaker. He had a wife and a son, twenty-two years old; they lived in Philadelphia, but Riddell had drifted away. He claimed that he had never been in trouble. One night to town, Riddell "got to drinking around." He rented a room, and "stupid with the drink," wandered into the Occidental Lodging House on Washington Street, in Oakland, about eight o'clock in the morning. John Kavathis, of Room 38, had gone to the toilet; Riddell picked up a pair of pants belonging to Kavathis's roommate. Kavathis came back and saw the defendant standing there, inanely, holding

27. *Oakland Tribune*, Aug. 17, 1883, p. 3, col. 1. Dodds was convicted of embezzlement, and sentenced to five years in San Quentin. He was pardoned by the governor after serving three and a half years of the sentence. J. J. McConnel, assistant secretary of Oakland Camp No. 95, Woodmen of the World, and a deputy in the assessor's office, was arrested in 1906 for taking money from the camp, and doctoring the records. *Berkeley Reporter*, Jan. 22, 1906, p. 6, col. 4.

28. *Berkeley Reporter*, May 16, 1906, p. 4, col. 2; for a report on a gang of burglars, see *Haywards Weekly Journal*, Feb. 14, 1880, p. 3, col. 3.

the corpus delicti. For this piece of drunken folly, Riddell got a year and a half in San Quentin.

Many burglary cases were more or less of this sort. They came from the world of unattached men, who drifted in and out of Oakland, working now and then, living as boarders in lodging houses. Often the crime was lifting something from another lodger. The victim, or the burglar, or both, were dead drunk. Charles Ross was another such burglar (no. 4691, 1909). George Collins, the victim, went to bed in his room "in a cheap lodging house on the corner of 7th and Washington Streets." It was November 13, 1909. He put his clothes on a chair. A window that faced on the hall was left open. The next morning, about five o'clock, Collins woke up; his clothes were missing. He found them on the back porch, minus a gold watch, chain, and locket; a bunch of keys, and a small amount of silver. The watch, chain, and keys turned up in Ross's pocket. Ross said it was all a joke. No one was amused. Ross had no record, and pleaded guilty to burglary. He got two and a half years in prison.

It is dangerous to generalize, because the data are poor; but what we have give off a strong impression. Here, too, defendants were not so much criminals as losers: failures at family and job, drifters, the unattached. Perhaps professionals were better at wriggling out of trouble, less likely to be caught. In any event, they seem less often in the dock than these drunken unfortunates. Judges were always talking about making examples of burglars, forgers, and so on. But, one wonders, examples of what? Many of the men were not the hard-core repeaters to whom the strong message needed to be sent.

In one sense, then, the felony process was a charade, a conceit, a trick on society. No doubt the world was full of brutal, thievish men; but these defendants were imposter knaves. They were charged with awful, heinous crimes; yet they strike us all too often as nothing worse than drunken fools, misfits, lost and lonely souls. The judges were often merciless. Edward Williams's case (1895) is a good example of this misplaced cruelty. The complaining witness was James Duffy, track walker for the Southern Pacific. Williams accosted him and demanded money and tobacco. By the time the case got to court, Duffy was reluctant to prosecute; Williams had been drunk, after all, and his mother begged Duffy for mercy. The prosecutor would not let go: Duffy believed that "a public offense had been committed," and yet did not want to prosecute? Browbeaten, Duffy gave way. Williams was bound over to Superior Court, convicted, and sent to jail for three months (no. 1700, 1895).

Preliminary Arraignment

Typically, the first stage in a felony prosecution was the filing of a complaint before a magistrate (usually a township or city justice, or a police court judge). The complaint was based on information given by the victim, or the witnesses, or the police. It described the crime, gave the date it was committed, and accused a particular person of committing it. Our sample of Superior Court case files shows that the filing was not usually much delayed: most complaints that led to prosecutions in Superior Court were filed less than five days after the crime took place.[29] Sometimes the accused was already in custody. If not, and if the complaint set out enough information to establish probable cause to believe the accused had committed the crime, the magistrate could issue an arrest warrant.

Under California law, anyone arrested for a felony had to be taken before a magistrate "without unnecessary delay" (§ 825; Calif. Const., Art. 1, § 8). In almost all cases, a person arrested for a felony appeared before a magistrate either on the day of his arrest or the next day. We examined the Oakland Arrest Books, and the only surviving Minute Book of the Oakland Police Court (covering a fourteen-month period in 1880–81); 34 percent of the people arrested on felony charges appeared before the police judge the day they were arrested, and 55 percent more the following day. Nearly 97 percent were brought before the police judge within forty-eight hours of arrest.

The prisoner's first appearance before the magistrate was called the "preliminary arraignment." The magistrate told the defendant what the charges were against him, and instructed him about his right to hire a lawyer. Preliminary arraignments generally were fairly perfunctory; the complaint was read out to the defendant, he was told about his right to counsel, a date was set for preliminary examination, and that was that.

Obtaining Counsel

The Penal Code required the magistrate to "allow the defendant a reasonable time to send for counsel" (§ 859). The defendant had a right to a lawyer's help at the preliminary examination. But this was a

---

29. The *median* length of time between the occurrence of the crime and the filing of the complaint for the cases in our Superior Court sample was 4.4 days. Other complaints were filed much later, perhaps because the crimes or the perpetrators were not promptly discovered; the *average* length of time between the crime and the filing of the complaint for the cases in our sample was 26 days.

right to *hire* a lawyer. At the trial stage the state would pay for the lawyer, if necessary. But there was no right to a free lawyer at the preliminary examination.[30] At that stage, if the accused had no money, he would have to do without. And many did. In police court, Michael Giger, charged with rolling a drunk, told the judge: "Your Honor, I would like to get an attorney, but I have no means." The judge was sympathetic but helpless: "there is no provision which authorizes the Court to appoint one in this Court. If you are held over in the Superior Court, the court there will provide you with an attorney" (no. 1828, 1896).[31] Louis Simonoff, arrested for burglary in 1898 (no. 2186), wanted the justice of Alameda Township to "send out for a state lawyer." The court pointed out that the "state lawyer" was already there—to prosecute, not defend.[32]

Money or no, it was hard to hire a lawyer out of a jail cell. Joseph Fortas, charged with grand larceny in 1903 (no. 2670), complained (through a French interpreter) that he had no chance "to write about getting" a lawyer. He had had "some money, but they had taken it away from me downstairs." The court volunteered "the services of an officer" to send for a lawyer.[33] But Fortas had no idea who to send for. Abe Halff, on the day of his hearing, told the judge he was waiting for a lawyer. The court recessed for an hour. Still no attorney. Halff admitted he was stalling; he was waiting for his father to come up from Los Angeles. The court pointed out that the father "couldn't add anything in the way of testimony." True, said Halff, but he "would have the money to procure this lawyer."[34]

The poor defendant, then, usually stood alone at this stage. Once in a while, someone volunteered to help the underdog. A black, James Jackson, was arrested for housebreaking in 1876; he wanted a lawyer, but he had no money. Lawyers, said the judge, "don't . . . attend to these cases for nothing; but . . . there is no accounting for

---

30. It was not until 1957 that the Penal Code was amended to permit appointment of counsel for indigent defendants at preliminary hearings (§ 859).

31. But Hugh Aldrich volunteered to defend the prisoner. The jury acquitted Giger in Superior Court.

32. Charles Brown, accused of burglary in 1896, knew the score. The judge asked him if he wanted time to get a lawyer. He replied: "I ain't got any money to get an attorney" (no. 1952).

33. The Penal Code directed the examining magistrate, "upon the request of the defendant, [to] require a peace officer to take a message to any counsel in the township or city the defendant may name. The officer must, without delay and without fee, perform that duty" (§ 859).

34. Nos. 4183–84. The court refused to give Halff a continuance, but the prosecution found a technical defect in the complaint. A new complaint had to be filed, so Halff gained some time. He hired George McDonough to represent him at the preliminary exam. Halff later pleaded guilty. He was, however, granted probation.

their eccentricities." Four or five "older attorneys" were in the court-room, but they ran away. Then a young lawyer, Gardner, "volunteered to defend the . . . darky in the Police Court," at the request of "several gentlemen whose only interest in the case was that arising from the peculiarly human sympathy which always goes out toward the bottom dog."

It is hard to tell how much it cost to hire a lawyer at this stage. A few scraps of information suggest that routine counseling at a preliminary examination could cost as little as $25.[35] Still, this might mean two weeks' wages, or even a month's. (In 1880 the average factory worker in Oakland earned $547 a year, if he worked full time; the average farm laborer on the West Coast made about $300 a year.)[36] Real wages rose between 1880 and 1910, and probably faster than attorney's fees. Still, hiring a lawyer was a hardship for a poor man. And most defendants were decidedly poor.

Preliminary Examination

The preliminary examination took place before the same judge who conducted the arraignment: in the police court (in Oakland), or in a justice court (elsewhere in the county). The preliminary exam was a screening device, a way to tell, at an early stage in the process, whether formal prosecution should go forward. The judge heard evidence and, at the end, decided if there was enough of a case to send ("bind over") the defendant to Superior Court for trial. The preliminary exam also served other functions. It permitted each side to learn something about the other's case and it was usually the stage at which bail was set to guarantee the defendant's appearance in Superior Court.

In theory, the preliminary exam could be held immediately after arraignment. In practice, it rarely was. The state needed time to round up witnesses, and defendants could use the time, too, to round up their own witnesses (and, it was hoped, find lawyers). Some defendants thought the preliminary exam an unnecessary bother; they wanted to throw in the towel and avoid further delay. B. C. Goodard, charged with forgery, told the court it could dispense with all formalities "because I am guilty of the crime and I acknowledge it" (no. 2594,

---

35. An article in the *San Francisco Bulletin* in 1903 refers to $25 for a small burglary case in the police court of that city. *Law Student's Helper* 11 (1903): 213.

36. U.S. Bureau of the Census, *Social Statistics of American Cities* (1880), 2:788; U.S. Department of Commerce, *Historical Statistics of the U.S. from Colonial Times to 1970* (1976), p. 135.

1902). The judge told Goodard that there was no way to waive the hearing. It was held, and Goodard was bound over to Superior Court.

Preliminary exams were typically held about a week after arraignment. Except in unusually complicated cases, they took a single day. Most defendants who made it to Superior Court had been bound over less than eight days after the complaint had been filed in the lower court.[37]

Both prosecution and defense were allowed to subpoena witnesses, who were examined and cross-examined at the hearing. Testimony had to be taken in the presence of the defendant (§ 865), but if the defendant so desired, the public could be excluded from the hearing (§ 868). This sometimes happened in rape cases.

A transcript was usually kept at the preliminary exam, and it was sent to the Superior Court, along with other papers in the case, after the defendant was bound over. These documents are a rich source, and sometimes our only source about the facts and the evidence in felony cases. The victim of the crime or the arresting officer usually presented testimony for the prosecution at the preliminary exam. The prosecuting attorney, normally an assistant district attorney, dominated the proceedings. Defendants often declined to put on a defense; only one-quarter elected to take the stand. As we have said before, many defendants were too poor to afford counsel. Overall, nearly half (about 45 percent) of all felony defendants bound over between 1890 and 1910 did without counsel at their preliminary examinations (see Table 5.2).[38]

Defendants without counsel did poorly at their preliminary exams. They were rarely able to cross-examine witnesses effectively. They were more likely to take the stand than defendants with counsel, giving the prosecution a fine opportunity to grill them for the record (see Table 5.3). Dan Morgan, in 1906, stood accused of burglary, for entering a room in the Eureka Hotel and rolling a drunk (Roland McKee). He had no lawyer and was foolish enough to take the stand at his preliminary exam. The prosecutor asked: "This is not your first experience at drunk rolling, is it?" Morgan fell into the trap. "This is

37. The *median* length of time between the filing of a complaint and bindover was 7.8 days for the cases in our Superior Court sample; some cases took much longer. The *mean* was 18.1 days.

38. Our sample can provide only a rough estimate of how many defendants actually went without counsel at preliminary hearings: it included only cases in which the defendant had been bound over; if the defendant was discharged in the lower court, the papers were never forwarded to Superior Court. Moreover, in some cases forwarded to Superior Court, it is not clear whether the defendant had a lawyer at his preliminary exam. Our estimate excludes 1880–89, because there are too many unknowns for that period.

Table 5.2. *Defendants in Superior Court Sample
with and without Counsel at Preliminary Examination, 1890–1910*

Counsel Status	1890–99		1900–1910		Weighted average 1890–1910
	No.	%	No.	%	
Defendants without counsel	64	42	139	47	45
Defendants with counsel	89	58	155	53	55
N	153		294		447

Source: Sample of Superior Court casefiles, 1890–1910.

Table 5.3. *Defendants in Superior Court Sample
Electing to Testify at the Preliminary Examination,
by Counsel Status, 1890–1910*

Counsel	Defendants testifying		Defendants not testifying	
	No.	%	No.	%
Defendants without counsel	50	32	106	68
Defendants with counsel	34	20	136	80
N	84		242	

Source: Sample of Superior Court casefiles, 1890–1910.

the first time," he blurted out (no. 4015). He was ultimately convicted of first-degree burglary.

The court often cautioned defendants that what they said on the stand could be used against them in Superior Court. But this did not seem enough to dissuade some defendants from testifying. Once on the stand, uncounseled defendants faced a hostile prosecutor intent on coaxing admissions from them. After a particularly grueling cross-examination, Edward Neal, accused of burglary in 1902, admitted that he was ready to plead guilty if he was bound over for trial (no. 2528). After another burglary defendant, Arthur Larson, took the stand in 1907, he was repeatedly asked by the court why he lied to the police who arrested him. He eventually admitted, "Because I didn't know what they were charging me with" (no. 4096). Other defendants took the stand to confess; they wanted to plead guilty and be done with it. Fred Herman, charged with grand larceny for stealing "one Columbia chainless bicycle," told the court, "I don't know what I have got to say, I plead guilty, that is all" (no. 2332, 1904).

Of course, not everyone accused of a felony at the preliminary examination ended up facing trial. Many of these poor fish wriggled through the nets, or were thrown back into the sea of life. We can gain a rough idea of how frequently defendants were discharged at the preliminary exam by tracing what happened to persons arrested for felonies in Oakland. Table 5.4 presents our results for all 175 felony defendants brought before the Oakland Police Court during a fourteen-month period in 1880 and 1881. Thirty-one of these defendants, or 18 percent, had the charges against them dismissed on motion of the prosecution; another 44, or 25 percent more, were discharged by the court. William Cullen, accused of grand larceny in 1888, was a defendant discharged after his preliminary exam. Melvin Chapman, one of the best criminal lawyers, later mayor of Oakland, represented Cullen. Chapman sharply cross-examined the police about their efforts to get confessions out of Cullen and his codefendant; he objected to admitting into evidence a statement by Cullen's codefendant; and he challenged an eyewitness who identified his client after the police told him (when showing him Cullen), "Here's the man." Cullen was discharged. The court explained that the co-defendant's statements were inadmissible hearsay; and the rest of the evidence was not enough to connect Cullen to the crime. Here a good lawyer helped scotch a shaky case before it ever got to Superior Court.

Eleven defendants, or 6 percent of those charged with felonies in police court during this period, were not bound over to Superior Court; instead, their charges were reduced to misdemeanor. John Hastie was one of these. He was charged with assault with a deadly weapon; apparently he "ran amuck with a butcher knife during the

Table 5.4. Disposition of Felony Cases before the Oakland Police Court, 1880–1881

Disposition	No.	%
Dismissed by prosecution	31	18
Discharged by court	44	25
Held to answer on felony charges	89	51
Reduced to misdemeanor charges	11	6
Total cases	175	100

Source: 100% sample of entries in Oakland Police Court Minute Books, 1880–81.

course of a row and tried to carve John Davies with the weapon." After Davies and two other witnesses testified, "an agreement was reached whereby the serious charge was withdrawn and a new one, alleging battery, was sworn to." Hastie pleaded guilty to the misdemeanor charge and was fined twenty dollars. He could thank his attorney, former Judge A. F. St. Sure, for sparing him a felony conviction.[39]

Just over half the felony defendants brought before police court—89, or 51 percent—were held to answer on felony charges. This did not mean that the committing magistrate was convinced they were guilty; it merely meant that he thought there was evidence enough to warrant prosecution. As an Alameda justice explained (when binding over a defendant accused of attempted rape), the evidence was conflicting; the case turned on who was telling the truth, the victim or the defendant. While the judge confessed some doubt, he concluded that "the opinion of twelve men would be better than any one man upon the question." A jury should hear the case (no. 1282, 1902). The defendant was later acquitted.

The percentages of persons held and discharged at the preliminary exam fluctuated over time. Examination of persons arrested for felonies in Oakland during 1890 and 1910 reveals that roughly one-half and three-fifths, respectively, were bound over to the Superior Court on felony charges. One-third and one-ninth of those arrested for felonies were released when the police declined to pursue the charges; one-fifth and one-fourth were discharged by the court after preliminary exams.

What happened at the preliminary exam could be crucial to the eventual outcome of the case. Naturally, this was true for those people who were discharged; it was the end of the line for the prosecution. But even for those held to answer on felony charges, what had gone on in the lower court could have a significant impact on the chances for success in Superior Court. Table 5.5 indicates that roughly five-sixths (84 percent) of the defendants bound over on felony charges who had *not* had lawyers at their preliminary examinations were ultimately convicted; but only slightly more than half (54 percent) of those *with* lawyers at the preliminary suffered this fate. The preliminary exam could therefore indeed be a "critical stage" in criminal process; and many years later, in 1970, the U.S. Supreme Court held that defendants had a right to counsel at that stage of proceedings, under federal constitutional law. If they could not pay, the state must provide.[40]

39. *Oakland Tribune*, Dec. 2, 1905, p. 2, col. 2.
40. Coleman v. Alabama, 399 U.S. 1 (1970).

Table 5.5. Outcome of Superior Court Prosecutions by Counsel Status at Preliminary Examination, 1890–1910

Counsel status	Defendants Convicted		Defendants not Convicted		N
	No.	%	No.	%	
Defendants with counsel at preliminary exam	143	54	124	46	267
Defendants without counsel at preliminary exam	186	84	36	16	222

Source: Sample of Superior Court casefiles, 1890–1910.

Bail

At the close of the preliminary exam, the judge who bound the defendant over also set bail to guarantee his appearance before Superior Court. Under California law, a defendant had a right to bail for any crime that did not carry the death penalty (Calif. Const., Art. 1, § 6; Penal Code, § 1271). Even in a capital case, the defendant could have bail unless the "proof of guilt" was "evident" or the "presumption" of guilt was "great."

The California Constitution, copying the Eighth Amendment of the federal Bill of Rights, forbade "excessive bail." Between 1880 and 1910, three-fourths of the defendants in our sample had their bail fixed at between $1,000 and $2,000. Some defendants had lower bail, some higher (see Table 5.6). Clara Windeberg was charged with assault with a deadly weapon; her bail was set at $500 (no. 2407, 1900). At another extreme was Anna Mantel, in a murder case, released on $20,000 bail in the winter of 1898–99.[41] The judge usually refused bail in capital cases; this was one of the exceptions. Another was Fred Jurgewitz, charged with murdering Claude F. Smith, one of his employees. He was released on $10,000 bail.[42] Jack London, the author, was one of his sureties. Jurgewitz was later acquitted.

41. The victim, William F. Mantel, seduced the defendant, made her pregnant, and then concocted a bogus marriage. He talked her into taking a drug that made her miscarry. He then planned to flee to the East Coast. Anna confronted him; a quarrel followed; she shot him to death on Dec. 1, 1898. She was charged with murder on Dec. 27, released on bail on Jan. 13, 1899, and acquitted at her trial on Apr. 6, 1899, after her attorney argued that she had killed in self-defense.

42. The defense lawyer, Frick, referred to a "conference with the district attorney" about bail. Ezra DeCoto, the deputy district attorney, said that he "would have no objection to the admission of this man to bail in the sum of $10,000." Frick reminded

Table 5.6. Amount of Bail Set at Bindover, 1880–1910

	1880–89	1890–99	1900–1910	1880–1910
Mean amount ($)	1,800	1,770	2,118	1,947
Median amount ($)	1,047	1,488	1,992	1,982
Modal amount ($)	1,000	1,000	2,000	2,000
Range ($)	100–25,000	200–15,000	100–18,000	100–25,000
N	141	169	297	607

Source: Sample of Superior Court casefiles, 1880–1910.

Courts have broad latitude in setting bail. Bail was not, in theory, a way of keeping dangerous people behind bars; it was only a way of making sure that they showed up for trail.[43] In the real world, however, bail *was* used to guarantee detention. Isabella Martin's crime— dynamiting the home of a Superior Court judge—shocked the community, or at least the judges. Her crime was not a capital offense. Under law, Isabella had an absolute right to bail. But the court set bail at $50,000—an astronomical sum in its day. This made sure that she stayed in jail.

The right to bail in felony cases was one thing, raising the money another. Most defendants, apparently, could not come up with the cash. Table 5.7 shows the percentages of defendants in our sample who made bail. One overall fact is clear: most defendants could not scrape up the money. A. W. Brodt was hauled before a magistrate for arraignment on January 21, 1909. The charge: committing a "lewd" act with Rosie Peterson. The judge set January 25, 1909, for preliminary examination and fixed bail at $2,000. Brodt wanted out; he pleaded his "advanced age and infirmity," and sixteen years of diabetes: "I have been unable to eat anything for the past few days, and I would ask permission of the Court that I obtain my release on my own recognizance." But the judge was unyielding: "You can phone

---

the judge (Smith, the Oakland justice of the peace) that under the statute "the defendant may be admitted to bail where the presumption is not great or the evidence strong enough to sustain a conviction of a capital offense." The judge said: "That is true, but yesterday I took the matter up with the district attorney myself, and I told him in my judgment, the People had made out a case against this defendant which would never warrant a conviction of murder in the second degree, or to sustain a conviction of manslaughter, and upon his recommendation, it is ordered that the defendant be admitted to bail in the sum of $10,000, and he stands committed to the custody of the Sheriff of the County of Alameda, until he gives such bail."

43. Bail was to be "sufficient" to guarantee "the appearance of the defendant" (§ 1269).

Table 5.7. *Percentages of Defendants Released on Bail, 1880–1910*

	1880–89	1890–99	1900–1910	1880–1910
Bail made	22.8	17.1	15.2	16.3
Bail not made	73.8	79.5	81.6	80.4
Bail not allowed	3.4	3.4	3.2	3.3
N	145	176	308	629

Source: Sample of Superior Court casefiles, 1880–1910.

from the County Jail for friends to file a bond."[44] David Mitchell—a lawyer—went on trial in 1906 for assaulting "pretty 14 year old Evelyn Walker," at his law office in Oakland. The police judge fixed bail at $10,000. Mitchell simply could not raise the money, either alone or with bondsmen. He had to sit in county jail.[45]

WHEN WAS BAIL GRANTED?

Although the committing judge set bail when binding defendants over to Superior Court, bail could also be fixed at other stages in the process. Bail could be set when an arrest warrant was issued. William A. Cox was arrested on August 16, 1909, on an assault charge. Two days before, the judge had issued a warrant for his arrest, and set bail at $2,000. Cox spent a day in jail, but then he found bondsmen: Ada Graber, a housewife, and Alfred C. Rulofsen, a manufacturer, both of Berkeley.[46]

Similarly, when a person was indicted by grand jury, he was usually taken in on a bench warrant; he might make bail when brought in to the judge (§ 1284). Bail was usually set when the indictment was filed; the defendant also usually came before the same judge who received the indictment.

A defendant out on bail *before* information or indictment did not

44. Brodt did get a lawyer, H. W. Brunk, in time for the court date, but he could not scrape up bail until Mar. 25, 1909, five weeks later.
45. *Berkeley Reporter*, Feb. 16, 1906, p. 4, col. 4.
46. Any magistrate with power to "issue the writ of habeas corpus" could admit a person to bail (§ 1277). This meant either the committing justice of the peace or police judge, or any judge of the Superior Court (prior to 1880, any judge of the County or District Court). Once in a while, a defendant, out on bond before his preliminary examination, had to file a new bond when held to answer. John Gray, for example, was arrested on Mar. 20, 1909, charged with assault to commit murder, and released on $5,000 bond on Apr. 19, 1909. When he was held to answer in Superior Court, on May 11, 1909, he posted a new $5,000 bond.

automatically keep his freedom during the rest of the process. Superior Court judges, by law, had the right to raise the amount of bail (§§ 985, 1310). This happened to Lester C. McNulty, accused of assault with intent to rape, in one of the most sensational cases of our period. McNulty filed a $2,000 bail bond when he was held to answer on December 4, 1905. His sureties were John W. Havens, a "capitalist," and George Schmidt, a postmaster, both of Berkeley. The information was filed in Superior Court on December 7, 1905. The judge increased McNulty's bail to $6,000. His parents, who were wealthy, stepped in as sureties the following day.

Overall, in twenty of a group of sixty-five bail bonds found in an old drawer, covering the years 1898–1910, the defendant made bail *after* an information was filed. On the average, it took the defendant two or three weeks to make bail. By contrast, indicted defendants who made bail at all usually made it on the day of indictment.

"Upon good cause shown," the court could raise or lower bail (§ 1289, added in 1874). There were occasional examples: bail for William Perrin, charged with grand larceny in 1906, rose from $2,000 to $3,000 one week before trial (no. 4078); for J. H. Russell, awaiting trial in December 1906, bail was cut in half, from $2,000 to $1,000 (no. 4199).

SURETIES

To "make bail," a defendant had to file a bail bond, with two "sufficient sureties" to back him up (§ 1278). Each surety had to be a "resident, householder, or freeholder within the state," whose assets were worth at least the amount of bail he was responsible for (§§ 1278–79). Bail bonds listed the addresses and occupations of sureties; an affidavit—a paragraph attached to the end of the bond—recited that they met the demands of the statute. Sureties signed their bonds before the county clerk, or before a notary public.[47]

With one dubious exception, every surety we found was a private person; no bail bond companies, apparently, did business in the county. Sureties were usually relatives or friends. In about one-quarter of the bonds in the bail bond drawer at least one surety had the same last name as the defendant. Some names appeared on bail bonds with suspicious frequency. F. S. Osgood and H. L. Osgood, who listed themselves as Oakland merchants or as Oakland druggists, appeared in many of the papers found in the drawer of old

47. Under § 1279, the court could refuse to accept someone who came from outside the county. We found, however, many such sureties. Their signatures were usually endorsed by a magistrate of their county; *his* endorsement was certified by the county clerk of that county.

bail bonds. Sometimes an Osgood was paired with someone else—possibly a relative of the defendant. Mostly the Osgoods appeared together. Clearly, they were in the bail bond business.

About nine-tenths of the bonds had two sureties; the rest had three or four.[48] A defendant needed extra sureties if he could not find two people rich enough to cover the bond twice over. J. Holliday, a burglary defendant with bail set at $2,000, needed four men—Thomas O'Donnell, D. Morrissey, Thomas A. Deasy, and J. Cohen—to cover his needs in 1902. O'Donnell assumed liability for a full $2,000; Morrissey, a railroad employee, went in for $250 and Cohen, a contract glazier, for $750; Deasy took up the last $1,000.

If a defendant on bail failed to show up in court at any time when he was ordered to do so, his bail was forfeited. The sureties might still avoid disaster, if they could come up with a good excuse for the defendant's absence. On May 10, 1880, John Bird's case was called. No John Bird appeared. The district attorney moved to have the bail bonds forfeited. The judge obliged, and issued a bench warrant. Then Bird's attorney, John Glascock, appeared, with an excuse; he was unaware the case had been called up. He promised to send for his client. The judge agreed to vacate his order, provided that Bird showed up.[49]

Of course, some defendants *did* skip bail: Ingram Chapman, charged with embezzlement and out on $1,500 bond, disappeared in the middle of his trial in 1910. Bail was forfeited, and a bench warrant issued for his arrest. Four years later, the case was dropped from the calendar; Chapman had never been found. Alfred Fassio, on trial for grand larceny, failed to appear on the third day of his trial in 1910; $2,000 bond was forfeited. A robbery defendant, in 1906, skipped out after one of his "confederates" got a long stretch in prison. A bond of $2,000 was lost.[50]

BAIL AND DISPOSITIONS

Some defendants went free on bail; others sat in jail. Did the bailed group do better in court? Apparently they did, according to our data. Table 5.8 gives the information. Defendants out on bail were much more likely to be acquitted or to have their charges dismissed than defendants who failed to make bail. Less than one-third of all defendants out on bail were convicted; nearly three-fourths of all other

48. Provision for more than two sureties is expressly recognized by the code, § 1279(2).
49. *Oakland Tribune*, May 10, 1880, p. 3, col. 3.
50. *Berkeley Reporter*, Feb. 20, 1906, p. 4, col. 3.

Table 5.8. Disposition of Felony Charges against Defendants Making and Not Making Bail, 1880–1910

Disposition	Defendants not making bail		Defendants making bail	
	No.	%	No.	%
Pleaded guilty	253	47	13	12
Convicted at trial	138	25	17	16
Acquitted at trial	74	14	32	30
Charges dismissed	75	14	39	36
Escaped/jumped bail	1	—	6	6
N	541		107	

Source: Sample of Superior Court casefiles & Registers of Actions, 1880–1910.

defendants were. Defendants released on bail were also more likely to escape; 6 percent of these defendants, in our sample, jumped bail.

There may be several reasons why defendants who made bail did so well. First, defendants who make bail probably have more money and better contacts than those who do not. They can afford private lawyers, and may mount a better defense. They were substantially more likely to have counsel at preliminary exam. Second, defendants find it easier to prepare their defense when out on bail than when sitting in a jail cell. They can better afford to maneuver and delay. Defendants free on bail even *look* better. They come into court with their lawyers, as free men; the others are brought in, handcuffed, by a sheriff's deputy. Other explanations are also possible. Lower bail may be set when a judge thinks the state's case is weak. Perhaps defendants out on bail were actually innocent more often than the others. At least they were better able to persuade a jury that they were.

The Filing of Charges: Indictments and Informations

As we said before, for most of our period there were two routes to felony court—indictment or information. Before the creation of Superior Court in 1880, indictment was the only way. People arrested for felonies before an indictment was returned were brought before a police judge or township justice for a preliminary examination. If the defendant was held to answer on felony charges at the preliminary examination, he could be detained (or released on bail) until his case was presented to the grand jury at its next sitting. If the grand jury failed to return an indictment, the defendant had to be released from custody (§ 1382).

The grand jury met only quarterly, usually for a week at a sitting. Hence, defendants might wait as much as three months before learning whether they would be indicted or not. It was by no means an open-and-shut matter. When the grand jury convened on Monday, January 3, 1876, there were fourteen prisoners "in the dock," waiting for their cases to go to the grand jury.[51] The grand jury returned its indictments the following Saturday. "True bills" (indictments) were returned against ten of the prisoners; four others went free when the grand jury "ignored" their bills.[52] The grand jury that convened in April 1877 returned twenty true bills, while ignoring six.[53]

Beginning in 1880, felony charges could be brought either by indictment or by information. As before, a grand jury could indict (with or without a preliminary exam). An information could be filed only after a preliminary exam, at which the judge bound over on felony charges. Within ten days after the defendant was bound over, a transcript of the preliminary exam was transmitted to the Superior Court (§ 869). Informations had to be filed by the district attorney within thirty days after the bindover (§ 1382).

Table 5.9 shows the source of felony prosecutions in our Superior Court sample. As the table indicates, information rapidly replaced indictment. During the 1880s, only one-ninth of the prosecutions in our sample were begun by indictments, and the percentage dropped to less than 3 in the 1900–1910 decade.[54]

51. *Oakland Tribune*, Jan. 3, 1876, p. 3, col. 4.
52. Ibid., Jan. 8, 1876, p. 3, col. 3.
53. Ibid., Apr. 7, 1877, p. 3, col. 3. A grand jury's decision to ignore a bill presented to it usually terminated the felony process. However, it did not always foreclose a subsequent prosecution for the same offense. In 1871, for example, the Alameda County grand jury at its April term declined to return an indictment against Frederick Clarke, a wealthy farmer who had been held to answer on a charge of murder for killing a squatter. The public was outraged, and the district attorney applied to the County Court for permission to resubmit the case to the next term of the grand jury. Permission was granted and, after two lengthy appellate challenges to the resubmission order, the case was presented once again, to the July 1874 term of the grand jury. The grand jury again refused to indict Clarke. In 1880 another effort was made to prosecute Clarke under the new procedures attendant on the creation of the Superior Court. After another lengthy appeal, it was determined that double jeopardy would not bar further prosecution of Clarke. Clarke, however, eventually won a dismissal of the charges against him in the Superior Court.
54. Prosecutions also could be commenced by "accusation," a rarely used procedure for charging misconduct by a public official and seeking his removal from office. Our sample uncovered only two cases in which the device was used.

Table 5.9. Sources of Felony Prosecutions in Superior Court, 1880–1910

Source of prosecutions	1880–89		1890–99	
	%	Est. no.	%	Est. no.
Grand jury indictment	11.1	81	4.3	35
Information after bindover by:				
Oakland Police Court	59.3	431	55.1	444
Oakland Township Court	4.9	36	8.6	69
Berkeley City Court	2.5	18	3.2	26
Emeryville Recorder	—	—	1.1	9
Brooklyn Township Court	1.2	9	1.1	39
Alameda Township Court	6.2	45	7.0	56
Alameda City Court	1.9	13	0.5	4
Eden Township Court	2.5	18	2.7	22
Washington Township	5.6	40	6.4	52
Murray Township Court	4.3	31	5.9	47
Pleasanton Township*	—	—	—	—
Accusation	0.6	4	0.5	4
Total prosecutions		728		807
N		162		187

Source: Sample of Superior Court casefiles, 1880–1910.

* Formed from Murray in 1902.

On the average, charges were filed in Superior Court about three weeks after bindover in the lower court; nearly all charges (97 percent) were filed within thirty days after the conclusion of the preliminary exam.[55] Although the information device was considered more efficient than indictment,[56] some defendants thought it impaired their rights. It took away the requirement that citizens, sitting on the grand jury, had to concur in the decision to file formal felony charges. It substituted a preliminary hearing, a proceeding that often served the prosecution's ends more than it served the defendants'. Information was never successfully challenged, however, and it survived and thrived.[57]

55. The average time between bindover and the filing of charges in the Superior Court for the cases in our sample was twenty days; the median was eighteen days. Approximately 97 percent of the charges were filed within thirty days of bindover.

56. See, e.g., R. Justin Miller, "Informations or Indictment in Criminal Cases," *Minn. L. Rev.* 8 (1924): 379; Raymond Moley, "The Initiation of Criminal Prosecutions by Indictment or Information," *Mich. L. Rev.* 29 (1931): 403.

57. In Hurtado v. California, 110 U.S. 516 (1884), the U.S. Supreme Court held that the Due Process Clause of the Fourteenth Amendment did not require the states to

1900–1910		1880–1910	
%	Est. no.	%	Est. no.
2.6	33	5.3	149
56.0	844	61.1	1719
3.5	45	5.3	150
6.4	82	4.5	126
0.6	8	0.6	17
4.5	57	3.8	107
2.2	29	4.6	130
3.5	45	2.2	62
2.6	33	2.6	73
2.6	33	4.4	125
3.8	49	4.5	127
1.6	20	0.7	20
—	—	0.3	8
	1,279		2,814
312		661	

Once a defendant was bound over at a preliminary examination, felony charges were filed in Superior Court as a matter of course, even if the district attorney was not enthusiastic about the strength of the case. In January 1910, for example, District Attorney Donahue filed an information charging three Chinese defendants with robbery; the crime allegedly took place during a "war" between rival Chinese tongs. Two months later the district attorney moved to dismiss the information, expressing doubt that the robbery had taken place at all. He thought that the prosecution's witnesses had committed perjury at the preliminary exam. A private attorney hired by a rival tong had

grant defendants the right to indictment by a grand jury. Now that defendants have the right to appointed counsel at preliminary examination, grand jury indictments have become more popular with prosecutors, who want to avoid premature disclosure of their cases to the defense. Comment, "The California Grand Jury—Two Current Problems," *Calif. L. Rev.* 52 (1964): 116, 118. Because the preliminary hearing has become an important tool for discovery by the defense, the California Supreme Court has recently held that defendants indicted by a grand jury have a right to a postindictment preliminary examination. Hawkins v. Superior Court, 150 Cal. Rptr. 435, 586 P. 2d 916 (1978).

conducted the prosecution's case at the hearing. The defendants were bound over, despite the district attorney's objections. "It is simply a case of one Chinese tong using the courts to fight another tong," he said, "and if these three cases go to trial it will be the cause of the expenditure of at least another $1,000.00 and there is no doubt that they would be acquitted" (no. 4720, 1910). Despite this, the motion to dismiss was denied, and the case went forward. As Donahue predicted, the defendants were acquitted.

The district attorney did have some discretion. He could decide the number of counts to lay at the defendant's door, and whether to charge the defendant with prior convictions. Overall one-eighth of the defendants in our sample were charged with more than one count; 9 percent were accused of "priors" in the charging papers. The district attorney could also decide to prosecute defendants jointly or severally. Less than 9 percent of the prosecutions in our sample involved multiple defendants.

Proceedings in Superior Court

ARRAIGNMENT IN THE SUPERIOR COURT

A defendant's first appearance in Superior Court was his arraignment. This typically occurred about a week after the indictment or information was filed.[58] At arraignment, the defendant was told the nature of the charges against him and of his right to counsel (§ 987). At this stage, if a defendant could not pay, the court would appoint an attorney.

COUNSEL IN SUPERIOR COURT

There was no system of public defenders in Alameda County before 1927. All defense lawyers in our period were lawyers in private practice. As we said, a poor defendant did not have to pay; in California, from 1872 on, he had a right to (free) counsel at a felony trial. (Many states provided no such service.) According to our figures, the great majority of felony defendants (about 85 percent) *did* have a lawyer's help, of one sort or another, in Superior Court (see Table 5.10).

If the defendant had a lawyer at some earlier stage of the process,

58. The average length of time between the filing of felony charges in the Superior Court and arraignment was 10 days for the cases in our sample; the median was 5.6 days. Nearly three-fourths of all defendants were arraigned within 1 week of the filing of charges; more than 90 percent were arraigned within 3 weeks of being charged.

Table 5.10. Legal Representation of Felony Defendants in Superior Court, 1880–1910

	1880–89	*1890–99*	*1900–1910*	*1880–1910*
Attorney waived	11	15	17	15
Represented by attorney	89	85	83	85
N	166	171	286	623

Source: Samples of Superior Court casefiles, 1880–1910.

he usually stayed with his lawyer through trial.[59] The others had three choices: they could hire their own lawyer, ask the court to appoint one, or waive the right to counsel. Those who waived counsel generally pleaded guilty. A few carried on their own defense.

We cannot always tell from the records whether counsel was hired or appointed. We do know that about one-quarter of the defendants in our sample *definitely* had appointed counsel. The practice was for the judge to ask the defendant at arraignment if he wanted a lawyer. If the defendant said yes, and had no money, the court appointed one.

Most of these were young lawyers waiting for Mr. Right Case; some were hangers-on in the courtroom, looking for crumbs of business.[60] Any criminal lawyer was willing to take on the really big cases, if only for the publicity. A person accused of murder had a peck of troubles, but finding a lawyer was not one of them. Criminal lawyers were not like business lawyers, with a regular clientele; their work was by and large a series of one-shot cases. Business lawyers were like farmers, raising the same crop of barley and wheat, year after year. Criminal lawyers were hunters and gatherers. To drum up trade, the criminal lawyer wanted publicity; he needed a jailhouse or newspaper reputation. He liked to see his name in print; the business

59. A few defendants changed lawyers in the Superior Court: e.g., James Gilligan (no. 2220, 1899).

60. A study, commissioned by the Department of Labor, noted that under the assigned counsel system,

> The lawyers selected are apt to be of two sorts, either young and inexperienced men who wish to gain experience at the expense of the client, or older men who are present in the court room expressly for the purpose of receiving these appointments. Neither group represents the best element at the bar and neither is able to afford the accused a first-class defense. The more able lawyers, whether in civil or criminal practice, are too busy to spare the time in such comparatively unremunerative work, and the courts rather hesitate to select the better lawyers because it seems like an imposition.

R. H. Smith and J. S. Bradway, *Growth of Legal Aid Work in the United States* (Washington, D.C., 1926), p. 48. We have every reason to believe that the situation was very much the same during our period.

lawyer, on the other hand, was content to be gray and anonymous, to blend into the background.

We know very little about *how* lawyers were selected in routine cases. In the files of a robbery case (1880), there is a tantalizing note. "H. M. Van Arman, Esq. was appointed attorney for three men accused of robbery. J. Mc H. Moore having been thrice called at the door by the sheriff and no answer" (Charles Cropper et al., no. 142). One wonders why Van Arman was so handy at the courtroom; and why Moore was expected "at the door." Some cases went, perhaps by default, to court commissioners. Fred Whitney, a commissioner, handled over 3 percent of the felony cases in the 1880s. Most of these were burglars who pleaded guilty.

Appointed attorneys, alas, received no fees. In theory, it was a lawyer's duty to help out the indigent.[61] Counsel was not even entitled to recoup his expenses. This cramped the style of defense lawyers, to say the least. Howard K. James represented Charles F. Hunt, accused of murder (1902). James asked the court for delay, to give Hunt a chance to raise some money. James was "content," he said, to "devote his every effort" for Hunt "without expectation or hope of remuneration." But he needed evidence from witnesses scattered about the country, and that cost money. Hunt was penniless; but his parents in St. Louis *might* send some cash. The judge postponed the case (no. 2608).

The percentage of defendants who waived the right to counsel in Superior Court was small, but it rose somewhat between 1880 and 1910. The reasons are a bit murky. Guilty pleas rose at the same time, and probation entered the system in 1903. These factors are probably connected, as we will see. Nearly all defendants who waived counsel pleaded guilty, perhaps out of shame or hopelessness, or perhaps just to get matters over with. Arthur F. Gunn, age twenty-one, was arrested in 1910 on a charge of burglary. He had a lawyer in justice court; but the magistrate bound him over to trial in Superior Court. Gunn needed more money, and wrote to his father in Portland, Oregon. His father turned him down cold. The letter, incidentally, sheds some light on the costs of a basic defense: "How in the world could you do such a foolish and wrong thing? Have you taken to drinking? or what Evil Impulse seized you—a Lawyer named Grijalva has written asking for $150 to defend you—If you are Guilty, I don't see what he could hope to do. If you are not—I judge you will be able to prove it—Just at present boy I cannot raise any money. . . . God help you."

61. Rowe v. Yuba County, 17 Cal. 62 (1860).

When this letter arrived, Gunn gave up and pleaded guilty. He got eighteen months in San Quentin (no. 4763).

In a few rare cases, the defendant waived counsel, not to plead guilty, but to fight the case himself. Charles Robinson, an attorney, was accused of pocketing $77.33 that belonged to a client. He won his own case (no. 780, 1887). James Bowen (no. 4241, 1907) was not a lawyer; he lost his case. A man who defends himself, the saying goes, has a fool for his client. This was probably true in our period, too, but our cases are too few for firm inference.

CASE DISPOSITION PATTERNS

Table 5.11 shows some basic facts about the fate of cases in Superior Court. During our period, about 40 percent of the defendants ended their cases by pleading guilty. (About a third of these began by pleading not guilty, but then later changed their pleas.) About one-sixth of the cases were dismissed. A few others were never pursued to a formal conclusion: they reached the limbo of "indefinite continuance" either because the defendant fled or because he was committed to a mental or juvenile institution. The rest, roughly 40 percent, actually went to trial. "Trial" in our period meant trial by jury; there was basically no such thing as a bench trial.[62] Still, the jury decided less than half the felony cases that began in Superior Court. And most "convictions" were the result of guilty pleas, not trials. Even so, trial by jury made a much better showing than in the 1970s, when only a tiny percentage of cases went to the jury. One study of Connecticut, covering 1972–73, for example, found that guilty pleas accounted for

Table 5.11. Disposition of Cases in Superior Court, 1880–1910

Disposition	1880–89	1890–99	1900–1910	1880–1910
Initial guilty plea	22	23	33	27
Not guilty plea changed to guilty plea	16	12	14	14
Dismissed by court	15	16	16	16
Indefinite continuance	2	9	3	5
Convicted by jury	26	21	23	23
Acquitted by jury	19	20	12	16
N	180	200	316	696

Source: Sample of Superior Court casefiles and Registers of Actions, 1880–1910.

62. In November 1928, Art. 1, § 7 of the California Constitution was amended to permit the defendant to waive a jury in all felony cases tried in Superior Court.

more than 70 percent of some 3,000 dispositions in Superior Court (the court that handles the cases of serious crime). Trials accounted for less than 4 percent of the total.[63] In California in 1977, out of 28,608 convictions in Superior Court, only 2,798—under 10 percent— were the result of jury trials. About 3 percent came from bench trials, and virtually all the rest from guilty pleas. (A mere 920 were acquitted, out of 33,146 *total* dispositions.) In Alameda County, 1978, about 4 percent of the cases were decided by juries.[64]

ENTERING THE PLEA

More than two-thirds of the defendants in our sample entered their initial pleas at the time of arraignment. Most of the rest entered their pleas within a week of arraignment.[65] As Table 5.12 demonstrates, most defendants pleaded not guilty; but the percentage of not guilty pleas declined over time. During the 1880s more than three-fourths of defendants who pleaded initially pleaded not guilty; from 1900 to 1910 less than two-thirds pleaded not guilty at the start. Overall, more than a quarter of all defendants pleaded guilty at the outset. Most of these pleas were entered by defendants who waived counsel in Superior Court.

Table 5.12. *Initial Pleas in Cases in Which Defendants Entered Pleas, 1880–1910*

Initial plea	1880–89	1890–99	1900–1910	1880–1910
Not guilty	78%	75%	64%	71%
Guilty as charged	12	19	32	23
Guilty of lesser offense or fewer counts	10	6	4	6
N	171	185	295	651

Source: Sample of Superior Court casefiles, 1880–1910.

63. Milton Heumann, *Plea Bargaining: The Experiences of Prosecutors, Judges and Defense Attorneys* (Chicago, 1978), p. 27. In a study of a California county, out of 965 felonies prosecuted in 1970 there were 680 guilty pleas, and only 97 trials in front of a jury; 28 defendants were acquitted, the rest convicted. Lief H. Carter, *The Limits of Order* (Lexington, Mass., 1974), 171.

64. California Bureau of Criminal Statistics, *Crime and Delinquency in California, 1977*, pt. 2, pp. 8, 9; *Alameda County Criminal Justice Profile* (1979); authors' sampling of Registers of Actions in Alameda County Clerk's Office.

65. Of the defendants in our sample who entered pleas, 69 percent did so at the time of arraignment; 92 percent had entered a plea within a week of arraignment, 97 percent within two weeks.

DISMISSALS

A handful of defendants sought to have the charges against them dismissed before entering pleas. Of the defendants in our sample, 4 percent made motions to set aside the charges they faced; 8 percent interposed demurrers challenging the legal sufficiency of the indictment or information. These motions were usually unsuccessful: only 1 percent of defendants had charges against them set aside; 2 percent had demurrers sustained. Overall, approximately 5 percent of all cases were dismissed before pleas were entered.

Dismissals were more common *after* defendants pleaded not guilty. Of all cases 8 percent were dismissed between the pleading stage and trial; 2 percent were dismissed after trial, usually following hung juries. Why were these cases abandoned?[66] Sometimes this happened because of plea bargaining, as we shall see. Sometimes the prosecutor realized that his case was thin, or that defendant was innocent; he then threw in the towel. William Cull was accused of stealing some sacks of barley. Cull convinced the district attorney that the barley belonged legally to him, and the case was dismissed (no. 804, 1887). Sometimes a key witness failed to appear, and the case blew up in the prosecutor's face. Joseph Sorrel (1883) was charged with assault with intent to rape. The victim, Ada Hall, disappeared, and that was the end of the case (no. 360). Once in a while, charges were dropped for technical reasons. The information against Victorio Garcia recited that the crime (theft of a horse) took place on June 1, 1885. This was a slip of the pen; the true date was 1884. The information was dismissed (but the prosecutor could amend and try again) (no. 593). Of course, magistrates screened out dozens of cases; these never reached Superior Court. Others were detoured for one reason or another. Lars Nelson, a thirty-year-old Scandinavian, attacked a policeman with an "ugly pocketknife" in May 1906. He was booked for attempted murder; but doctors, who examined him, decided that he was suffering from "extreme melancholia." Judge Waste sent him to Ukiah Asylum, and he never stood trial.[67]

PLEA BARGAINING

Plea bargaining is a pervasive system today, in many parts of the United States. The defendant "cops a plea"—makes a deal, promising to plead guilty, in exchange for some break. Often, as part of the

66. Sometimes, although the record and file do not clearly show the dismissal, the case was in fact never prosecuted. But this was not the usual practice.

67. *Berkeley Reporter*, May 22, 1906, p. 2, col. 6, May 25, 1906, p. 5, col. 6.

bargain, he pleads guilty to a lesser charge. Sometimes what he gets in return is a lighter sentence, or probation. Sometimes some of the charges are dropped.[68]

Plea bargaining was a bone of contention in the 1970s, attacked from left and right. Many of its critics felt that it was a sign of great decay in criminal justice, something both awful and new. Awful it may be, but hardly new. True, plea bargaining was less common in 1880–1910 than it is today, by a country mile. But it was real, and far from rare. It is not always easy, of course, to show plea bargaining at work. Deals were made outside the formal record. Our figures no doubt understate it. But about 14 percent of the defendants in our sample changed their pleas from not guilty to guilty. Some half of *these* pleaded guilty "on the nose," that is, guilty as charged: Emma Delacey, in 1895 (no. 1728), took back a plea of not guilty, pleaded guilty to the charges of petty larceny and three prior offenses, and got eighteen months in San Quentin. But other defendants changed from not guilty to guilty of some lesser charge, or fewer charges. This is almost unmistakably the sign of a bargain. These bargains, conservatively, account for something on the order of 8 percent of all pleas; and no doubt the true figure was higher. Plea bargaining was also present in other Bay Area counties.[69]

Examples can be found as early as 1880, the first year of our felony sample. Here, for instance, is the case of Albert McKenzie, charged with embezzlement (no. 51). Albert was agent for Willcox and Gibbs,

68. Nowadays, it is common practice in Alameda County to charge a defendant with a whole barrage of "counts"; then, as part of the bargain, the prosecution drops all but one or two. This was not the practice in our period. Only 12 percent of defendants were charged with more than one count; 4 percent of defendants were booked for more than one crime, each with its own separate file number, which amounts to much the same thing. Here, as part of a bargain, the defendant might plead guilty in one of the "cases"; the district attorney would move to dismiss the rest. In 1881, for example, a Chinese defendant was charged with burglary, grand larceny, and assault with intent to commit murder, all out of one incident. These were three separates cases (nos. 291, 292, 293). He pleaded not guilty to all three, initially. Then he recanted on the assault charge. The other two were dropped.

There is a huge literature on plea bargaining today, including Heumann, *Plea Bargaining*; John F. Klein, *Let's Make a Deal: Negotiating Justice* (Lexington, Mass., 1976) (plea bargaining in Canada); Pamela J. Utz, *Settling the Facts: Discretion and Negotiation in Criminal Court* (Lexington, Mass., 1978). Vol. 13, no. 2, of the *Law & Soc. Rev.* (1979) is entirely devoted to plea bargaining. The issue also includes some historical material on the subject. Some of the information in this section is discussed, in a bit more detail, in Lawrence M. Friedman, "Plea Bargaining in Historical Perspective," in this special issue, p. 247.

69. In San Francisco, in 1908, plea bargaining was found in something on the order of 10 percent of the cases, and this too is probably a very conservative estimate. John Broadhurst, "An Analysis of the Criminal Justice System in San Francisco County in 1908" (unpublished term paper, Stanford Law School, 1978).

a sewing machine concern. According to the charge, he collected $52.50, in gold coin, and kept the money. On December 15, 1880, he pleaded not guilty in Superior Court. The judge set the trial for February 6, 1881. On that day, McKenzie, his lawyer, and the district attorney appeared in court. Albert withdrew his plea, and pleaded guilty to embezzling an amount less than $50. This was a misdemeanor, with a much lighter penalty than the felony charge.[70] The court, "with the consent of the District Attorney," accepted the new plea, and sentenced Albert to six months in jail—a light sentence, considering. Notice that the defendant was convicted of a crime he probably did not commit: he either stole *more* than $50, or he stole nothing. But the illogic did not seem to bother anyone. Judges were perfectly willing to accept pleas that, under the facts, were absurd. In one case, in 1888, three men were accused of breaking into a railway car belonging to the Southern Pacific. E. H. Howard was tried and convicted of first-degree burglary (burglary at night). John Feno took a wiser course and pleaded guilty—to second-degree burglary (burglary by day). This meant that this one burglary took place both by day and by night. No one seemed to mind the impossibility.[71]

The judges, of course, knew all about plea bargaining; they apparently approved. After all, they had to accept any changes of plea. It was very, very rare for a judge to refuse. It did happen to a certain Ah Young in 1887. He stood accused of petty larceny, but with a prior offense, which made it a felony. He offered to plead guilty to his current charge, if the court would forget the prior. But the judge refused to deal, and Ah Young pleaded guilty as charged (no. 756). Judges also seemed anxious, at times, to keep up appearances. A defendant in 1910, William Carlin, faced two charges: rape and abduction (putting a woman under eighteen into a house of prostitution) (nos. 4766, 4767). He pleaded guilty to the second charge. The judge, Everett Brown, lectured him sternly about morality, and complained that the law was too lenient (five years in prison was the most he could give). A girl who "becomes a common prostitute . . . is far worse than dead"; hence this was "one of the most awful crimes, I believe, a human being can commit." Still, William had pleaded guilty, which showed a "certain amount of penitence." Therefore, said the judge, "you deserve a certain amount of credit for the fact that you

70. Under § 514, the punishment of embezzlement was the same as "for feloniously stealing property of the value of that embezzled," and $50 was the boundary between grand and petty larceny (§ 487).

71. No. 840 (1888). Feno, who pleaded guilty, got five years; Howard, who was convicted, got six. Feno's reward for his plea, in other words, was one year off the sentence. This is real enough, though a bit on the skimpy side.

did plead guilty." He promised to give "a lighter sentence." That turned out to mean four years.

Now it was time to deal with the other charge: rape. Satterwhite, deputy district attorney, moved to dismiss the charge. The defendant had "already been sentenced for the crime of abduction . . . I have had a talk with this defendant . . . and he stated to me that he would plead guilty to the charge of abduction if we would dismiss the charge of rape. In response to his promise, he came into court and pleaded guilty to the charge of abduction. I am now keeping my promise to him in dismissing this charge of rape."

Judge Brown behaved as if he were deaf. He turned to the defendant and said: "You did not believe that there was any understanding with the court that the case would be dismissed, so far as the court was concerned." This, naturally enough, confused the defendant. He said: "I pleaded guilty because I had talked to my attorney." Judge Brown went right on: "You didn't feel you were making any bargain . . . by pleading guilty, did you?" Of course, there *was* a bargain; but the lawyer quickly said, "Oh no, sir." Defendant, too, now got the point, and chimed in, "No, I would have pleaded guilty anyway." His conscience clear, Judge Brown dismissed the rape case, "on motion of the district attorney." Strange were the ways of the law.

Most of the time, as far as we can tell, the defendant's lawyer carried on the bargaining. Sometimes the prosecutor made the first move, perhaps if his case was weak. A prosecutor with a shaky case might try to induce the accused to plead guilty to *something*. This would salvage a sort of conviction. In 1902, William McCormick, a horse trainer, shot and killed a man on a ranch. The victim was Thomas Cullen, a groom. McCormick, it seems, was dead drunk, and wildly firing bullets. After he shot Cullen he fell asleep on a bed of straw in one of the stalls. The initial charge was murder. McCormick pleaded not guilty. Then the prosecutor moved to reduce the charge, to manslaughter. There was no legal "malice," he said, because "the man had shot at random, not firing at anyone in particular." The court granted the motion, "after which McCormick entered a plea of guilty to a charge of manslaughter."[72]

---

72. *Oakland Tribune*, May 15, 1902, p. 1, col. 4. But the judge gave the defendant ten years, the maximum sentence for manslaughter.

In a case from another Bay county (San Mateo) in 1886, Frank Williams and George Brown were charged with robbery. They waived counsel, and pleaded not guilty to the charge. They then "acknowledged" in open court that they *were* guilty of an assault on Ah Louis, the victim, and wanted to plead guilty. The district attorney did not object to this change of plea; he had his own admission to make: the only evidence he had, on the robbery charge, was the "uncorroborated" word of the complaining witness; "a conviction would be 'doubtful.'" No. 711, San Mateo County Superior Court (1886).

IMPLICIT BARGAINING

Guilty pleas were often the result of obvious, open bargaining. But many more defendants—hundreds and hundreds, in fact—pleaded guilty, with no *overt* evidence of bargaining. The guilty plea was an everyday affair in Superior Court. It became more and more common over the years. By the end of our period, as we see from Table 5.12, more than a *third* of all first pleas were guilty pleas. Even more remarkable is the rise in the number of people who pleaded guilty as charged. Only 12 percent did this in 1880–89; this figure rose to 19 percent in 1890–99, and 32 percent in 1900–1910 (Table 5.12). It would go even higher in the 1920s and 1930s.

The guilty plea is a striking feature of American law. (It shares this trait, to be sure, with other common-law countries. In some legal systems, there is no guilty plea, at least in theory; the prosecution must *always* prove its case.) The tendency toward more and more guilty pleas was nationwide; it was by no means confined to California.[73] A plea of guilty, of course, abandons all hope of acquittal, all hope of total exoneration. Why, then, do so many plead guilty?

No one can read minds; but clearly, some defendants pleaded guilty from shame and remorse. They were sorry for what they had done; they wanted to be punished. Charles Wilson, charged with sodomy in 1906, was one of these. He did not lift a finger in his own behalf. He was overwhelmed with guilt and regret. At the preliminary hearing, he begged the judge not to "humiliate" the "little boy" who testified against him; and he cried out, "Punish me . . . I am guilty" (no. 4218). Others, too, no doubt pleaded guilty because of hopelessness, or to avoid the stigma of trial, or to get the damn thing over with. Two "disreputable tramps," L. W. Oliphant and George Riley, broke into a station and rifled a valise; they admitted their guilt, and said they wanted to go to San Quentin "as speedily as possible."[74] A few defendants pleaded guilty out of some ulterior motive. This was hinted at in the case of Fred Lee. Lee, in 1908, supposedly stole diamonds from Katherine Grasso. (They were hidden in her mattress.) Lee told the judge he was guilty and wanted to spare the county the

---

We are indebted to Michael Rosiello, J.D. 1976, Stanford Law School, for this example, drawn from a term paper, "Plea Bargaining in San Mateo County, 1881–1920," June 1976.

73. See the material on trends in New York in Raymond Moley, *Politics and Criminal Prosecution* (New York, 1929), pp. 163–65. Out of a sample of 100 felony cases in Placer County, Calif., 1880–1910, no less than 55 were disposed of through a plea of guilty. Placer County is in the gold country. (Information on this county comes from Mark Chavez.)

74. *Oakland Tribune*, Aug. 28, 1883, p. 3, col. 2.

expense of a trial. But the court was suspicious of his "haste"; perhaps he wanted "to get the case settled before a prior conviction is dug up and the penalty is increased accordingly."[75] Other defendants pleaded guilty in return for the withdrawal of "priors." Overall, about one-ninth of the defendants in our sample who were charged with repeat offenses succeeded in getting the "priors" dismissed; this came to about 1 percent of the cases in Superior Court.

But all of this still leaves a huge residue of pleas unaccounted for. People *wanted* to plead guilty. They must have gotten something out of it, but what? Surely what they got—or expected to get—was lighter treatment. Milton Heumann has called this system "implicit" bargaining.[76] Defendants feel, in other words, that they will be better off if they plead guilty than if they go to trial and lose. Many plead guilty to avoid the risk of heavy sentence. Prosecutors and judges also understand that there is a price attached to a plea of not guilty. Hence a defendant strikes a bargain, in a way, when he pleads guilty, even though not a word about bargains is spoken.[77]

Beyond a doubt, defendants did believe that it paid to plead guilty. From the case records, it is hard to sift out one kind of bargaining from another. The district attorney, for example, might promise to put in a word for probation, provided that the defendant pleaded guilty. This is plea bargaining, but the documents will be ambiguous. Explicit plea bargaining can be safely assumed only when the defendant changed his plea to guilty of some lesser offense.[78] We probably *understate*, then, the amount of "real" plea bargaining, and overstate the amount of implicit. But implicit plea bargaining was certainly common.

Were defendants right? *Was* there a reward for pleading guilty? Judge Everett Brown, for one, believed in paying a price to get defendants to plead. By chance, a report about probation in Judge Brown's court survives for the years 1909–10.[79] Forty-two adults won proba-

75. *Alameda Argus*, Apr. 3, 1908, p. 5, col. 2. According to the *San Leandro Reporter*, a "hardened criminal," Albert Andrews, decided to plead guilty to keep out evidence of old convictions. *San Leandro Reporter*, Sept. 12, 1908, p. 3, col. 4.

76. Milton Heumann, "A Note on Plea Bargaining and Case Pressure," *Law & Soc. Rev.* 9 (1975): 515.

77. A survey of prisoners at Folsom in the late 1880s, for what it is worth, reported that of 330 inmates who pleaded guilty, 120 did so "in order to mitigate the penalty"; 112 pleaded guilty because they "had neither money nor friends"; 36 claimed "ignorance of the law"; 40 so pleaded "because of prior convictions"; 19 wanted "to avoid prosecution for other crimes." *Eight Annual Report, State Board of Prison Directors, 1887*, p. 88.

78. See also Arthur Train, *The Prisoner at the Bar* (New York, 1906), pp. 223–25, describing the situation in New York.

79. The three-page report, "In the Matter of Applicants for Probation and Court

tion during the year. Of these forty-two, forty-one had pleaded guilty; only one defendant who insisted, stubbornly, on trial, also talked his way to probation. Cases that went to trial *might* differ systematically from those that did not, in ways that *might* influence probation. But the figures are so one-sided that this cannot be the whole story. Clearly, a guilty plea opened the doors to probation. Word of this must have gotten around to defendants and defense. The message— "plead guilty"—rang through loud and clear.

Implicit bargaining, to be sure, was risky. No one promised anything. (In Judge Brown's court, many who pleaded guilty did *not* get probation after all.) A man's hopes might be cruelly dashed. This happened to John Brown, charged with grand larceny in 1902; he pleaded guilty, expecting a light sentence. Judge Melvin saw matters differently, and sent him to Folsom for a nine-year stretch.[80]

These were, perhaps, exceptions. There is no doubt that implicit bargaining was part of the understanding of prisoners—and of judges as well. It is hard to show this directly. But once in a while, the curtain lifts a bit. Judge Everett Brown was unusually open about "credit" for guilty pleas. In the case of Louis Schroeder (no. 4825, 1910), who pleaded guilty to grand larceny, Brown repeated this theme:

> I am going to be lenient now and give you the full benefit . . . for the plea of guilty . . . I am going to give you the credit of it. I am going to give you a great deal lighter sentence than I would have given you. You can rest assured if you had gone on the witness stand and told some perjured tale about this affair, you would have received a heavier sentence. It is true you pleaded guilty after the case of the People had been closed, but you didn't go upon the witness stand and commit perjury. You are entitled to . . . credit . . . for having entered a plea of guilty.[81]

Action Thereon, Summaries and Statistics, Judge Brown's Probationers, 1909–1910," dated June 8, 1910, was found in a file drawer in the basement of the Alameda County Courthouse. We found no other documents of this type.

80. *Berkeley Reporter*, May 26, 1906, p. 8, col. 2. The story appeared in the paper after Brown broke jail.

81. Louis Schroeder, Proceedings upon Sentence, 5–6 (no. 4025, 1910). The defendant said: "I didn't pick this man's pocket, although I pled guilty to it. . . . I am willing to throw myself on the mercy of the court." These remarks only made Judge Brown angry. The defendant was breaking the rules of the game. "There is no more question about you having picked this man's pocket than there is about your standing there. . . . You pleaded guilty. . . . There is positive testimony here . . . you were caught red-handed. . . . The statement . . . is the statement of a foolish boy. I am not going to be prejudiced. . . . " Ibid., 9–10.

182 | *The Roots of Justice*

TRIAL BY JURY

For defendants unable or unwilling to strike a bargain, there was always trial. Overall, 43 percent of the cases in our sample went to trial: 48 percent in the 1880s, but only 40 percent between 1900 and 1910. The more serious the offense, the more likely it was that the case would go to trial. Murder cases overwhelmingly went to trial (85 percent of the murder cases in our sample went to the jury). More than half (52 percent) of the robbery cases in our sample went to trial, but less than one-third of all burglary and grand larceny charges.

By law, trials were to commence within sixty days of the filing of the indictment or information, unless the defendant wanted more time. In practice, about two-thirds of the trials began within sixty days of the filing of charges. Defendants had to be given at least two days in which to prepare for trial after entering their pleas (§ 1049). On the average, trials began less than two months after defendants entered these initial pleas. In some cases there were long delays before trial; but about half of all cases went to trial little more than a month after the pleading stage.[82]

Table 5.13 shows what happened at trial. Statistically speaking, the defendant had a fighting chance. The jury acquitted more than one-third of those whose cases went to trial (16 percent of all cases in the Superior Court). Another 54 percent were convicted, but nearly a third of these were found guilty of reduced charges. In 11 percent of the cases, the jury was unable to agree or, rarely, a mistrial was declared. Most of these cases eventually were dismissed; about a third were retried, but most of these defendants were acquitted on retrial.

Statistics cannot tell the whole story of what happened at trial.

Table 5.13. Verdict of First Trial in Cases Tried, 1880–1910

Verdict	1880–89	1890–99	1900–1910	1880–1910
Guilty as charged	36%	33%	42%	38%
Guilty of lesser offense	15	17	16	16
Not guilty	39	40	30	35
Hung jury	10	10	13	11
N	87	90	125	302

Source: Sample of Superior Court casefiles and Registers of Actions, 1880–1910.

82. The average length of time between the filing of charges in Superior Court and commencement of trial was sixty-seven days; the median was forty-four days. On the average, fifty-five days elapsed between pleading and trial; the median time between these two stages was thirty-three days.

Oddly enough, we know more about preliminary exams than about the trials themselves. Trial transcripts were not preserved anywhere near as often as transcripts of preliminary examinations. But we do have access to newspaper accounts (a very skewed sample), excerpts from appealed cases (equally skewed), and other scraps of information here and there.

It is clear that the jury had a great effect on the way a trial was carried on. American law displays contradictory attitudes toward juries. The jury has truly awesome power—power over life and death. Most modern legal systems do not give this power to amateurs, to people virtually picked up off the streets. Yet the common law, in a way, seemed to assume that juries were made up of idiots, or at best of weak-minded people easily swayed or impressed. The law of evidence reflects this paradox. American rules of evidence were and are more complicated than those in any other legal system. The law gives the jury great power with one hand, and takes some of it away with the other. This is in the form of a giant cardhouse of rules, whose point is to make sure that jurymen eat nothing but the safest, softest Pablum of evidence. Whether the rules work—whether they keep out biased or improper information—is another question. The rules could hardly hope to capture and contain the subtle, shifting give-and-take of trials. And they are impossibly complex: the rules have exceptions, and exceptions to exceptions; and these in turn have exceptions.

In California, in our period, the Penal Code laid down that the general rules of evidence in civil cases applied in criminal cases, too (§ 1102), with a few special twists. One special rule, for example, applied to perjury cases: two witnesses (or one witness and "corroborating circumstances") were required to convict. The Penal Code also contained a handful of special provisions on what was needed or not needed to prove specific crimes (§ 1106, for instance, on bigamy, stated that it was not necessary "to prove either of the marriages by the register, certificate, or other record evidence," but that the state could use "such evidence as is advisable to prove a marriage in other cases"). One section laid down the rule that no one could be convicted of a crime solely through the word of an accomplice (§ 1111). And, of course, the idea of proof "beyond a reasonable doubt" was peculiar to criminal justice.

The general shape of trial by jury was simple and familiar. First, a jury had to be selected. In big cases, this was a long, drawn-out process. In ordinary cases, it was short, almost routine. In Chapter 3, we described how the jury list was made up. The names of prospective jurors were drawn from these lists. But there was many a slip twixt the list and the jurybox. Some prospects were excused, for sickness or other reasons. Still others were *challenged*. Lawyers for both sides had the right to challenge a juror, and get him off the case. If the challenge was "for cause," there was no limit to the number. Either side could challenge for cause a juror who was prejudiced— who had a state of mind that kept him "from acting with entire impartiality" (§ 1073). Each side also had a number of *peremptory challenges*. These were challenges for which the lawyer did not need any (overt) reason. He could dismiss any juror who somehow looked or smelled wrong for the case. These challenges were a precious resource, and not to be wasted. A defendant had only ten of them, and the state only five, except in cases that carried the death penalty or life imprisonment, where each side had twice as many (§ 1070). Naturally, lawyers preferred to challenge for cause, rather than use up the precious stock of peremptory challenges.

Jury selection, then as now, was a delicate lawyering art. The sifting of jurors took place at a preliminary hearing called *voir dire*. Here, in big cases, the lawyers sniffed and probed for hidden prejudices, for facts about a man that made him dangerous to the lawyer's side. Questioning could be sharp, even brutal. The lawyers, "full of legal peccadillos," often made "green" jurymen squirm. To the layman, *voir dire* seemed like an ordeal of ridiculous questions. The *Tribune* mocked these questions in 1875: "How long since your youngest child had the whooping-cough?" or "How would you prefer to die— with the jaundice, or to fall off a church?"[83]

In routine cases, choosing a jury was itself routine; challenges played no part. They were used in more serious or sensational trials. In 1890, George C. Pratt stood accused of a murderous assault on Colonel Bromwell. Pratt's defense was temporary insanity. It was crucial to find out what prospective jurors thought of this fishy defense. The two sides jockeyed for position. James Gorie, a "coal dealer with the face of a bank president," admitted that he had "heard a great deal of talk about the case"; he also had "a decided opinion in favor of the defendant, though he did not believe in the plea of momentary insanity." His wife, he said, "goes over to Oakland and hears a great deal of talk about the case, and we talk the matter over, and—you know how it is." Defendant's lawyer, Foote, laughed and said, "No I don't know how it is." The district attorney was not amused. He challenged Gorie. Foote objected, hoping to save this excellent juror. But the judge sent Gorie home.

Solomon Zeekind, a "solid looking citizen," was another prospect. He was against the idea of temporary insanity. Could "disclosures as

83. *Oakland Tribune*, Feb. 18, 1875, p. 3, col. 3.

to a wife's unchastity . . . unbalance a man so as to render him legally irresponsible?" Zeekind doubted it. This made him dangerous to the defense, and Foote immediately challenged him, for cause. The prosecution objected. Half an hour of wrangling followed. In the end, the judge disallowed the challenge. This forced Foote to use up one of his precious stock of peremptory challenges; but Zeekind had to go.[84]

In big, tough cases, the two sides sometimes ran through the whole stock of jurors, without settling on twelve unchallenged men. The court would then have to call for a special panel. This happened, for example, in the murder trial of Edward Flanigan (1902). The court spent an entire morning trying to pick a jury; at noon, when the court recessed, only eleven had been chosen, and the regular panel was exhausted. The judge had to issue a "special venire for six jurors . . . returnable at 1:30 o'clock." Eventually, of course, the panels were always filled. When the jury was in place, lawyers on both sides could make opening statements, if they wished. They then called witnesses. Witnesses told their stories through questions and answers. The prosecution presented its side first. Each side had the right to cross-examine witnesses for the other side. In some cases, documents, papers, or physical evidence were presented as "exhibits." Lawyers might "object" to evidence or to decisions by the judge that hurt their cause and were wrong (they thought) as a matter of law. But such "objections" were common only in big cases. In a few trials, expert witnesses took the stand: doctors, scientists, professionals.

The typical trial was quite short. The average was 2.6 days. Even this figure is misleading, because a few very long trials distort the figures. The median length was only 1.6 days. As one might expect, the more serious the offense, the longer the trial. Murder trials in our sample took, on the average, more than 7 full court days; burglary and grand larceny trials took less than 2 days. Trials got somewhat longer over the period; between 1880 and 1889, the average length was 1.5 days, the median 1.2; between 1890 and 1899, the average was 2.6, the median 1.7; between 1900 and 1910, the average was 3.2, the median 2.0. This was probably because a smaller percentage of cases went to trial. Those that did were probably the more bitterly contested. Some cases that might have gone to trial in 1880 or 1890 ended with guilty pleas in (say) 1905.

After the evidence was in, both sides made final arguments in front of the jury. These were usually fairly brief. In exceptional cases, they could go on for hours, even days. (In the trial of Lester McNulty, in 1906, for "ruining" young Dorothy Olson, A. L. Frick pulled out all

84. Ibid., May 1, 1890, p. 3, col. 3.

the stops. By the third day of argument, even the defendant was yawning; he "manicured his nails" to keep away boredom. Meanwhile, Frick "gesticulated nervously and shouted vehemently in a strenuous endeavor to keep the minds of the jurymen alert.")[85] After the arguments were over, the judge gave his "instructions" to the jury. That is, he told them about the *law*, which they in turn applied (or were supposed to apply) to the *facts* of the case.

There was a fantastic contrast between final argument and the judge's instructions. The lawyers could, if they wished, appeal to the emotions, harangue, plead, posture, shout. P. David Kiniry, in 1905, was charged with first-degree murder. The victim was James H. Smith, a policeman who died in the line of duty, trying to stop a burglary. The prosecutor boiled over in wrath: "If you can transform a rattlesnake into a human being," he said, you would still "have a man better than Smith's murderer," because at least "his rattles . . . would . . . give a warning." Kiniry had a "cold . . . relentless heart, mind and soul." He had killed a "noble, kindly young man." The jury should show no mercy; Kiniry could beg for mercy "on the border of eternity," when he passed "the great divide" and met Smith "face to face." (Apparently they were going to the same afterworld.) A. L. Frick, Kiniry's lawyer, was not to be outdone. He begged the jury to "remember that this lad has a mother." "Do not commit yourself," he said, "to a vote that will afterward cause you to regret your action to the day that you leave this earth."[86]

The judge's instructions were an entirely different kettle of fish. They were supposed to be in writing; but if both parties agreed, the judge gave them orally. This often happened, and a "phonographic reporter" (stenographer) recorded them. Both parties had the right to suggest instructions. Often both sides submitted lists of proposed instructions. In other words, the lawyers wrote the instructions. They drew up statements of law that (they felt) leaned toward their side of the case. The judge had to pick out those that were legally "correct and pertinent," and reject the others.

Many drafts of instructions can be found in the case files, with each section duly endorsed by the judge as "given" or "refused." Either way, the instructions were not very illuminating. They were standardized, boring, abstract—written in deadly legal language. They were connected with the actual case only in a very general way. In a murder trial, for example, the instructions would tell the jury the definitions of first- and second-degree murder, and inform them what

85. *Berkeley Reporter*, Apr. 4, 1906, p. 1, col. 7.
86. *Oakland Tribune*, May 22, 1905, p. 12, col. 1, Mar. 23, 1905, p. 3, col. 4.

added up to a reasonable doubt. But apparently the judge said nothing to connect these instructions to *this* man or *this* woman on trial.

As an example, we can take the charge to the jury in the case of William Butts (no. 1562, 1895). Butts was accused of manslaughter. The instructions came to thirteen legal-size pages, typed double-spaced. It probably took an hour or two to read all this to the jury. In the thirteen pages, not once is there any reference to the facts of the case. Only one proper noun appears in the text at all; it is the victim's name—William Greene. The instructions were a chain of abstract propositions. No one who read them would have the slightest notion what the case was actually about. One instruction, defining manslaughter, began this way: "Manslaughter is the unlawful killing of a human being without malice. It is of two kinds: voluntary, upon a sudden quarrel or heat of passion; involuntary, in the commission of an unlawful act which might produce death in an unlawful manner, or without due caution or circumspection." Not a word on how to fit this dreary verbiage to the case of the late William Greene. Indeed, the court told the jury flat out that it would express no "opinion" about the evidence. That would be "eminently improper." The jury was also told to decide on the basis of "absolute justice." "With the policy of the law you have . . . no concern. No sentiment, no consideration . . . should move you in your deliberations." These pious platitudes, and various stock phrases of black-letter law, were repeated again and again with only tiny differences in wording, in charges to juries. Indeed, the biggest change in the whole period was the shift from handwritten charges to charges neatly typed.

In the Butts case, the jury retired, discussed the case for three hours or so, and then sent word that they wanted "further instructions." The judge called them back into court, and asked them what was on their minds. The foreman said, humbly, "We would like to have some further instruction what is the nature of self-defense." Clearly, they wanted help. But the judge would have none of it. He simply reread the page and a half of jargon he originally read them on the subject ("It must be an imperious necessity, or such an apparent necessity as would impress a reasonably prudent man that it existed . . . "). Plainly, nothing could induce the judge to step out of role and give them an honest explanation. All he would do was "instruct," in the technical sense.[87]

87. In some cases, the instructions did track the facts of the case, though her too in a rather abstract form. We may take as an example the defendant's draft instructions (which Judge Gibson accepted and gave) in a case from 1890 (Gilbert, no. 1126). The following is a fair sample: "If you find, from the evidence, that said defendant falsely represented to . . . Clason, with intent to deceive him, that the owner of said block of

It was not always so. In the early nineteenth century, judges truly "instructed," in the sense that a teacher does. They commented freely on the evidence. They spoke to the jury in everyday language, explaining how rules of law fit the facts of the case. The habit continued in some places. We examined trial transcripts from New York City around the turn of the century. In this court (the Court of General Sessions of the Peace), instructions were much less formal. To take one example: Richard Moore was on trial, in 1908, for murdering Isaiah Rhett. The jury, said the judge, had to decide whether Moore planned the crime ahead of time. "Was the defendant jealous of Rhett . . . when did he learn that the woman and Rhett had left Long Island City? Did he follow them to New York City? Did he lurk about the place near 39th Street on the afternoon of September 7?"[88] These were real questions, about real facts of real cases, not a bundle of dry bones of law. There is no trace of such instructions in the files of Alameda County.

Why give instructions, if they do not instruct? What earthly advantage could there be to the California system? One explanation springs to mind: dry, standard phrases cut out one source of a judge's power. A judge *might* use vivid, free-form instructions to lead a jury by the nose. By a lift of his eyebrows, by his tone of voice, by his phrasing, he can give them hints how the case should come out. This "danger" was, in theory, greater in New York than in California. A layman might wonder why it would be so bad for the judge to play a guiding role. But power *to* the judge is taken *from* the jury; and the law of process and evidence at trial was a kind of elaborate balancing game, in which every grant of power was confronted with some counterpower.

There is another point to dry, stereotyped instructions. When a defendant decided to appeal, he had to show some "error" at his trial. Appeal courts were at times very finicky about the way trials were conducted. One main source of "error" was faulty instructions. As we will see in Chapter 8, most defendants did not appeal; this factor, then, was of marginal importance. Nevertheless, it seemed better—especially for the state—to use safe, antiseptic instructions, instructions in stereotyped language, language that appeal courts had perhaps already approved.

---

land, 138, resided in the City of Philadelphia, when as a matter of fact he resided elsewhere, but that said Clason was not induced thereby to part with his money or transfer the same to said defendant, then I charge you that such false representation will not warrant or justify you in finding the defendant guilty."

88. People v. Richard Moore, Court of General Sessions of the Peace, City and County of New York, 1908, Case no. 10, p. 405. The collection is in the library of John Jay College of Criminal Justice, New York City. Professor Eli Faber was kind enough to tell us about this collection, and we thank him for taking the trouble to show it to us.

Instructions were instructions about *law*. In theory, the jury took the judge's word about the law, but decided all questions of fact for itself. In reality, the jury simply came in with a verdict—guilty or not guilty. No one could really tell if the jury understood the "law," or applied it correctly, or even tried. Nothing in the process prevented the jury from following its own gut reactions. Undoubtedly, some cases were decided on grounds that were quite illegitimate in law— the so-called unwritten law, for example, that excused a man who shot his wife's lover. How much passion and prejudice entered into decisions is something we will never know. The jury debated in secret. Sometimes newspapers claimed to know how and why the jury voted. In David Kiniry's trial (for murder), the jury deadlocked on whether to sentence him to death. Four jurors held out against the gallows, and vowed through seventeen ballots that "we would turn him loose before we would hang him." These stories came from loose-lipped jurors. The jury had pledged themselves to secrecy, but two jurors later "consented to talk" for the *Oakland Tribune*.[89]

The jury made short work of some cases. After the charge in one case in 1907, the jury took a vote without leaving the room, and found G. H. Anderson guilty of second-degree burglary (no. 4123). But normally, the jury retired to a separate room, to talk things over. According to law, the room had to be furnished with "suitable furniture, fuel, lights and stationery" (§ 1135). If the jury spent the night, beds were provided. The jury could take along any documents in the case, and the written instructions (if any). They could use notes they took by themselves, "but none taken by any other person" (§ 1137). In this room, the jury stayed put until they could all agree on a verdict—or until they gave up.

Our data do not allow us to say how long the jury took, on the average. Once in a while, they reached a verdict very quickly. In one case it took three minutes.[90] The median length of time was probably an hour or two. Some difficult cases took a good deal longer. In the trial of David Kiniry, the jury was out for almost twenty-four hours, trying to reach a decision. They retired at 2:45 in the afternoon; it was 2:00 the next afternoon when the jury, sleepless and "careworn after their long vigil," announced their verdict: guilty.[91]

A verdict seems, in a way, like an all-or-nothing proposition: guilty or innocent. Yet a jury could (and often did) reach what amounted to a sort of compromise. They could find the defendant guilty of what is

89. *Oakland Tribune*, Mar. 25, 1905, p. 3, col. 5.
90. H. C. Allen's case, *Oakland Tribune*, Feb. 28, 1881, p. 1, col. 5.
91. *Oakland Tribune*, Mar. 25, 1905, p. 5, col. 3.

known as a "lesser included offense" (§ 1159). This occurred in 16 percent of the cases in our sample (see Table 5.13). If a man is accused of murder, for beating his victim to death with a club, the charge necessarily "includes" an assault. The jury could, if it wished, find the defendant guilty of assault, and let him go on the charge of murder. There are many examples in the files. In the Brandes trial (see Chapter 7), the defendant was tried twice for first-degree murder; the jury at the second trial found him guilty of manslaughter, a lesser included offense.

Sometimes the jury could not agree. This was the so-called hung jury, which occurred in almost one-ninth of all trials (see Table 5.13). Judges did not like hung juries: a hung jury meant that everyone's time had been wasted. Judges often coaxed and wheedled their juries, trying to get them to agree on a verdict. In the trial of Charles J. Kindleberger, in 1893, the judge went too far. The charge was assault with intent to rape. The jury began to deliberate at around nine o'clock in the evening, February 17, 1893. At midnight they were deadlocked, and had to be shut up for the night. At ten o'clock in the morning, they told the judge that they had "no prospect" of any agreement. The judge was greatly annoyed, and scolded the jury: "Honest men," he said, should have no trouble with the case. No doubt the jurors thought of themselves as "smart men, prominent men, with large heads and big capacity"; and they stuck stubbornly to "ill-digested" opinions, "right or wrong." The judge demanded a verdict, and a straight verdict, not some "compromise verdict. If you believe this defendant guilty as charged in the information, you have no right to render a verdict of guilty of assault." The jury went back to its room and came out later with a verdict of guilty. The judge gave Kindleberger seven years in prison; but the case was reversed on appeal. The judge's lecture had prejudiced the case.[92]

The Louis Matheny case, also in 1893, also produced a hung jury. Matheny was accused of killing a police officer who caught him in the act of robbing a saloon. The evidence was circumstantial; the defense was clever and tough. For almost twenty-four hours, the jury was locked in a stuffy room. They ate restaurant food, delivered in a big basket, and wrangled over the case. The first vote was nine to three

92. Charles J. Kindleberger, no. 1389, 1893. The second time around, Kindleberger struck a bargain: he pleaded guilty to assault. So a compromise—which the judge had said was legally impossible—came about after all. There is a certificate in the file, dated Feb. 7, 1894, in which Dr. L. R. Webster explains that Mrs. Jesse Hartnett (the complaining witness) had been "recently confined" and was not "in a physical condition to attend a trial at court." This fact, along with the bad news from the California Supreme Court, no doubt put the prosecutor in a bargaining mood.

for acquittal. They argued away into the night and took another ballot —it came out exactly the same. Then they dropped the case and played cards. A few of the jurors on Matheny's side later wavered; but there was no way to reach a unanimous verdict. The count stood seven to five for conviction when the judge let the jury go.[93]

If the jury acquitted, of course, the case was over. If the jury hung, the prosecution could try again. Or it could give up, or try to strike a bargain. There are examples in the files of each of these tactics. If defendant was convicted, he could appeal to a higher court. (We take up appeals in Chapter 8.) About a third of the defendants convicted at trial asked the trial judge for new trials, on one ground or another; a small number of these got what they asked for (see Table 5.14). Of the defendants in our overall sample, 3 percent were tried twice. A handful—1 percent of our overall sample—were tried three times, before finally going free or going to jail. These long, drawn-out (and costly) affairs occurred mostly in sensational cases of murder and rape. We shall see some examples in Chapter 7.

A verdict of guilty (or not guilty) had to be unanimous. What happened if one of the jurors got sick or died before the end of the trial? The court could swear in a new juror; or let the old jurors go and choose twelve new men. In either case, the trial had to begin all over again (§ 1123). In the more elaborate, protracted trials, there was a real danger of losing a juror. The Percy Pembroke trial, a sensation in 1906, had to start over again when one of the panel had a heart attack. To avoid this awful waste, the court had the power to empanel one or two "alternate" jurors. The alternate sat in the jury box, along with the regular jurors, ready to leap into the breach (§ 1089). In ordinary cases, of course, no such measures were needed.

In a handful of cases, the defendant's sanity became an issue. This could happen in a number of ways. First, the defendant might plead not guilty by reason of insanity. Or the defendant could claim the right to a special trial to test his sanity. This was because an insane man could not stand trial, even if he was sane when the deed was

Table 5.14. Motion for New Trial
Following Convictions at Trial, 1880–1910

No motion made	67%
Motion made & denied	28%
Motion made & granted	5%
N	172

93. *Oakland Tribune*, Oct. 14, 1893, p. 2, col. 4, Oct. 17, 1893, p. 8, col. 4.

done. If a doubt about the defendant's sanity arose at any time during trial, the court had to suspend trial and put the question of sanity to a jury. If the jury found the defendant sane, the trial went on; otherwise, the court would send the defendant to a state hospital (§§ 1368, 1370). In 1890, B. H. Dawson was tried for assault with a deadly weapon (no. 1120). He pleaded not guilty. His lawyer suggested to the court that Dawson might be insane. Two doctors testified, and the jury, without even leaving the box, found him insane. The judge suspended the trial, and sent Dawson away to Stockton until he might come to his senses.[94] A jury found Frank Cheeseman insane in 1898. Cheeseman had been accused of murder, but he was committed to Mendocino State Hospital rather than put on trial. The hospital sent him back three months later, thinking him recovered. But another jury "inquired into his sanity" and found him insane. He was sent to Napa State Hospital for his second stay (no. 2155, 1898).

A sanity trial might take place after trial, but before sentence. Luigi Tempio, a laborer, burned down Patricio Marsicano's barn in 1908. The jury took twenty minutes to decide that he was guilty of arson. E. E. Gehring, Luigi's lawyer, then asked for a sanity hearing; the district attorney consented. The jury found Tempio insane, and off he went to Napa State Hospital. If he recovered, he could be brought back to court for his sentence (no. 4466, 1908).

THE TWILIGHT OF TRIAL BY JURY

It certainly did not escape notice, in the twentieth century, that trial by jury was not what it used to be (if it ever was). Raymond Moley, in 1930, found many "symptoms which suggest the decline, if not the utter dissolution, of trial by jury in criminal cases."[95] The rise of the guilty plea was, of course, one of these "symptoms." Our slice of time is one in which we can, quite clearly, see the institution declining. Even at the beginning of our period, somewhat less than half the defendants in Superior Court went to trial (48 percent to be exact, in the period 1880–89). By 1900–1910, this had fallen to 40 percent. The percentage then continued to drop. In the 1960s and 1970s, "deals"

94. Of course, many sanity trials in Superior Court did not come out of criminal proceedings. One hotly contested case, in 1894, concerned the mental states of Mary and Catherine Colehan, two sisters from Livermore; their brother Daniel had them arrested. According to Daniel, they believed that "everything about the house has been poisoned, including the water in the water pipes." The sisters fought hard to stay out of the asylum, and a jury found them sane. *Oakland Tribune*, Aug. 14, 1894, p. 7, col. 1, and succeeding days.
95. *Our Criminal Courts* (New York, 1930), p. 107.

determined the fate of most accused felons. Only a few of the people who were convicted went to prison because of a jury's verdict. We also should not forget that most people who were *acquitted* were not acquitted by a jury. They were "acquitted" because the case was dismissed by the judge, or dropped by the prosecution.

We have, then, a number of phenomena, rather closely bound up together: (1) fewer trials, proportionately; (2) the rise of plea bargaining; (3) the flowering of the guilty plea; (4) for those who did go to trial, less chance of outright acquittal. More defendants seemed to "give up"; waivers of counsel, for example, increased somewhat. The system became (in result) harsher in some ways, more lenient in others. There seemed less chance to escape the guilty *label*; but there were more second chances (probation and parole), as we will see in a later chapter. We can sum up the changes by describing the system as more *administrative* than before, and rather less *adjudicative*. The center of gravity shifted from judge and jury to full-time crime handlers (prosecutors and police). This was a marked trend, between 1880 and 1910, though not an outright stampede: that came later, in our own times.

Two things, indeed, were happening: a shift in theory, and a shift in arrangements. The shift in arrangements was the shift to administered justice. The shift in theory was a new, heightened, special emphasis on *who* the criminal was (rather than his crime). This is, of course, a matter of more or less: murderers never got probation, regardless of their personal habits or family background. But for the middling sort of felon, the system was geared to close examination of character, to sift "real" criminals from others who were "weak" or "made a mistake," and who could be reformed. We will say more about this, too, in Chapter 6.

Trial by jury is a noble ideal, enshrined in the Constitution; many people deplore its slow disappearance. There is certainly nothing noble about plea bargaining. A vile dickering and haggling has replaced an age-old system of justice. So runs one line of criticism. But it is interesting to look at some places where (in our period) disposition patterns, at least superficially, were very different from those of Alameda County. The patterns we found held true generally in the Bay Area[96] and were typical of many, perhaps most, jurisdictions. But

96. For example, in the Federal District Court for the Northern District of California. A sample was drawn of 55 cases in 1899–1901. Of these, 10, or 18 percent, went to trial; 21 ended in guilty pleas (38 percent); in 12, either the grand jury ignored the charge or the case ended with a *nolle prosequi*. Robert B. Bell, "Turn-of-the-Century Criminal Justice: A Case Study of the Federal District Court for the Northern District of California, 1899–1901" (unpublished term paper, Stanford Law School, 1979). In rural San

by no means all. In some counties, almost every defendant went to trial. (This is even true today.) We have to ask, however, what kind of trial? "Trial" to most of us conjures up a definite image: a real courtroom battle, with two sides struggling like young stags and the judge acting as umpire, applying fair and honorable rules. Reality was quite different. In many places, the normal case was nasty and short. We examined the minute books of a Florida county from the 1890s. Here "trials" took, on the average, half an hour at most. A jury was hurriedly thrown together. Case after case paraded before them. The complaining witness told his story; sometimes another witness or two appeared; the defendant told *his* story, with or without witnesses; the lawyers (if any) spoke; the judge charged the jury. The jury retired, voted, and returned. Then the court went immediately into the next case on its list.[97]

Perhaps there never was a golden age of trials. Except for really big cases, English trials in the eighteenth and nineteenth centuries were even swifter than those of Florida.[98] At any rate, the rise of the police and full-time prosecutors changed the conditions of criminal justice; so did "police science"—fingerprinting, blood tests, and so on. In a system run by amateurs, or lawyers who spent little bits of their time and energy, with no technology of detection or proof, a trial was perhaps as good a way as any to strain the guilty from the innocent. During the nineteenth century, however, criminal justice shifted away from amateurs and part-timers toward full-time crime handlers. Once this change took place, it could no longer be assumed that trial by jury (in the idealized sense) was the normal way to handle a criminal case. After all, police and prosecutors had already "tried" the defendant. Why not leave it to them? Crime was their job. Why go through a long, expensive process? Trials for the obviously guilty were a waste of good money and time. Everywhere the police had power (unoffi-

---

Benito County, between 1880 and 1910, of 120 felony cases for which disposition is known, 56, or almost half, ended with guilty pleas; 49, or about 43 percent, went to trial. Lawrence Ponoroff and Nannette Schulze, "Criminal Justice in San Benito County, 1880–1910: An Empirical Analysis" (unpublished term paper, Stanford Law School, 1978). In San Francisco in 1908, of some 400 cases in Superior Court, about 30 percent went to trial; just over half (51.8 percent) ended with guilty pleas. Broadhurst, "Analysis of the Criminal Justice System in San Francisco County in 1908."

97. Minute Books, vol. 10, Circuit Court, Leon County, Fla. (Tallahassee is the county seat). Here one finds up to six complete "trials" a day. The same jury heard all the day's cases; it was not the practice to impanel a fresh jury for each case. And the court handled other business besides these cases of serious crime! Cases probably took between twenty and forty minutes each.

98. For nineteenth-century England, the sources are the authors' unpublished data. For eighteenth-century England, see John H. Langbein, "The Criminal Trial before the Lawyers," *U. Chi. L. Rev.* 45 (1978): 263.

cially) to shortcut the frills of due process. "Police brutality" was an everyday matter. Most people did not know about it; if they did, judging from the immunity and persistence of brutality, they did not care. People probably felt, then as now, that police *had* to be tough to deal with "hardened criminals." The beauty of the jury was that it kept the state under citizen control. But this was true only of big, political cases. Long before 1880, this dropped away as a major issue. To the middle class, there was no tyranny, no George III. But crime stalked the streets every day.

Plea bargaining (explicit and implicit) was part of the new system; it was part of a more "rational," "professional" process. Once the system got underway, it affected resources—how money was spent, and on whom. Plea bargaining was well established in the late nineteenth century. It can hardly be blamed on crowded urban courts (as it is, conventionally, today). The courts were not that crowded, and it was common in places that were not urban at all. But by the time a flood of arrests engulfed the system, plea bargaining had become indispensable. And plea bargaining was not by any means the first sign of creeping routine in criminal justice. It was only a symptom—neither the first nor the last of its kind.

Chapter 6
The Fate of the Guilty:
Sentencing in Alameda County

Criminal justice has been described as a giant filtering system. Not everyone is caught, or arrested, or charged. Of those who are, some are dismissed; some are acquitted. At the last, a few are left: the guilty or unlucky. Some have pleaded guilty, some were convicted by a jury. The last word belongs to the judge, who will sentence the accused and thereby fix the punishment.

In our period, the judge's power to sentence fell within definite limits, limits set by law. Sometimes the jury shared in the sentencing power. Murder, for example, carried the death penalty; but the jury, if it so pleased, could sentence a murderer to life imprisonment (§ 190). For most crimes, the judge made the choices, and he had wide discretion. Inside statutory boundaries he could do as he pleased. For robbery he could fix sentence at "not less than one year" in prison; for assault with intent to commit murder, "not less than one nor more than 14" (§§ 213, 217). It was an old, persistent complaint that this was far too much discretion. Sentences varied wildly, from one judge to another, from one day to another. Hence punishment was a lottery, a poker game, a toss of the dice.

It was certainly true that the judge had, for some crimes, amazing latitude. The committed robber could go to jail for life, for one year— or for anything in between. The sentence could be molded to the particular case. Discretion lived on despite criticism; indeed, as we shall see, it became broader than ever in our period.

In one key regard, the judge in 1880 had little choice. Prison was the basic punishment for felonies. The judge could say how long the defendant would be there; but he had to go. Suspended sentences were very rare.[1] Even for juveniles, there was no real alternative before 1889. The convicted felon—no matter how young, how penitent, how unfortunate—was prison-bound.

This period, then, did not have the system of fixed, flat sentences

---

1. Stanley Watteen, a minor, pleaded guilty to grand larceny in 1890; judgment was suspended, and he was sent to his family in England (no. 1045).

that we hear so much of today. Nor did it have the indeterminate sentence (in the technical sense). In the indeterminate sentence system, the judge sets a minimum sentence (usually a year), but does not fix a maximum. That is done later, by a prison board or agency that has looked the man over, checked his record, seen him in action in his prison year. It is the board that decides how long the prisoner will serve. Some states adopted the indeterminate sentence long before 1900. California, in the event, waited until 1917.

A simple idea lay behind the indeterminate sentence. Punishment had to fit the criminal, not the crime. Some men (and women) were born criminals; some were hopelessly degenerate. Others could be saved. The state should lock up the criminal until he was ready for society—not a minute more or less. When would this be—a year later, ten years later, never? The judge, certainly, could not tell; not even Solomon in his wisdom could do that. It was a job for "careful officials" (prison officials); they would have the man "in their continuous charge"; they could study and observe him "for months and years."[2] The prisoner carried "the key of his prison in his own pocket." Some prisoners would (and should) never get out—"regardless of the offense committed." These were the hopeless, the damned. It was as pointless to let them go as to let loose "persons suffering from leprosy."[3] The same sort of theory underlay a cluster of other reforms: probation, parole, juvenile justice. These, indeed, did enter California's system during our period—probation, for example, in 1903. The reforms, including probation, increased the power of the judge. They opened the gates to a broader, freer search for the soul of the man in the dock. On the surface, the new penology was more humane than the old penology. But it cut out some of the niceties of due process; it had to, as we shall see.

One theme of this study is the drift in criminal justice from an affair of amateurs to a serious, professional job. Sentencing and corrections, too, are rich in examples. Parole replaced the governor's pardon; prison boards and probation officers crowded judge and jury out of part of their ancient role. In part, this took place openly; in sentencing the focus shifted, at least somewhat, from judge (and jury), to the prosecutor (who made "deals" in exchange for pleas), the probation officer (who recommended for or against probation), and the far-off parole board. Criminal justice became, then, more *administrative*. All this was done in the name of rational policy; but a

2. John C. Taylor, "The Need for a 'Sure Enough' Indeterminate Sentence," *Charities*, Sept. 17, 1904.
3. Report of the California Crime Commission, 1929, p. 65; see also Charlton L. Lewis, "The Indeterminate Sentence," *Yale L.J.* 9 (1899); 17, 19.

modern reader, poring over old files, is struck by how biased and superstitious much of this seems today. To be sure, less depended on the whims and bias of a jury; but new whims and biases took their place. A figleaf of science barely covered these naked whims. In 1910 people *thought* that their system was better, more intelligent, more rational than the system of the 1880s. From our standpoint, the case is not so clear.

California judges had great leeway, as we said, in deciding on sentences. Table 6.1 gives some idea of the range of penalties for different crimes. The ranges are impressive. For attempted robbery,

Table 6.1. Statutory Range of Prison Sentences for Various Felonies

Range of possible sentence	Crime for which sentencing range applicable
Death	Treason, perjury leading to a wrongful execution, first-degree murder (before 1874), assault with a deadly weapon by a life prisoner (after 1909)
Death or life imprisonment	First-degree murder (after 1874), train wrecking (after 1905)
Life imprisonment	Any crime punishable by life imprisonment when defendant has a prior conviction of petty larceny or attempt to commit a felony (before 1903)
10 years to life	Second-degree murder, kidnapping for purpose of extortion or robbery (after 1901), any felony punishable by more than 5 years' imprisonment when defendant has a prior felony conviction (or, after 1903, a petty larceny conviction)
5 years to life	Rape, crime against nature (sodomy or bestiality)
2 years to life	First-degree arson
1 year to life	Robbery, dynamiting (after 1887), lewd acts with a child under 14 years of age
Up to life imprisonment	Attempted robbery, attempted crime against nature

Table 6.1. (continued)

Range of possible sentence	Crime for which sentencing range applicable
1 to 25 years	Second-degree arson
1 to 15 years	Burglary (until 1876), first-degree burglary (after 1876)
2 to 14 years	Abduction
1 to 14 years	Forgery, assault with intent to murder or to rape or to rob, assault with a deadly weapon with intent to murder, passing fictitious checks, perjury, forging public records
3 to 10 years	Placing wife in house of prostitution
1 to 10 years	Grand larceny, kidnapping, felony embezzlement, bribery, obtaining goods or money under false pretenses (after 1889)
Up to 10 years and fine up to $10,000	Aiding an escape from jail
Up to 10 years and/ or fine up to $5,000	Bigamy (after 1905)
Up to 10 years	Manslaughter, any felony punishable by no more than 5 years in prison when defendant has prior felony conviction (or, after 1903, a prior petty larceny conviction)
Up to 7 years	Attempted first-degree burglary
2 to 5 years	Performing an abortion
1 to 5 years	Housebreaking (until 1876), submitting to an abortion, third poison law offense
Up to 5 years and/ or fine up to $5,000	Seduction
Up to 5 years and/ or fine up to $1,000	Abduction for prostitution, placing girl under 18 in house of prostitution
Up to 5 years	Second-degree burglary (after 1876), dynamiting (before 1887), extortion, attempted grand larceny, smuggling opium into jail, injuring public jail, any crime committed by defendant with prior conviction of petty

Table 6.1. (continued)

Range of possible sentence	Crime for which sentencing range applicable
	larceny or attempted felony (until 1903), petty larceny with prior conviction
Up to 5 years prison or up to 6 months county jail	Receiving stolen property
Up to 3 years prison and/or fine up to $2,000	Bigamy (until 1905)
1 to 3 years prison and $1,000 to $5,000 fine	Prizefighting
Up to 2 years prison or jail and/or fine up to $5,000	Assault with deadly weapon, assault with intent to injure
Up to 2 years prison or jail and/or fine up to $1,000	Failure to provide

for example, the judge could give a sentence of *any* length, including life. Robbery carried a term of one year to life. First-degree burglary (burglary at night) could carry one to fifteen years; second-degree burglary (the daytime variety) could carry up to five years. For some crimes, the law *insisted* on long terms: a minimum of ten years for second-degree murder, five years for sodomy or rape.

Sentencing Procedures

Table 6.1 shows the statutory boundaries. But what were the actual results? We begin with a look at the process.

In Superior Court, sentencing was a special proceeding, separate from the trial itself. At the sentencing hearing, defendant had the right to raise legal points bearing on his conviction, which showed "good cause . . . in arrest of judgment or for a new trial" (§ 1201). He could also bring out any "circumstances in . . . mitigation of punishment." The judge in turn could also consider "aggravating" facts (§ 1203). From 1901 on, the court was supposed to ask questions and

gather information that might help guide later decisions about parole
—whether the defendant had a trade, and what, for example, lay
behind his "criminal character" (§ 1192a).[4] (We will say a little more
about these proceedings at the end of this chapter.)

Sentencing was usually a fairly rapid process. After conviction, the
judge was supposed to wait at least two days before fixing sentence
(§ 1191). But over one-third of the defendants waived their rights and
were sentenced the day they were convicted. Half of all defendants
were sentenced in less than three days. Posttrial motions, of course,
took more time. The average time between conviction and sentencing
increased between 1880 and 1910, especially after probation came in, in
1903 (see Table 6.2).[5] In the 1880s, 14 percent of the cases were continued for sentencing; that is, the sentencing proceeding was postponed at least once from the originally scheduled date. This happened in 21 percent of the cases in the 1890s and in over 36 percent
between 1900 and 1910. As Table 6.3 shows, the more serious crimes
took the longest. Sentencing also took longer for defendants who had
lawyers (see Table 6.4): lawyers were more likely to file motions and
to argue mitigating circumstances.

A convicted felon had to be present for his sentencing. The judge
followed a little ritual: he asked whether the defendant had "any legal cause to show why judgment should not be pronounced" (§ 1200).
Around one out of eight had legal cause, or thought so, and filed
motions for new trials. Another few (less than 5 percent) filed motions in arrest of judgment. These almost never got anywhere. Motions for new trials were filed in about one-third of the cases in the
sample where a trial ended in conviction. There were fifty-six of these
motions; eight were granted.[6] Rudolph E. Perwein, convicted of se-

Table 6.2. Days between Conviction and Sentencing, 1880–1910

No. days	1880–89	1890–99	1900–1910	1880–1910
Mean	6.3	8.5	9.6	8.5
Median	2.3	1.9	3.6	2.6
N	115	112	219	446

4. The district attorney and the judge had to file statements giving their opinions
concerning the defendant's character and how much of his sentence he should be
required to serve.
5. In 1905, § 1191 was amended to impose a five-day time limit, with ten more days
possible if the defendant moved for a new trial or to arrest judgment. Twenty days was
allowed if the court was considering probation. If the court had reasonable ground to
believe the defendant insane, sentencing could be further put off, until the defendant's
sanity was determined. Beginning in 1909, the defendant was entitled to a new trial, if
the time limitations on sentencing were not complied with (§§ 119, 1202).
6. Not one motion in arrest of judgment succeeded.

202 | *The Roots of Justice*

Table 6.3. Days between Conviction and
Sentencing by Offense, 1880–1910

Offense	Average no. days	N
First-degree murder	26	3
Robbery	10	21
Grand larceny	11	75
Forgery	10	22
First-degree burglary	8	54
Second-degree burglary	7	112
Assault with a deadly weapon	7	30
Simple assault	5	37
Petty larceny	3	35

Source: Sample of cases in Register of Actions, 1880–1910.

Table 6.4. Days between Conviction and
Sentencing by Attorney Status in Superior Court, 1880–1910

Attorney status of defendant	Average no. days	N
Waived counsel	3.6	86
Counsel appointed by court	6.6	95
Counsel hired by defendant	10.8	248

Source: Sample of cases in Register of Actions, 1880–1910.

duction in 1899, was one of these lucky few. His lawyer, Welles Whitmore, claimed "newly discovered evidence": three men who said they slept with Hattie Isaacs, the "victim," before Perwein supposedly seduced her. The judge granted a new trial, and indeed, the prosecution then abandoned the case (no. 2255). Far more often, the motion accomplished nothing but delay.

The defendant had one last hope for a mild sentence: he could try to persuade His Honor to be lenient. Some begged for mercy and forgiveness. Richard C. Beggs had embezzled from the Oakland Street Railway Company. His wife and children were in court as he told his story: "My reputation is gone and my family is scattered and dependent upon strangers. There are my little ones and in their innocent faces I can see myself. Oh, Judge, their innocence condemns me. I beg of you to have mercy upon me, Judge. For their sake have mercy on me." There were "few dry eyes in the courtroom." As for Beggs, "His eyes were moist, his lips trembled and his frame quivered as he waited to hear his fate." Judge Greene put off sentencing for ten days, but he was hardhearted enough to give Beggs five years in San Quentin.[7] Frank E. Parlin, who pleaded guilty to bigamy, tried to excuse himself; but there was nothing, said the judge, that could condone this "cold-blooded, atrocious crime."[8]

Defendants sometimes brought in character witnesses. When John Schaetz pleaded guilty to robbery in 1910, his lawyer, A. L. Frick, paraded in fourteen witnesses, including two lawyers, two policemen, a doctor, and the defendant's wife. They all swore that the defendant had an impeccable character, and they all told how amazed they were to hear about the robbery. The crime was too serious for probation, but Frick asked for "extreme leniency," and quoted Shakespeare's lines about the quality of mercy ("twice blessed"); the deputy district attorney joined in, asking for "a very light sentence." Judge Brown gave Schaetz four years in San Quentin—it could have been worse—and he was paroled after eighteen months (Proceedings upon Sentence, no. 4758). Albert Luckhardt, who pleaded guilty to second-degree burglary in 1897, did even better with character witnesses. The judge sent him to San Quentin—but for only ten days.[9]

When a defendant asked for leniency, he said whatever he wished, talking freely and openly about himself. Before the days of probation reports, this was one way for the judge to get some sort of insight about the defendant and his case. Some judges read the transcript of the preliminary hearing, at least in serious cases. Yet the judge often knew next to nothing about the man or woman in front of him. William Henry, in 1909, had "nothing to say" during his short trial, or afterwards (except to insist that he was innocent). Judge Brown admitted that he had no "accurate opinion" of Henry's character. But he sent him to San Quentin for a six-year term (no. 4591).

7. *Oakland Tribune*, July 19, 1892, p. 1, col. 7. Beggs's sentence was commuted to time served in April 1894, after he had served only a third of his five-year term.

8. *Oakland Tribune*, July 18, 1892, p. 2, col. 6.

9. The prosecution could also speak its mind at the sentencing hearing. It could rebut the defendant's evidence. This rarely happened, but Henry L. Lewis, convicted of first-degree burglary, enraged the prosecution by filing a motion for a new trial. The motion was probably based on lies—a false attempt to blame the burglary on another man. Apparently, Lewis persuaded a fellow prisoner in county jail, Michael J. Hart, to take the blame for the burglary. The prosecution was able to poke holes in the story. "It is seldom that the District Attorney of this County ever asked the Court in passing sentence to pass a severe sentence. Ordinarily it has been the policy of the District Attorney's office of this county to confine our efforts to putting in the testimony at the time of the trial, and when a verdict has been rendered, this concludes our efforts." This case, however, called for sterner measures. The judge obliged with a very heavy sentence. Proceedings upon Sentence, 5 (no. 4670, 1909).

Death and Iron Bars

The most wicked crimes, of course, brought the heaviest punishment (see Table 6.5). For the entire period, 1880–1910, two-thirds of the defendants convicted in Superior Court were sentenced to state prison. Another fifth were fined, or sent to county jail for short terms. These were defendants originally charged with felonies, but convicted of misdemeanors. Edward Macomber, for example, accused of robbery in 1897, pleaded guilty to petty larceny, a misdemeanor, and got six months in county jail (no. 1958). Probation was the outcome for roughly 6 percent of the sample, and 5 percent went to juvenile institutions. Probation began only in 1903; for the subsequent years, 20 percent of the convicted defendants won probation.

Table 6.5. Sentences Following Convictions in Superior Court by Time Period, 1880–1910

Period	Death	State prison	County jail	Jail and fine	Jail or fine
1880–89	0.7%	73.2%	14.8%	1.7%	7.0%
1890–99	0.4	66.1	16.7	—	4.5
1900–1910	0.2	64.9	16.4	—	0.5
1880–1910	0.4	68.2	16.1	0.4	3.1

Source: Sample of cases in Register of Actions, 1880–1910.

There were a few crimes—assault with a deadly weapon, attempted burglary, and receiving stolen property—that could be punished either by prison or by jail. For these crimes, the tail wagged the dog: that is, the sentence determined the degree of crime. If the defendant was sent to county jail, he had committed a misdemeanor; he was a felon if he went to state prison.[10] As Table 6.6 shows, most defendants convicted of assault with a deadly weapon avoided prison. In the case of petty larceny, first offenses were misdemeanors; the defendant might go to county jail for six months or less. A *second* petty larceny was a felony, a ticket to state prison. Just under half the petty larceny convictions in Superior Court took the defendant to prison.

Fines were an everyday affair in police court, but were rare for

10. On the legality of this situation, see In re Shea, 11 Cal. App. 568 (1909).

felonies in Superior Court. In theory, the judge could impose fines for assault with a deadly weapon, bigamy, seduction, and assisting escape, or add fines on top of a stretch in prison. But fines for felonies were quite scarce. In forty years (1870–1910), the state prison register listed only two felons from Alameda County who were fined in addition to being given sentences to prison. One was Robert Mitchell, sentenced to two years and fined $4,000 for assault with a deadly weapon in 1886. A court order set him free in 1887, "he having a fine to pay which was unconstitutional."[11] The second was W. B. Gay, sentenced to three years in prison and fined $100 for bigamy in 1897.[12] The Penal Code (§ 672) permitted the judge to impose a fine up to $200 for any felony, unless the law specifically set some other fine. We found no case in which this section was used.

Fine alone	Susp. judgment or probation	Juven. inst.	N
).9 %	—	1.7 %	115
—	0.9 %	11.5	113
—	14.5	3.7	218
).2	6.4	5.1	446

Judges did hand out fines, but only when a felony charge dropped off to a mere misdemeanor. Jee Ham was accused of assault with intent to kill, in 1887. He was found guilty of simple assault. He paid a $5 fine on the spot and went free (no. 764).[13] George Bonde was fined $400 for assault with a deadly weapon. If he could not pay, he was to sit in jail until the fine was satisfied, at $2 per day (no. 2059, 1897). The average fine in Superior Court was $250, the median $205. Of course, not every defendant could come up with the money. The poor and luckless paid off their fines behind bars. The rate could go no lower than $1 per day, and it was fixed at $2 in 1891.

11. California State Prison Registers, San Quentin, no. 12050.
12. Ibid., no. 17197.
13. Another man, Walton, accused of assault with a deadly weapon, was convicted of battery only by the jury. He was fined $300 (no. 174, 1881).

Table 6.6. Sentences Following Convictions in
Superior Court by Offense, 1880–1910

Offense	Death	State prison	County jail	Jail and fine
First-degree murder	41 %	59 %	—	—
Second-degree murder	—	100	—	—
Manslaughter	—	100	—	—
Robbery	—	91	—	—
Assault w. deadly weapon	—	27	57%	3%
First-degree burglary	—	90	—	—
Second-degree burglary	—	95	—	—
Grand larceny	—	80	—	—
Petty larceny	—	43	46	3
Forgery	—	73	—	—
Embezzlement	—	89	—	—
Passing fictitious check	—	82	—	—
Simple assault	—	—	79	—

Source: Sample of convictions in Register of Actions, 1880–1910.
Note: Percentages may add up to 101 because of rounding off.

Death was a rare and awesome penalty. It was mandatory for first-degree murder until 1874. After that, the jury had the choice of death or a life sentence; if the defendant pleaded guilty,[14] the choice was the judge's.[15] Between 1872 and 1910, only seventeen people were convicted of first-degree murder—about one every other year. Ten were sentenced to life imprisonment. Seven were sentenced to hang. Five actually died on the gallows. We will follow their fates in Chapter 9.

The Prison Decision: Days, Months, and Years

The penalties set out in Table 6.1 are a rough index of what crimes people (and judges) considered most grievous. The actual sentences

14. Wong Git, on trial for first-degree murder in 1908, was allowed to change his plea to guilty of second-degree murder after "[i]t was shown that the defendant had been mentally incompetent for a number of years." *Oakland Tribune*, Sept. 25, 1908, p. 7, col. 3. Git was the only Alameda County defendant to plead guilty to murder during our period. He was sentenced to life imprisonment. He served nearly thirty-four years in San Quentin, and was pardoned in 1942.

15. A San Francisco defendant, Louis Dabner, against the advice of three different sets of court-appointed attorneys, pleaded guilty to first-degree murder. (He killed a

Jail or fine	Fine alone	Probation	Juven. inst.	N
—	—	—	—	17*
—	—	—	—	4
—	—	—	—	5
—	—	9%	—	21
10%	—	3	—	30
—	—	7	3%	59
—	—	2	4	112
—	—	13	7	76
3	—	—	6	35
—	—	23	5	22
—	—	11	—	9
—	—	18	—	11
18	3%	—	—	38

* 100% sample of first-degree murder cases between 1872 and 1910.

handed out followed more or less the same pattern. Table 6.7 shows mean and median prison sentences imposed, by type of crime. A man convicted of second-degree murder was likely to go to prison for a very long term: the median was twenty-two years. Prison sentences for robbery averaged more than ten years. Sex crimes were harshly dealt with (if the state could convict)—more than fifteen years, on the average, for rape; even for *statutory* rape, the median was ten years in prison. Sodomy was also treated severely. Charles Wilson pleaded guilty to sodomy in 1907, full of remorse; the judge gave him twenty-five years in San Quentin (no. 4218). Frank Pierce pleaded guilty to sodomy in 1902. His victim was a ten-year-old boy. Pierce got fourteen years at Folsom (no. 2546).

Burglars also went to prison, but for shorter terms. Charles Bender, who pleaded guilty, got a year in San Quentin (no. 1286, 1892). Some defendants, however, "got the book." Olaf Jensen, a young Danish immigrant, never in trouble, broke into a store on Seventh Street and

---

bank manager during a robbery in 1906.) Dabner was sentenced to death. At this point, he decided to change his plea. The judge said no; Dabner appealed, and lost. People v. Dabner, 153 Cal. 398 (1908). When he died on the gallows, he was eighteen years old.

*Table 6.7. Prison Sentences of
Alameda County Prisoners by Offense, 1870–1911*

Offense	Including priors & multiples		
	Mean months	Median months	N
First-degree murder	*	*	1
Second-degree murder	207 (+4 Life)	264	1
Manslaughter	95	96	2
Robbery	129 (+2 Life)	120	6
Assault to kill	88 (+1 Life)	78	2
Assault with deadly weapon	36 (+1 Life)	24	2
Assault to rape	138	96	1
Assault to rob	88	96	
Assault to injure	47	24	
Forcible rape	266	198	
Statutory rape	157	120	1
First-degree burglary	60	36	21
Second-degree burglary	37	36	38
Burglary (pre-1876)	30	29	1
Housebreaking (pre-1876)	23	18	1
Attempted burglary	36	29	1
Grand larceny	42	24	25
Petty larceny & prior conviction	36	27	5
Forgery	47	37	8
Embezzlement	47	36	3
Passing fictitious check	47	38	4
Arson	125	60	
Sodomy	157	151	1
Bigamy	25	27	
Perjury	36	27	1
Escape from jail	24	20	1
All Crimes	57	36	1,46

Source: 100% sample of California State Prison Registers, 1870–1911 (plus fiftee
prison sentences that were reversed on appeal and never appeared in the priso
registers). The first two columns give total sentences for each defendant who went
prison; if a defendant was charged with more than one offense, the table uses the mo
serious offense he was *convicted* of. Thus it may slightly overstate the average senten

	Excluding priors & multiples		
Mean months	*Median months*	*N*
*	*	17
67 (+4 Life)	264	18
36	94	19
26	86	52
76	71	19
36	23	19
08	93	13
80	60	5
56	42	4
56	198	6
54	90	14
38	30	135
36	24	257
27	27	15
21	17	14
27	24	9
35	24	186
—	—	—
43	36	69
44	37	30
33	27	30
48	48	2
46	144	11
25	27	8
27	21	8
22	18	9
50	36	1,006

received for each *count*. The second two columns show sentences received by first-termers only. Prisoners who had prior convictions or who served any previous time in prison have been excluded. Prisoners convicted of more than one crime have also been excluded.

* There were seven death and ten life sentences for first-degree murder.

stole some gloves. He pleaded guilty, and said he was drunk at the time. Judge Harris sentenced him to five years at Folsom (January 2, 1906). The median prison term for burglary (both degrees) was about three years. David Riddell, a drunken boilermaker, pleaded guilty to second-degree burglary in 1909; he got a year and six months at San Quentin; Judge Brown considered this "lenient" (no. 4681, 1909). Perhaps it was: James R. Williams got a two-year "jolt" in 1897 for stealing eight chickens (no. 2010).

Averages, of course, are averages; they can be misleading. There was a great deal of variation from case to case—too much, according to some. The California State Penological Commission, in 1885, looked at prison terms and found the variations unsettling.[16] Warden Aull of Folsom made a similar complaint. "Harsh" sentences for small crimes only cause resentment; light sentences for heavy crimes breed contempt for law. The legislature must find a way to "equalize." Judges, he felt, allow "lapses" to occur, when "the criminal has position and influence"; then to soothe their consciences, they inflict an "extreme penalty" on "some poor sinner who has only committed crime to satisfy the demands of hunger, or to protect himself from the winter winds."[17]

Prior Convictions

Having a "record" made a dramatic difference in a defendant's sentence. Petty larceny, a misdemeanor, became a felony (up to five years in prison) the second time around. For other felonies, by law a two-time (or n-time) loser might suffer much stiffer penalties than a first offender—either a longer minimum, or a higher maximum. For example, a second conviction for first-degree burglary carried ten years to life (§ 666). A two- or three-time loser for certain offenses automatically received the *maximum* sentence for his most recent crime.[18] Thus, Bert Hodges (1910), convicted of second-degree burglary, admitted a

---

16. *Report of the California State Penological Commission* (1885), p. 56.

17. Warden Charles Aull, Folsom State Prison, in *Report, State Board of Prison Directors* (1891), p. 42.

18. Before 1903, this was true for anyone committing a felony who had been convicted of petty larceny or an attempted felony. After 1909, the automatic maximum applied to felons who had served time for any previous felony (§ 667). It did not matter whether the prior conviction was in California or not (§ 668).

There were all sorts of anomalies in the laws about recidivism. For example, until 1903, a robber with a prior conviction of petty larceny (a misdemeanor) faced a *life* sentence; a robber with a prior *felony* conviction (even murder) might escape (if that is the word) with as little as ten years in prison. See People v. Stanley, 47 Cal. 223 (1874).

prior felony conviction and automatically got the maximum—five years.[19] A seventeen-year-old boy, Walter Kavanaugh, stole a 25-cent purse with $1.65 in it "from the person of . . . Annie Ratto." This was grand larceny ("grand" because he stole from the *person* of the victim). The jury recommended mercy. But he had two prior convictions. The sentence was ten years in San Quentin (no. 1406, 1893). Louis Long, who stole a bolt of blue cloth in 1907, had done a stretch in San Quentin; his sentence was thirteen years in prison (no. 4242).

Table 6.8 compares sentences for particular crimes, showing the effect of prior convictions. It comes as no surprise that "priors" cost defendants dearly. Their sentences were, in general, about 50 percent longer than first offenders'.

It was not always easy to prove a prior record. No fingerprinting system was in everyday use; there was no simple way to connect with police files elsewhere in the country. Prison photographs, along with marks, blemishes, and tattoos, were the best way to identify a veteran. Some cases were doubtful. In 1895, John Kearns, a sixty-five-year-old, was on trial for burglary before Judge Frick. Yes, he had been in trouble before, but only for drunkenness and petty larceny (he said). An Oakland detective combed the "rogues' gallery" in San Francisco; he found a picture of a three-time felon, John McDonald, who looked a lot like Kearns. McDonald had spent fifteen years at

Table 6.8. Average Sentences (in Months) for Various Offenses with and without Inclusion of Prior Conviction Cases, 1880–1910 (N in parentheses)

Offense	All Cases	First offenders only	Recidivists
First-degree burglary	69 (54)	49 (46)	188 (8)
Second-degree burglary	33 (106)	29 (98)	84 (8)
Grand larceny	49 (62)	40 (54)	110 (8)
Petty larceny	15 (34)	5 (17)	26 (17)

Source: Sample of cases in Registers of Actions, 1880–1910.

19. The district attorney complained that the "jury found him guilty of burglary in the second degree, disregarding absolutely the testimony in the case, which showed it was a burglary committed about midnight." Opinion of the District Attorney 1, Bert Hodges, no. 4801. If the jury had convicted him of first-degree burglary, a fifteen-year sentence was mandatory. The jury may just possibly have known this fact and taken it into account.
At least one judge thought recidivists were treated too lightly under § 667. Charles Johnson was convicted of burglary in 1909 (no. 4679). He was a second-timer. The judge gave him five years, the most he could under the law. This was "inadequate" and showed that the law was "unwise." The judge thought the defendant knew "that the court had no discretion . . . and received his sentence with an entire air of indifference."

Folsom and San Quentin. "In '66," said Kearns, "I was a miner at Folsom, but I never was in the prison." Detective Tim Bainbridge of San Francisco, who knew "every criminal that ever served a term in the state prison," was called in to identify Kearns; a deputy sheriff went to San Quentin to fetch photographs and more details. In the end, Judge Frick decided that Kearns did have a record; he received the five-year term mandatory for second offenders.[20]

Convictions in other states were, in practice, hard to prove. Ira Butler was arrested for robbery in Oakland (1907). The police suspected that he had served time in Tennessee. But they had no hard information, and they did not charge him with "priors." The mere suspicion probably affected his sentence. In Butler's file is a letter from the chief of police at Nashville, who sent prison descriptions and records. Prison officials had "positively identified" Butler. In Nashville they were sure he was a "traveling thief. . . . We do not know anything of him in this department, but he is the holdup man you think he is without doubt."[21] The letter was never introduced at the trial; but the judge read it before sentencing Butler. Butler's sentence was twenty years.[22]

Bargain Justice

In the last chapter, we discussed plea bargaining in Superior Court. Defendants, we saw, sometimes pleaded guilty, as part of a deal or because they hoped to get easier treatment. Were they right? Did the court reward the person who pleaded guilty? As we shall see, when probation came into the system (after 1903), a guilty plea was the best way to earn a crack at freedom. As for actual sentences, Table 6.9 shows the data we have. The sample size is small; but the figures show more or less what we expected. Except for first-degree burglary, defendants who went to trial and lost got longer sentences, on the

20. "Is He an Ex-Convict?" *Oakland Tribune*, Oct. 9, 1895, p. 1, col. 6; "Gets Another Respite," *Oakland Tribune*, Oct. 3, 1895, p. 6, col. 1. Judge Frick was afraid that he had, in effect, sentenced the old man to life; but four years later he walked out of Folsom.

21. Letter from Henry Lumons, Nashville Chief of Police, to A. W. Wilson, Oakland Chief of Police, Mar. 14, 1907, filed in case papers of Ira Butler (no. 4121).

22. Local prior convictions were easier to prove. When Bessie Barclay was on trial in 1909, the district attorney's office had only to telephone the judge of the San Francisco Superior Court to line up witnesses to her prior record. She had been convicted of grand larceny in San Francisco in 1904. The earthquake destroyed the records in her case; but the judge arranged for her former probation officer to testify, along with a San Francisco police sergeant. Letter from Judge William Lawlor, San Francisco Superior Court, to Phillip M. Carey, Chief Deputy District Attorney, Sept. 6, 1909, filed in case papers of Jennie Thurnher (no. 4602).

Table 6.9. *Average Sentences (in Months) by*
Method of Conviction, 1880–1910 (N in parentheses)

Offense	Initial guilty plea	Not guilty plea changed to guilty	Convicted by jury
Robbery	108 (3)	88 (3)	230 (11)
First-degree burglary	50 (24)	24 (2)	49 (20)
Second-degree burglary	31 (56)	30 (20)	40 (30)
Assault with deadly weapon	15 (6)	9 (5)	18 (17)
Grand larceny	37 (38)	52 (13)	63 (21)

Source: Sample of cases in Registers of Actions, 1880–1910.

average, than defendants who pleaded guilty at the outset, or after a bargain was struck. The differences are not great, but they are in a consistent direction.

Table 6.10 redoes Table 6.9, dropping out cases in which the defendant had prior convictions, or multiple counts that were later abandoned.[23] These dropped counts and charges might well influence a judge. Table 6.10 confirms the impression that the judge rewarded those who pleaded guilty. In Table 6.10, in fact, even the figures for first-degree burglary are in the predicted direction. We must remem-

Table 6.10. *Average Sentences (in Months) by*
Method of Conviction, Excluding Cases of Prior Convictions, Multiple
Charges, or Lesser Convictions, 1880–1910 (N in parentheses)

Offense	Initial guilty plea	Not guilty plea changed to guilty	Convicted by jury
Robbery	108 (3)	48 (1)	226 (10)
First-degree burglary	42 (18)	24 (2)	47 (18)
Second-degree burglary	29 (42)	25 (14)	31 (21)
Assault with deadly weapon	14 (4)	5 (4)	17 (11)
Grand larceny	29 (22)	45 (9)	46 (15)

Source: Sample of cases in Registers of Actions, 1880–1910.

23. Are the data influenced by prior convictions that are not dropped? Suppose men with records choose to go to trial rather than plead guilty. To test this we recomputed the data, dropping out defendants with records. The differences were slight. For example, the spread narrows a bit for second-degree burglary (twenty-nine months for guilty pleas, twenty-six for pleas changed to guilty, thirty-two for people convicted by jury). But the general results are unaltered.

214 | *The Roots of Justice*

ber, of course, that sample cells are too small for solid statistical inference. Still, it seems that those who *changed* their pleas did best; by playing hard to get, they extracted a better bargain. Those who pleaded guilty right away got *something*, but not very much.

Defendants, to be sure, did not know these statistics. They knew about rumors, hints, veiled threats, and guarded promises. These led them to think that they were better off pleading guilty. Ella Hargens pleaded guilty to burglary in 1910 (no. 4841). Her lawyer, George McDonough, pointed out that she had "shown repentence" by "confessing her guilt." She "saved the county money, and the District Attorney's office time, and we ask the court to be as lenient as possible in sentencing." Judge Harris gave her a year in prison. (Through McDonough, Ella thanked His Honor for this "leniency." Judge Harris replied: "It is a question of doing my duty, that is all.")

Defendants may have known about the other side of the bargain, too: the "punishment" for going to trial. And, after all, if a jury convicted a man, didn't that mean he was lying when he pleaded not guilty? Daniel Sullivan was tried for grand larceny in 1910 (no. 4837). Sullivan was a laborer and a drifter; he got drunk one night and roamed the saloons with John Shannon, who was even drunker. Sullivan went through his buddy's pockets and took $3.15. At the trial, Sullivan told a different story: Shannon gave him the money to "go to a car on a siding at Niles Depot and buy something to eat from the Chinese cook." A number of witnesses poked holes in this story. The jury found Sullivan guilty, and the judge, at the sentencing proceeding, unleashed his wrath: it was bad enough to roll a drunk, it was even worse to commit "wilful perjury. . . . You were not only willing to commit the offense, you were willing to go upon the witness stand and state that which was not true." The wages of these sins was five years in San Quentin.

Sometimes juries convicted but recommended mercy. When this happened, sentences did tend to get lighter. Michael Dean was convicted of assault after a two-day trial in 1890. The jury recommended mercy, and Dean got off with a fine of $250 (no. 1086). J. W. Saunders was tried on two counts of burglary in 1895. The two trials were held on consecutive days. Both juries convicted Saunders of second-degree burglary; both recommended mercy. The sentence was one year for each conviction (no. 941). Sometimes, to be sure, the judge turned a deaf ear: James Hunter got eight years in prison for grand larceny, despite the jury's call for mercy (no. 1990, 1897).

Sentencing: The Ebbs and Flows

So far, our figures on sentence length have covered the entire period. In fact, sentences varied over time, as well as from case to case. The warden of Folsom, in a report, voiced the opinion that sentences ebbed and flowed with public pressures. When communities were "seized with spasms of virtue," the judges gave long, severe sentences. Public energy would then "flag," and sentences would fall.[24] But our figures suggest that there was a good deal more to the story.

Table 6.11 shows sentence lengths, broken down by time periods. The average jumped in the 1880s, dipped a bit between 1890 and 1893, spurted up in the period 1894–99, slid back down somewhat until 1908, and then rose again. What accounts for these patterns? One factor is reform in the law. The Goodwin Act (1878) liberalized "good time" credit for prisoners. A prisoner serving five years could go free in three years and seven months after this act, a gain of six months. A ten-year prisoner could go free after six and a half years, a gain of fifteen months. In 1893 came another reform: parole. First-term prisoners who served at least one year might be paroled, at the discretion of a parole committee.

Table 6.11 suggests that these reforms brought on longer sentences at the level of Superior Court. In the five years after the Goodwin Act, the average felony sentence was more than 30 percent longer than in the previous decade. Parole was followed by an even greater

Table 6.11. Prison sentences of Alameda County Prisoners by Time Period, 1870–1911

Period	Mean months	Median months	N
1870–78	36	24	180
1879–83	47	30	171
1884–89	54	36	196
1890–93	49	31	114
1894–99	77	42	153
1900–1903	64	39	153
1904–7	52	35	171
1908–11	67	45	309

Source: 100% sample of Alameda County prisoners in California State Prison Registers, 1870–1911.

24. *Report, State Board of Prison Directors* (1891), p. 42.

effect; the average sentence between 1894 and 1899 was nearly two and one-half years *longer* than in 1890–93.[25]

It certainly leaps to mind that judges adjusted to the new policies by passing out longer sentences. The reaction, of course, may have been temporary, and perhaps it was not true of the state as a whole.[26] But the numbers rather boldly suggest that the judges in Alameda County threw in extra years to counterbalance parole or to sour chances of early parole. That is, they wanted to make sure that there would be no change in actual time served (or, possibly, to add to the total time of state supervision inside or outside prison). Judge Everett Brown, sentencing Phillip Wolf in 1909—Wolf had passed a bad ten-dollar check—said that he hoped "the Prison Board will keep you confined in prison for a part [of the sentence] . . . and then . . . parole you, so you may be out, but not absolutely free." He warned the defendant: Wolf would go back to prison if he turned to drink or evil ways (no. 4612).[27]

Sentencing: Race and Sex

What factors made a difference in sentencing? Did judges favor men over women? whites over blacks and Chinese? rich over poor? Type of crime was, of course, a factor. As to other variables, nothing was said openly; and we have no way to measure except for race and sex. The overwhelming majority of defendants were males and were white. If we control for type of crime, the numbers shrink drastically in each category and statistical inference becomes impossible. Still, for what it is worth, Table 6.12 shows prison sentences for prisoners of three races in state prisons between 1870 and 1911. (Prisoners with

25. The increased length was even more dramatic if we look at the time period right after the parole law went into effect. Between 1894 and 1896, the average sentence was ninety-two months in prison.

26. The largest increase in length came in the first few years after parole was instituted. Between 1897 and 1899, the average length of sentences fell *below* that of the 1894–96 period. Tirey Ford, a member of the State Board of Prison Directors, gathered figures showing that between 1880 and 1885 the average length of sentences increased, while between 1885 and 1895 sentences grew shorter on the average. From 1895 to 1905, Ford's results show sentences again increasing in length. Tirey L. Ford, *California State Prisons: Their History, Development, and Management* (San Francisco, 1910), p. 45. It is possible, of course, that there was a different mix of crimes for which people were sentenced in the years after parole. But this is unlikely; our data rest on a 100 percent sample of prison sentences.

27. Brown was a good prophet in this case. Wolf was paroled after twenty-two months of a three-year "jolt." Within nine days, he was sent back to San Quentin as a parole violator. In the end, he served eight months *longer* than if he had stayed in prison without parole and earned the normal "good time" in prison.

Table 6.12. *Prison Sentences (in Months) for Selected Offenses by Race of Prisoner, 1870–1911 (N in parentheses)*

Offense	White	Black	Oriental
Robbery	116 (47)	213 (4)	240 (1)
First-degree burglary	38 (115)	44 (11)	41 (9)
Second-degree burglary	29 (226)	42 (12)	34 (18)
Grand larceny	34 (165)	44 (7)	31 (12)

Source: 100% sample of Alameda County prisoners in California State Prison Registers, 1870–1911. Excludes all prisoners convicted of prior offenses or multiple charges.

prior offenses or multiple convictions are excluded.) Blacks and Orientals got longer sentences than whites; this result holds consistently except for Orientals convicted of grand larceny.[28]

Women make an even poorer showing than blacks or Orientals in our sample. There are so few for most crimes that comparison with men's sentences is useless. One thing seems clear: defense attorneys *thought* or *hoped* that conventional sentiment about the gentler sex would help. In 1909, Jennie Thurnher was convicted of burglary (a very rare crime for a woman). Her lawyer argued for leniency. He spoke of her first as a "little girl," and then as "a woman filled with womanly qualities." She was (he said) "an absolute virgin up to the time of her wedding. Yonder sits her husband whose arms are extended to her, willing to take her to his home, to his bosom." He begged the judge to remember that the defendant was "a woman," and one with a "sweet disposition." The judge was touched. The case, he said, caused him "a great deal of worry. Under the law of this state a woman who transgresses the law must be treated the same as a man. That is of course an extremely difficult thing for a man to do, but it must be done." He wanted to give "the shortest sentence" he had ever given for this crime. In the event, this was a one-year term (no. 4602).

The evidence, though fragmentary, suggests a different story. From Alameda County, 11 women first offenders went to prison for grand larceny between 1870 and 1911. Their average sentence was forty-two months. At the same time 173 men, also first offenders, went to prison on this charge. *Their* average sentence was thirty-four months. This implies at least some slight discrimination against women. But

28. Of course, it is possible—though unlikely—that blacks and Orientals committed more savage and less excusable crimes.

these are figures only for women sent to prison; perhaps these were the worst of the lot.

The evidence, then, is inconclusive. We know that the races were *not* equal in the white man's mind, that women belonged in the home, that the double standard was rampant. But variables like sex, race, or age do not explain very well the range in sentencing. Overall, it seems as if practice did follow theory in one regard: judges, juries, and prosecutors assessed *this* man or woman, *this* crime, one by one. All the baggage of contemporary prejudice—against people who drank, against tramps, against drifters, and so on—entered into the judgment, along with popular theories about deterrence, and whatever else rattled about in the attic of the mind. The best predictor of sentence is the gravity of the crime; but the gravity of a crime is itself a shifting social judgment. And much of the variance is left unexplained —a residue not easily accounted for except by the rather lame and empty proposition that popular prejudices and ideas molded results. Middle-class norms wrote the script in criminal justice; and nothing stood in the way—certainly not any timeless conception of justice or law, or the lawyer's litany of "rights." Criminal justice was not a watertight box, but a membrane; outside values and forces constantly flowed through. These conclusions are strengthened when we consider how reforms of the period—juvenile justice and probation— worked out in practice. To this matter we now turn.

Juvenile Justice

At the beginning of our period, California had no special court for children who committed crimes. In fact, no state did: the first juvenile court in the United States was set up in Illinois in 1899. In 1870, California had no special institutions of any kind for young offenders. The young went to jail or prison along with everybody else. Indeed, in the list of prisoners sent to San Quentin and Folsom from Alameda County, we find two twelve-year-olds, three fourteen-year-olds, three fifteen-year-olds, twenty-four sixteen-year-olds, and twenty-eight seventeen-year-olds.

In practice, throughout the period, police, prosecutors, and judges probably did treat children in a special way. Very young boys or girls were likely to arouse pity, especially if the crime was minor, or looked like a simple case of wild oats. In 1900, for example, Officer McKinley arrested Joe Willie, a boy of fifteen. Joe had stolen bolts and tools belonging to the Southern Pacific line. Judge Smith dismissed the case, but told Joe to report every week to the chief of police, "until further notice."[29] When three boys—the oldest was thirteen—stole seventy-five dollars from a quarryman in Berkeley (1906), they were "mildly" whipped by Chief Vollmer, and handed over to indignant parents.[30] A sour old scrooge of a candy-store owner had two boys arrested in 1901 for stealing a nickel's worth of candy. But Police Judge Smith "considered their tender years" and sent them home.[31]

From the beginning, press and pulpit clucked over a system that let children go to prison. Prisons were "houses of corruption," and "schools of crime"; they were no place for the young. In 1889 the legislature finally made a move. Two state reform schools were established, one in Whittier and one (the Preston School of Industry) at Ione, in Amador County.

The original site of Preston was a tract of state land, near Folsom; and the Board of Prison Directors was to double as Preston's trustees. But the site was shifted, and an independent board (of three members) was provided. Construction seemed to proceed in fits and starts; at one point money ran out, and the building stood "roofless and windowless," its tower "only half completed," exposed to "winter storms and summer sun."[32] Preston finally opened for business in 1894; carpets arrived on May 6 and 7 boys from San Quentin on June 13. In 1894–95, Preston held 167 boys; 24 of them, or 14.6 percent, came from Alameda County. There was one eight-year-old among the first 167 and two ten-year-olds, but the overwhelming majority were fourteen and above. The average age was in fact something over fifteen.[33]

Under the law of 1889, the judge could send a young offender (under sixteen) to Preston or Whittier for a term of one to five years, for any felony that did not carry the death sentence. (Juveniles convicted of misdemeanors could be sent to Whittier or Preston or to

---

29. *Oakland Tribune*, Mar. 31, 1900, p. 5, col. 5.
30. *Berkeley Reporter*, June 13, 1906, p. 1, col. 8.
31. *Oakland Tribune*, Apr. 23, 1901, p. 3, col. 3.
32. *First Biennial Report, Board of Trustees, Preston School of Industry*, July 1, 1892 to June 30, 1894, Sacramento, 1894, p. 6. In the meantime, some young felons were diverted to social agencies. George S. Kernan, convicted of first-degree burglary, went to the Boys' and Girls' Aid Society (no. 948, 1889).

The law of 1889 (Laws Cal. 1889, p. 111) authorized judges to commit young people to juvenile institutions. Under this law, young people between the ages of ten and sixteen who had been convicted of noncapital felonies were to be committed to one of the institutions, for a term of between one and five years. Juveniles convicted of misdemeanors could either be sentenced to county jail or be sent to one of the institutions. If the defendant consented, the judge could suspend criminal proceedings before trial, and send the boy or girl to a juvenile institution.

Whittier was a standard reform school; both boys and girls were sent there. Preston was all male and was designed to teach young men a trade.

33. *Second Biennial Report*, 1896, pp. 8–9.

county jail.)[34] In 1893, the one-to-five-year term was dropped; and any child eight to eighteen could be committed to Whittier or Preston for any length of time, up to age twenty-one. It was usual to commit for exactly that period; so Charles Veara, just short of seventeen and accused of burglary, was sent (without trial, at his request) to Whittier, for four years, one month, and eleven days (no. 1498, 1893). As this example shows, the judge could also suspend proceedings *before* trial and commit the young offender (if he or she agreed). The Superior Court could also take charge of incorrigible, vagrant, or destitute children, and park them with some welfare agency. Kate Donaldson, a "wayward young miss of fourteen," was committed to the Humane Society in 1891; her brother brought her to court, explaining that she spent her nights away from home, in bad company.[35] California was thus edging toward the system of juvenile courts: special proceedings (or no proceedings) for the young and a common jurisdiction over all children who needed "care," whether because they broke the law, or because they were destitute or simply hard to handle.

It is not easy to tell what life was like at Whittier and Preston. A description of Preston much later, from the 1940s, paints a grim picture.[36] Rules and regulations issued in the 1890s express a sober but not oppressive ideal. A superintendent and his assistant ran the school. Also on board were a secretary, a commissary (a "male officer" in charge of supplies), and a military instructor. This man, through "military training of his pupils," was supposed to instill "pleasure and pride" in the boys. There was also a matron, teachers, a steam engineer, a watchman to make the rounds every hour, and a farmer to take "general care of the farm and stock." The general regulations were fairly bland. Tobacco and liquor were forbidden, of course. The school was a *reform* school; every employee had the duty of inspiring the boys "with a love for study, morality, and a correct mode of living." There would be discipline, to be sure, but "the discipline of the family home, the school, the shop," not "that of a penal institution." Corporal punishment would be used only "after all else has failed"; "kind words fitly spoken are of more avail and exert a better influence

34. When a juvenile was convicted of a misdemeanor in the lower courts, he could be committed to a state institution. After conviction, a petition had to be filed in Superior Court, outlining the circumstances of the conviction and praying for a commitment order. In 1898, for example, Robert Ash and Henry Simons were convicted of petty larceny in Oakland Police Court, and committed to the Preston School of Industry by Judge Frank Ogden in Superior Court. Ash was sixteen, Simons fifteen (nos. 2167, 2168).

35. *Oakland Tribune*, June 23, 1891, p. 3, col. 3.

36. Malcolm Braly, *False Starts* (Boston, 1976) (describing life at Preston in the years beginning with 1943).

than harsh or unkind treatment." But Preston was decidedly no country club. Friends could visit only once every two months. The boys could write once every four weeks at the state's expense, once every four weeks at their own expense. They could receive letters, home newspapers and periodicals (including the *Youth's Companion* and *Golden Days*), but "no literature of the sensational kind."[37]

In the 1890s, more than 10 percent of the convictions in Superior Court ended with juvenile commitments—cases of precocious burglary, larceny, and forgery, among others.[38] After the juvenile court was created, in the 1900s, courts were encouraged to use the new process, and avoid "criminal" trials as much as possible. Finally, in 1909, the law directed magistrates, at preliminary examinations, to refer *all* juvenile cases to juvenile court. Naturally, then, fewer convictions in Superior Court resulted in commitments to Preston and Whittier (less than 4 percent between 1900 and 1910).

The first true juvenile court began in Cook County, Illinois, at the very end of the nineteenth century.[39] In theory, it was no criminal court at all, but a forum for young people in trouble, whatever the cause. The Illinois law applied to children who were "destitute or homeless or abandoned," or who begged or "lacked proper parental care," or who were "living in a house of ill-fame or with any vicious or disreputable person," or whose homes were unfit because of "neglect, cruelty or depravity on the part of . . . parents." It also applied to children under eight found "peddling or selling any article, or singing or playing any musical instrument upon the street or giving any public entertainment."

The California law, passed in 1903, contains very similar language. The law did not actually set up a separate court. There would be a "juvenile court" in any county with more than one Superior Court judge; but the "court" was nothing but one of the regular judges, wearing a different hat. The judge had power to commit a "dependent" child to a society for the care of dependent or neglected chil-

37. *Preston School of Industry at Ione, Rules and Regulations* (Sacramento, 1894).
38. Some young people ended up spending more years in confinement than if they had gone to prison. But this was all right, according to the California Supreme Court, because Whittier and Preston were places not of punishment, but of "reformation, discipline and education." Ex parte Liddell, 93 Cal. 638, 640 (1892); Ex parte Nichols, 110 Cal. 651 (1896).
39. Laws Ill. 1899, p. 131. On the rise of the juvenile court, see Robert M. Mennel, *Thorns and Thistles: Juvenile Delinquents in the United States, 1825–1940* (Hanover, N.H., 1973); Anthony M. Platt, *The Child Savers: The Invention of Delinquency* (Chicago, 1969); Steven L. Schlossman, *Love and the American Delinquent: The Theory and Practice of 'Progressive' Juvenile Justice, 1825–1920* (Chicago, 1977); Sanford Fox, "Juvenile Justice Reform," *Stanford L. Rev.* 20 (1970): 1191.

dren, or to a "respectable citizen of good moral character." The options were wider for delinquent children; the child could remain home (under the eye of the probation officer), be boarded out, be committed to an agency, or be sent to reform school.[40] The idea in California, as elsewhere, was to handle each child individually, to protect children, to spare them entry into criminal society. The judge would be a "friend" to those who behaved and an "avenger" to bad boys and girls. But even for these, the "fears thus implanted" by the process would hopefully "contribute toward . . . reformation."[41]

The first juvenile case in Alameda County—case no. 1—was filed on June 30, 1903. The subject was twelve-year-old Earl A. McArthur, of Peralta Street, Oakland, a "dependent and delinquent minor." His mother, Israella F. Very, signed the petition. Earl, she said, was "unmanageable" and "very abusive." If she tried to discipline him, he threatened her and used "profane language." He was dishonest at work and a persistent truant at school. On July 9, 1903, Judge Melvin signed an order committing the boy to the custody of a probation officer, Charlotte Anita Whitney.[42]

As far as we can tell, juvenile court proceedings were used rather sparingly at first: there were 15 filings in 1903, 25 in 1904, 23 in 1905, and 15 in 1906. After 1906, there was a sharp rise in filings: 92 in 1907, 153 in 1908, 175 in 1909, and 283 in 1910. The total, through the end of 1910, was 782.

These early files have (more or less) survived. They are, alas, quite sketchy, and from them we harvested a most meager crop of information. Table 6.13 shows what we were able to find about the types of complaint. The complaints, of course, reflect the mixed nature of juvenile justice. Many of these boys and girls were accused of acts that would have been crimes for adults as well: for example, Richard Fought, sixteen, who in December 1900 "did . . . feloniously enter the building . . . of V. W. McCoy with . . . intent to commit larceny" (no. 505). Even here one sometimes wonders: Levi Meiss, sixteen, was delinquent because he "maliciously" overdrove a horse (no. 601, 1910). Still others were "truant" or "incorrigible"—terms

---

40. Laws Cal. 1903, ch. 43.
41. This is from a talk given by Judge Waste to the West Berkeley Mothers' Club. *Berkeley Reporter*, June 6, 1908, p. 8, col. 3.
42. Charlotte Anita Whitney, born in 1867, was secretary of Associated Charities, and a woman of strong left-wing sympathies. In 1919 she was arrested in Oakland and charged with violating the Criminal Syndicalism Act. She was convicted and appealed to the U.S. Supreme Court. She lost there in the famous case of Whitney v. California, 274 U.S. 357 (1927). She was then sixty years old. The governor, C. C. Young, pardoned her in June 1927, and she was spared a term in prison. *Reprieves, Commutations and Pardons, 1927–1928*, pp. 6, 23–29.

Table 6.13. Types of Complaint in Juvenile Cases, 1903–1910

Complaint	No.	%	Complaint	No.	%
Crime v. persons	15	8	Multiple charges	11	6
Crime v. property	45	23	Drunkenness	3	2
Sex offense	21	11	Destitution	18	9
Incorrigibility	16	8	Unknown	4	2
Truancy	26	14	Other	15	8
Unfit home	18	9	Total	192	100

Source: Sample of juvenile files: first 30 cases; then every fifth case, through Dec. 31, 1910.

certainly not part of the penal code. Others were homeless, for example, Joseph Chambers, ten, "found wandering without any home or proper guardianship or any visible means of subsistence" (no. 593, 1910). Little Lillian King, one year old in 1907, had done nothing wrong except to be born to a broken family, the "destitute" daughter of an "immoral" mother. Another unfortunate was William Phal, four years old, whose father was dead and whose mother, Julia, was "not sufficiently strong" to support him and his older brother Albert. Little William, declared "destitute," went in January 1908 to the Golden Gate Orphanage and Industrial Farm.

The double standard was in full operation. Charges of immorality were leveled mostly at girls: for example, Enid Foss, age sixteen, turned in by her mother in December 1908, accused of "immoral" sex relations; or seventeen-year-old Verenice Antissime, guilty in 1909 of an "immoral life"; or Katie Walsh, a fourteen-year-old prostitute, sent to Whittier in December 1900 (her father was dead, her mother a "victim of melancholia"). May Fittock, fifteen, kept late hours; so did Ethel Jacobsen, thirteen (both in 1908). Boys were not totally immune: a fourteen-year-old, in 1910, was accused of indecent exposure; in the same year two seventeen-year-olds and a fifteen-year-old stood charged with statutory rape. These acts, to be sure, were also crimes for adults; an "immoral life" as such was not.

An ungrateful child may be sharper than a serpent's tooth; but Shakespeare gave us no metaphor for the mother who throws up her hands and delivers a child to the juvenile court. Louise Rolland's mother called her daughter "incorrigible." She had made (she said) "every effort" to walk Louise in paths of decency. It was no use. Louise at thirteen kept company with "bad and dissolute characters"; she even stayed out all night (no. 93, 1907).

Petitions from parents occur with monotonous regularity. Minnie W.

Young was the mother of George Oscar Young, three months short of eighteen. She was a widow, unable to control her "incorrigible" and "vicious" son—a son who paid her "no respect whatsoever." She was afraid he would "commit some act . . . which will bring great disgrace upon himself and his family." The cure was Whittier (no. 86, 1907). Bartolomeo Comella, a widower, also had an "incorrigible" son—Salvatorio, fifteen years old. The boy stayed out "late at night and . . . upon his return he does not explain to his father where he has been." Also, on April 29, 1907, he stole $100 from his father's trunk (no. 100, 1907). Mary A. Coburn's son, Charles, thirteen years and five months old, "frequents the company of reputed criminals" and "habitually visits saloons"; he also went to "places of entertainment" where liquor was sold. Charles was incorrigible, and a truant besides (no. 28, 1904). The cross Mrs. Adelia Duvernay had to bear was her boy Arnold, sixteen, who did not "obey . . . reasonable orders," stayed out late, and finally ran away (no. 513, 1910). These were all cases of breakdown in parental authority. It is striking that many of the parents were immigrants, whose children lacked Old World respect. Others were parents without partners, pathetically unable to cope as the family crumbled. In desperation, baffled and angry, these parents turned to the state.

What happened to their children? Unfortunately, the records are poor. In a sample of 180, we find very few dismissals (3); but for 35 percent of the cases (65 out of 180), the file does not tell us disposition at all. For 125 cases disposition is known; of these, 50 ended in probation. Seventy children were removed from home and placed elsewhere: some with the Boys' and Girls' Aid Society, or Associated Charities, or an orphanage; some were sent to Whittier or Preston.

Probation

For adults, probation entered California law in 1903. From that year on, the code provided that a judge could put a defendant on probation, if the judge found "circumstances in mitigation of . . . punishment." The law also spoke of probation officers and probation reports.[43] If a case seemed a good candidate for probation, the judge

43. Cal. Penal Code, § 1203. This section, enacted in 1872, spoke of the judge s right to take into account "circumstances . . . either in aggravation or mitigation of . . . punishment." The section was changed in 1903, to add the power to put the defendant on probation. The section was further amended in 1911. This amendment referred specifically to the work of the probation officer, who was to investigate and make a report, "recommending either for or against release upon probation." But this had been the practice since 1903, in any event.

turned it over to the probation officer. He filed a report; then the court made up its mind after reading what the officer said. Benjamin Boynton, who pleaded guilty to grand larceny in July 1903, was the first defendant granted probation in the county (no. 2690).

If a defendant won probation, he was usually put in custody of a relative, friend, or employer. He also had to report every week to his probation officer. Manuel Alveo, for example, pleaded guilty to a serious charge of assault in 1907; he was put on probation for two years, in his father's custody (no. 4701). Probationers could not leave the county without permission. Sometimes probation was combined with a prison term. This increased the state's power to supervise defendants after release. Joe King and John Swanson, for example, pleaded guilty to two counts of second-degree burglary in 1910. On one count, King was sentenced to four years in San Quentin, Swanson to three years. For the second count, each defendant was placed on probation (nos. 4782, 4783).

Probation was a two-edged sword. It brought some humanity into sentencing. A poor first offender did not *have* to go to prison. It was a godsend for people like Lewis Bobroskie. Bobroskie, in 1905, pleaded guilty to statutory rape. He had never been arrested before. Before probation, the judge would have had little choice: the minimum sentence for rape—of all sorts—was five years. Instead, the judge put Bobroskie on seven years probation (no. 3021).[44]

But there was another face to probation. It was a grant of vast power to judges (and probation officers).[45] If a defendant wanted probation, his fate was in the hands of a man (the probation officer) who was free to take into account all sorts of "evidence" that a jury could not legally hear. "Due process," in the strict lawyer's sense, was a kind of fairy tale to begin with; probation made it more so.

The probation law said nothing about pleading guilty; but in the real world, a defendant who insisted on his right to trial by jury gave up any chance for probation. As we saw, in Judge Brown's court (1909–10), forty-one out of forty-two adults put on probation had pleaded guilty. In our sample, thirty-two defendants were released on probation; all but one of these had pleaded guilty. The one exception was a certain Alexander Sevilio. Sevilio was convicted of grand larceny; his attorney, Heim Goldman, made a heroic effort to save him from prison. Goldman paid back the stolen money, out of his

44. Bobroskie kept his nose clean; five years later the charges against him were dismissed.
45. In Judge Everett Brown's court, we hear that it was a "rule" that "where the district attorney opposes probation . . . the court will not refer it to the probation officer" (McCauley, no. 4564, 1909). Probably other judges followed a similar practice.

own pocket (his client agreed to repay him at two or three dollars a week); Goldman also lined up jobs for Sevilio—in construction work, and then as a dishwasher. The judge gave Sevilio four years on probation. But obviously, this level of lawyerly devotion was rare.[46]

There was, then, an unwritten rule: for any reasonable chance at probation, you *must* plead guilty. How this worked can be seen in a case from 1910 (no. 4866). The crime was arson; there were three defendants. Israel Liever was twenty-two, a Russian Jew struggling to succeed in the clothing business. Arthur Nagel was his partner. Israel was courting the daughter of a man named Schoenfeld. Schoenfeld talked Liever and Nagel into a scheme to cheat the insurance company. He gave the two partners a stock of goods, insured for twice its value. He moved into an apartment above the clothing store; here he overinsured his household effects. At 1:00 A.M. on August 19, 1910, the three men doused the store with gasoline, opened a gas jet, and set fire to the building. The building was destroyed, but bits of stock survived; the evidence was damning, and the three men were arrested.

Liever was tried first and convicted, after a fifteen-day trial. He then confessed, as did Nagel, who pleaded guilty. So did Schoenfeld. Schoenfeld had an arson record; everyone agreed he was the evil genius behind the crime. He was sentenced to fourteen years in prison. Nagel was released on five years' probation. Liever was in as deep as Nagel, but no deeper. He was a first offender, and even the district attorney had to admit that he was "of good moral habits . . . industrious and ambitious to make a success in the business world." But he had made the mistake of going to trial. Liever got five years in prison, while Nagel went free.[47]

Trial by jury was already, in 1903, a declining institution. But probation hurried it along toward obsolescence; it gave the guilty plea a powerful thrust. Between 1880 and 1902—before probation—guilty pleas disposed of about 35 percent of the felony cases. *After* probation, between 1903 and 1910, the percentage rose to nearly 50 (see Table 6.14).

A guilty plea, of course, did not guarantee probation. By no means: it only opened the door to a *chance* at probation. Many defendants who pleaded guilty, in hopes of probation, went away disappointed.

46. Statement of H. Goldman, People v. Sevilio, no. 4873, 1910.
47. The judge felt that Liever did not belong in prison, with "hardened criminals"; if there were such a thing as a state reformatory for first offenders, Liever belonged *there*. Unfortunately, there was not. The district attorney added that Liever "ought to be released on parole just as soon as it is compatible with the prison rules." Liever served out his five-year sentence.

*Table 6.14. Percentage of Guilty Pleas in
Felony Cases by Time Periods, 1880–1910*

	Before probation			After probation
	1880–89	*1890–99*	*1900–1902*	*1903–10*
Guilty pleas	68	69	19	127
N	180	200	59	257
% guilty pleas	37.8	34.5	32.2	49.4

Source: Sample of cases in Registers of Actions, 1880–1910.

Harry Hodges, a morphine addict, pleaded guilty to burglary in 1910. Judge Wells denied probation, in large part because of Hodges's habit. At San Quentin, as the judge was well aware, it was easier to get *on* morphine than off. But Judge Wells had a rule: no probation for drug addicts; and that was that.[48]

Hodges was bitterly disappointed—so much so that he wanted to change his plea. The judge would have none of this:

THE COURT: Did anyone tell you before you pleaded guilty you would be given probation if you did plead guilty?

HODGES: That is the only way you can get probation.

THE COURT: Did anybody tell you if you would do that you would be placed on probation?

HODGES: No, sir.

THE COURT: Then you pleaded guilty to the crime charged, did you?

HODGES: I pleaded guilty because you can't try to get probation otherwise.

THE COURT: Well, probation is denied.

HODGES: I would like to withdraw my plea.

THE COURT: You cannot withdraw your plea.[49]

48. Probation Officer Ruess told the judge: "I understand the situation at San Quentin and Folsom is very different from what it has been before. . . . One of the prison commissioners was talking to me two or three days ago. He said he felt absolutely certain from his dealings . . . that whatever morphine or other drugs there are in San Quentin or Folsom, it is mighty small in quantity." Ruess also noted: "I don't think anyone with the drug habit has ever been placed on probation here except one young man here recently who was not insane enough to go to the Insane Asylum, but too insane to be kept at Preston. We placed him on probation and sent him back to Ohio. On the way back he got out and put his hand on the track to see how it would feel to have it cut off. His hand was cut off on the railroad track." Proceedings upon Sentence, 8–10 (no. 4801, 1910).

49. Hodges was sentenced to one year in San Quentin, the minimum prison term for

Another defendant, Walter Tracy Teale, was luckier; perhaps Judge Ogden was more accommodating. The charge was writing a bad check (for $15.10) (no. 4226, 1908). Teale pleaded guilty. He was confident about probation, since the district attorney promised to cooperate. But Teale ran afoul of another rule of thumb: the judge gave probation only to the young, and Teale was forty-two. When Teale heard the bad news, he demanded the right to change his plea. He had a good defense, he insisted; he had pleaded guilty only to avoid "publicity and notoriety," and to spare his aged parents. Surprisingly, the judge let him change his plea. This story had a happy ending; a jury acquitted Teale. One cautious defendant, J. D. Waters, refused to plead at all until he saw the probation report (no. 2973). But the courts rarely allowed such dallying. The defendant first had to plead—then take his chances.

The first probation officer in Alameda County was a lawyer named Ezra DeCoto, later the district attorney. He was succeeded by Christopher Ruess. So far as we can tell, the probation officer followed this course of action: first he read the transcript of the preliminary hearing. Then he interviewed the defendant's family, and wrote (or telephoned) employers, schoolteachers, relatives, and others who knew the defendant. Usually local police were asked about the defendant's record. Sometimes they had other bits of information to contribute: in a rape case, the police told DeCoto the girl was nothing but "a common prostitute" (Gardiner, no. 3049, 1906). Most important of all, the probation officer talked to the defendant, trying to get some measure of the man. It was this, above all, that determined the defendant's fate. Was he worth saving, *could* he be saved, or not?

The *reports*, then, were crucial. Usually, the judge did what the probation officer recommended. These reports were the judge's main window on the defendant's soul, except for what his own eyes, ears, and insides told him. The judge was inclined to go along with a strong recommendation *for* probation; he almost never overrode a negative report. Raphael Scott, who pleaded guilty to burglary, was one of the few who succeeded. Scott, a first offender, wrote a pitiful letter from jail to the district attorney (April 20, 1908). Scott was the thirteenth of sixteen children, from a family so "humble" that the kids did not know their own birthdays; the father was dead; Scott went to work at fourteen; he worked for lumber companies and a street-sweeping contractor and also "engaged in sea-faring"; he was

---

first-degree burglary. Judge Wells thought Hodges "should be kept in confinement . . . to break him of the morphine habit if possible." Chief Deputy District Attorney Carey described Hodges as a "lazy, useless, weak and shiftless sort of [man], who could not be successful on parole."

a member of the sailors' union. He was about to sail for Alaska when an "impulse" overcame him. He tried to steal a "talking machine," thinking it would give him "companionship in that lonely place." He begged for probation, to spare his mother "the sorrow and disgrace I have brought on her (I being the only one who has made a mistake of the sixteen)." Probation Officer Ruess was unmoved, because Scott was "an habitual intermittent drunkard, with all the risk that implies." But the judge gave Scott his chance (no. 4349).

Such grace and favor was rare. It was somewhat more common for the judge to *deny* probation, even though DeCoto or Ruess recommended it. These were usually the weaker, more hesitant reports, the reports that said "on balance." Lee Von Jacobs was a first offender, twenty-two, son of a German saloonkeeper who owned a ranch outside Los Angeles. Young Lee played piano in a roadhouse. He got drunk, broke into the bartender's room, and stole twenty-seven dollars. Reuss called him a "third grade risk," but worth a chance— maybe. He could be sent to the family ranch. The judge denied probation: first, because Von Jacobs had failed to "provide for his wife"; second, because he was "a confirmed drinker"; and third, because it was not court policy to release probationers outside the county.[50]

Occasionally, the judge said no even over a strong recommendation. Judges had their views; certain crimes, they felt, *deserved* prison; and certain patterns of behavior showed that defendants needed harsher medicine than the syrup of probation. Judge Brown was particularly stern. He sentenced Donald A. Moore in 1910 (no. 4831) even though (he said) the scene in court was the saddest he had ever seen. To send Moore to prison, Judge Brown had to conquer his own heart (this was easier to manage than the judge thought it was). Moore was twenty years old, a forger, on his own since age sixteen, married, with a pregnant wife. His father, a respectable businessman, begged and pleaded for him, so piteously that it would have melted a stone. Even the district attorney joined in. But the judge thought probation was out of the question: young Moore had a history of forgery; he had never gone to prison, but he had never learned a lesson either. Judge Brown was afraid of setting a "precedent." He sent Moore to San Quentin for a two-year term.

If an offender was over sixteen but under eighteen, the judge could choose between probation and juvenile commitment. Leo Udell and Johnnie Hall (no. 4330) pleaded guilty to burglary in 1908. The court asked for a probation report. Udell was sixteen, the son of a poor

50. But it was occasionally done. Abe Halff, a forger, was released in 1907 on probation, in custody of his brother in San Antonio, Tex. (nos. 4183, 4184, 1907).

plasterer, living in a crowded part of West Oakland. There were five other children. Once he had been arrested for stealing chickens, and in the fifth grade, he had been kicked out of school for misbehavior. He and Johnnie Hall broke into a dry goods store and took twenty-five dollars. Ruess felt Udell's home was "not as strong as it needs to be in keeping him from further idleness and crime." This appealed to the judge: he sent Udell to Preston, during minority, which meant until July 12, 1913. Udell's father had to pay eleven dollars a month for his upkeep there.[51]

Johnnie Hall (probably only fifteen years old) lived with his mother, who was twice divorced and once deserted. Johnnie had been arrested as a vagrant, and put on juvenile probation. He had had "sexual relations with two different girls." One of these girls gave him VD. His mother was frank with Ruess; after a boy reached twelve, she expected him "to have relations with girls of a sexual nature." This candor convinced Ruess that the "boy had not been subjected to severe standards of clean manhood." If Johnnie *was* fifteen, he should be sent out of Oakland to live with an uncle. If he was sixteen, Ruess recommended a suspended judgment and long probation. Preston, he thought, was a poor choice; it did not remove the dangers of bad company. The judge decided Johnnie Hall was only fifteen, and returned him to juvenile court. There he was declared delinquent, and put on probation.

Was probation a success? The probation officers, who had an axe to grind, certainly thought so. In 1904, when Ezra DeCoto had a mere six probationers in tow, he was sure they would "live good, decent, honest lives." The program had, in one year, already saved the state at least $744, by keeping men out of jail.[52] Christopher Ruess's report, in 1908, noted 75 adults and 100 juveniles put on probation in a two-year period. Most, he felt, stayed out of trouble and jail.[53] Indeed, most probationers did serve out their time without incident. The practice was to let them, when their time ran out, retract their guilty pleas;

---

51. Udell behaved himself at Preston, and was out, in fact, two years early.

52. *Proceedings of the Third California State Conference of Charities and Correction* (1904), pp. 120, 126–28.

53. Some adults (twenty-five) had been released on "voluntary probation." There was no legal basis for this practice (it was very common for juveniles), and Ruess did not think much of it for adults, even though it spared the defendant "the record of a plea or verdict of guilty." *Third Biennial Rpt. State Board of Charities and Corrections* (1908), pp. 173, 175. Robert Hildebrand, for one, charged with statutory rape in 1906, was released on his own recognizance for a four-month period, under orders to report to the court every two weeks; afterwards, he had to report to the probation officer (Ruess). This went on for years. Hildebrand behaved himself, got a job and a wife. In 1909, Ruess asked the court to dismiss the information, which it did.

the state then dismissed the charges, and wiped their records clean. William S. Guest, for example, pleaded guilty to grand larceny in 1905, and was released on two years' probation. In 1907, after two years as "a law-abiding citizen," he was discharged from probation. He then withdrew his guilty plea, and, on motion of the district attorney, the court dismissed the charge (no. 2943). Of forty-two probationers in 1909–10, one disappeared, one went to jail for other crimes, three violated the terms of probation; for thirty-four the system worked. It saved money, and it also saved their "manly self-respect."

Inevitably, some probationers fell from grace. Elmer Wells was a fifteen-year-old, charged with robbery. Probation was rare for this crime, but Elmer got it. Two and a half years later, he was arrested for violating his probation and sent to Preston (no. 4081). Fred Stevenson (grand larceny) lasted only three months out of a ten-year probation (1908). For his violations, he was sent to San Quentin to serve a six-year term (no. 4351).

The petition to revoke probation was usually filed by the probation officer. It recited the violation and asked for a hearing in court. At the hearing, the judge generally asked for a new probation report. The process sometimes took considerable time. On December 8, 1909, a petition was filed to revoke the probation of William Walderman, a forger. The hearing was first held on December 14, 1909, and continued twice for further information. On February 16, 1910, the court denied the petition; Walderman walked out (more or less) free. On May 18, 1910, a new petition was filed; again a hearing was held. The hearing lasted four days. This time, on August 10, 1910, the court revoked probation and sent Walderman to prison (no. 4161).

On what basis did a defendant win—or lose—his right to probation? It is not always easy to tell. Early probation reports are quite sketchy. William S. Guest's took up less than a page, but it was favorable. Guest belonged to the Twenty-third Avenue Methodist Church; he had always been considered a "man of good standing." He was a veteran of the Spanish War; he served in Company C, Second Regiment, Georgia Volunteers, in 1898, and did "honest and faithful" service. DeCoto recommended probation.[54]

Later reports are fuller, and go into greater detail. They were meant to shed a bright light on the defendant's soul. This they sometimes did; they also shed a bright light on the soul of the probation officer, and the respectable citizens of Alameda County. Clearly, DeCoto,

54. Alas, it was later revoked; Guest "commenced to drink steadily," and was several times "under the influence of liquor." Still later Guest was more successful at probation; see text following note 53.

Ruess—and the judges—believed in the current jumble of theories about crime and criminal personalities, about the role of heredity and environment in crime. They were not deep thinkers, to be sure; neither more or less humane, one suspects, than the average of their class and sort. They were sure that drink, bad company, and loose habits were evils. They were certain that family background was decisive, that "weakness" or strength of character helped bend the twig. Church was good; theater was bad. Literature was good; dime novels were bad. Marriage was good; masturbation and brothels were bad. Cigarette smoking was bad. The ultimate question was one of personality, of character. Prison was for the unregenerate. Judges often spoke about sending a man to San Quentin, to "cure" him of drink, or opium—or crime in general. One wonders if, in their hearts, they really believed in such "cures." San Quentin was in fact a place for incurables. For those who could be saved, probation was the answer.

To find out about character, habits, inheritance; to serve up a stew of gossip, intimate detail, and hocus-pocus—this required hard work, and dogged certainty. It meant snooping into corners of the defendant's life, for "evidence" that had no *legal* bearing on innocence or guilt, and that no lawyer could get before a jury, except by some trick. Yet these things *had* to be uncovered, because the theory of probation demanded them. Ruess, speaking to the ladies of the Fannie J. Coppin Club, in 1908, compared his investigations to a doctor's diagnosis. He had to know his man "through and through." In ordinary criminal process, the lawyers tried to keep out important information, on this or that legal grounds. Ruess's job was the opposite. He had to bring information *in*.[55]

It might be useful to look at examples, to see what reports were really like. L. Howard Mendell, guilty of forgery (no. 4296, 1908), was a first offender. Investigation turned up some troublesome facts: Mendell had been in trouble in the army; his reputation was bad back home in Missouri. Mendell's old doctor wrote a damning letter: the man was "guilty of theft and forgery"; only "the respect in which his father, mother, and brother are held" prevented prosecution. The doctor thought he was a "dangerous criminal." This was the rankest sort of hearsay; but it ruined any hope of probation. John Martindale, who pleaded guilty to petit larceny (with a prior conviction), came from a family of "fair, if not good, grade." John had "practiced masturbation to extreme degree, he says, till of late." Then he began to visit prostitutes, "about two or three times a week." He also drank considerably. "Says he doesn't know why he steals. Says he doesn't

---

55. *Alameda Argus*, Jan. 30, 1908, p. 2, col. 3.

think hanging would be too good for him." Ruess certainly did not disagree; Martindale was "so degenerated that he is truly not responsible. Ought to live in a walled town for such persons, if there was such a place." The nearest approximation was prison, and Ruess "decidedly" recommended against probation (no. 4163, 1907). Still another man was written off as "a human being and yet not a human being, deprived of mind or cultivation of mind, dull and illiterate. . . . The temptation to steal was probably too great for his weak mind to resist" (no. 4729, 1909). Another offender was damned by bad habits: he had "masturbated since about 14," and was still not in total control; he resorted to houses of prostitution ("three times"), and was "fond of theatre." He had "no library card"—no doubt a sign of deep degeneracy (no. 4347, 1907).

Does all this mean that decisions were harsh and arbitrary? Yes and no. After all, jury decisions, and bench decisions, could be just as harsh and arbitrary. Discretion was everywhere: in police decisions, prosecutor decisions, bench decisions, jury decisions. This was, however, a rather higher grade of discretion than that which the jury (for example) bootlegged into law. It was lodged in a single man. He represented community opinion, but without the discipline of eleven peers. There are signs that probation officers learned something over the years; their attitudes softened somewhat. Ruess decided, for example, to stop reporting what he learned about the sex life of women. Good probation work required "full confessions of life habits." But the "double standard of morals" and the "unfairness of society toward woman" made it "impossible to get girls or women to tell the truth," unless they were sure "their confidence would be held sacred" (no. 4520). We must not forget, too, that probation gave some men (and women) a second chance, a chance that would have been impossible before. They escaped thereby the rot and ruin of prison.

Proceedings upon Sentence

A law of 1909 created a new little process, to take place after conviction. The court ("assisted by the district attorney") was to hold a hearing, to find out certain information that would help in fixing sentence, or in guiding a parole board later on. Did the defendant, for example, have any "mechanical or other trade"? What "facts" shed light on the causes of his "criminal character or conduct"?[56] The little inquiry was called "proceedings upon sentence." These proceedings

56. Laws Cal. 1909, p. 365, adding Penal Code § 1192a.

were recorded, typed, and put in the files. They can be very illuminating. They also give us a vivid, racy look at the minds of such
judges as His Honor, Everett Brown. "Judicial discretion" is a dull
phrase, but it hides an awesome reality: the power, almost of life and
death, held by a single man. He could be merciful, but he could also
be petulant, harsh, unyielding. His firm ideas about right and wrong,
about the evils of drink, about sex and family life, translated into
years in prison, or conversely, into at least conditional freedom. During these "proceedings," the court was able to shoehorn in a great
deal of material that did not measure up to legal standards of evidence. Like the probation report, this evidence bore on sentencing
and parole, not on guilt or innocence. But these proceedings could
mean as much for the defendant's fate as his own plea, or a jury's
verdict. We give an example to show the process at work.

It is the case of Charles Ross (no. 4691), standing before Judge
Everett Brown in January 1910. Ross has stolen money and some
gewgaws from a man in a boardinghouse. Ross is divorced and a
drinker. He has been arrested once in San Jose, it turns out, for
assault with intent to commit rape; but the case was dismissed. Ross
was, he says, as innocent as the driven snow; anyway, they "let me
go." The judge asks question after question, about Ross's record. Yes,
Ross admits, he was once arrested for drunkenness. Then he contra-
dicts himself, and gets in deeper and deeper. Back to the San Jose
incident: was Ross bound over to Superior Court? the judge wonders.
Then he asks about the present offense: what was Ross doing in the
boardinghouse? Ross says he went there to meet someone living
there: "a young lady, a girl I knew in Los Angeles." The judge presses
on: "was your purpose in going up there to have sexual intercourse
with that girl?" Ross (rather weakly, one supposes) denies this dreadful charge: he "just went up to see her and talk to her." Brown keeps
hammering away: "have you ever had sexual intercourse with this
girl?" Ross—a divorced man, mind you—says no. The next line of
attack is to inquire why Ross took the goods. He says: "I did not take
them intending to steal them. . . . I knew the man. The window was
open, I just took them to scare him."

> THE JUDGE: What did you plead guilty to burglary for?
> ROSS: Because — I didn't understand the law, if you
>   reached in a window it was burglary.

But this is the wrong answer, most definitely. Brown thunders down
at him: "Burglary . . . is a serious offense . . . don't make it any more
serious by adding perjury to it."

Ross retreats; his next ploy is to say he took the goods to scare the victim, nothing more. Another mistake. It goads Judge Brown into saying, ominously, that the case was "becoming more serious, now that the defendant is trying to make the court think that he committed this burglary as a joke, when he did not. It makes the offense a more serious matter." In the end, the judge hands Ross a "light" sentence —two and a half years at San Quentin. He drops a hint Ross *might* have been put on probation—but he lost his chances when he told his terrible lies.

Conclusion

In this chapter, we tried (among other things) to dig underneath the formal law, and to see what sentencing processes were really like. What we found, in essence, was this: sentencing was an intensely personal, intensely particular process. The statutes spoke mostly in terms of offenses; but judges had wide discretion, and the discretion if anything got wider with time. Such reforms as probation and juvenile justice saw to that.

To say that sentencing was very personal, and very particular, does not mean that it was arbitrary, random, unpatterned. Obviously the kind of offense did make a difference. Murderers were severely punished, and were *never* given probation. What we mean is that, for any given offense, there were great variations: one thief got probation, another went to prison for a nice long stretch. What explains these differences? We cannot tell for sure: but what information we have at least suggests that the usual mess of variables in the social scientist's bag (age, race, sex, social class) do not carry as much punch as one might guess.

This calls for some comment. We have no direct, systematic evidence of social class. It is perfectly obvious, of course, that the rich and respectable are not often found squirming in the dock. But neither do we find the respectable poor. Rather, our defendants seem to be, first of all, an unlucky bunch, and second of all, *social* misfits, rather than the poor as such. Most were no doubt guilty, though perhaps no more so than others who slipped through the meshes of the process. Those who were convicted were dealt with more harshly if they made a bad impression, or had defects of character, family, inheritance, or background, even if (from our modern perspective) these factors had little or nothing to do with their crimes, and should have had little or nothing to do with the punishment.

Our period was a period of science, of rationality; we are not dealing with the Dark Ages. What looks to the modern observer like prejudice and unreason, paradoxically, comes from the search for rational decision. The whole system was moving, growing, changing —away from laymen, part-timers, pure common sense, toward science, experts, professionals. But the science was the pseudo-science of the day. Popular opinion about the deserving and the undeserving among transgressors was the ultimate judge. Criminal justice rose no higher than its source.

Chapter 7
Front Page: Sensations
in the Courtroom

Every year, there were a handful of cases at the apex of the system different from all the others. These were the big cases, the celebrated cases, the notorious cases: cases that made a splash in the papers, cases that people talked about in the streets. They were more mysterious or sensational than all the others; they dragged on longer, ate up more resources, and demanded more time and attention. There is no easy line between a "great" and an "ordinary" case. It is a matter of judgment or taste to guess how many "great" cases came up in any particular year. Five to ten at the most is a fair estimate. There was no mistaking the *really* big ones. In these, reporters crowded into the courtroom, and the public fought for seats. Every step was hotly contested, from jury selection to final verdict; clever, expensive lawyers pitted their cunning against the state; and each day brought fresh shock and surprise.

What set these cases apart? First of all, the crime itself. When some miserable wretch was caught taking cash from the till, or forging a twenty-dollar check, nobody much cared, outside his circle and the circle of the victim. But the lurid, bloody offenses, the murders and the great crimes of passion: these were a different story. Murder cases, too, had the smell of death at both ends. The victim's ghost hung over the courtroom. At the same time, the shadow of the gallows fell across the prisoner. Most of the sensational cases, then, were cases of murder; a few were cases of rape or seduction. One was a bombing. It was not always the crime itself that caused the sensation. Sometimes the criminal had the limelight, if he was rich, famous, or socially prominent. In one case at least, the *victim* was part of the shock: Isabella Martin was accused of planting a bomb at the house of a judge of Superior Court.

What do we learn from these big cases? We will set out a few examples, then try to pull together some general notions. Before we begin, however, a word of caution is in order. Much of what we know has been filtered through newspaper reports. This was, of course, the age of the yellow press. Crime news was shrill and sensational. Trials were described in tones of "coarse buffoonery and brutality." The press created "morbid tastes," then pandered to them. Arthur Train, who voiced these views, accused the press of gross indifference to justice. All that the newspapers wanted was good copy: "as many highly colored 'stories' as possible." Train blamed the press for the spread of the "unwritten law." If newspapers "united in demanding that private vengeance must cease," the "unwritten law" would die a natural death. The duty of the press was to give "an accurate report" of the evidence at trial, nothing more. Photographers, along with "sympathy sisters," should be banned from the courtroom.[1] This was, of course, an idle dream. Big cases made big news. They attracted crowds; the crowds generated stories; the stories generated crowds. At a good murder trial, like that of Benjamin Lichtenstein, in 1888, it was standing room only in the courtroom.

The question remains: how much of what we read was puffery or lies? There is no easy way to be sure. The papers did report testimony, some of it verbatim. The press was probably a more reliable witness about what happened at the trial itself than about background information, about what went on *before* trial. The press also had the bad habit of jumping to conclusions. For example, on July 10, 1883, the *Tribune* reported, in almost hysterical tones, the fiendish acts of a certain Andrew Sands. Sands, a "very powerful man, a carpenter by trade," abused his stepson, Charlie, a boy about ten years old. Sands stripped the boy naked, put his head between his knees and whipped him with a braided strap: "with terrific force . . . the relentless leather cut deep into the tender flesh of the boy . . . the hissing thong also cut into the muscle of the child, and when the horrible torture ended, the victim was a mass of blood and bruises." Clearly, Sands was an "unnatural wretch," possessed by a "demon of rage." He locked poor, helpless Charlie in a room, but Charlie—a "frail, gaunt, delicate boy weighing not more than 50 pounds"—managed to escape.[2] All well and good; yet, a few days later the following bland entry appeared in the *Tribune*: "Andrew Sands, charged with battery upon his little stepson, was acquitted in the police court yesterday, the jury considering that he was acting only on the desires of the mother, and that he did not whip the boy maliciously."[3]

1. Arthur Train, *Courts, Criminals and the Camorra* (New York, 1912), p. 62. W. I. Thomas wrote in 1908 that the yellow journal, "advocating" crime, vice and vulgarity, "becomes one of the forces making for immorality." Quoted in Edwin H. Sutherland, *Criminology* (Philadelphia, 1924), p. 166.

2. *Oakland Tribune*, July 10, 1883, p. 3, col. 3.

3. Ibid., July 14, 1883, p. 1, col. 5.

A Bouquet of Violets

On August 2, 1897, Clara Fallmer shot and killed her lover, Charles LaDue. Clara was fifteen years old, and she was pregnant. She wanted Charles LaDue to marry her. He refused. This cost him his life.

Joe Luque, a barber in Alameda, saw the crime. Joe was standing opposite Van Vorhies Drug Store, chatting with a friend. Charles LaDue got off the train; Joe saw him talking to a young girl. He heard a shot; Charles fell to the ground. Clara then turned the pistol on herself. Johnny Manuel, who worked in a borax refinery, had just gotten off the train himself. He and some others dragged Charles into the drug store; later they took him to his mother's house, on Webb Avenue. Dr. C. H. Lubbock examined him. Charles had a gunshot wound in the left breast. The doctor saw at once that the wound was "necessarily fatal"; sure enough, a week later Charles was dead. Clara, however, did not die. She recovered, and was charged with murder. On October 16, 1897, she appeared before H. T. Morris, justice of the peace in Alameda Township. Lin S. Church, chief deputy district attorney, represented the state; George W. Reed appeared for Clara. The result was a foregone conclusion. Clearly, there was evidence enough to bind her over for murder. No bail was set, and Clara was taken to jail.[4]

The trial in Superior Court was the sensation of the Christmas season. Clara was arraigned on November 17, 1897; she pleaded not guilty. Her trial began in the middle of December. A. L. Frick joined Reed on Clara's team; thus she had the very best legal talent on her side. The *Tribune*'s account of opening day was short, colorless, demure; but as the trial went on, headlines got thicker, the story gobbled up more printer's ink, and it moved to the front page, elbowing out other news of the day.

From the first, Clara herself was the center of attraction. She sat in court with her sister, and a friend, Cora Whitstone. Clara wore "a blue cloth suit with hat to match." A thin veil covered her face, and she clutched in her hands a bouquet of violets.[5] This bouquet, or its

4. Under § 1270, a defendant charged with a capital crime "cannot be admitted to bail when the proof of his guilt is evident or the presumption thereof great."

The account of Clara Fallmer's case is taken, in part from the files (no. 2073, 1897), in part from coverage of the trial in the *Oakland Tribune*. Compare the treatment in detail of a group of nineteenth-century trials, analyzed as morality plays, in Mary Hartman's *Victorian Murderesses* (New York, 1977).

5. The press meticulously reported what women victims wore. In the trial of Lester McNulty for assaulting Dorothy Olson, one of the great cases of 1906, we are told, for example, that she appeared in court "dressed in a stylish long automobile coat of gray

replacement, appeared again and again; it became, in a way, her trademark. The *Tribune* soon warmed to the subject: Clara, "pale and trembling, pitiably frail and delicate," faced the jury, "her face gray with a shadow of a great fear." She was a symphony in blue: "neatly gowned in a blue serge suit, with an Alpine hat of blue bound in leather. In her neatly gloved hands was a small bunch of violets. A dark veil screened the white, frightened face."

From the newspapers, no clear picture of Clara emerges. We never learn what she was really like. She was young, perhaps impulsive, perhaps a bit foolish. But the real Clara was hidden—under a veil, so to speak. The real Clara, of course, never walked the streets clutching violets. Violets, veil, and the rest sprang, no doubt, from the fertile brains of her lawyers. They had their work cut out for them. In at least one primitive sense, Clara Fallmer was guilty as sin: eyewitnesses saw her pull the trigger, wounding Charlie so severely that he died within a week. There was no question of self-defense. Because young girls do not usually run around with revolvers—any more than with violets—her behavior smacked of premeditation. There was no way to wriggle out of these facts.

But there was more to the case than facts. Clara Fallmer was fifteen, she was pregnant, she was, in her view, seduced and abandoned. In short, she had a powerful story to tell. Her story was not an excuse for murder, as far as the Penal Code was concerned. But the case was tried in front of a jury, not the draftsmen of the code. Clara's hope sat before her, in the jury box. She had to turn her trial into theater. If Clara pleaded guilty (as well she might) or bargained with the prosecutors (as well she might) or if she went through trial in any ordinary way, she faced long years of prison. (The gallows was most unlikely.) In a sense, it was scandal that saved her from this fate. The scandal, like her crime, was shocking and open. She chose trial by jury, and her lawyers built up a case out of an imaginary Clara: they turned her into an act, a role, a part in a drama, a player on a stage, pale, pathetic, clutching her violets.

Both sides were well aware that the case turned on theater. The lawyers haggled and jostled and struggled for position. Picking a jury was crucial. Attorney Melvin, for the prosecution, asked prospects if "the spectacle of a young girl charged with the killing of a man" would sway them. The defense asked: "Have you a young daughter?" Clara's counsel also dropped the first hint of his basic legal tactic: "Did you recognize the justice and humanity of the law

color and wearing a new hat entirely covered with white lace and a large spray of red roses." *Berkeley Reporter*, Mar. 16, 1906, p. 1, col. 2.

that protected the person who committed a crime while insane?" E. Q. Turner, a grocer from Berkeley, said he was biased against the insanity plea: "I am willing to be convinced, but I would like to see the man who could convince me." The defense challenged him on the spot. Two men were excused because they were deaf. One man was a lawyer; he too was excused. Challenges flew back and forth. The regular panel was exhausted; the sheriff brought in a special panel, forty new faces. Not until five in the afternoon, December 16, was the jury in place.

As the trial began, a crowd filled Judge Ogden's court. The mob was "hungry for sensation." Clara Fallmer sat "calm and immovable"; now and again, she lifted "her little bouquet of violets," and sniffed at their "perfume." The prosecution brought in its eyewitnesses. From the jury box, Dr. Dawborn of San Leandro, "an old man with a benevolent countenance," posed a question. A "bloomer girl" came to the trial in the afternoon. She sat "directly behind the prisoner . . . dressed in a fawn-colored suit with a wide velvet collar. . . . She attracted plenty of attention which she apparently enjoyed." Mrs. LaDue, the victim's mother, "in deep mourning," her voice "frequently broken with emotion," testified; her dead son had been twenty-one years old. The prosecution closed its case.

Now came the defense: Clara shot her lover "during a state of emotional insanity." She was "brooding over her delicate condition and LaDue's refusal to right the wrong by marrying her"; she became "unhinged." Her mind was "already frail by inheritance." Insanity ran in the family of "this little girl." Her sister, Mary, had been twice committed to Agnews Insane Asylum; she died there at age sixteen. Clara's mother was mentally unbalanced, "ever since the birth of her second child." She had a mania for throwing things—dishes, biscuits, wood. A grandfather committed suicide. Clara, as a child, had "malarial intermittent fever." She was delirious for two months, and "never entirely recovered. Her mind was left in a diseased and disordered condition." These skeletons in the closet were revealed by Clara's father, Rudolph Fallmer, "a red-faced and bald-headed German," who had a "choleric temper," and spoke poor English. Louise Fallmer, Clara's sister—"though only 24 years of age," she had been "married and divorced"—confirmed the sad family history. So did her brother, Rudolph.

Wednesday, December 22. The crowd, "as agape for a sensation as a thirsty man for water, surged into Judge Ogden's court . . . to gloat over the details of the inmost life of a young girl." Clara herself took the stand. "The blood receded from the full curling lips and the clear hazel eyes had an agonized expression, like the eyes of a terror-stricken fawn facing its enemies. . . . " When the lawyers "persisted in asking embarrassing questions," a "flush of shame dyed her cheeks." She told the jury "a miserable, shameful story. . . . Young as she was, she had drunk deeply of the poisoned cup of pleasure, and its dregs had been bitter to her taste." She told how she met LaDue, how they began to keep company. He asked her (she said) to marry him; he gave her a ring. She lived with him, and found herself, after a while, "in a delicate condition." Charlie knew what to do: he sent her to a Mrs. Smith, formerly Kitty Knight, in San Francisco. Clara took some "medicine," and was "very ill for a week or two." This worked; but in July she was pregnant again. She told Charlie the bad news. She said that he promised to marry her, when she turned sixteen. But instead, he began to see another woman. He was tired of Clara, she felt. She confronted him at a Grant Street restaurant, in San Francisco. She begged him to help her. He laughed.

Next in the trial came a battle of experts, squabbling over the insanity issue. The doctors argued, pontificated, nagged about "melancholia" and "transitory mania." Dawborn, the juror, asked whether there could be "mania without illusion, delusion or hallucination." Dr. H. N. Rucker gave "an informal lecture, telling the difference between melancholy and melancholia" (one came from disease, the other was "a functional disturbance"). The lawyers, too, wrangled and sputtered. They dickered over words. Yet, in a sense, it was all a charade. Insanity was not the real issue; the issue was Clara. The prosecution tried, a bit feebly, to break through the masks and disguises. They wanted to show she was not so innocent as she claimed, not quite the victim of a cad. They hinted she was older than she said. But the strategy failed.

It was, after all, 1897. There were two ways to look at the short, tragic life of Clara Fallmer. She might be a fallen woman, depraved, a creature of the lower depths. The prosecution hinted as much. Or, as the defense described her, she was a lonely, pathetic child, weak in mind, seduced and destroyed. Neither side could face the third possibility: that Clara was nothing special at all—a bit precocious, no doubt, high-strung, old beyond her years, but essentially a woman, with ordinary feelings and passions. Both sides accepted a Victorian picture of Clara, and of Charles LaDue. She had to be unbalanced or depraved—one or the other. He had to be a monster or a cad.

There is not a hint in the record that the sex life of Clara and Charles was anything special, nothing that had not gone on infinite times since Adam and Eve. Yet the *Tribune*, in its lust to sell newspapers, huffed and puffed with a prurient tone, proclaimed its horror and shock, leered and sneered, hinted at unspeakable acts and amazing debauchery. The *Tribune* also clucked in indignation over the women who came to watch, when they should have stayed home and read the *Tribune*. They "sat within the rail and listened . . . with the eager eyes and attentive ears of gossips." (Less fuss was made, of course, about the men who came, although one day the *Tribune* did call them "vampires.")

As the trial went on, the moral climate darkened: women, old and young, "swelled" the "female colony inside the bar." Women with "grim visages" came, regulars at many trials. What "attractive power," the *Tribune* moaned, led these women "to so present themselves in public?" These trials, after all, had "features of a repulsive character, which most women would blush to hear discussed elsewhere save in a murder trial." On December 28, the *Tribune*'s prudery reached some sort of climax. A large, "morbid crowd" had gathered at the trial. Blessedly, "the canaille was not permitted to listen"; Judge Ogden chased out the "scandal-seekers," using "the danger of suffocation" as an excuse. He also asked "beardless youths" to leave, lest their minds be poisoned by testimony "which discloses the life of the lowest of the demi-mondaines."[6]

Meanwhile, the trial drew to a close. It was time for concluding argument. A. A. Moore, Jr., for the prosecution, spoke for nearly two hours. He conceded that Clara "probably" deserved some sympathy. But the jury had sworn an oath to uphold the law. "We do not ask you to hang her. She is too young to die." But he did demand some punishment. They had to remember the danger of acquittal: other girls and women, "guilty of what she has been guilty," might fasten themselves on men and force them to marriage "at the point of a pistol." The jury must not let Clara free, "unwhipped of justice." That would set up a "bulwark" for "disreputable women," who might "point their pistols at men" and "demand to be made their wives," on pain of a bullet.

George W. Reed spoke first for the defense. Clara was young and unstable, he said. He leaned heavily on the defense of "temporary insanity." He drew a sad picture of her life: "Against her wish . . . she consented to improper conduct." She was "desperately in love." And Charles LaDue had betrayed her. Yes, she had done disreputable things, "things she ought not to have done." She had gone to a "dance house" in San Francisco, on Grant Avenue, for example, but

6. The trial was not good box office every day. One "raw and chilly" morning, the courtroom was only half full. The medical testimony was quite tedious, too; even the defendant "looked bored" at one point. The session was "tiresome in the extreme," the *Tribune* complained, as if the main function of the trial was to provide them with good copy.

she went there to talk to Charles, to demand her due. And who had introduced Clara Fallmer to such places? No one but Charlie LaDue.

Judge Frick came next, the big gun of the defense. He brought Clara into court—without her veil. "Can you see the defendant?" he asked the jury. A row of chairs stood between Clara and the jury. The chairs were taken away, and Clara sat in plain view. Frick asked: "Who does she look more like, her father or her mother?" The answer was obvious: the father was "round and rubicund," the mother "pale and thin." There was no question but that Clara favored her poor, distracted mother.

Frick played on the jury's sympathy, for hours on end. His strategy worked. On December 31, 1897, the jury gave Clara and her family a wonderful gift to start the New Year. It was a few minutes after 3:00 P.M. when the jury came back to court with a verdict. Clara Fallmer was innocent of murder. Clara fell into the arms of her sister, Louise. The jury had taken only two ballots. In the first, they stood eleven to one for acquittal. The second was unanimous. Mrs. LaDue stormed out, vowing revenge.

And so the curtain fell. Clara Fallmer left the courtroom, and the limelight; she faded away into the shadows. But in a sense she had always been in the shadows. Neither side cared about the *real* Clara Fallmer—or indeed, the real Charles LaDue. The necessities of trial turned them into roles, played on the courtroom stage. These roles were stock roles in some Victorian melodrama. They tell us more about the audience than about the actors or the play. And the system of criminal justice that tried Clara—and then let her go—was geared, as it always is, to the scripts and the values of the day, to a set of external values, as specific to the time and place as a lady's dress, or the shoes men wore on their feet.

Isabella's Bomb

The case of Clara Fallmer was as sensational as anyone could wish. But from the standpoint of legal process, it was plain, unvarnished, and relatively swift. For a vexed and tortuous life course without equal in our period, we turn to the case of Isabella Martin. *People* v. *Martin* swallows five whole pages in the Register of Superior Court; the case papers hog an entire file drawer, yards of documents and pleadings. Gallons of printer's ink and tons of newsprint were expended before the matter came to a close. Isabella Martin was tried twice and convicted twice; she appealed twice, and was finally dragged off to prison. All this took years.

The charge against Isabella was heavy. It was a crime against the very court that tried her. Isabella plotted to blow up the home of Judge Ogden. She had a grudge against Ogden, because of the way he handled a civil case in Superior Court. According to the prosecution, Isabella planned and directed the crime; but she did not plant the dynamite herself. Her tool was "Baby John," her foster son. He was sixteen years old. He was also the star witness for the prosecution.

The dynamite went off on March 19, 1907. The blast made a mess of the Ogden home, but no one was hurt. Nearly a year later, on March 2, 1908, Mrs. Martin was indicted. Her bail was set at $50,000—an astronomical figure. Naturally, she could not raise this amount. The issue of bail was only the start of four years of maneuvering. On March 25, 1908, Mrs. Martin's lawyer tried to quash the indictment. A grand juror, James P. Taylor, had talked to Judge Ogden, had heard the judge say Mrs. Martin was guilty. On April 17, 1908, the court granted the motion, and set the indictment aside. But Mrs. Martin did not go free. Immediately, the district attorney's office swore out a complaint charging her with the bombing. Isabella was rearrested. On May 22, 1908, Isabella went to trial. It was one of the longest trials in our period. The court sat in trial session for forty-three days. On December 15, 1908, the jury found Isabella guilty. The judge sentenced her to life at San Quentin. Mrs. Martin appealed; on March 30, 1910, the District Court of Appeal reversed her conviction, and ordered a new trial. Her second trial began on November 1, 1910, and lasted until December 23, 1910. This time the trial took thirty-seven days. Once again, Isabella was convicted; once again she was sentenced to life imprisonment in San Quentin. And once again, Mrs. Martin appealed. But this time, her luck, or her bag of tricks, had exhausted itself. She went off to San Quentin, on February 10, 1911, to wait for the ruling of the District Court of Appeal.[7] The court affirmed her conviction, on June 20, 1912. Less than a year later, on April 15, 1913, Isabella Martin, then fifty-one years old, was found to be insane; she left San Quentin for the Napa Insane Asylum.

Nothing in the files or records indicates what all this cost Isabella, or how she raised the money—or for that matter, what it cost the state of California. Clara Fallmer's case shows how time, money, skill, and the right set of facts might twist and deform the official rules of the Penal Code; Isabella's case shows how time, money, skill, and patience could contort ordinary rules of procedure. In the everyday

7. The trial court refused to give her a certificate of probable cause (see "Probable Cause" in Chap. 8, below); this meant that Isabella had to go to prison right then and there, while the appeal was pending.

case, the system moved along with fair speed and efficiency. In each case, the state and its agents had to make a kind of rough judgment: how much effort and time was *this* matter worth? The rules were bent and cut, for the sake of economy and speed. In a big case, on the other hand, a defendant with money and will could bend the rules in the other direction. His lawyer could play to the hilt every motion, technicality, and safeguard; he could seize every opportunity. Tiny points of law lay buried like dormant seeds; the right mix of chance and will could rouse them into furious life.

The Monsters of Telegraph Avenue

On November 9, 1898, the *Tribune* reported a terrible tragedy. A young girl named Lillian Brandes, of 2234 Telegraph Avenue, Berkeley, took her own life. Her family found her hanging from a post at the head of her bed, her "slender form" wrapped in a night robe.

Lillian lived in a two story house with her father, William Brandes, her stepmother, Etta, and her younger brother. Brandes was a night watchman and patrolman in Berkeley. Lillian had a "passion for reading works of romance." These books—which included tales of murders—provided "undue exercise of the emotions"; this may have unhinged her mind.

So the *Tribune* reported. But the very next day there were dramatic developments. Dr. S. H. Buteau had performed an autopsy. Lillian, it seems, had not killed herself at all. She died of a blow on the head; and she was hanged *after* her death. Her body was "covered with bruises from head to foot"; she had head wounds, possibly from a rubber hose. William and Etta Brandes were arrested on suspicion of murder. Thus began one of the most sensational cases ever tried in Alameda County. The *Tribune* decided, immediately, that Brandes was guilty; he had beaten his daughter to death, then tried to hang her, to cover up his crime. Other people felt the same way. There was even "talk of lynching." No case, it was said, had ever aroused such "widespread interest" as this one: a "little defenseless girl," murdered by "heartless parents."

The *Tribune*'s theory was confirmed by the coroner's jury. The jury found that "death was caused by injuries on the head inflicted by a blunt instrument in the hands of W. A. Brandes." Brandes appeared in Judge Fred Clift's court for his preliminary examination; the crowd was so huge that the judge had to clear out the overflow. The evidence seemed damning. Lillian had not lived very long on Telegraph Avenue. For most of her short, bitter life, she lived with an aunt in

Santa Cruz. Then she came to live with her father, exchanging a good home for a bad one. Mrs. Nina Richardson, a neighbor, had heard Brandes beating the girl, who begged him to stop.[8] Neighbors said she was yelled at. There was an obscure affair of some fifteen dollars, which Lillian may or may not have stolen, and which may or may not have touched off great rage on the part of father and stepmother. Brandes, everyone agreed, swore a lot. Some said the girl did not eat with the rest of the family; she lived a sort of Cinderella life—without glass slippers or prince.

Later the *Tribune* announced an even greater sensation: Etta Brandes was not married to Brandes at all! Mary Brandes, Lillian's mother, who lived in San Francisco, came forward with her story. She and Brandes had been married by a priest. Four years later they separated; but Mary never got a divorce. Brandes was living in sin! Even worse things were laid at his door. It seems he paid court to a Miss Emma Oliver, whose testimony added "another chapter to the volume of his misdeeds. It showed that he was steeped in a perfidy which stopped at nothing." Miss Oliver, twenty years old, was a nurse; she worked in the home of a "prominent family" in North Berkeley. Brandes told her his name was Ralph; he said he was single. After his arrest, he wrote her a "dear Emma" letter. He said he could not call on her for some time, that he had to go East; he advised her "to marry someone if she wished." She "deserved a good man," and she should find one. (But, he warned, never marry a "Spaniard or a waiter.") There were other women, too, in Brandes's life; but he flatly denied that his relations were "improper."

Clearly, he was a dubious, difficult man.[9] A deputy sheriff reported that people in Berkeley were afraid of him. He was a night watchman; but he made people feel nervous, not secure. Some customers subscribed to his watchman service "merely through fear"; they paid "their regular monthly allowance, believing it cheaper to pay the night watchman than to have his ill will." He followed women home and propositioned them.

The case seemed plain enough. Judge Clift bound Brandes over to Superior Court, to be tried on a murder charge. Etta was bound over, too. (As it turned out, she was never tried.) The trial of William Brandes was long, exciting, bitterly contested. The defense wheeled up big guns of its own. One was Dr. E. H. Woolsey, who contradicted all the other doctors. Lillian Brandes, he said, was *not* beaten to death.

8. The *Tribune* reported that Brandes broke down and sobbed when he heard this.

9. He was an uncooperative prisoner, too. He objected to having his picture taken for the rogue's gallery, and ruined the photographs by making faces. *Oakland Tribune*, Nov. 3, 1898, p. 4, col. 4.

She died of strangulation. To prove this point, the defense passed around a piece of Lillian's skull. Bennett, Brandes's lawyer, got this "gruesome relic" from the Berkeley morgue. Just before the funeral, Bennett and Dr. Woolsey came to examine the body; while no one was watching, they took away part of the skull. "The head was stuffed with excelsior and neatly sewed over and presented in no way a disarranged appearance." Bennett never bothered to tell the undertakers (or anybody else) what he had done. (He explained lamely that he had no chance at the time: "it was within a half hour of the . . . funeral. People were already beginning to rap at the door for admittance.") In any event, everybody got a chance to ogle Lillian's head-bone, and compare it with other skulls—this to bolster the theory that Lillian did *not* die of blows to the head.

Etta provided another sensation. Brandes never beat Lillian, she said; *she* beat the child. This was a noble attempt, the papers thought, to save her "husband's" neck. The trial went on and on; but interest never flagged. The strain was great; one of the jurors came close to "nervous prostration," and all the others suffered from "fearful strain." March 17, 1899, was "another day of sensations," according to the *Tribune*. As usual, the courtroom was packed, with "men of morbid natures and empty pocketbooks" and women "who feed on the sensation instead of attending to their household duties." The main event of the day was that Brandes fainted. He was taken to the washroom, where he revived, and sat for ten minutes "by an open window, sighing and moaning. He appeared overcome, or else a wreck mentally and physically." The *Tribune* dismissed him as "an actor"; a deputy sheriff called him a great faker. Actor or not, Brandes took the stand in his own defense, and sobbed and wailed to the jury "in a theatrical manner." He insisted that he loved his Lillian dearly; he was distraught to think she took her own life.

Finally, after fifty days of trial, the case went to jury; waves of rhetoric sped it on its way. Henry A. Melvin, assistant district attorney, described Brandes as a monster. Lillian, in happier days, had lived in a "beautiful city by the sea"—Santa Cruz—nurtured by her aunt, "a motherly old lady." She never missed "the father who had practically deserted her." Why did Brandes finally fetch her to his house? It was because she was "old enough to assist in the household drudgery." "Pause for a moment and think of the place to which he brought her," a place where he was "always swearing and cursing," a house where he lived "with a woman who called herself Etta Brandes, but who will not tell what relationship she bears to him" because the answer "would tend to degrade her." In this house of sin and foul English, the poor child was mercilessly beaten. "Her tender body was covered all over with bruises." Now Lillian's lips were "sealed with the great silence of death"; she could not "plead for justice." Nobody, however, had sealed the prosecutor's lips. He waved photographs in front of the jury, showing "the tender body of Lillian Brandes, marred by the foulest murderer that ever disgraced the image of his God . . . or ever desecrated the sacred name of 'father,' which he by his inhuman cruelty translated into murderer." Death by hanging was too good for such a man.

But Brandes was not bound for the gallows. True, the jury found him guilty, but of a somewhat lesser charge—murder in the second degree. This ruled out hanging. The judge delayed sentencing, at the defense's request. One of Brandes's lawyers had a case of "follicular tonsilitis." The delay irritated the *Tribune* and evoked a long, bitter editorial. Why this "paltering with justice?" Did only murderers have rights? Why cater to the "mawkish minds" that made the guilty "a subject of petting and sympathy?" Besides, tonsilitis was sometimes a "very obstinate malady." What if the attorney had to go to Arizona or Hawaii for his cure? It would be dreadful if "the moss of forgetfulness" covered up Brandes's "cruel, awful crime," like the moss on "the grave of his little . . . victim."[10] But in fact the tonsilitis ebbed; Judge Hall sentenced Brandes to life in prison.

This too was not the end. Brandes appealed, and the California Supreme Court listened. The court sent the case back to be retried. The Supreme Court did not write an opinion, and its reasons are obscure; but in any event, Brandes won a second trial. A. L. Frick took over Brandes's case. He tried a new line of defense. He gave up the claim that Lillian hanged herself. In essence, he conceded that she died after some sort of beating. But who struck the blows? Most likely Etta. This was a bold tack, but apparently it worked. Etta herself ran little risk. The district attorney had dropped the charges against her; he felt the case was hopeless. Yet this hopeless case was a godsend for Brandes and his lawyers. Frick needed only to plant seeds of doubt in the jury's mind; this might be enough to ruin the state's case. For nearly twenty-one hours, the jury was out; finally, in an obvious compromise, they found Brandes guilty of manslaughter. Judge Ogden gave him as stiff a sentence as he could: ten years at Folsom. It was, said the judge, "a wonder . . . that you were convicted only of manslaughter." To Judge Ogden, Brandes had gotten away with murder. Brandes himself insisted to the end he was an innocent lamb. In his own mind, *he* was the victim. His first trial he had called a farce and a mockery. He had been tried, he said, by the

10. Ibid., May 1, 1899, p. 9, col. 5.

newspapers, not by the jury. Except for the lying newspapers, he would have gone free. Now his second trial was over, and he faced ten years in a hellhole. Already he had lost two and a half years in county jail, years of strain and notoriety, years in which insults streamed in on him like so much garbage and rotten tomatoes. It was more than a man could bear.

Yet, curiously enough, *because* of publicity, because the crime was so dreadful, Brandes escaped from the gallows. This was a great case, and a great case has to be a perfect case for the prosecution. The defense fought tooth and nail; it exploited every chink in the prosecution's armor. The skull trick in the first trial, the bold use of Etta in the second—these saved Brandes's life. It was good lawyering and good theater. The state portrayed him as a monster, a vampire, a beast in human form. This was, perhaps, fatally exaggerated. When the state's case crumbled a bit around the edges, the jury questioned all of it; it fell like a house of cards.

In the end, the jury members saw the case in their own light. They read life more realistically, perhaps, than the *Tribune*. And, to be fair, no one knows what went on in the house on Telegraph Avenue. It remains a mystery. The one sure fact was that Lillian was dead. The hanging was almost certainly a fake. That Lillian was badly treated, beaten, seems also certain. Quite possibly she died after a beating, but who struck the blow, Etta or William? We will never know. That anyone *intended* to kill her seems unlikely. Brandes was probably no monster at all, only a harsh, impulsive, ignorant man, a man with a temper and a streak of cruelty—an old-fashioned man, authoritarian, impatient with children. It is even possible that he struck his daughter in a fit of misguided love. If so, then the second jury hit on a verdict that fit the case like a glove: manslaughter. Perhaps the lesson of the Brandes's case is that twelve real people, living in real homes with real families, in a case that touched on tensions and emotions they all may have shared in some form, could cut through the rhetoric, the cant, the purple prose, and reach the inner core.

The Curse of Drink

Charles G. Adams was another unlikely murderer. His victim was Dr. John G. Jessup. Adams was an Episcopalian minister, fifty years old at the time (1901). He was a widower, with two children. The older child was a daughter, Agnes, who was twenty-two. The Reverend Adams was a chronic drunkard. He started drinking in Southport, Connecticut, in 1888, where he had a pulpit. Later, he moved from city to city, job to job. He was too drunk to keep any post. Things went no better for Adams in California. In the end, drink addled his brain. Like many children of alcoholics, Agnes suffered terribly. The Reverend Adams was a good man, but he was cruel and abusive when drunk.

The tragedy occurred on June 18, 1901. Agnes was at a neighbor's house; she was afraid of her father, who was drunk as usual. He called the neighbor's house, on the phone, and asked Agnes to return. She was afraid to go alone, and she begged Dr. Jessup, her father's friend, a man in his fifties, to come with her. When they arrived, her father, completely drunk, called out to ask who was there. Dr. Jessup said, "It is I, Charlie. . . . You've got to stop abusing this girl." Adams shouted, "Don't come up the stairs, or I will shoot." But Jessup went anyway; when he got to the head of the stairs, he took off his coat and "hung it on a post at the end of the stairs." Adams was lying across the bed in the middle bedroom. He fired his revolver. Jessup staggered back, then dashed forward and wrenched the pistol from Adams. Then Jessup stumbled downstairs; Agnes rushed to help him. "Keep away from me," he said. "You will get covered with blood." He made light of his wounds; but in fact, the bullet sent him to his grave.[11]

In Berkeley's justice court, the judge was sympathetic, even warm, to Dr. Adams. He did not "believe for one moment" that the defendant should be "held on a charge of murder." Manslaughter, perhaps; he might even walk out unpunished. In the end, the judge bound Adams over on a manslaughter charge. In few cases do we sniff so strong a smell of class bias; Adams was not a tramp, not a foreigner, but a "reverend," brought to his knees by drink. And yet, surprisingly, the information filed in Superior Court charged the Reverend Adams with murder, not manslaughter.[12] Snook and Church, hired for the defense, moved to kill the information; Adams had "not been legally committed by a magistrate for the offense charged." Nevertheless, the trial went forward. But the reverend was clearly an object of sympathy—a victim of drink, a good man gone astray. The jury found him not guilty, by reason of insanity. A second "trial" followed immediately, to decide if Adams was still insane. Dr. D. D. Lustig, one of the examiners for the insane in San Francisco, testified. Dr. Adams was indeed insane. A chronic alcoholic, his morals were

11. Jessup was married, but separated. There are hints that he had been paying "marked attention" to Agnes, although this was by all accounts not a factor in the killing. See *Oakland Tribune,* June 18, 1901, p. 2, col. 3.

12. In California, the information could legally charge any crime supported by the evidence in the transcript of the preliminary hearing.

"mentally . . . so warped that he cannot reason with any degree of judgment." Dr. Rowell and Dr. Hatch agreed. On October 17, 1901, the jury took twenty minutes to decide that the Reverend Adams was still insane. The judge committed him to Agnews Insane Asylum, for as long as it might take to work a cure.

The Vice Hunter's Vice

Assault with intent to murder was not usually a sensational crime. But it was the basis of one of the most newsworthy trials of 1893. The defendant, George Gray, was also not the usual defendant. He was old, and had lived a life of spotless honor. He was, however, not the center of attraction at all. All eyes were on the victim, G. R. Bennett. Bennett—"holy" Bennett, as the *Tribune* called him, sarcastically— had been secretary of the Society for the Suppression of Vice. Apparently he was not much good at suppressing his own. In a real sense, Bennett, not Gray, was on trial. There was a third character in the drama, too: Gray's daughter, Ella, a young woman Bennett had "ruined."

The incident that led to the trial took place on cars of the Southern Pacific. C. J. Benjamin, a gateman, saw Gray and his daughter get on a local, traveling between Twenty-third Avenue and East Oakland. Bennett was already aboard; he was sitting in a corner, reading. Gray came up behind him and fired two shots. The first shot broke a window; the second struck nearby. Bennett jumped up and ran; Gray burst after him, firing again. Bennett sprang from the car; Gray ran to the door and fired a fourth shot. A group of men now grabbed Gray, and disarmed him. Then Bennett came back with *his* gun, and raised it to fire. A quick-witted bystander struck Bennett's hand with a cane; the pistol went off, but no one was hurt. Then the crowd disarmed Bennett too.

The whole affair was a draw, and perhaps it should have been left at that. But Bennett insisted on prosecuting Gray. At preliminary examination, Gray was duly held to answer; he came to trial before Judge Greene, in a courtroom "thronged . . . with people." "Long before the doors were opened," they clamored to get in.

The sensation, of course, was Bennett's double life, and what a handy villain and hypocrite he made. The name of the case was *People* v. *Gray*; but George Gray, the defendant, was totally upstaged. "That strict judge, 'Public Opinion'" was trying Bennett, not Gray. The *Tribune* had no doubt Bennett was "guilty"; the "vast Crowd" in Judge Greene's courtroom had "nothing but contempt for him. He is despised of men." He had—so claimed his wife—once before "ruined" a girl, in New York. Now he had shattered the life of Ella Gray.

The climax of the trial came the day Ella Gray took the stand. She told the classic tale of a good girl led astray. She had been a stenographer, working for Mr. Heap at the Boys' and Girls' Aid Society. She met Bennett, and fell deeply in love. They went for long walks together; they made "excursions on the bay." All the while, Bennett "represented himself as a single man." Ella assumed they would marry. She yielded to him, and committed "indiscretion." Later, to her horror, she found out Bennett had a wife. By this time, her "indiscretion" had put her in a certain "condition." Eventually, she had a miscarriage. But meanwhile she told her story to her parents, who were devastated, outraged, shamed.

George Gray's crime grew out of this background. What normal father would have done anything different? Public opinion (and the jury) convicted Bennett; the result was almost a foregone conclusion. George Gray went free.

The trial was thus another sentimental drama, on a Victorian stage; as such it has to be judged. What, we wonder, drove Bennett on? What could he hope to gain from the case? At the trial, he played the role of the villain; Ella was Miss Innocence, led astray by a deep-dyed cad; her father was Outraged Morality. These were the parts in the play; and the "court" of "public opinion" trapped the three players in these roles. We would see things rather differently today. Bennett was certainly weak, foolish, passionate, hasty, but no monster of vice; we might look at Ella's innocence, too, with a slightly jaundiced eye. The nineteenth century had its own way of ordering reality.

Still, the case has its puzzles. Why prosecute a case so obviously doomed? Some clues come out of the preliminary examination. In police court, the case was as lopsided as it was at the trial—but in the other direction. The background (Ella's fall) never came to light. The only testimony was about the deed itself: bare, physical facts. The first witness was B. C. Robinson, a commission merchant from San Francisco, a passenger on the train where the shooting took place. He saw everything, and helped to separate Bennett and Gray. When he was holding Bennett down, Robinson asked, "What are you doing . . . do you want to follow this thing to perdition?" And Bennett said: "Oh my wife, my wife." In the pages and pages of testimony, pages and pages of newsprint, this is the only hint that Bennett had a soul.

No witness, however, said anything about motive; and Gray put up no defense at the preliminary hearing. One can hardly blame the judge for binding Gray over to Superior Court. This was one of those rare cases where the defendant *had* to go to trial; his only hope—like Clara Fallmer's—was to appeal above and beyond the law, to turn his case into a morality play, to win the jury to his cause. The price was high, in grief and notoriety; but role-playing saved Gray from prison, as it saved Clara Fallmer.

But this was not the end of the story. The salvation of George Gray was the doom of his enemy, Bennett. Bennett was the villain; the scarlet brand of immorality blazed on his forehead. He could not accept the label. He was now more "ruined" than Ella: a bitter, dangerous man. Now he had to play out the drama to the end.

In May 1894, Bennett and Gray had another set-to, as the two of them rode on a car of the broad gauge train in Oakland. This time, Bennett shot four bullets at Gray. (Railroad trains seemed to arouse their instinct for blood. On the other hand, in all the shooting, neither Gray nor Bennett ever hit a living soul.) Gray ran off; Bennett was arrested, and charged with assault with intent to kill. At the end of July, he was brought to court for arraignment. Gray, of course, was the darling of public opinion. Bennett was "sulky and savage," a caged animal, frustrated, sour, unable to hire a lawyer or make bail— a man "without a friend in the world."[13]

And this time it was Bennett who had to face the jury. He was charged with assault with intent to kill. He would not give in easily. A long road lay ahead, with many procedural twists and turns. The trial began in January 1895. Bennett was "a great drawing card"; the courtroom was crowded.[14] He claimed self-defense. But the jury found him guilty (assault with a deadly weapon). On February 11, 1895, Bennett's attorneys, Hewitt and Connors, asked for a new trial. The motion was argued on February 11, on February 16, and on February 23. On February 25, the judge granted Bennett's request. The verdict, assault with a deadly weapon, was not supported by the evidence.

After some delays, the second trial began on May 24. Again the jury found Bennett guilty (assault with intent to murder). On June 10, his lawyer filed a motion in arrest of judgment; the judge turned it down. Then Bennett asked for a new trial; the motion was argued on June 17—and, on June 25, the motion was granted! The jury in trial number one had convicted Bennett of assault with a deadly weapon; the original charge was assault with intent to murder. But, said Bennett's lawyer, this in effect acquitted Bennett of the heavier charge. If so, the jury in trial number two could not convict him of assault with intent to murder; that was double jeopardy. The judge, on reflection, agreed.

13. *Oakland Tribune*, July 31, 1894, p. 5, col. 5.
14. Ibid., Jan. 9, 1895, p. 3, col. 3.

This was too much for the prosecution. The state decided to appeal. Normally, of course, only the defense can appeal, but California law allowed a few exceptions. One was the prosecution's right to appeal from an order granting a new trial (§ 1237). The third trial was put off, while both sides waited to see what would happen on appeal. On August 15, 1896, the California Supreme Court decided against Bennett. The court rejected the argument of double jeopardy; the case was sent back to Superior Court, with orders to pass sentence on Bennett.[15] On August 17, 1896, Bennett's bail bond was raised to $2,000 and a bench warrant issued for his arrest. On September 21, 1896 the judge sentenced him to a year in San Quentin. Once more he tried to appeal. In October 1897 the Supreme Court dashed his final hope. On November 12, 1897, three and a half years after his shootout on the train, Bennett became convict number 17,478, locked behind bars in San Quentin. He served ten months, behaved himself, kept out of trouble, and left prison in September 1898.

Double and Triple Jeopardy—and More

Even this brief account of the steps in Bennett's case shows how a determined, desperate defendant could drag the process out. This was, of course, an unusual instance. But there were other examples where the law moved at a snail's pace. One defendant who wriggled and squirmed, legally speaking, trying to stay out of prison, was James O'Brien. O'Brien was accused of drugging and raping Miss Nina de Lopez (a "beautiful young girl, with unassuming ways and cultured speech," born of "ancient Spanish blood although the name is the only evidence of the fact"). Miss de Lopez had some drinks at a hotel, became unconscious and "remembered nothing" until hours later, when she "discovered that she had been ruined."[16] The information was filed on March 19, 1898. The trial began on May 6 and lasted until May 28. The jury convicted O'Brien; but he won a new trial. The second trial ended in a hung jury. There was a great hue and cry about bribery and perjury; three jurors, who held out for acquittal, were "under a shadow."[17] There was still a third trial, which ended June 1, 1899. O'Brien lost, and appealed. The Supreme Court of California reversed. By then, the struggle had entered the twentieth century. Unlike Bennett, James O'Brien won out in the end. On September 25, 1901, after three and a half years, three trials and

15. People v. Bennett, 114 Cal. 56 (1896).
16. *Oakland Tribune*, Feb. 25, 1899, p. 3, col. 3.
17. Ibid., Mar. 13, 1899; p. 3, col. 3.

countless motions, the case collapsed. Miss de Lopez was away in England; the prosecution threw in the towel, and the charges were dropped.

Only a few defendants (2 percent or less) were tried more than once for the same transgression. These were mostly defendants whose juries hung; a few were cases where the defendant talked the judge into a new trial or perfected a successful appeal. A handful of defendants had three trials, like James O'Brien. Percy Pembroke, accused of murder, was another of these. The first jury in this long-drawn-out battle hung. During the second trial, a juror, H. I. Mathos, became gravely ill with heart disease. This happened after the evidence was in, but before the final argument. The judge put the trial off for two weeks, hoping Mathos would recover. But his health remained poor, and the judge had to let the jury go. This was on April 17, 1906; he set the third trial for May 7. But on April 18, the great killer earthquake struck. Not until June did the courts even open their doors. In the end, Percy beat the murder charge. In great cases, time and delay were often on the defendant's side.

Tricks of the Trade

The criminal justice system in 1880, or 1900, was not at the heart of controversy as it is today, but it was hardly immune to criticism. One stock complaint centered on what Roscoe Pound called the "sporting" theory of justice.[18] Trial was a kind of game, in which lawyers struggled like gladiators, before a mob of spectators. The judge was a mere "umpire"; he did not sift the facts "independently," in search of justice or truth. He kept the lawyers from hitting too far below the belt, but little more. The stronger, more cunning lawyer won the case. Justice lost.

This complaint, of course, in no way described what happened in the *ordinary* case, That, as we saw, was much more cut-and-dried. Even in big cases, to judge from our data, the "sporting" theory, in Pound's sense, did not quite fit the facts. These trials were not so much games as dramas; they were morality plays, dished up by lawyers, before an audience of jurors and newspaper readers. Yes, the lawyers used tricks; but *legal* tricks were not usually the decisive ones; tricks to win sympathy or moral approval were far more important. The audience seemed eager to be drawn into the drama. The

18. Roscoe Pound, "The Causes of Popular Dissatisfaction with the Administration of Justice," *Rep. Am. Bar Ass'n* 29 (1906): pt. 1, pp. 305, 405–6.

winning side was the one that acted out the more appealing or persuasive role.

In that kind of case, lawyers had to be drama coaches; this was perhaps more vital than legal cunning. A striking instance comes from the case of Percy Pembroke. Percy was in a desperate struggle against a murder charge. The victim was shot during a holdup. Unquestionably, Percy was part of the holdup gang; but was he guilty of murder? At the second trial, reporters noticed a change in the way he wore his hair. Young Percy was "a remarkably handsome lad"; at his first trial, in 1905, he "wore his hair combed down over his forehead in a long curly bang." The trial ended in a hung jury. A single juror held out for conviction. This stubborn fellow had made a "contemptuous" comment about "the effeminate way that Pembroke combed his hair." Lin Church, Percy's lawyer, took no chances. At the second trial, the "offending bang" was brushed back from Percy's forehead, "in manly fashion, making a striking difference in his looks."[19]

Percy's trial was as sensational and difficult as any discussed in this chapter. It took at least four days to pick the jury for the second trial. The trial itself went on for days. To arouse sympathy, Percy's lawyers trotted out members of his family. Kinfolk always surrounded him. His father and mother both took the stand. His mother was particularly dramatic. Her "whole figure trembled" as she told her tale, "in a voice scarcely above a whisper." Several times "she broke down completely and wept. Her daughter-in-law went to her assistance and brought her around with smelling salts."[20]

Clara Fallmer's relatives, too, were conspicuous in the courtroom. In rape and seduction cases, defense lawyers were eager to show that the wife (if any) "stood by" her husband. When Benjamin Lichtenstein was tried for murder in 1888, his wife and little boy were always there. In police court, during preliminary examination, the boy brought his "papa" a bag of cherries.[21] At the trial, Mrs. Lichtenstein, "plain looking, and neat in dress" sat by her husband's side. The "baby boy" was brought in, and she "tenderly kissed and caressed him." The defendant also joined in the show of parental love.[22] Closing argument made much of Lichtenstein's family life. Lichtenstein, a hot-headed tailor, was acquitted. In the trial of Lloyd Majors for murder (1883), his wife appeared, "her young babe clasped to her bosom," her "once pretty" face now "distorted by the agonies of a heart broken by the terrible sorrow that will embitter her whole

---

19. *Berkeley Reporter*, Feb. 15, 1906, p. 6, col. 2.
20. Ibid., Mar. 16, 1906, p. 1, col. 5.
21. *Oakland Tribune*, May 2, 1888, p. 1, col. 6.
22. Ibid., July 17, 1888, p. 1, col. 7.

life."[23] In this case, sympathy did not save Majors from the gallows. And, of course, two could play at the relatives game. In murder cases, the prosecution dragged out mothers of dead sons, swaddled in yards of black. Relatives evoked sympathy; they also fixed a person's place in society: a defendant with a loyal mother and father, sisters, brothers, a wife, little children, especially if the family made a good (or pitiful) appearance, was unlikely to be judged a "tramp," a "born criminal," or any of the stock villains of the day.

Roscoe Pound, of course, did have a point. The sporting theory was not wholly fanciful. The great cases were cases in which lawyers unloaded all the tricks in their bag; and *some* of these were tricks of law. Some show trials mixed dry law with high drama. Louis Matheny was the defendant in one of the mightiest cases in our period. It was 1893, and the charge was murder. The dead man was a police officer—then, as now, the most serious, most dangerous victim for any defendant. Matheny's lawyer tried to get a change of venue. All through the trial, he raised technical points, particularly in matters of evidence. In big cases, lawyers for the defense hoped for the best, but prepared for the worst; if they could not squeeze out an acquittal, they might at least lay the groundwork for appeal on points of law.

It is too bad that we know so little about the cost of these trials. Often it is a wonder where the defendant got the money. Long-drawn-out trials, with two lawyers or more, out of private practice— these *must* have cost a fortune. Lawyers, to be sure, were eager to handle big cases—they had great publicity value—and they may have shaved their fees. A few defendants had money of their own. Matheny's father, for example, was a doctor. The Matheny case was a perfect demonstration of the way time and money paid off; they saved the defendant's hide. The evidence was largely circumstantial; but Matheny was in deep, deep trouble. Officer Cashin, the dead man, was with another policeman; they interrupted a burglary in an Oakland saloon. It was a stormy night; rain came down in buckets. Shots were fired; Officer Cashin was fatally wounded; the next day, the dead body of a burglar was found. There were probably *two* burglars, though no one could swear they saw the second one. (Matheny's lawyer exploited this doubt to the hilt.) Somebody left a gun and a hat at the scene of the crime. It *seemed* at least that burglar number two jumped out the window and ran away. Detectives tracked down Matheny and arrested him in San Francisco, in a rooming house. In his room were wet, muddy clothes. A cab driver

---

23. Ibid., Nov. 13, 1883, p. 3, col. 1. At Percy Pembroke's trial, his mother, father, brother, and sister-in-law sat with him. Ibid., Nov. 28, 1905, p. 3, col. 6.

swore he drove Matheny to a place near the scene of the crime. Matheny was a friend and associate of the dead burglar. Suspicion tightened like a noose about Matheny's neck.

Yet he escaped the gallows; indeed, after a long ordeal, he went completely free. The first jury hung; the second acquitted him. Without good lawyering, and good detective work, the case was hopeless. Matheny had hired a private detective, Teague; Teague was worth every penny. The defense was able to attack, brick by brick, every bit of the prosecution's structure. A professor of chemistry, from the Cooper Medical College, even testified about the mud on Matheny's clothes. It was racetrack mud, he reported, not mud from near the saloon. By a "chemical test," the professor said, he could tell if the mud from the shoes "was salt or whether the clothing in evidence was wet with salt water." Of course, this sort of thing cost money, and plenty of it—but it saved the defendant's life.

Symbols and Myths

The great cases were, as we have seen, great theater. Trials were full of "sensations," grisly photographs, secrets revealed, defendants fainting, wives unmasked as concubines, women sobbing and telling how they were "ruined." The cases twisted and turned, in and out; spectators hung breathless on the outcome. The atmosphere in the courtroom was charged and electric. At the Lester McNulty case, in 1906, one of the regular spectators, L. D. Gooch, an "extra man" for the Oakland Traction Company, died of heart failure, brought on, we are told, by the "hot close atmosphere of the courtroom and the nervous tension prevailing among the spectators."[24] Sometimes, as in a good play, there was a surprise in the very last act. Sometimes the normal rules of law were confounded. Some defendants escaped scot-free, even though—Clara Fallmer is a perfect example—the evidence of guilt, in the legal sense at least, was overwhelming.

What did these cases accomplish? What function was served by these proceedings? Mostly, they taught the rules of the game of life. The trials were propaganda plays, plays of morality, cautionary tales. They were not subtle. The norms were crude, the rhetoric shrill. But they flashed a powerful message, reinforcing some moral postulates, weakening others. What *total* effect they had we can hardly tell. But it is clear that trials were, at least potentially, powerful teachers and preachers of conventional morality.

24. *Berkeley Reporter*, Jan. 24, 1906, p. 1, col. 3.

Arguably, in most cases, too, justice was done. These were cases where the norms, the ideals, of due process became reality. They were also the cases in which justice verged on show business. Indeed, show business was necessary to build and hold an audience. In older days, in small communities, literally everybody came to the trials. In Alameda County, only a few "morbid" people attended; there were not enough seats for the rest. *They* had to attend, vicariously, through reading the papers. And this they did, absorbing, in this way, lessons about the law at work. The Superior Court did most of its work in obscurity—*except* for these cases. Hence what people knew about criminal justice they learned mostly from these show trials, and from nowhere else.

But what did they learn about the law, when they learned it this way? First of all, they learned about rights, about due process. They learned that there were many safeguards; that America left no stone unturned to protect the rights of people accused of crime. They saw that judges and juries were fair and impartial. They saw the wicked (sometimes) punished, the innocent (usually) vindicated. These were important, vital, essential things to learn. Great symbols and myths were trotted out and displayed, for the people to see and to worship.

Trotted out and displayed: but the symbols and myths took grotesque forms. They were huge, bloated shapes—puffed-up bodies and heads of papier-mâché, garishly colored, effigies at some great Mardi Gras. This was the price paid for spreading the word about law. People saw that justice was real, but also absurd. The contradiction persists to this day. The normal work of the law is obscure, quiet, hidden from view; what people see, or think they see, is a caricature. They learn that defendants have many chances and rights —too many perhaps—whether or not this is true in the usual case. They also see justice as a ham, a mountebank, a fool. The other face of justice—efficient, callous, crude—is rarely revealed to the public; it is dry and obscure, and grinds out its work in deep shadow.

Chapter 8
On Appeal: Review of
Criminal Cases in a Higher Court

For most defendants who lost their cases, sentencing was the end of the road; their hopes and their chances were over. A handful—with money, energy, and (they hoped) an issue—took an appeal. During most of the period, only one court in the state, the Supreme Court of California, heard appeals from Superior Court. A few defendants found good fortune there; the rest merely postponed the day of reckoning. Appeals gave the higher court a chance to correct mistakes in the lower courts; appeal cases also generated written opinions. These made up a kind of running commentary on criminal law. They were the cases (if any) that lawyers read and studied and that jurists wrote about. A few became famous or notorious; hence they possibly had some effect on what a broader public thought about criminal justice, too.

Appeals: How Many?

Under California law, either party in a felony case could take "questions of law" to the Supreme Court (§ 1235).[1] The defendant could appeal if he was convicted, or if the judge denied his motion for a new trial.[2] The state had to swallow an acquittal, no matter how wrong-headed it was; there was no right to complain. The state did have a limited right to appeal; it could challenge a demurrer, an order for a new trial, an order arresting judgment, or an order affecting "the substantial rights of the people" (§ 1237).[3] Petitions for habeas corpus could also go to the high court (§ 1473).

Before 1880, criminal appeals were rare in Alameda County. On the

1. In 1905, § 1235 was amended so that a defendant could appeal from a conviction in a misdemeanor case in the Superior Court.
2. He could also appeal any postconviction order that affected his "substantial rights."
3. Between 1880 and 1905, prosecutors also were permitted to appeal directed verdicts in favor of defendants. Beginning in 1897, prosecutors were allowed to appeal an

average, there was fewer than one a year. Only about 1 percent of felony prosecutions made it all the way up the ladder to the Supreme Court. Before 1880, the loser had to pay costs; this no doubt discouraged many potential customers. After 1880, the appeal rate went up, though it fell again after the turn of the century (see Table 8.1). During the period 1880–1910, there were appeals in about 3 percent of the felony *prosecutions* in Alameda County, in about 5 percent of the felony *convictions*, and in roughly one out of seven cases in which the *jury* returned a verdict of guilty. (Naturally enough, acquitted people never appealed, and people who pleaded guilty appealed very rarely.)

The writ of habeas corpus was the only other way to get the ear of the Supreme Court. Between 1870 and 1910, there were forty-two cases of habeas corpus from Alameda County.[4] Most came out of misdemeanor cases in justice or police courts.[5] A few petitioners were felony defendants; a few had also filed appeals. A citation for contempt of court produced one habeas petition. Petitions for habeas corpus usually failed. The courts set the petitioner free in only three of the forty-two cases, all of them misdemeanors.

Table 8.1. Number and Rate of
Felony Appeals in Alameda County, 1870–1910

Period	No. cases appealed	Appeals/100 felony charges	Appeals/100 convictions	Appeals/100 trial convictions
1870–74	4			
1875–79	3			
1880–84	8	2.1	3.4	8.4
1885–89	7	2.0		
1890–94	12	2.7	6.7	17.7
1895–99	20	5.7		
1900–1904	8	2.0		
1905–8	13	2.4	4.7	14.2
1909–10	20	6.0		

Sources for all tables in this chapter except table 8.4: Annual Reports of California Attorneys General; Alameda County Registers Actions, 1870–1910.

---

order setting aside an indictment or information. No case in Alameda County was ever appealed on these grounds.

4. Twenty-two were reported; twenty more, unreported, were located in the records of the Supreme Court. It is possible that there are others, in the records of the District Court of Appeal, that we have not found.

5. Habeas petitions probably were used in misdemeanor cases because there was no other way, before 1905, to get to the Supreme Court.

Appeals: Who and What?

Naturally enough, defendants appealed mostly when the stakes were high, when the case was serious and the sentence harsh. Every death sentence was appealed. Sex crimes and murder made up 10 percent of the prosecutions, but spawned 30 percent of the appeals (see Table 8.2). For defendants who appealed, prison sentences were on the average nearly eight years; for defendants who did not appeal, the average was under five years.[6] Of defendants sentenced to life

Table 8.2. Cases Appealed in Alameda County by Offense, 1870–1910

Offense	No. appeals	% of total appeals	% of total prosecutions
Against persons	35	34	28
Murder	11	11	4
Manslaughter	1	1	0
Robbery	2	2	4
Assault to kill	8	8	4
Assault with deadly weapon	2	2	10
Assault with deadly weapon & to kill	5	5	2
Forcible rape	5	5	1
Assault to rape	1	1	1
Against property	49	48	58
Burglary	19	18	28
Grand larceny	13	13	15
Forgery	6	6	6
Embezzlement	6	6	3
Arson	2	2	1
False pretenses	3	3	1
Morals offenses	14	14	5
Statutory rape	6	6	2
Other sex offenses	7	7	2
Gambling	1	1	1
Public order	5	5	5
Perjury	3	3	1
Other public order	2	2	4

6. The mean for all defendants sentenced to prison was 57 months; the median, 36 months. For defendants who *appealed*, the mean was 92 months; the median, 70.

imprisonment, after trial, one out of four appealed; of those sentenced to prison, but not for life, 18 percent appealed. Only three defendants in forty years appealed from a "jolt" in county jail (see Table 8.3).

The long-drawn-out case went up on appeal, not the run-of-the-mill felony. Most cases went to verdict within a month and a half after charges were filed; cases that were appealed took, on the average, nearly four months to crawl to a verdict.[7] The trials themselves were more than twice as long as in the average case (5.6 days, as opposed to 2.3 days).[8] These long trials also gave the judge more chance to slip up and hand the defendant some grounds for appeal. Long trials were of course also cases of heavy crimes, and cases where defendants were willing and able to fight (and spend) for their freedom. Appeal cases tended to have histories of hung juries and multiple trials. Fifteen percent came from cases tried more than once, though these made up only 6 percent of our sample.

There were 103 appeals in our period. *Prosecutors* brought only 4. (Curiously, all 4 occurred within a single period of two and a half years.) The other 99 appeals were brought by 100 different defendants. (We have to add appeals by codefendants, and subtract defendants who appealed more than once.) Of these 100, 5 were women, which is more than expected, though the numbers are too small to make any inference. Some of the women's appeals are puzzling. Annie Cameron was accused of assault with intent to murder; the jury convicted her of simple assault, but she appealed anyway. Daisy Curtis, convicted of perjury, appealed from a one-year sentence, even though it was the minimum sentence for this offense.

Table 8.3. Cases Appealed in
Alameda County by Type of Sentence Received, 1870–1910

Type of sentence	No. appeals	% of appeals	% receiving sentence who appealed	% receiving sentence after trial who appealed
Death	7	7	100	100
Life imprisonment	5	5	24	25
Other prison term	80	82	6	18
Juvenile institution	1	1	1	13
County jail	3	3	1	2
Fines	2	2	2	4

7. For all felony cases, the mean number of days between filing of charges and trial verdicts was 69 days, the median 45; for appealed cases, the mean was 115 days, the median, 83.

8. The *medians* were 1.5 days for all cases, 2.9 days for appealed cases.

Grounds for Appeals

Table 8.4 summarizes the main grounds for appeals in Alameda County, at least as the Supreme Court saw them.[9] Defendants (or their lawyers) typically raised as many objections as they could; some threw in everything but the kitchen sink. Table 8.4 is based on grounds for review that the Supreme Court actually considered. Two types dominated, one or the other appearing in well over half the appeals. One was the jury charge; the other, the handling of evidence: did the judge let in evidence that was "incompetent, irrelevant and immaterial"? or did he keep good evidence out? The law of evidence in the United States was more complex than in any other system in the world. This was a most dubious distinction; but it's an ill wind that blows no one any good. These complex rules gave some defendants a chance they would not otherwise have had.

Mostly, of course, evidence consisted of testimony—words. In a few cases, the problem was "physical" evidence—things. In Elmer Letterell's trial for burglary, in 1897, the prosecution introduced a pair of nippers and a skeleton key found at the Hotel Metropole, the scene of the crime. The prosecution tried to show that expert burglars used

Table 8.4. *Principal Grounds for Appeals in Alameda County, 1870–1910*

Principal grounds for appeal	No. appeals	% of appeals
Error in admission or exclusion of evidence at trial	25	36
Misinstruction of the jury by trial judge	15	22
Defect in pleadings	7	10
Interpretation of substantive law	6	9
Sufficiency of evidence to support verdict	4	6
Double jeopardy	3	4
Conduct of district attorney	2	3
Jurisdiction and venue	2	3
Statute of limitations	2	3
Juror misconduct	1	1
Exercise of peremptory challenges	1	1
Appealability of pretrial order	1	1

Source: Opinions of the California Supreme Court and the California Court of Appeals.

9. The high court had wide latitude in reviewing criminal cases. It could review any ruling by the trial court that might have influenced the outcome; on the other hand, the court could disregard any technical errors that did not affect "substantial rights" (§§ 1258, 1259).

such tools. Letterell argued that *he* had never used them, so it was "error" to introduce the tools at trial. The California Supreme Court affirmed his conviction. At the trial of Mark Wilkins for murder, in 1907, the prosecution showed the jury the rotted scalp of the victim (nine months dead). Wilkins's lawyer raised an objection, but the appeal court was unmoved.

There were many examples of more standard evidence matters. S. J. Thomas was charged in 1894 with burglary, and a prior conviction. At arraignment, he admitted the conviction, to keep the jury from hearing about it at the trial. A prosecution witness let the cat out of the bag: "I says to the defendant, 'Ain't it a fact that you served two years in San Quentin, from Alameda County, for burglary?' He said: 'No, I served two years in Folsom for burglary.'" Naturally, the defendant objected. The California Supreme Court agreed that the testimony was "highly prejudicial"; the court reversed Thomas's conviction.[10] Abraham Kafoury was convicted of a "murderous assault" on his sister-in-law. In front of her screaming children, he shot her, shattering her hip bone; she grappled with him, and he dragged her into another room, choking her until she lost consciousness. A doctor testified at the trial that the woman was pregnant (she lost the baby). The court found Kafoury's behavior revolting (a "brutal, unprovoked" crime); this probably made it easier for the court to conclude that the doctor's evidence was competent, "under the peculiar circumstances of this case."[11] Benjamin Hill was tried for murdering his wife, in 1896. His defense was insanity. Hill was sentenced to death, and on appeal, raised a number of arguments. For one thing, his lawyer had tried to show that his wife "had been guilty of unchaste conduct with other men." The trial judge held that this evidence was irrelevant, and kept it out. The Supreme Court agreed. There was no showing Hill knew about these goings-on; the evidence was "wholly immaterial."[12] In a few cases, defendants argued that they had "newly discovered" evidence. Under the law, new evidence could lead to a retrial, but only when the defendant had no way to get the evidence in time for the first trial. The Supreme Court looked suspiciously ("with distrust and disfavor") on claims of newly discovered evidence. Nathan Sutton was convicted of murder in 1887. He argued, on appeal, that he had proof of a clutch of insane relatives. The Supreme Court affirmed.[13] In many appeals, the defendant threw in

10. 110 Cal. 41, 44 (1895).
11. People v. Kafoury, 16 Cal. App. 718 (1911).
12. People v. Hill, 116 Cal. 562 (1897).
13. 73 Cal. 243, 248 (1887).

the argument that the conviction was "against the weight of evidence." This was a weak, last-ditch makeweight; it usually lost.[14]

Instructions to the jury were in second place as a source of "error." John H. Young burglarized a ticket office of the Central Pacific Railroad. He wanted the judge to tell the jury that the ticket office was not really a "room"; it did not have a partition reaching up to the ceiling, shutting it off from the main waiting room. The court refused, and the Supreme Court affirmed.[15] Thomas Hickey was convicted of sodomy in 1895. The trial judge at first refused to tell the jury that they could, if they wished, find him guilty of simple assault. Then the judge had a change of heart, and granted Hickey a new trial. This was one of the rare cases in which the *state* appealed (and lost).

Jury instructions could be oral or written.[16] If the judge gave oral instructions, a court reporter took down his words. Usually, the judge read from a written text. In big cases, lawyers proposed dozens of complex, wordy instructions—a trap for the unwary judge. Oral charges were even more of a trap. Attorney General Hart suggested, in 1882, that they should be abolished. Criminal law was so "unsettled," he said, that no one could deliver a "lengthy dissertation" on the law without a written text; oral charges led to "errors," and "errors" led to reversals. After 1897, instructions had to be in writing, but the parties could agree among themselves to allow oral instructions (§ 1127). Because they usually did agree, nothing much changed.

The attorney general did have a point. A slip of the tongue could be fatal. Ah Sing was convicted of burglary in 1880. The judge told the jury that if a person possessed stolen goods right after a burglary, and could not explain why, this was "a strong circumstance tending to show guilt." The Supreme Court reversed, in a nine-line opinion. The word "strong" was error; it was the jury's job, not the judge's, to decide whether evidence was "strong" or only "slight."[17] In Charles Swarbrick's case, in one instruction, the judge talked about a line of defense the defendant had "attempted" to show. His lawyer pounced on the word "attempted." It was a slur on Swarbrick's case, he said,

14. In People v. Boero, 13 Cal. App. 686 (1910), the defendant was convicted of rape. The girl was sixteen. She testified that Boero's wife was in the room at the time of the dastardly deed. Boero said this evidence was "unreasonable," but the argument lost, along with a whole grocery list of objections to various aspects of the trial.

15. 65 Cal. 225, 226 (1884). Apparently the point was this: the defendant was convicted of burglary. His theory was that he first went into the waiting room, without any plan to steal; hence to enter the ticket office, if it was not a separate *room*, was not burglary.

16. See "Trial by Jury" in Chap. 5, above.

17. 59 Cal. 400 (1881).

and prejudiced the jury. (Here the Supreme Court disagreed.)[18] In a burglary case (1891) the judge told the jury that in every crime there was "a union . . . of act *or* intent"; he meant "act *and* intent." The Supreme Court agreed that the charge was incorrect. But the court did not reverse; the mistake had been neutralized by other instructions.[19]

The Pleadings

Defects in pleadings made up the third common grounds for appeal. For its day, the Penal Code was quite liberal about pleading errors. A court was not supposed to dismiss any case simply because the pleadings were wrong or imperfect; only a mistake that substantially impaired the defendant's right was fatal to the case (§§ 960, 1404). This gave a court a good deal of leeway; it could be liberal or tight, as it wished. In 1880 the Supreme Court threw out an indictment because one letter was missing. The indictment charged the defendant with "intent to commit larcey." The lost "n" was fatal. The prosecution could not even amend the pleading here. The state had to start all over again, or else give up.[20]

Defendants raised all sorts of objections to the *form* of informations. Usually, the courts were not impressed. In 1891, Manuel Lopez was accused of "stealing, taking and driving away" a horse. The information left out the word "feloniously." That, argued Lopez, was fatally defective. (He lost.) John Taylor's information for burglary (1897) left out the words "contrary to the form, force and effect of the statute." The information against Frank Oliveria, Jr., at one point left off the "Jr." These farfetched arguments got nowhere. A certain Ah Sam had better luck, in 1892. Ah Sam, it was charged, perjured himself at a trial about illegal sales of lottery tickets. In the information was a photo of the ticket, written entirely in Chinese. The Supreme Court felt that the information should have translated the document. Otherwise, the reader who knew no Chinese could not be sure it was a lottery ticket at all.[21] Albert Monteith stole a horse, and was arrested (he was so drunk he nearly fell off the horse). He was convicted (1886); on appeal, his lawyer argued that the pleadings and the proofs

18. People v. Swarbrick, 77 Cal. 125 (1888).
19. People v. Winters, 93 Cal. 277 (1892).
20. People v. St. Clair, 55 Cal. 524 (1880), *rehearing* 56 Cal. 406 (1880).
21. People v. Ah Sam, 92 Cal. 648 (1892). Art. 4, § 24, of the California Constitution required judicial proceedings to be carried on in English. The Penal Code (§ 950) required informations to be written in "ordinary . . . language." The court relied on these two provisions in reversing.

did not match. The charge was stealing a horse, but one witness called the animal "a gelding." Whitmore, Albert's lawyer, claimed that a horse, by law, "is a stallion, not a gelding or a mare." But both layers of courts dismissed this argument; there was no true "variance" between information and proof.[22]

These, then, were the major grounds for appeal. Others were scattered about the cases. Most challenges were procedural, but not all. A few were questions of substantive law: what, legally speaking, did embezzlement consist of, or forgery? One case, *People* v. *W. D. Miller*, turned on whether a confession was valid. Miller killed an old man. He was arrested, and admitted his crime. When he confessed, he was lying on the ground, dazed by a bullet in his head. The court allowed this confession in as evidence; and the appeal court affirmed. The jury could make up its own mind whether the confession was credible.[23]

Appeals today are peppered with arguments based on *constitutional* rights. According to a recent study, almost *half* of all criminal appeals to state supreme courts in 1965–70 raised some constitutional issue.[24] These issues were rare in 1870–1910 in California; to say that 3 percent of appeals presented a constitutional issue would be a generous estimate. In the few cases, defendants turned to the California Constitution, not the federal. Lloyd Majors raised the defense of double jeopardy. He was sentenced to life imprisonment, for killing William P. Renowden. Then, in a separate trial, he was sentenced to death for killing Archibald McIntyre. The two killings took place at the same time. The Supreme Court held that they were two separate offenses.[25]

Appellate Procedures

THE STRUCTURE OF APPELLATE COURTS

Figure 8.1 shows the paths that appeals from Alameda County could travel between 1870 and 1910. Between 1870 and 1879, the California

22. 73 Cal. 7 (1887).
23. 135 Cal. 69 (1901).
24. Robert Kagan, Bliss Cartwright, Lawrence M. Friedman, and Stanton Wheeler, "The Business of State Supreme Courts, 1870–1970," *Stan. L. Rev.* 30 (1977): 121, 147. It must be recalled that in our period the state Constitution was just about the only source for defendants' constitutional rights; the process of applying the federal Bill of Rights to the states through the Fourteenth Amendment had barely begun. The state Constitution did provide a battery of procedural rights, but the cases only rarely invoked them.
25. See William W. Blume, "California Courts in Historical Perspective," *Hastings L.J.* 22 (1970): 121, 169 (1970).

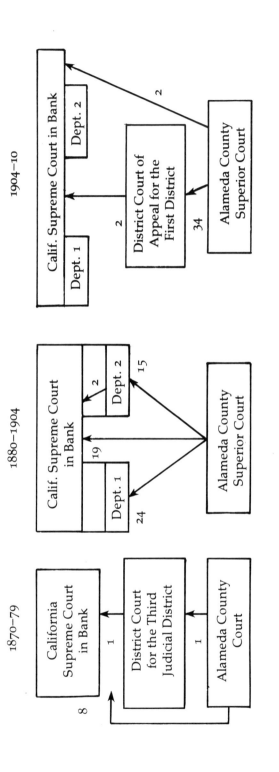

FIGURE 8.1
Procedural Route of Alameda County Appeals, 1870–1910

Supreme Court was the only statewide court that heard appeals. It heard only nine criminal appeals from Alameda County in the decade. Eight came directly from County Court; one case first went to District Court on appeal. The Supreme Court was made up of five judges, a chief justice and four associates. The court heard all its cases "in bank"; that is, the court sat as a whole. The District Court was the trial court for murder, manslaughter, and arson; it also heard appeals from County Court. None of its original cases was appealed between 1870 and 1879.

In 1879, the state got rid of County and District Courts, and established a single trial court for felony cases—the Superior Court. The Supreme Court was expanded to seven judges; and it was divided into two "departments." Each department had three justices. The chief (the seventh man) assigned cases between departments; he, or any four justices, could order a case to be heard in bank. A case decided by one department could go to the full court, if four justices (three, if one was the chief) so decided. Of fifty-eight Alameda appeals (1880–1904), the full court decided about one-third; two-thirds went to departments. Two cases were reheard in bank.

The department scheme was supposed to cut down the court's nagging backlog. But it did not do the job. The legislature then set up a system of "court commissioners," to help the Supreme Court out.[26] Commissioners ("persons of legal learning and personal worth") were appointed by the Supreme Court for four-year terms; they earned the same salary as justices. The commissioners were treated as another department. Commissioners wrote opinions, which the court could adopt officially as its own. Commissioners wrote about 30 percent of the opinions in our appeals after 1885.[27]

A constitutional amendment in 1904 abolished the commissioners, and drastically reorganized appellate justice in California. The state was divided into three appellate *districts*; in each district, there was a District Court of Appeal, made up of three judges. The first district sat in San Francisco; its domain included Alameda County. The District Courts were not really *intermediate* courts. They were supposed to be the end of the line for "ordinary" appellate cases, leaving the

26. Laws Cal. 1885, ch. 120, § 1, p. 101; Laws Cal. 1889, ch. 16, § 1, p. 13. The 1885 law set the number at three; the 1889 law raised it to five. When there were five, three at a time acted as a department; the other two were free to write opinions. See Roscoe Pound, *Organization of Courts* (Boston, 1940), pp. 204–5. When there were only three commissioners, two commissioners sometimes sat with one Supreme Court justice to hear cases. The commissioners would write the opinion; the regular justices would add a *per curiam*.

27. In People ex rel. Morgan v. Hayne, 83 Cal. 111, 23 Pac. 1 (1890), the Supreme Court upheld the commission system, against the claim that it was unconstitutional.

Supreme Court free to deal with high and mighty matters. All felony appeals, except death penalty cases, went first to the new court. Death penalty cases went directly to the Supreme Court. There were only two death cases in 1905–10; the other appeals (thirty-four) were heard first by the District Court. The Supreme Court or the District Court could issue a writ of habeas corpus. Of the habeas cases, seventeen were in the Supreme Court, three in the District Court of Appeal.[28]

As we saw, a defendant might appeal from a conviction, or from certain unfavorable rulings and motions. In practice, nearly all appeals came after the judge refused to grant a new trial to a defendant just convicted (see Table 8.5). When a jury convicted, one out of four defendants filed a motion for a new trial; of the total number of defendants who appealed, 83 percent filed such motions. The motion nearly always lost. Twenty defendants asked for a new trial; only one of them got it. Usually the judge said no on the very day the motion was made; occasionally the judge heard argument, and took time to consider the question. Motions for a new trial came *after* verdict but *before* sentence; hence, they slowed up sentencing a good deal.

A person could file a writ of habeas corpus any time he felt that he was unlawfully imprisoned; but notices of appeal carried a definite time limit. Before 1907, defendants had a full year after judgment to

Table 8.5. Stage of Proceedings from Which Appeals Were Taken in Alameda County, 1870–1910

Stage of proceedings	No. appeals	% of appeals
Before trial	2	2
By defendant after charge submitted to grand jury	1	1
By prosecution after dismissal	1	1
After conviction	101	98
By prosecution after new trial granted	3	3
By defendant after new trial denied	52	50
By defendant after new trial & motion to arrest judgment denied	29	28
By defendant after conviction alone	17	17

28. After 1905, amendments to § 1475 made the writ harder to get, and the number of petitions dropped off.

file notice of appeal with the trial court.[29] Beginning in 1907, the period was drastically shortened. Defendants had only ninety days to decide to appeal. Two years later even this period was wiped out. Defendants had to announce their decision to appeal "in open court" at the time of sentencing. But, in fact, this had always been the practice in Alameda County; the change, then, was largely formal.

PROBABLE CAUSE

Defendants acted quickly for a simple reason: they wanted to "stay" (put off) execution of their sentences. After 1874, an appeal did this automatically for anybody sentenced to death. Other defendants had to start doing their time, unless they could get the judge to issue a certificate of probable cause for appeal (§ 1243).[30] Trial judges had wide discretion in deciding whether there was "probable cause" for appeal. Appellants in Alameda County who asked got certificates only about half of the time. The others had to go to prison or jail while their appeals were pending.

Trial judges seemed fairly astute at predicting how appeals would turn out. There were forty-four defendants who did *not* get their certificates. Only three of them (see Table 8.6) were successful on appeal. Of forty-seven who did get certificates, seventeen won on appeal. Ludwig Streuber was one of the few who beat the odds. He was

Table 8.6. *Outcome of Appeals by Grant or*
Refusal of Stay Pending Appeal, 1870–1910

	Won by prosecution on appeal		Won by defendant on appeal	
	No.	%	No.	%
No certificate of probable cause for appeal: sentence in effect	41	93	3	7
Certificate of probable cause for appeal: stays of execution of sentence	30	64	17	36
Automatic stay because of death penalty	4	80	1	20

29. Defendants appealing from a court order, rather than from the judgment itself, had sixty days; and so did the prosecution, in appealing a court order (§ 1239).

30. The certificate could be issued by the trial judge, or by a justice of the state Supreme Court (§§ 1244–45). Appeals by the prosecution did not stay rulings or orders favoring the defendant (§ 1242).

sentenced to three years in Folsom for keeping his wife in a house of prostitution. His certificate was denied, and off he went to Folsom on January 25, 1898; when he arrived and "donned his striped attire," he "broke down completely."[31] But six months later, Streuber's conviction was reversed, and he left Folsom never to return.[32]

A stay of sentence was not an unmixed blessing, unless the defendant faced the gallows. Under the law (§ 670), a defendant got no credit for time served while he waited for the appeal court to act. If he was sitting in county jail, and lost his appeal, all he had for his pains was extra time behind bars. Hard-luck Albert Monteith, for example, was sentenced in August 1886 to four years in Folsom. Normally, he could expect to go free, if he behaved in prison, in August 1889. Instead, Monteith asked for a stay to appeal his case. He got it. He sat in county jail for nearly a year. The Supreme Court affirmed his conviction. In July 1897 he started his prison term. With time off for good behavior, he went free in July 1890. By contrast, Daisy Curtis began her prison sentence (eighteen months) the day she was sentenced in August 1874. Her conviction was affirmed in April 1875; by this time, she had only seven months to go.

A handful of defendants went free on bail while they appealed. But bail after conviction was not easy to get. A convicted felon had no right to bail. It was completely up to the court (§ 1272). The district attorney had to have "reasonable notice" of any application for bail (§ 1274). Only eight appellants succeeded in getting bail pending appeal; two of these had won new trials and were waiting while the prosecution appealed. Only five of the eight came up with enough bond to go free. One defendant, Fred W. Scott, with two years in prison staring him in the face, made a desperate argument for bail. His appeal would take "at least eight months"; his health could not hold out if he had to wait in jail.[33] But the court turned a deaf ear; Scott lost heart and dropped his appeal altogether.

Still, many defendants (forty-one out of forty-seven who had certificates of probable cause *without* bail) were willing to wait out their time in county jail, rather than go to state prison. Apparently, it was worth the gamble. Perhaps they thought the mere fact that a judge felt they had probable cause helped their chances on appeal. There was a rumor in later years that some lawyers told their clients to use

31. *Oakland Tribune*, Jan. 27, 1898, p. 3, col. 4.
32. In part, a stay of sentence may have been a kind of self-fulfilling prophecy. If the trial judge certified probable cause, the appeal court may have taken a closer look at the case. Still, the facts do suggest that trial judges (and perhaps defendants, who had to decide whether to ask for certificates) were reasonably good at prediction.
33. Affidavit of F. W. Scott, Dec. 1, 1901, case file no. 2469.

this tactic.[34] Some defendants probably wanted to stay out of Folsom or San Quentin as long as humanly possible. County jail was no paradise; but it seemed better than the violence, forced labor, and barbaric discipline of prison. One defendant, Ah Sing, spent three years of an eight-year term at San Quention, then asked for a writ of probable cause; with this writ, he could sit in county jail while waiting word on his appeal.[35]

And wait one did. The wheels of appellate justice turned slowly. First the defendant had to prepare a "record," which the clerk of court sent on to the higher court. This record was a formidable document. It included pleadings, a chronology of the proceedings, instructions to the jury (including those that were refused), and the judgment roll. Along with it went a *bill of exceptions*. This was supposed to sum up, concisely, the evidence, testimony, and rulings on which the defendant based his appeal (§ 1175). (In practice, defendants threw in a lot more, hoping that the high court would find *something* wrong.) The defendant had to submit a draft of his bill of exceptions to the trial judge within ten days of his notice of appeal (§ 1174). The district attorney could object to the draft. The trial judge then met with both sides, to work out a bill of exceptions agreeable to everybody.[36] The code assumed that this process would take at most a couple of weeks. In practice it took months, sometimes years, to settle on a bill of exceptions. The files are full of petitions asking for extensions of time; the court seemed to grant them almost automatically. On the average, three *months* went by between final judgment and settlement of the bill of exceptions.[37]

The exact causes of this delay are somewhat murky. Both sides did a good deal of jockeying for position; they tried to make sure that the bill of exceptions was full of what they hoped were the choicest mor-

34. We have no direct evidence that this happened; but Alameda County's first public defender remembers the practice from the time when he took office in the 1920s. The hint was that unscrupulous lawyers puffed up the chances for success, to encourage clients to choose a more expensive course of action. (Willard Shea, Oral History, Bancroft Library, University of California).

35. Once a conviction was affirmed, there was no longer any need for delay; the case was lost. When Arthur Crane heard that the District Court of Appeals had affirmed his conviction, in 1906, he went to court and moved to vacate the writ of probable cause. This was done, and Crane began serving his sentence seven weeks earlier than if he had waited for the Superior Court to get the formal remittitur and opinion.

36. A judge's refusal to allow an exception could itself form the basis of an exception.

37. This was a statewide problem. See *Annual Report of the California Attorney General, 1902–04* (1904), p. 15.

sels. The lawyers were also, it seems, indulgent to each other. Each allowed his brother lawyer on the other side endless extensions.[38] The judge too was in an uncomfortable position. He wanted to avoid reversal. The best way was to give each side as much time and scope as it wanted. Before 1889 the bill of exceptions was written out in longhand. Many were "almost illegible," Attorney General Johnson reported in 1888: it was "a great waste of time" for his office to decipher them.[39] A new law of 1889 called for fifteen *printed* copies of the bill of exceptions. But this created problems of its own. Because the county paid the printing bill, records became fatter and fatter.[40] In one appeal from Alameda County—not by any means extraordinary —the bill of exceptions ran to 193 pages (1889).[41]

In 1909, the procedure was thoroughly revamped. The bill of exceptions was done away with. Now the clerk of court was to forward a typewritten copy of the papers in the case—minutes of trial, any written or printed exhibits—within twenty days of notice of appeal. Each party got a carbon copy of the papers.

This system was swift and efficient. Before 1909, the transcript on appeal was not filed, on the average, until nearly five months after judgment; and the process had been getting slower and slower (see Table 8.7). In the two years *after* the change, the average fell to less than one month. A disinterested third party now enforced strict time limits. The clerk of court was in charge; there was no more haggling

Table 8.7. *Days between Trial Judgment and Filing of Transcript on Appeal, 1870–1910*

No. days	1870–79	1880–89	1890–99	1900–1908	1909–10	All periods
Mean	103	109	120	142	26	102
Median	78	83	114	133	21	80
N	9	15	31	23	21	99

38. M. C. Sloss, "Reform of Criminal Procedure," *J. Crim. L.* 1 (1911): 705, 714.

39. *Annual Report of the California Attorney General, 1887–88* (1888), p. 6.

40. Attorney General U. S. Webb complained in 1904: "Transcripts have reached the office in which lengthy instructions, as given or refused by the trial court, have been printed in full as many as three times. . . . Another phase of this same abuse is the printing of the testimony in extenso, as transcribed by the court reporter, instead of reducing it to a condensed narrative form, as required by law." *Annual Report of the California Attorney General, 1902–04* (1904), p. 14.

41. The amount of paper sent up varied, of course, from case to case. Charles Kindleberger was able to appeal in 1893 without *any* bill of exceptions. He based his appeal on a single "dynamite charge" addressed to the jury. Instructions were part of the record, so there was no need for a bill of exceptions.

over the bill of exceptions. But the price was more paper. The extreme case was Isabella Martin's in 1910; the record contained the judgment roll and a full transcript of "all the proceedings before the trial court." This came to "five volumes consisting of 2,770 pages of printed matter." Today, the courts face even more inflated paper work, but in 1910 the work seemed staggering. No wonder the court was thankful when it got "systematic and lawyer-like" briefs.[42]

Hearing the Appeal

The higher court docketed cases in order, as their transcripts were filed; but each term criminal cases went to the head of the line.[43] In most instances (80 to 90 percent) the defendant's trial lawyer was also his lawyer on appeal. (Sometimes another lawyer or two joined the defense.) There were some notable exceptions. Isabella Martin prosecuted her second appeal without counsel. (Her "brief" was more than

42. People v. Martin, 13 Cal. App. 96 (1910). Apparently some defendants filed appeals with no real intention of going on with them, because they could not afford lawyers; but they could get automatic transcripts by filing a notice of appeal. District Attorney W. H. Donahue of Alameda County told the state bar convention: "[I]f you will go to the office of the clerk of the First Appellate District Court in San Francisco at the present time, you will find there transcript after transcript that has not been gone through, for the reason that no further action was ever taken, or the appeal was dismissed. As it is at the present time, the counsel representing the defendant must, when the motion for a new trial is denied, immediately give his notice of appeal, and ask that the testimony be written up. All of the testimony is written up, at the expense of the county of a great sum of money, without any good to the defendant, because in very many cases he does not intend to go on with his appeal. . . . I know that, as things now are, it has cost the County of Alameda $150,000 a year for unnecessary and useless appeals, and that the Appellate Court's records and pigeon holes have been filled with waste matter. . . ." California Bar Association, *Proceedings of First Annual Convention* (1910), pp. 98–99.

Former Alameda County District Attorney Charles E. Snook told the bar association: "In my brief experience as district attorney of Alameda County some few years ago, there was then no provision made for a transcript on appeal to be furnished by the county, nor was there any provision for the reporters to write up the testimony. I never knew a case with any merit in it at all where the lawyer did not take an appeal if he had half an opportunity to appeal to the Supreme Court. In other words, proportionately speaking, there were practically as many appeals then as there are now. Then followed the law providing for the transcript to be printed by the State, which was a very good thing in our county for some of the printers who did the public printing there." Ibid., p. 126.

43. Rules of the California Supreme Court, Rules IV & XVII, adopted Apr. 13, 1892. The California Supreme Court sat in three cities: San Francisco, Sacramento, and Los Angeles, by rotation. All Alameda County appeals were heard in San Francisco. This is also where the relevant District Court of Appeals sat, after 1905. All Alameda County appeals, thus, were decided in San Francisco.

500 pages long.) Charles Kinard, who defended himself at his trial, hired a lawyer to appeal when he lost.

For the prosecution, appeal meant a drastic change of guard. The attorney general, a newcomer to the case, represented the state. His office did not always have good contact with the local district attorney. In 1888, for example, the attorney general admitted that his staff often had no idea at all what line the defendant would take; they were in the dark until oral argument.[44] In 1892 the Supreme Court stepped in to remedy the situation. The defendant, it was decreed, had to provide "points" and authority for the attorney general within ten days after filing a transcript.[45] This probably helped somewhat. But the attorney general's office was thinly staffed. In 1892 he had only two deputies to work on criminal briefs.[46] Later, the office leaned much more on local district attorneys.

At oral argument, the Supreme Court allowed one attorney per side, except for "peculiar and important cases,"[47] and death penalty cases, where two were permitted (§ 1254). Normally, each side had one hour to argue. Table 8.8 shows how long it took the court to come to a decision, once the transcript was filed. The process became slower and slower, until 1905, when the new District Courts helped out.[48] We see the same general pattern if we look at the time from judgment below to judgment above (see Table 8.9). Habeas corpus petitions, however, were heard and decided very quickly, within a matter of days or weeks.

Table 8.8. Days between Filing of Appellate Transcript and Decision of Appellate Court, 1870–1910

No. days	1870–79	1880–89	1890–1904	1905–10	All periods
Mean	99	145	237	168	189
Median	66	138	231	121	150
N	8	15	36	35	94

44. *Annual Report of the California Attorney General, 1887–&88* (1888), p. 6.

45. Rules of the California Supreme Court, Rule II, adopted Apr. 13, 1892. The attorney general had ten days to respond; the appellant could file a reply brief up to five days later.

46. *Annual Report of the California Attorney General, 1891–92* (1892), p. 3.

47. Rules of the California Supreme Court, Rule XIX, adopted Apr. 13, 1892.

48. During the 1870s, the Supreme Court, by law, had to hear and decide all criminal appeals before the end of the first term after the record had been filed (§ 1252). In 1880 a new time limit was imposed: sixty days after "submission" except for cases "continued on motion or with the consent of the defendant." "Submission" is a rather ambiguous term. It is usually used by appellate courts to refer to the fact that a case is ripe for consideration, that is, after oral argument, when all the proper papers have been filed,

*Table 8.9. Days between Trial Court Judgment and
Appellate Decision, 1870–1910*

No. days	1870–79	1880–89	1890–1904	1905–10	All periods
Mean	209	306	375	259	309
Median	181	220	372	182	245
N	7	15	39	35	96

Winners and Losers

Only about one out of four of the defendants from Alameda County won on appeal (see Table 8.10). Prosecutors won two of their four appeals. In four cases, there were rehearings: in two, the District Court of Appeals had been unable to agree; in two, departments of the Supreme Court had made the original decision. The full Supreme Court affirmed two of the cases and reversed the other two. Altogether the prosecution won in more than three-quarters of the cases.[49] De-

*Table 8.10. Final Appellate Decisions in Alameda County
Cases by Party Bringing Appeal, 1870–1910*

	Judgment affirmed		Appeal dismissed		Judgment reversed	
Party bringing appeal	No.	%	No.	%	No.	%
Cases appealed by defendants	70	71	7	7	21	21
Cases appealed by prosecution	2	50	0	0	2	50

Note: the prevailing party on appeal was the prosecution in 79 cases (77%) and the defendant in 23 cases (23%).

---

and there is no other case pending that affects the present case and might be cause for postponement. Because there is no requirement that a case must be "submitted" at any particular time, appellate courts can make their dockets look good by deferring "submissions," and then claiming that they dispose of cases after "submission" very rapidly.

The Constitution of 1880 had a novel cure for delay: no Supreme Court judge could be paid, after July 1, 1880, unless he signed an affidavit that he had cleared all cases within ninety days. Cal. Const. 1879, art. 6, § 24. The Supreme Court's Rule XXX stated that opinions would be filed in all cases within ninety days of submission, if there were enough votes to decide the case.

The court has developed an easy way around the ninety-day rule. It simply defers "submission" of the case, and so the clock does not start running until the court wants it to.

49. A study of criminal cases in the California Supreme Court, published in 1928, found that the reversal rate declined steadily between 1850 and 1926. C. G. Vernier and Philip Selig, Jr., "The Reversal of Criminal Cases in the Supreme Court of California,"

fendants also did poorly in habeas corpus cases; they won only three out of forty-two.

Why did some appeals win and some lose? In theory, the court's opinion tells us. In two-thirds of the decisions, the court wrote opinions. Except for one case in 1892, no justice published a dissenting opinion.[50] Opinions were quite short, by modern standards: they averaged four pages; the longest was thirteen pages.

The court could dismiss an appeal if it was "irregular in any substantial particular" (§ 1248); this happened in seven cases. A few defendants abandoned their appeals. Two defendants—Annie Cameron and William Allen—died before their cases were heard. Most of the other aborted appeals were probably cases where the defendant could not scrape up money for a lawyer. In a few cases, the appellant failed to file a brief, or appear for oral argument, and the court summarily affirmed. William Day, convicted of sodomy in 1901, did not file a brief, bill of exceptions, or any statement of grounds for appeal. The court affirmed his conviction, in a five-sentence opinion. Some appeals, according to the attorney general in 1902, were "frivolous," even "absurd"; they had nothing new to say, and their points of law had been time and again "emphatically . . . passed upon by our Supreme Court." (Of course, to each defendant *his* case was new, and close to the bone.) Technically, many appeals were poorly put together. The brief for Percy Pembroke asserted that certain instructions ("set out in folio 93 to 102 . . . of the transcript") were wrongly refused. But the brief did not explain *why* the judge should have given these instructions. To put the question this way, the court said caustically, "has the merit of brevity, if no other." It refused to rule on the point.[51]

A few appeals were sensational or politically delicate. In a few cases, the publicity itself was an issue. Wong Loung was convicted of murdering Lee Chung, member of a rival tong, during Chinese gang violence in 1907. He was sentenced to death. A story in the *Oakland*

S. Cal. L. Rev. 2 (1928): 21. Our data show that the reversal rate held steady in the 1880s and 1890s. In the 1870s, few cases were appealed—perhaps only the ripest cases. The rate of reversal dropped between 1900 and 1909; this may have had something to do with changes in appellate structure. But it is interesting to note that reversals in criminal cases went down substantially in the Wisconsin Supreme Court after 1900—from 39 percent in the 1900s to 12 percent in the 1910s. Edward L. Kimball, "Criminal Cases in a State Appellate Court, 1839–1959," *Am. J. Legal Hist.* 9 (1965): 95, 98.

50. People v. McNutt, 93 Cal. 658 (1892). There may have been other cases in which one or more judges did not agree with the majority, but did not record a dissent. The records of the Supreme Court show that one justice "dissented" in People v. Ah Sam, 92 Cal. 648 (1892); but the published opinion makes no mention of this dissent.

51. People v. Pembroke, 6 Cal. App. 588 (1907).

Tribune claimed that Wong Loung had killed once before, in San Francisco. He was convicted, the article went on, but won on appeal. Then the earthquake and fire destroyed the evidence, and Loung went free. The story was strongly prejudicial; it called the defendant "a noted highbinder," and was couched in tones of high indignation. The day after this article appeared, Loung's case went to the jury. Some jurors had read the story; one had it in his pocket in the jury room; a juror's wife swore she read the account to her husband; and all of the jurors discussed the article. They insisted that the story made no difference to them; but the Supreme Court reversed the conviction, and ordered a new trial.[52] The next time around, Wong Loung was acquitted.

The saga of Isabella Martin has been told in Chapter 7. Mrs. Martin was convicted of dynamiting the home of Judge Ogden. In 1908 she was sentenced to life imprisonment. But the prosecution had made what turned out to be a major blunder. Its star witness was "Baby John," Isabella's foster son, a boy of sixteen. John said he planted the explosives, under Isabella's orders. Normally, this would make him an accomplice. On appeal, the high court insisted that an accomplice's testimony had to be "corroborated." The prosecution's line was that John was *not* an accomplice. John lived, they claimed, in deadly fear of his mother; she threatened him with arrest, and said she would bash his head in with a sledgehammer, or put powder under him and blow him up, if he did not do as he was told. To shore up this tale, the prosecution brought in all sorts of "evidence" about Isabella: stories accusing her of arson, dynamite plots, and a scheme to poison the water supply of Weaverville. The prosecution also dredged up obscene letters, and proof that Isabella owned poison at the time of her arrest. All this had only the flimsiest connection with the crime for which she sat in the dock. "However depraved and vicious she might be, she was entitled to be tried only for the crime charged against her," said the District Court of Appeals. Besides, Baby John's story did not prove he was in "imminent" danger from his mother. This made him, legally, an accomplice. Isabella had to be tried again.[53]

As Table 8.10 shows, few cases were reversed. It was not easy to convince the high court that the trial was tainted with so much "error" that the whole thing had to start all over again. In general, appeal courts brushed technicalities aside. There were a few interest-

52. Case file no. 4225 contains the slip opinion. The decision is reported as People v. Wong Loung, 159 Cal. 520, 114 P. 828 (1911).
53. People v. Martin, 13 Cal. App. 96 (1910). The prosecution petitioned for a rehearing before the Supreme Court in bank. The petition was denied.

ing exceptions. Fred Miles was accused of raping Carrie Welte (1907). His first trial ended in a hung jury; the second jury convicted him, and he was sentenced to thirty-five years in prison. On appeal, his lawyer argued that the information was defective; it never said, in so many words, that Carrie Welte was not his wife. (Under California law, a man could not rape his own wife.) Of course, she was *not* his wife, as everybody knew; and the prosecution proved it at trial. Despite this, the court reversed. Crimes must be charged in the language of the Penal Code; this was a "fundamental rule." The information here was legally "insufficient."[54] Of course, we cannot read the judges' minds. But perhaps the long, long sentence stuck in their craw. It was harsh indeed—the longest sentence for rape in the county for forty years. This, rather than the paltry mistake in the information, may have moved the court. Two months later, the charges against Miles were quietly dropped.

A year later, Clara Newton came to judgment. She was accused of abducting Lizzie Wright, for purposes of prostitution. The information said that Lizzie, who was sixteen, was unmarried at the time of the crime. Lizzie's testimony was fairly damning: she had been combing Clara's hair, she said, when Clara promised her "a silk kimono and chemise," ten dollars a night, and other glittering inducements. Lizzie, bedazzled, sprinkled with perfume, went off with Clara to her ruin. On appeal, Clara Newton argued that the state's case was incomplete; the state never *proved* that Lizzie was single at the time of this terrible deed. But this time the high court was less concerned with dotting *i*'s and crossing *t*'s. The prosecution did not have to prove every minor allegation in the information; in any event, it was easy to infer, from circumstantial evidence, that Lizzie was single.[55]

We can usually make a good guess about motives, in the handful of hyper-technical reversals. James O'Brien, Jr., was convicted of rape in 1909; the court reversed for a flock of minor errors. The victim insisted that O'Brien had raped her after she passed out from drink. The evidence was shaky, and it took three trials before a jury convicted.[56] In some cases where the court reversed on technical grounds, the defendants were Chinese. Five out of eight appeals by Chinese defendants were successful. Did the high court smell bias, and react against it? It is at least possible.

A few cases turned on the meaning of words or phrases in the Penal Code itself. In 1903, F. K. Lewis was convicted of "taking" a girl

54. People v. Miles, 9 Cal. App. 312 (1908).
55. People v. Newton, 11 Cal. App. 762 (1909).
56. People v. O'Brien, 130 Cal. 1 (1900).

away from home, "for the purpose of prostitution" (§ 266a). Lewis transported the girl from San Juan Bautista, in San Benito County, to Oakland. She ended up in a house of ill fame. On appeal, Lewis argued that the crime was not committed in Alameda County, but rather in San Benito, because the "taking" happened there. Hence the trial was held in the wrong place. But the court felt otherwise. The offense was not complete until the abductor decided to turn the girl into a prostitute. This notion, perhaps, did not pop into Lewis's head until he crossed into Alameda County; at any rate, the jury might have thought so. The case was affirmed. In another case, William Proctor was convicted of grand larceny. Proctor met an old woman, Amaline Tyson, at the station, struck up a friendship, sold her a pair of glasses, and told her he had fallen in love. She gave him $108, as a "loan," to help him in a real estate deal. This, said the court, was not grand larceny; the money was given voluntarily. True, Proctor was guilty of a crime: obtaining money "under false pretenses." But he had been convicted of grand larceny, the wrong crime, and the case had to be reversed.[57]

Constitutional decisions were extremely rare. J. H. Russell was convicted under § 476, the bad check law. He argued, rather feebly, that the law was "special legislation," forbidden by the California Constitution. The statute, he said, made it a crime to draw false orders on bankers, but not on other people. The court dismissed this flimsy argument. C. R. Bennett, as we saw, had been granted a new trial on grounds of double jeopardy; the state appealed and won.[58] Constitutional arguments were a bit more frequent in petitions for habeas corpus. A. L. Thomas was convicted in 1886, under a license ordinance. The ordinance taxed peddlers and hawkers, but exempted people who sold goods made in California. The court agreed that the ordinance violated the federal commerce clause; only Congress could regulate interstate commerce.[59] Another case, in 1905, overturned a conviction under a law banning usury in chattel mortgages. The act applied only to loans on furniture, fixtures, pianos, and an assorted lot of other goods. The court thought it was unreasonable to single out certain goods and not others; this violated the defendant's right to "equal protection of the laws."[60] Robert Mitchell was convicted of assault with a deadly weapon, and sentenced to pay $4,000 and serve two years in prison. This, he claimed, was cruel and unusual punish-

57. On the meaning of "false pretenses," see also People v. Mary Martin, 102 Cal. 558 (1894).

58. People v. Bennett, 114 Cal. 56 (1896).

59. Ex parte Thomas, 71 Cal. 204 (1886).

60. Ex parte Sohncke, 148 Cal. 262 (1905). The statute was Laws Cal. 1905, ch. 354.

ment. If he could not pay the fine, he pointed out, he would have to spend four thousand extra days in prison. This was longer than a man would serve for manslaughter, or assault with intent to kill—crimes much more serious than his. The Supreme Court disagreed on the constitutional point, but reserved judgment on whether Mitchell had a right to go free after two years in prison, fine or no fine. In the end Mitchell served his time and went free without paying.

Starting Over

When a defendant "won," this did not mean, necessarily, immediate freedom. About two-thirds of the time, a new trial was ordered. Yet defendants had an excellent chance after reversal. There were twenty-one convictions reversed, but only six reconvictions; and in three of these, the defendant got a lighter sentence his second time around.

When a case was reversed, the district attorney had to take a fresh look at the case. He had to decide if it was worth the effort to mount a new trial. Normally, he would schedule one, then look the evidence over, read the decision, and decide what to do. In thirteen of the twenty-one cases, trials were scheduled; in eight, charges were dismissed. Two were prosecuted under new informations. One of these ended in a conviction. Only seven of the thirteen scheduled retrials actually took place. Four were dismissed. After James O'Brien's conviction for rape was reversed, the prosecution dawdled for a year, then moved to dismiss, "for want of evidence." This ended a drama that lasted three and a half years, and stretched over three trials. Charles Kindleberger (also convicted of rape) came back from San Quentin when the high court reversed; he agreed to plead guilty to a charge of simple assault. In the process, his seven-year sentence shrank to three months in county jail.

George Jones was, perhaps, the luckiest of all the defendants who appealed. Jones was condemned to death for first-degree murder. In 1886, his conviction was reversed. Then Jones fell ill; his doctors swore he was too sick to stand trial. Four years went by. The court inquired again into Jones's condition. Again, the doctors reported bad news: Jones could not live out the year. Yet in January 1892, the *Tribune* claimed he was "frisky as a colt." Jones was housed in county jail; the jailer expected him to die, but Jones, it seems, had "vitality": "He's getting better. . . . When I go to see him in the mornings he is as gay as you please. But if you want to make old Jones very sick just tell him that they are going to bring him into court and try him and in a day he'll become the sickest man in Alameda County. The old man don't want to have anything to do with the law. He simply wants to be let alone and is satisfied to die in jail."[61] Jones was never retried.

Only seven defendants, then, went to trial again on their original informations, after a reversal. Two were acquitted: Adolph Silva on charges of grand larceny, Wong Loung on a charge of murder. W. A. Brandes, charged with murder, was convicted of manslaughter; the jury recommended mercy. Brandes was sentenced to ten years in prison, a considerable improvement over his first sentence (life).[62] Three defendants were reconvicted, and did no better than before. Isabella Martin was one of these. Her second trial lasted thirty-seven days, only six less than the first. She was convicted, and sentenced to life in prison.

One retrial ended in a hung jury. The defendant, David Mitchell, was a lawyer, fifty-four years old. It was a lurid case. A fourteen-year-old girl accused him of making love to her in his law office; meanwhile, her friend, Bernice (seventeen), who arranged the whole thing, waited patiently outside. Mitchell then gave the girl $2.50, to buy a costume for a skating carnival. At the first trial, Bernice was the star witness for the prosecution. Mitchell tried to show that Bernice had a record. She had been arrested for vagrancy; now she faced the reform school at Whittier, unless she testified. The trial court refused to allow this line of attack. The appeal court felt that it was "error" to keep this evidence out, and reversed the case. At the second trial, the jury hung, and the prosecution gave up.

Habeas Corpus and Federal Court

In our system, a defendant can also "appeal" to federal courts—if he or she has appropriate *federal* grounds. This was exceptionally rare in our period. In 1880 the federal courts let go Tiburcio Parrott, on a writ of habeas corpus. Parrott was prosecuted under a state law, which restricted hiring Chinese for certain jobs. The federal court ruled that state law had to give way to federal law or, as here, to the United States treaty with China.

C. R. Bennett, whose trials and tribulations we followed in Chapter 7, applied for the writ, in federal district court (1897). His argument was based on the Bill of Rights (double jeopardy). Judge DeHaven, the federal district judge, agreed that Bennett's conviction was "void."[63]

61. *Oakland Tribune*, Jan. 11, 1892, p. 2, col. 3.
62. The Brandes case was discussed in more detail in Chap. 7.
63. In re Bennett, 84 Fed. 324, 326 (1897).

But DeHaven thought he had no power to let Bennett go, without a writ of error from the U.S. Supreme Court. In fact, Bennett served out his year in San Quentin.

Benjamin Hill also applied for a writ in 1897, in the very shadow of the gallows. On August 27, the court denied his petition. Hill then tried to appeal to the U.S. Supreme Court. On September 23, 1897, he filed his appellate transcript. The case was scheduled for argument on December 6, 1897. But the court dismissed the case when Hill failed to produce a printed record. Four months later, Hill was put to death as ordered.

None of this suggests excessive use of federal courts, to say the least. Yet Attorney General Fitzgerald of California took a dim view of Hill's maneuvers. It was an abuse, he felt, to run to federal court "for the sole purpose of delaying the execution" of a condemned murderer. He was afraid that "the machinery prescribed by the Federal statutes could and would be successfully used by all persons under sentence of death to indefinitely stay the execution of their sentences." This is why he moved so "promptly and vigorously" to get the Supreme Court to hear these cases. The Supreme Court's speed "had a very salutary effect"; Hill and three others were executed "and no further attempts have been made on behalf of that class of criminals to invoke the aid of the Federal courts."[64]

Appeals: A Summary Word

What do we conclude from this brief walk through the cases on appeal? The most striking fact is how few there were: three or so a year from Alameda County. In theory, higher courts controlled the work of the lower courts. They made sure injustice was corrected. No doubt appellate courts took their duties seriously, but the process was too sporadic, too technical, to provide *real* supervision. Basically, Alameda County ran itself. The higher courts were rare and distant thunder. The federal courts were no factor at all.

Can we be sure? Sometimes the most powerful bosses are those who never need to interfere. The courts of Alameda County were courts of *law*; they followed, in general, what they understood were the norms and principles of justice. They took their law from the Penal Code, from state statutes, from the two constitutions, from case

---

64. *Biennial Report of the California Attorney General, 1896–98* (1898), pp. 3–4. Fitzgerald also claimed that he "succeeded in obtaining from the Federal courts a construction of the Federal statutes relative to the law of habeas corpus which materially curtailed the dilatory uses to which those statutes have heretofore been put by the criminal classes."

law. In some broad sense appellate reports had (we assume) a certain impact on Superior Court. Yet very likely this was true, not because judges were afraid of reversal, or ashamed of it, or felt coerced, but rather because of duty, tradition, morality, habits of obedience, a sense of role. It was what judges felt they had to do.

A second striking fact is how poorly defendants did on appeal: even the few who made it to the high court usually lost there. As we saw, prosecutors won 77 percent of the appeals. Roscoe Pound, writing in 1930, complained about the "hypertrophy of procedure," a deadly disease of appellate courts, causing them to reverse in criminal cases on absurd and technical grounds.[65] He was not alone in this view. It is an old idea that appellate courts are too tender to criminals, and ignore the poor bleeding victims. Judge I. C. Parker, writing in 1892 on how to "arrest the increase of homicides in America," offered this advice: special courts of criminal appeals, "made up of judges learned in the criminal law, and governed by a desire for its speedy and vigorous enforcement." Such a court would "brush aside all technicalities," and ignore "technical pleas concocted by cunning minds."[66] Perhaps Pound and Parker had a point—but not in California. There was, on our evidence, no more than a pinhead of "hypertrophy," and precious little sign of appellate coddling. There may have been a case of "hypertrophy" here and there; these could well mislead an observer. Bad cases make bad law—and deceptive impressions.

The study of law in this country is mainly the study of appellate case law. In a common-law system, high court judges are supposed to play a huge role in making the law. This was not true of criminal justice in Alameda County. The Penal Code—that was law. So too was local practice. (There was not a word of guidance in appellate case law about plea bargaining, for example.) The probation system, to mention one great innovation of our period, owed nothing at all to appellate courts. It owed a great deal to the legislature, and the rest to local practice. Of course, if a court *really* got out of line, the high court was willing and able to slap its wrists; but for the most part, Alameda County carried on by itself, in obscure autonomy.

65. Roscoe Pound, *Criminal Justice in America* (Cambridge, Mass., 1930), p. 161. Apparently some courts did reverse a good deal. A journal article claimed that the Texas Court of Appeals did nothing but "overrule and reverse." This court, supposedly, reversed by a two to one margin in the 1870s and 1880s. Note, "Overruled their Judicial Superiors," *Am. L. Rev.* 21 (1887): 610. See *Oakland Herald*, Oct. 1, 1903, p. 4, col. 4.

66. Hon. I. C. Parker, "How to Arrest the Increase of Homicides in America," *N. Am. Rev.* 162 (June 1892): 667, 672–73. The notion that criminals used technicalities to delay and obstruct was probably widespread. See *Oakland Tribune*, Dec. 2, 1897, p. 3, col. 5, about a stay granted to a condemned San Diego murderer, Joseph E. Davis, which was called "another remarkable instance of the success of purely technical defense in the courts."

Chapter 9

Iron Bars, Cages, and Gallows:
Some Words about Prisons and Jails

Criminal justice was a long and rocky road. For those swept up by the police, there were many points at which one could wriggle out of the net. But if all these failed, and a prisoner was convicted, through a guilty plea or by a jury, the end result was iron bars. As we saw, loss of freedom was *the* mode of punishment in Alameda County: not reprimand, not fines, not whippings, but a "jolt" in prison or jail. This was overwhelmingly true of felony defendants, somewhat less so of petty criminals. As we follow our defendants to the bitter end, we shall have to say a word or two about prisons and jails.

There was a fundamental distinction between prison and jail. The state ran *prisons;* counties and cities ran *jails.* Indeed, the line between felony and misdemeanor, in California, was in part a line between prison and jail. A felony was a crime "punishable with death or . . . imprisonment in the state prison." Anything else was a misdemeanor (§ 17).[1] Prisons and jails were very different in looks, architecture, and purpose. Not everybody in a jail was there to be punished; some were merely waiting for trial. But there was one purpose and one only for a prison.

In eighteenth-century America, there were no "prisons" as such; there were only jails. Imprisonment was *not* the normal way of punishing criminals. Fines and whippings were far more common. The nineteenth century invented the true prison or penitentiary. These were grim, silent fortresses, constructed on a kind of monastic principle. They quarantined criminals from a corrupting social environment and bent their spirits toward conformity, through solitude and iron discipline.[2] These new and revolutionary prisons were first built in

---

1. If a crime was punishable either by imprisonment in the state prison *or* by fine or imprisonment in a county jail, in the court's discretion, then "it shall be deemed a misdemeanor for all purposes after a judgment imposing a punishment other than imprisonment in the state prison" (§ 17).

2. The literature on prison history is enormous. See, especially, David Rothman, *The Discovery of the Asylum* (Boston, 1971); see also W. David Lewis, *From Newgate to Dannemora: The Rise of the Penitentiary in New York, 1796–1848* (Ithaca, N.Y., 1965); on

the East—New York and Pennsylvania, in particular. The essence of the system was total silence, solitude, hard labor, and uniform discipline. Each prisoner was dressed the same, fed the same, treated the same; when prisoners moved, they walked in lockstep. Prisoners lived one to a cell in complete isolation. Not a word was ever to be spoken. No prison was able to sustain this hellish purity for long; for one thing, the "correct" sort of prison was expensive to build, and expensive to keep up. When prison became too crowded, more than one prisoner had to be shoehorned into a cell; silence and solitude went out the window. After the Civil War, new fashions in penology took over. Basically, the key notion was to differentiate between prisoners, sifting good ones from bad ones, the savable from the damned. We have seen this idea at work in other parts of the criminal justice system. Parole, time off for good behavior, and the indeterminate sentence reflected the trend. California, generally speaking, went along with these national movements.

The State Prison System

The first state prison opened for business in December 1851.[3] But this was no classic "penitentiary." Rather, it was a floating prison—a ship, sitting off Vallejo, in San Pablo Bay. State prisoners were under the tender care of M. G. Vallejo and James M. Estell. These two gentlemen rented the prisoners from the state. They promised to keep them healthy, safe—and well locked up. They had to feed, clothe, and guard the prisoners; despite this, they hoped they would turn a profit by making the prisoners work.

This floating prison was only a makeshift. Soon the state picked a spot for a permanent prison: Point San Quentin, north of San Francisco, across the Golden Gate, on a neck of land that looks out over the upper sweep of the Bay. Here a mighty prison was built. Administratively, it had a checkered career. First it was run by three directors; in 1856 the legislature changed its mind, and went back to the leasing system. James M. Estell rented San Quentin. But his regime was brutal. A report in 1858 described the convicts as tattered and filthy; the "commonest street beggars" looked like "newly Parisian clad gen-

---

parallel developments in England, see Michael Ignatieff, *A Just Measure of Pain: The Penitentiary in the Industrial Revolution, 1750–1850* (New York, 1978).

3. On the California prisons, specifically, see Tirey L. Ford, *California State Prisons: Their History, Development and Management* (San Francisco, 1910); Blake McKelvey, *American Prisons: A Study in American Social History prior to 1915* (reprint ed., Montclair, N.J., 1968), pp. 191–95.

tlemen" in comparison. Prisoners slept in tiny cells on straw mattresses; a "coarse, shaggy double blanket," usually crawling with lice, kept off the cold. Once more, the state took over. Reforms in the 1860s included a library, bath facilities, chaplains, and prison uniforms. But the prison was chronically overcrowded. In 1871 the directors complained that they needed 400 new cells. San Quentin was a warehouse, not a "reformatory." Another investigation took place in 1881. Again, the prison was branded a failure. It made no real attempt to follow the rules of modern penology. To turn San Quentin into a "progressive" prison, the state would have to classify and separate prisoners, instead of lumping together the worst and the best. Capt. I. W. Lees of San Francisco pressed for the use of the "silent system": isolating prisoners in utter silence. Professional criminals dreaded this system; it would "deter them . . . when nothing else will."[4] Most of those who spoke to the investigators wanted reform in one direction: more rigor. San Quentin should be utterly terrible, a place of total dread. But no real changes were made, one way or the other.

Meanwhile the state planned and built a second prison, Folsom, on the bank of the American River, twenty miles east of Sacramento. Work began in 1874; the south wing was ready in 1880. In 1910, Folsom's granite walls held something over 1,000 prisoners, in 394 cells. San Quentin was larger. It had 1,900 inmates in 1910, locked in 4 cell houses. It also had a sash and blind factory (fully equipped with a machine shop); a hospital; chapel; women's department; jute mill; and commissary, offices, and quarters for officers and guards. The prison officers lived in homes built outside the walls; here too stood the administrative offices. Death row was on the top floor of the blind factory. There were two exercise yards. Watchtowers, two or three stories high, were scattered about the grounds. There were sentry boxes along the top of the walls. The State Board of Prison Directors, with five (unpaid) members, stood nominally at the head of the prison system. The board appointed a warden; the warden appointed guards. The warden was in charge, but the board was not always a paper tiger; in 1905, for example, it fired Warden Tompkins, on the grounds that he was plainly "incompetent."[5]

4. *Oakland Daily Times*, July 28, 1881, p. 3, col. 5; *San Francisco Call*, July 27, 1881, p. 4, col. 2.

5. Minutes, State Board of Prison Directors, p. 217 (State Archives, Sacramento).

Inside the Big House

Anyone who has seen a movie about the "big house" would recognize the structure of the California prisons. Inside San Quentin, cells were arranged in long parallel rows, three tiers high. Each cell was separately locked. They varied in size. In 1910 the cells were without heat or toilet facilities. In that year, 396 prisoners lived in single cells; 408 in double cells; 126 were crowded into forty-eight other cells; the rest of the prisoners, 744 in all, were jammed into ten rooms and two large dormitories. The prison, everybody agreed, was terribly overcrowded.

Between 1880 and 1910, somewhat over 40 percent of the state's prisoners were in their twenties; something over 20 percent, in their thirties. In 1882, 17 percent of the prisoners were quite young (under twenty); the percentage fell to some 7 percent in 1910, doubtless because juveniles went to Whittier or Preston, or were otherwise handled. Four out of every five prisoners had committed property crimes.[6] This figure stayed stable over the whole thirty years. Crimes against the person, however, fell from 19 percent to 12.5 percent; the sharpest drop (from 15.6 percent to 12.5 percent) came between 1905 and 1910. Crimes against "decency" (the phrase is Tirey Ford's—a member of the State Board of Prison Directors) contributed only 1.5 percent of the prisoners in 1880, 3.3 percent in 1905; the figure rose to 7.3 percent in 1910. These crimes included bigamy, adultery, and rape. Over the whole period, about 20 percent of the prisoners were repeaters, back for a second "jolt."

Table 9.1 gives some information about the lost souls in San Quentin or Folsom who came from Alameda County. They were quite typical of the general prison population. These prisoners were, overwhelmingly, young men. (But compared to prisoners today, they were not so *very* young.) Property crimes dominated. Burglary alone accounted for 681 prisoners, or 46.3 percent of the total.[7] Prisoners, like people arrested in general, were overwhelmingly male; only 29 women went to prison during the whole period, or less than one a

6. In 1894, 796 out of 1,287 convicts had committed property crimes. Of these, 358 were burglars. There were 343 commitments for assaults and murder, 85 for "rape and other sex crimes." Charles H. Shinn, "The California Penal System," *Popular Science Monthly*, March 1899, pp. 644, 652–53.

7. Of these, 247, or 16.8 percent, were sent up for first-degree burglary; 419, or 28.5 percent, for second-degree burglary; 15, or 1 percent, for attempted burglary. Before 1876, the crimes of "burglary" and "housebreaking" corresponded to what became first- and second-degree burglary (§ 460). The first-degree burglary figures include 18 convicted of "burglary" before 1876. The second-degree figures include 15 convicted of "housebreaking" before 1876.

Table 9.1. Characteristics of Alameda County Prisoners in State Prisons, 1870–1911

A. Prison sent to	1870–1911 No.	1870–1911 %	1870–83 (no.)	1884–89 (no.)	1890–99 (no.)	1900–1905 (no.)	1906–11 (no.)
San Quentin	1,081	73.5	356	111	154	131	329
Folsom	390	26.5	0	87	114	92	97
Total	1,471	100	356	198	268	223	426

B. Sex	1870–1911 No.	1870–1911 %	1870–83 (no.)	1884–89 (no.)	1890–99 (no.)	1900–1905 (no.)	1906–11 (no.)
Male	1,442	98.0	350	194	264	221	413
Female	29	2.0	6	4	4	2	13

C. Nativity	1870–1911 No.	1870–1911 %	1870–83 (%)	1884–89 (%)	1890–99 (%)	1900–1905 (%)	1906–11 (%)
USA	962	65.7	51	60	66	79	74
China	99	6.8	16	10	3	1	2
Ireland	82	5.6	9	10	3	3	3
Germany	74	5.1	6	9	5	2	4
England	47	3.2	3	2	5	4	3
Canada	40	2.7	4	2	4	2	2
Mexico	18	1.2	1	2	1	2	2
Italy	17	1.2	1	0	0	1	2
France	14	1.0	1	1	2	0	0
Scotland	12	0.8	1	0	1	1	1
Sweden	12	0.7	1	1	0	0	1
Denmark	10	0.7	1	1	0	0	1

D. Race	1870–1911 No.	1870–1911 %	1870–83 (%)	1884–89 (%)	1890–99 (%)	1900–1905 (%)	1906–11 (%)
White	1,292	87.8	82	88	91	90	90
Black	74	5.0	2	2	6	8	7
Oriental	102	6.9	16	10	3	2	3
Indian	3	0.2	1	0	0	0	0

E. Age at commitment	1870–1911 (yrs.)	1870–83 (yrs.)	1884–89 (yrs.)	1890–99 (yrs.)	1900–1905 (yrs.)	1906–11 (yrs.)
Mean	30.6	29.2	31.2	30.1	29.4	32.2
Median	27.6	25.8	29.1	27.1	26.2	29.1
Youngest	12	12	16	15	16	18
Oldest	73	73	63	72	69	68
Mode	25	25	20	23	24	25

F. Class of crime	1870–1911 No.	%	1870–83 (%)	1884–89 (%)	1890–99 (%)	1900–1905 (%)	1906–11 (%)
Against persons	218	14.8	15	13	14	18	14
Against property	1,170	79.6	80	81	79	76	81
Morals	46	3.1	1	2	6	4	4
Public order	34	2.3	3	5	1	2	2
Regulatory	1	0.1	1	0	0	0	0

G. Number of times previously committed to California state prisons

	1870–1911 No.	%
None (first timers)	1,157	78.6
One	213	14.5
Two	69	4.7
Three	18	1.2
Four	8	0.5
Five	5	0.3
Six	1	0.1

H. Average sentence	Months	N
San Quentin	51.1	1,062
Folsom	72.1	384

Source: 100% sample of Alameda County prisoners committed to state prisons, 1870–1911.

Note: Figures in part G include only previous commitments to California state prisons. Of the prisoners, 4.3% had previously done time in a county jail, federal prison, state prison in another state, or reform school.

year. Prisoners were mostly native born; but the Chinese were much overrepresented, particularly before 1890. This is almost certainly a result of the virulent race feeling in California. After 1890, there is nothing in the numbers to suggest that Chinese were singled out for prison sentences. Table 9.1 also shows that most prisoners were first-timers.

Folsom was entirely a prison for men. The few women prisoners were all at San Quentin, in a special walled section of the prison. They spent their days sewing underwear for the men. Donald Lowrie, who did time at San Quentin, described them as "wrecks from the underworld," women without any "sense of delicacy. Their speech and actions are of the lowest order." This was perhaps just as well, as San Quentin was no place for a "woman of refinement or culture."[8] Life in the women's department, by all accounts, was as cruel, unhealthy, and barbaric as in the men's.[9]

Donald Lowrie was sentenced to fifteen years in San Quentin just after the turn of the century. He has left us a striking picture of life in the big house. It was a bleak, ugly dungeon; life inside the walls was brutal and harsh. Lowrie himself was locked up in a cell eight feet by ten feet, with four other men. In this narrow room, dressed in prison stripes, his head shaven, he passed much of his time. He has described for us the yard, the jute mill, and most vividly, the mess hall with its damp asphalt floor, whitewashed walls, and long tables made of plain boards. The men ate with rusty tinware. There were no tablecloths or napkins. The meals were served up in pans, without ladles; every prisoner dipped his own spoon "into the common receptable."[10] The place smelled worse than a stable. The Chinese sat apart. The men had twelve minutes to gulp down their food. After 1906, prisoners without teeth sat at a special table. There, at the "toothless table," the men chewed slowly; graciously, the warden granted them more time to eat than the others.

Official reports tended to be rose-colored. Lowrie draws us a picture of hell. Most convicts did not write books; but when they talked, their accounts agreed with Lowrie's. In 1903 the prisons were investigated once more. A lot of stones were turned over; what came crawling out was hardly pretty. A prisoner at Folsom talked about the straitjacket. He described the practice of "tricing": "They have rings

8. *My Life in Prison* (New York, 1912), p. 213; another vivid description of San Quentin life is Col. Griffith J. Griffith's, in Prison Reform League, *Crime and Criminals* (San Francisco, 1910), pp. 55–93.

9. "San Quentin, as a Female Prisoner Saw It," in Prison Reform League, *Crime and Criminals*, p. 94.

10. Lowrie, *My Life*, p. 35.

in the wall, and a strap on the rings and hand-cuffs buckled on to that, and by means of that buckle they can trice you up higher or lower."[11] At Folsom, the men in straitjackets yelled so loud they could be heard on the highway, six hundred yards away.[12] Prison officials defended the straitjacket as a harmless mode of discipline. But it was undeniably humiliating—the men lay helplessly in their own filth for a day, two days, even three. Griffith J. Griffith, who fell from great heights and did time in San Quentin, told a more sinister story. Laced too closely or too long, the jacket cut off circulation; it was always painful, sometimes crippling, and could even kill.[13] Griffith told an audience in Los Angeles, in 1908, that San Quentin was backward and tyrannical—a "school for crime." There was general agreement that "dope" was everywhere in the prisons—"plenty of it"—morphine and opium (although Lowrie thought the problem had been cured at San Quentin around 1907). The San Quentin doctors, Griffith said, were "heartless," loathsome men. One of them "had a cure-all that was called a 'bombshell,'" another used a "32-inch hose and a gallon of water for every sickness."[14] Torture was an everyday affair.

For many prisoners, the days crawled by in excruciating idleness. Others worked in the jute mill, or in the sash and blind factory. (The jute mill, "with its dark corners and piles of material," was also the scene of many "degenerate acts.")[15] Work was one way to kill time; prison specialists also considered it one of the ways to reform a criminal. But the outside world was hostile to prison labor, especially the unions. To them, prison labor was cheap, unfair competition. Under the California Constitution (Art. 10, § 6) "the labor of convicts" could not be leased out to private parties (this was common practice in the South). Prisoners were to work "for the benefit of the State." But doing what? Organized labor protested against convict-made goods; prison products "demoralized" the market.[16] Workers at the California Cotton Mills, in 1893, denounced plans to make rope, hemp, and twine at Folsom. A middle-aged woman at the mills said that the convicts were taking "the bread and butter out of our mouths"; a factory engineer talked about slave labor and falling wages. If prison labor went unchecked, he said, "we will have to knock at the doors of

11. Testimony of Joseph Bryan, Feb. 27, 1903, in *Investigation by Assembly Committee on State Prisons*, p. 42.

12. Ibid., pp. 66, 73.

13. Griffith, in Prison Reform League, *Crime and Criminals*, p. 82.

14. *Oakland Tribune*, Apr. 12, 1908, p. 17, col. 4.

15. Prison Reform League, *Crime and Criminals*, pp. 87–88.

16. U.S. Bureau of Labor, *20th Ann. Rpt. Comm. of Labor, 1905: Convict Labor* (1905), p. 11.

San Quentin and ask for a job.''[17] One compromise had prisoners at San Quentin making grain bags out of jute. This was acceptable; it gave "needed exercise to the prisoners and cheap grain sacks to the farmers.''[18] Folsom's main product in the early twentieth century was clothing—1,953 undershirts, 1,871 bedclothes—but mostly for the prisoners' own use.[19]

Getting Out

A ten-year sentence did not mean, necessarily, ten full years in prison. From 1868 on, a prisoner who behaved himself got "credit" for good behavior. These credits were fixed in 1889 at two months a year for the first two years, four months a year for the third and fourth years, five months for all later years (§ 1588).[20]

The quickest way out of prison (short of a jailbreak) was the governor's pardon. By law, the governor could grant reprieves, commutations, and pardons for all offenses, except treason and impeachment (§ 1417). Generally speaking, the governor had total discretion: he could pardon "upon such conditions and with such restrictions and limitations" as he thought "proper." (After 1880, however, anyone "twice convicted of felony" could not be pardoned by the governor unless a majority of the judges of the Supreme Court recommended a pardon in writing.) In each session of the legislature, the governor presented a list of those convicts he pardoned, reprieved, or commuted, and the reasons why. A prisoner who wanted a pardon had to apply for it. He also had to give "written notice" of his application to the district attorney of the county where he had been convicted. The notice was also published for thirty days in one of that county's newspapers (§§ 1421, 1422). These provisions, quite obviously, were meant to inform the prisoner's victims and the people who prosecuted him, and give them a chance to raise any objections.

Whom did the governor pardon? In a few cases justice had plainly miscarried. In 1876, Governor William Irwin pardoned William Cloonan, doing time at San Quentin for grand larceny. Cloonan's so-called

17. *Oakland Tribune*, Jan. 25, 1893, p. 1, col. 3.

18. Shinn, "California Penal System," pp. 644, 647. The Penal Code in 1907 made this explicit: "At San Quentin no articles shall be manufactured for sale except jute fabrics" (§ 1586).

19. U.S. Bureau of Labor, *20th Ann. Rpt. Comm. of Labor*, pp. 346–47.

20. The language of this section refers to a convict "who shall have no infractions of the rules and regulations of the prison, or laws of the state, recorded against him, and who performs in a faithful, orderly, and peaceable manner the duties assigned to him."

accomplices swore, before a notary public, that Cloonan was "entirely innocent."[21] Edward Moan was convicted of manslaughter in 1884; but "post-mortem examination of the body . . . proved the strong probability that death was caused by disease" (Oct. 8, 1884). Sometimes the governor pardoned sick or dying prisoners. Governor Perkins pardoned H. C. Holder, of Butte County, convicted of manslaughter in 1879; the prisoner was "an old man," lying "very sick" in the Prison Hospital; according to the prison doctor, Holder would not live long if he stayed behind bars (Feb. 18, 1882). George Gleason, convicted of burglary, was "incurably ill" and wanted to die "outside the prison gates" (Feb. 27, 1884). Others touched the governor's heart for one reason or another. Frank Rhodes of Alameda County, sentenced to two years in prison for burglary, was a "mere child, but twelve years old—a homeless wanderer, his father and mother being dead." Frank's uncle in Oregon promised to take him in (July 9, 1881). George Riley, age sixteen, pardoned in 1884, had committed his burglary out of "youthful impulse" (Sept. 30, 1884). Some pardons came in response to letters and petitions. Fredrick Maurer, also of Alameda County, convicted of grand larceny in June 1881, won a pardon six months later. The pardon was recommended by "numerous well known citizens of Alameda County, including the twelve jurors who tried the case, the prosecuting witness, the judge who sentenced him, the District Attorney . . . and other county officers." The Prison Directors concurred, and a merchant in Oakland promised to give Maurer a job.[22] Sometimes the governor pardoned because he felt the punishment was too severe. In 1891, Governor Markham pardoned Joseph Peralta on this basis. Peralta was arrested on two charges of petty larceny, for taking oysters from beds near San Leandro. He was convicted by a jury and sentenced to 100 days in county jail for each charge. This was a "severe" sentence; after Peralta served half his time, the governor "deemed that he had been punished enough."[23]

Over the years, as population grew, the job became (apparently) more onerous. In 1893, Governor Markham complained that petitions for pardon took up much of his time. He tried to set up a better

21. Cal. St. Prison at San Quentin, Diary, Dec. 1, 1874–Mar. 31, 1878, p. 143 (May 31, 1876). The warden's office houses this diary, and the warden was kind enough to let us see it.
22. These examples are drawn from the appendix to *Biennial Message of Governor George C. Perkins to the Legislature of the State of California, 25th Session* (Sacramento, 1883), pp. 31, 33, 34; and the appendix to the *First Biennial Message of Governor George Stoneman, 26th Session* (Sacramento, 1885), pp. 36, 47, 48.
23. *Oakland Tribune*, June 17, 1891, p. 2, col. 4. Peralta was listed as a farmer in Brooklyn Township in 1884, aged twenty-one. *Great Register, Alameda County*, 1884, p. 142.

system, in which the work, after an initial screening of petitions, was turned over to the Board of State Prison Directors.[24] A more structured alternative was the parole law, passed that very year.[25] Parole, in effect, replaced pardon. Between 1863 and 1891, pardon or commutation accounted for 11 percent of all prisoner releases; in 1901–11, the percentage dropped to less than 2.[26] Governor Henry Gage told the legislature in 1901 that he had pardoned only one man in two years: William Nagel, a seventy-year-old butcher of Modoc County, who "pleaded guilty to the crime of furnishing liquor to an Indian," and was sentenced to eight months in county jail (he was himself dead drunk at the time of this "crime").[27]

Under the parole law, the prisoner, as before, had to apply for release. First, he was to write up a sketch of his life. News of the application was released to the press in the city or county where the man or woman had been tried. The Parole Board asked the views of the sentencing judge, the defense attorney, and the district attorney, sheriff, or chief of police. The board could make further inquiries, too, among employers and others. The prisoner had to try to line up a job, and show he had some place to go if set free. The board would look at his prison record, and (finally) talk to the prisoner himself. No one was eligible before serving half his term, less credits (or eight years, whichever was less).

With provisions like these, parole was hardly automatic. The prisoner had to advertise his plans; this exposed him, in Donald Lowrie's view, to his "enemies" or to "prejudiced persons." Another stumbling block was the job requirement: "How many businessmen are there who can assure a man a position two or three months hence?"[28] And another requirement—a twenty-five-dollar deposit—was a hardship for many men. Still, according to Tirey Ford, 844 prisoners were paroled between 1893 and December 31, 1909—about 50 a year. Only 93 of these—11 percent—broke parole. Of these, 67 went back to prison, 26 slipped out of sight.

The law vested enormous discretion in the board. Its decisions

24. *Oakland Tribune*, Jan. 4, 1892, p. 6, col. 3.
25. Laws Cal. 1893, ch. 153, p. 183.
26. These figures are from "Discretion over Prison Sentences in California," unpublished paper, 1978, by Professor Sheldon Messinger of the University of California, Berkeley, who was kind enough to let us use his materials.
27. *Biennial Message of Governor Henry T. Gage, Jan. 7, 1901* (Sacramento, 1901), p. 38. The offense was proscribed by § 397. The governor commuted one sentence and granted two short reprieves. Governor Gillett, however, followed the practice of granting a pardon to prisoners released on parole. *Second Biennial Message of Governor Gillett, Jan. 2, 1911* (Sacramento, 1911), p. 13.
28. Lowrie, *My Life*, p. 342.

were absolutely final. The board's minutes are laconic, to say the least: an entry for June 1905 reads, "On motion duly made, seconded and unanimously carried the application of P. J. Wynn (20696) for parole was granted to take effect at once." But Mr. 18618 was denied parole, with no further ado or explanation. The board sometimes postponed its decision, for six months or so; and sometimes the board attached conditions: Thomas Galvin, no. 19832, was granted a parole, to take effect in ninety days, "provided that in the meantime he secure employment other than in San Francisco and prove to the satisfaction of the Board that he will abstain from the use of any intoxicating liquors." In no case did the board write down its reasons.[29]

A paroled convict had to toe the mark. Offenses that would bring nothing worse than a paltry fine to anybody else might put him back in his cage. Albert Marcus, a second-degree burglar from Alameda County, was paroled on July 13, 1908. He was brought back before the board later on for parole violation. His sin? "Having become intoxicated." Marcus pleaded not guilty; but the board "adjudged him to be guilty," and he became no. 22230 once more.[30]

Parole spared governor and staff the burden of handling applications for release. More important, parole suited the temper of the times. It gave the decision about early release to experts, not amateurs. Parole was conditional, like probation; and it was more in line with current theories of crime control, as we saw in Chapter 6.

County Jail

San Quentin was the big house, and so was Folsom; but the county jail was also an important house of criminal justice. Here prisoners were kept while they waited for trial; and here petty offenders and small sinners served out their time.[31]

The county jail was located on Washington Street, between Fourth and Fifth, in Oakland. It was finished in 1875, and was described as a "two-story and basement structure, built of brick with stone facings. The outside was cemented." It cost about $80,000. It had at first thirty-two cells. The cells came from the old jail at San Leandro, and were brought to Oakland and installed in 1875.[32]

29. Minutes, State Board of Prison Directors, p. 158 (June 1905).
30. Ibid., p. 465 (August 1908).
31. On the generally deplorable conditions in local jails, see Prison Reform League, *Crime and Criminals*, chap. 10.
32. C. W. Taylor and Theodor H. Chapin, *Bench and Bar of Alameda County, Calif.* (Angwin, Calif., 1953), p. 12.

The numbers locked up in county jail fluctuated a good deal. In January 1877 there were fifty prisoners. This included twenty-five U.S. prisoners, mostly Chinese sentenced for "peddling or selling unstamped matches or cigars," a federal tax offense. (There were no federal prisons anywhere before 1891, and none at all in our region in the nineteenth century; the federal government farmed out its convicts to local prisons and jails. These prisoners were treated somewhat specially. In 1905, we read, the U.S. government allowed forty cents a day to the sheriff to take care of them; county prisoners were taken care of for a mere twenty-five cents or less. County prisoners had two meals a day; federal prisoners three.)[33] The rest were a miscellaneous lot: three "Spaniards," waiting for the grand jury to decide whether to indict them for cattle theft; a "shootist" named Joseph Barker, who filled his brother James with lead; a seventy-five-year-old chicken thief; a stagecoach robber; a peg-legged burglar; and a certain "Liverpool Jack."[34] In 1883 there were only twenty-one inmates, two of them federal prisoners. At the end of December 1887, there were thirty-two prisoners; in 1894 there were seventy, and this was (we are told) only half the jail's capacity.[35]

The grand jury looked over the jail every year. In 1878 the grand jury praised the jail as "neat, clean and comfortable," but found the meat not "wholesome."[36] The report in 1883 allowed that prisoners were treated "kindly and considerately," but the food (as the inmates complained) was scanty and vile. Grand juries were sometimes unhappy about security. The grand jury in 1874 complained that "one full blow with a heavy instrument" could smash in the bars. In 1902 the jury demanded a "more modern structure," in which prisoners would be locked up more snugly. Jailers were so careless that the grand jury thought seriously about handing down indictments.[37] In 1906, after the great earthquake, prisoners were brought over from San Francisco; 104 prisoners were crowded into 46 cells, and the "hopheads" (drug addicts) made the nights "hideous" with their "wailing petitions [for] . . . drugs."[38]

Prisoners, as we saw,[39] preferred jail to prison. It was the lesser of

33. Expert's Report for the Grand Jury, for the year 1905, filed July 24, 1906, p. 8.
34. *Oakland Tribune*, Jan. 30, 1877, p. 3, col. 2.
35. *Oakland Citizen*, Mar. 5, 1894, p. 3, col. 1.
36. Grand Jury Report, April Term 1878, filed July 16, 1878.
37. Grand Jury Report, Sept. Term 1874, filed Sept. 25, 1874; *Oakland Tribune*, May 20, 1902, p. 1, col. 4. In 1906 the sheriff complained of "faulty construction," and claimed that it was the "poorest" jail in the state, and had the most escapes. *Berkeley Reporter*, Jan. 2, 1906, p. 5, col. 4.
38. *Berkeley Reporter*, Apr. 28, 1906, p. 5, col. 4.
39. See Chap. 8.

two evils. But evil it was. In 1893 there was a riot of sorts in the jail; James O'Connelly, a burglar and "confirmed opium fiend," led the revolt, out of drug desperation. The "revolt" failed, naturally enough, and the sheriff promised a good "dose of discipline"—enough to "make these fellows dance."[40]

Before the reform schools and juvenile court, one heard the usual complaints about mixing young boys with hardened criminals. In 1890 a twelve-year-old went to jail for thirty days for stealing eggs. He was, supposedly, quite a "vicious little fellow"; even so, it was unseemly to put him away with drunks and thugs.[41] There was mixing, too, of the innocent and the guilty: people charged with crimes sat in county jail when they could not make bail, although they were supposed to be kept in different rooms (§ 1599). Indeed, the most common way out of jail was a simple release, after charges were dismissed or the defendant was acquitted. For those who did time, there were credits for good behavior (five days for each month served, as a reward for "cheerful and willing obedience" to rules, and conduct that was "positively good," § 1614). A few prisoners were pardoned by the governor. For still others, "release" meant transfer—to the big house.

City Jails

Cities too had jails. In Oakland the city jail, sometimes called the city prison, was a "wretchedly gloomy" basement lockup, in the bowels of the old city hall.[42] The city also ran some "scattered, ill kept and unsanitary lockups," used as detaining jails.

On August 25, 1877, the city hall burned down.[43] The building was a complete loss; but the "howling prisoners in the basement" got out "before they could be roasted." After the fire, things returned to normal; the new jail was still noxious and overcrowded in 1879. The mayor wanted to build solid cells of brick and iron; and (as usual) he complained about "boys and petty offenders" brought "into contact with hardened criminals."[44] The grand jury in 1883 thought the city

40. *Oakland Tribune*, Aug. 26, 1893, p. 1, col. 5.
41. Ibid., May 12, 1908, p. 3, col. 4.
42. Frank Clinton Merritt, *History of Alameda County, California* (Chicago, 1928), 1:276, 292. A vivid description of the San Francisco city prison was reprinted in *Haywards Weekly Journal*, Aug. 31, 1878, p. 1, col. 1.
43. G. A. Cummings and E. S. Pladwell, *Oakland: A History* (Oakland, 1942), p. 63.
44. Ibid., p. 287. The 1878 grand jury called the jail a "disgrace . . . it can never be made a proper place for the confinement of human beings." Grand Jury Report, September Term 1878, filed Sept. 27, 1878.

jail was clean and "well ventilated"; the food was good.[45] The report of 1885 described the jail as consisting of six "strong and well made iron cells, ten wooden cells, and one large and very secure stone cell"; a "large and well ventilated room" served as "the female department," furnished with bathtubs, "hot and cold water, patent water closets, clean and tidy," along with other facilities.[46] Yet in 1888, a *Tribune* editorial spoke about dampness, prisoner escapes, and a "disgusting" smell.[47] In September 1894 prison officials and the Board of Health described city prison as a "hell hole." A sewer ran under what was called the old jail, where petty offenders were kept, next to the "boys' prison." The sewer pipe was "honeycombed with corrosion and rot"; it produced a "great pool of stagnant and disease-breeding water and filth." People passing on the street could smell the "rank odors" that "exuded" from this "pestiferous spot." A plan was drawn up to drain the water out, remove the "rotten and vermin-infested wooden floors," and put in cement. For this work, the city council appropriated the princely sum of fifty dollars.[48] Much later, in 1915, the city jail moved to the top floor of the new "skyscraper" City Hall.

The dry figures of police reports give some hints about life in city prison. In June 1, 1883, for example, the Oakland jail housed thirty-nine prisoners; on the average day in June, there were about twenty-seven or twenty-eight. The month's food (2,492 meals) cost $115.40, which, it was said, worked out to about 4 ⅝ cents a meal.[49] The prisoners were mostly idle; a few worked as trusties, doing odd jobs about the place, cooking, cleaning. Some prisoners worked outdoors, in chain gangs. In 1883, for example, the city marshall asked for a gang of twelve men to clean the streets.[50] These prisoners tended to slip loose; to avoid this, the chief of police in 1890 restricted work on the gang to men with seven days or less to go.[51] Nor did the jail avoid jumbling together the innocent and the not-so-innocent. The chief of police complained in 1897 that because of space problems, "young girls and drunken old women, and children are necessarily herded together"; it was a scandal, he thought, that women, boys, and girls were "unceremoniously dumped" in with "rougher criminal elements."[52]

Drink and drugs were constant headaches. An Oakland ordinance

45. *Oakland Tribune*, Oct. 9, 1883, p. 3, col. 1.
46. Committee Report to Grand Jury, Oct. 27, 1885, p. 3.
47. *Oakland Tribune*, Mar. 19, 1888, p. 4, col. 1.
48. Ibid., Sept. 13, 1894, p. 6, col. 2.
49. Ibid., July 3, 1883, p. 2, col. 2.
50. Ibid., Sept. 28, 1883, p. 3, col. 1.
51. Ibid., May 26, 1890, p. 1, col. 2.
52. *San Francisco Call*, Feb. 20, 1897, p. 11, col. 2.

of 1879 made it unlawful to "bring or pass any intoxicating liquor" into city prison; an ordinance of 1887 made it unlawful for a prisoner to possess opium.[53] But the problems would not go away. Addicts in jail were desperate for a "fix"; Chinese prisoners (1883), "confirmed opium fiends," went "almost insane" in their cells, because of "deprivation." Their friends outside tried desperately to help them: "The opium cake has been thrown from the city hall park through the bars . . . It has been conveyed . . . in platters of rice," smuggled in hidden in coat linings or in the thick paper soles of shoes. Prisoners found "ingenious" ways to make opium pipes: "They will take a potato and hollow it out for a lamp," collect fat from their beef and use it for oil, twist a wick "out of some threads from a blanket." Somehow, they managed to drill a hole in the bottom of a medicine bottle; they "steal a broom-handle and split it from end to end and then they break a pane of glass. With the glass they drill a groove in the center of the handle and then bind it together and tie greased rags on the outside. . . . This gives them a stem and a bowl for the pipe, and with the lamp they have a complete layout."[54]

Other towns also had jails. The grand jury report of 1885 mentioned township jails in Berkeley, Alameda, East Oakland, San Leandro, Hayward, Centerville, and Livermore, all "in good condition, containing from two to four large cells and large enough for their necessary wants" (October 27, 1885). This happy state, if it existed, did not last. The Berkeley jail, on Addison Street, was completely decrepit in 1892, to the point where prisoners could take "French leave" almost at will. The jail was so useless that the authorities locked one prisoner to a railing in the courtroom while he waited for his case to be called. And a "vagrant" was chained to a fence until he could be shipped off to Oakland.[55]

The Ultimate Price: The Death Penalty in Alameda County

Of all the pains and penalties that criminal justice inflicted, the most notorious, and rarest, was death. California law provided one way and one way only: "hanging the defendant by the neck until he is dead" (§ 1228). This was the penalty for first-degree murder; but "at the discretion of the jury," the defendant could be sentenced to life imprisonment instead (§ 190). The death penalty was also theoretically

53. *General Municipal Ordinances of the City of Oakland* (1895), p. 208 (ord. of May 10, 1879), p. 213 (ord. of June 8, 1887).
54. *Oakland Tribune*, Sept. 20, 1883, p. 3, col. 2, Sept. 27, 1883, p. 3, col. 2.
55. Ibid., July 25, 1892, p. 6, col. 1.

possible for treason (§ 37); but apparently no one tried to overthrow California. Another capital crime was train wrecking (§ 219). Some arrests were made in 1894, amid the turmoil of the great railroad strikes;[56] but no one went to the gallows for this crime. In 1901, alarmed at prison violence, the legislature added a new capital crime, for lifers who committed aggravated assault (§ 246). There were no examples from Alameda County during our period.[57] Despite or because of the hullabaloo over the death penalty, it was rarely inflicted in California,[58] and very rarely indeed in Alameda County. Between 1880 and 1910, only seven men were sentenced to die by hanging.[59] Only five were actually hanged: Lloyd Majors, Nathan Sutton, Benjamin Hill, Joaquin Eslabe, and Mark Wilkins.

Executions in the eighteenth and most of the nineteenth century were popular, if dreadful shows, in full view of the public. California banned this practice in the late 1850s. Until 1891, each county was in charge of hanging its own. Majors and Sutton died in Oakland, on the premises of the county jail. For Lloyd Majors, the bell tolled on May 23, 1884. The *Tribune*, naturally, gave a blow-by-blow description. As the "fatal hour of 11:00 drew on," people began to gather on the streets near the jail. Their "numbers were not large," the *Tribune* piously intoned, which was most "creditable to Oakland." They came "in the faint hope of catching . . . a glimpse of the top of the scaffold." The authorities foiled their morbid curiosity by stretching blankets "across the jail yard in front of the scaffold." Undaunted, some people climbed onto nearby roofs; a few of them, on top of the "high Sagehorn Building on Sixth Street," may have actually watched Majors die. One man paid a dollar to borrow a pair of opera glasses.

If we can believe the *Tribune*, the condemned man spent his last night sleeping soundly. At half past six in the morning, the coffin arrived in the wagon of H. B. McEvoy and Company ("polished

56. See, for example, ibid., Aug. 13, 1894, p. 2, col. 2.

57. On the constitutionality of § 246, see In re Finley, 1 Cal. App. 198, 81 Pac. 1041 (1905); People v. Oppenheimer, 156 Cal. 733, 106 Pac. 74 (1909); People v. Finley, 222 U.S. 28 (1911). Harry Eldridge, a cook from Alameda County serving a 30-year prison term in Folsom, was executed in 1905 for his part in an escape during which a guard was killed.

58. Annual Reports of the California District Attorneys indicate that, on the average, there were only eight death sentences a year imposed in the state between 1898 and 1910. Governor Markham, in his message to the legislature in 1893, remarked that juries seemed to be less likely than before to impose the death penalty: "it would seem to be almost conclusive that the verdicts of juries in murder cases indicate that . . . the people . . . are no longer in favor of capital punishment." *First Biennial Message, Gov. H. H. Markham, Jan. 3, 1893* (Sacramento, 1893), p. 47.

59. Under the code, if a pregnant woman was sentenced to death, she could not be hanged until she was "no longer pregnant" (§§ 1225, 1226). But no woman, pregnant or otherwise, was sentenced to die in Alameda County during our period.

redwood with silver trimmings," with six handles and "lined with the usual white stuff"). At 9:00 A.M., Majors ate the proverbial "hearty" breakfast—three soft-boiled eggs, a loaf of German bread, a pat of butter, and a cup of coffee. Then he talked to reporters for the *Tribune* and the *San Francisco Morning Call*. A "reverend" arrived and conducted religious services. At ten minutes to eleven the sheriff walked into the cell; he asked Majors if he wanted to hear the death warrant read. Majors was willing to forgo this entertainment. Instead, he gulped down a glass of whiskey.

Meanwhile, the jail yard was ready. The rope was adjusted, with a drop of seven feet. The knots were tried, the noose inspected. Excitement was in the air. At 10:15 "the jail yard was crowded to overflowing"; the lucky spectators jostled each other, "as they moved about in their nervous eagerness to lose none of the ghastly details." Outside, "several boys had climbed into a tall poplar tree in front of the jail, in full view of the scaffold." At nine minutes past eleven the sheriff and his deputies brought Majors in. He looked at the gallows, and at the crowd, and walked slowly and firmly to the scaffold. The execution itself went off smoothly. When the body dropped, doctors rushed up and surrounded it. They recorded the dying man's pulse rate. After nine minutes, there was nothing but "an occasional flicker of the wrist, barely perceptible." They pronounced Majors dead. At 11:29 A.M., the sheriff cut the body down. The black cap was removed. The face was "frightfully discolored . . . congested and livid. It was a face naturally ugly, but at that moment it was positively hideous. . . . The pupils of the eyes were contracted, the eyes were set, and the neck bruised." The body was put on a stretcher, then into the coffin, and taken off to the undertaker's. The drama was over.[60]

The hanging of Nathan Sutton, in January 1888, was given the same blow-by-blow treatment. Licking its chops, the *Tribune* recounted every gruesome detail. Once again, a crowd gathered. People climbed the housetops in their lust for a view. When Sutton was dropped, the rope cut deeply through his neck, almost severing his head from his body. The *Tribune*'s account could have been written by Count Dracula: "A noise was heard . . . like the gurgle of wind. . . . " A man in the crowd cried out "It's blood!" and blood it was: "spurting from the left side of his neck . . . bubbling from the right side . . . welling from in front—rushing in a thick crimson torrent over the

60. Or not quite. There was an autopsy, and though this, of course, was private, the *Tribune* did its duty: "The brain was . . . unusually large. . . . The neck was broken. . . . The arm . . . was found to have a fracture of the ulna." After the autopsy, the remains, in their "plain rosewood coffin," were "viewed by many people." *Oakland Tribune*, May 24, 1884, p. 1, col. 1.

bosom of the dead man's shirt—blood staining the cruel rope as it cut deeper and deeper through the tissues. . . . Blood that dripped, dripped from his feet, forming a sanguinary pool on the ground which sucked it voraciously, leaving only a dark clouded stain in the moist sand. The crowd stood spell-bound with horror."

This was the last of these shows to take place in Alameda County. In 1891 a new law ended county executions. The "judgment of death" was to be carried out inside the walls of state prisons. The warden would be there, and a doctor, the attorney general, twelve "respectable citizens," up to five relatives and friends, plus peace officers— but no one else (§ 1229). Hill, Eslabe, and Wilkins were hanged at San Quentin. At this austere and distant place, only a few eyes watched, and the public stayed home. But executions still made thick, black headlines; the press was there, relishing every detail of death row and the dead man's agony. The execution of William Henry Theodore Durrant, the "demon of the belfry," on July 7, 1898, took up the entire front page of the *Tribune*, and covered every detail, from his tearful farewell to his mom ("Goodbye, Mother. . . . We will meet in heaven"), to his pulse rate as he died. Because local executions were few and far between, the papers took up the slack with out-of-state hangings. In 1894, Eugene Prendergast, who killed the mayor of Chicago, Carter Harrison, died "within the gloomy walls of Cook County Jail," in Chicago. The *Tribune* gave this event its fullest attention. Oakland subscribers could read, for example, a full description of the corpse: the "bluish tint" of the face, the "unkempt reddish hair," the protruding tongue.[61]

Still, the move to San Quentin was part of a process that made hanging more and more vicarious. People were fascinated by the death penalty, but horrified as well. They believed in it, and doubted it, too. We have no hard data on what people thought about the death penalty in Alameda County. But there are unmistakable signs of confusion, hesitancy, ambivalence. The long painful road to the scaffold was one of these signs. Durrant died on July 7, 1898. He had kept the hangman at bay (according to the *Tribune*) for three years "solely by recourse to the technicalities with which the statute law of California abounds." This, the *Tribune* thought, made justice "farcical." Particularly noxious was the habit of "staying a State process by recourse to Federal writs."[62] But the process never got faster. Mark A. Wilkins was hanged at San Quentin at 10:30 A.M., January 12, 1912.[63] The

61. Ibid., July 13, 1894, p. 5, col. 2.
62. Ibid., Jan. 7, 1898, p. 5, col. 1.
63. Ibid., Jan. 12, 1912, p. 1, col. 1.

crime he died for was committed in July 1907—almost five years before. Caryl Chessman fought for twelve years before he died in the gas chamber in the 1960s.

Technicalities piled on technicalities, endless appeals and writs— these were signs that society feared and loathed its ultimate weapon. At this writing (1980), the death penalty is in a kind of limbo, despite or because of cases without number in state courts, a handful of Supreme Court cases that have thrown out many (but not all) state statutes, and a literature that stretches from here to eternity. Even in 1900, no one knew quite what to make of the death penalty. Society was not ready to give it up; but it filled people with a kind of dread. California used it only rarely, for "demons" and "fiends," and banished it from view, to the darkest corners of San Quentin, the slag heap of California life.

Cages: Some Concluding Remarks

Our information about local jails is scattered and fragmentary; our information on state prisons is somewhat better. But it is hard to draw firm conclusions. We have too many impressions and too few facts. A few features come through quite clearly. First of all, we see our familiar trend toward professionalization. It took place everywhere in criminal justice, and in the system of corrections as well. Even before our period began, the old jail system had been replaced by the penitentiary. After 1870, there were further attempts to make prisons more than cages and warehouses. The key was to rationalize correction, to tailor it to different classes of offenders. Juveniles, for example, were plucked out of San Quentin and Folsom and sent to their own institutions. Pardon, a loose and amateurish system, gave way to parole, which was more "scientific" and precise. The prisons drew lines between types of prisoner and types of criminal, in a way that fit current theories about crime and the soul of the criminal. The result was to place a layer of skilled and professional insulation on top of the raw, naked acts of the layman. It may not be too fanciful to see the same process at work in the history of hangings, the shift from public to private spectacle, from a general show to a party for professionals, deep inside San Quentin's walls.

There is another striking point about prisons and jails. At all three levels—state, county, and city—the gap between theory and practice was enormous. We have little information on out-and-out corruption. But we see a great deal of a more indirect corruption, the corruption of professed ideals. In this country, there are ideals about due process, and pious hopes about reform and rehabilitation. There are norms about the treatment of women and children, and against cruel and brutal punishment. Torture was something unspeakable that died out in the Middle Ages; in this country it was not supposed to exist. Corporal punishment, too, had been abolished for good.

Yet even a scratch at the surface shows that prisons and jails violated all of these norms. The cruelty of prison life was not even much of a secret. Prison abuse was constantly exposed and deplored—then forgotten, papered over, ignored. It shared this trait with police brutality, and other illegalities small and large that we have seen in these pages, and that did not seem to trouble the conscience of the county.

Prison, to be sure, was somewhat different, and worse. Prison was a sort of private vice, like a collection of dirty books, whips, and torture tools, in a corner of an otherwise respectable house. Prisons were supposed to punish and reform; they punished, in theory, in *order* to reform. Punishment theoretically had to be clean, severe, ennobling. The practice was lawlessness, brutality, savage neglect. Society, it seems, did not really *believe* in reformation, whatever it said—not for "real criminals," at any rate. Those who were lost, degenerate, unredeemable (or simply different) were shoved behind bars and left to their fates, by and large. The reforms, as far as they went, were supposed to sift out some salvage from this dross. The rest could rot.

Society built walls, then, to keep prisoners in, but also to keep them out of sight. In their cages, prisoners seemed almost forgotten. Yet not quite. Some pages back, we quoted an article from the *Tribune*, about Chinese prisoners in local jails: how they made opium pipes for themselves, how dope was smuggled in for their use. The tone of the article was one of detached amusement. It seemed to escape the *Tribune* that these men were human beings, that they were suffering. The agony of a horse or a dog might have touched the *Tribune*'s heart rather more. Prisoners were not worth any pity or effort. Perhaps this is why wave after wave of exposure and scandal never left much residue behind. Prison life, visible or invisible, never mattered. When the curtain was raised, people saw what they wanted to see.

This is understandable only if we assume some reason, if we assume that society gained something precious (or thought it did) by locking people up, and mistreating them. We can only guess what this was. Perhaps it was a sense that the social fabric was infinitely delicate and fragile; people saw all about them in America (rightly or wrongly) a system of wide-open spaces, vast personal freedom, endless opportunity, and absence of restraint. All this made society exceedingly brittle. People were free to choose the pattern of their lives;

but the whole structure depended on right choices. When people overstepped the boundaries, or defied the norms, they were unfit for democracy; they endangered society in some terrible, fundamental way. The prisons were the only place for such people. Society in effect drew a line: on one side law, on the other side, lawlessness. Freedom stops here.

Chapter 10
A Concluding Word

We have traveled a fairly long road, from the beginning to the end of the processes of criminal justice in Alameda County. In this brief chapter, we will try to sum up a few of our basic findings, for the patient reader who has come along this far. Later, we will discuss a few of these results in a bit more detail, and engage in further speculation. But first, some selected conclusions:

1. Criminal justice in Alameda County was structurally very complex. It was arranged in definite "layers," each with its own procedure and function.

2. Serious crime was on the decline in Alameda County. Much police effort went into order and discipline—enforcing rules about how to behave in public. The "students" in this school of the streets were overwhelmingly adult working-class men. The modal crimes were crimes of drunkenness and brawling. The police (and petty courts) also served, as they do now, as social agencies of last resort.

3. Compared to today, accused felons were much more likely to go to trial. But even in 1880, judge and jury decided the fate of less than half of such defendants. The system became less adjudicative over the years. Plea bargaining was present from the start. The guilty plea was frequent, and became more so. Trial by jury slowly declined. Fewer defendants took advantage of their "rights," although most defendants had attorneys at the trial stage. Appeals were few, and mostly unsuccessful.

4. Property felonies were much more common than felonies of personal violence in Superior Court. Sex offenses were not terribly common, but carried harsh penalties. The period seemed to evince a growing concern about sexual morality, at least at the level of law making.

5. A handful of great cases each year took advantage of the full panoply of "rights"; these cases made good stories, were eagerly followed by the reading public, and seemed to teach important moral and legal lessons to onlookers and to society in general.

6. There was a shift in emphasis, all up and down the system, from the crime itself to the criminal. Punishment was supposed to be cut to the individual case. The question was, Could the defendant be re-

formed or cured, or not? To answer this question, one had to know background, character, habits. Probation, parole, and juvenile justice were signs of great concern for the defendant's personality, family, and inheritance.

7. Those who "failed" the tests imposed by the system—those who were convicted by juries, and who were denied probation—went to prison. Fines were uncommon, corporal punishment illegal, the death penalty rare. Prison was a harsh, rather brutal world, about which society seemed to care very little. *why ?*

8. Overall, the system became more professional between 1870 and *What does this mean?* 1910. In 1870 the system was dominated by laymen and part-timers: jurymen, district attorneys who practiced law on the side, policemen who were chosen any which way. By the end of the period, there were a number of at least semiprofessional newcomers: probation officers, members of parole boards. Prosecutors were by then full-time workers in the system. The police, too, had become more professional. After 1910, of course, this trend continued, and became much stronger.

We tried to base these results (and others) on hard data. Whenever we could, as often as we could, we used numbers, tables, simple statistics. Still, we often had to lean on impressions, stories, testimony. And we were always aware that this is a case study. Of course, every study, even the most rigorous, is in a sense a case study. Numbers only "prove" this or that statement about the immediate subject. There is always a question: how far beyond the case can the data be pushed? We have shown certain things about Alameda County, California, between 1870 and 1910. What more can we claim? How many of our findings stop right there? How much is true of California, as a whole, at that time? of the United States in general? Do we dare reach dizzier heights of abstraction? The answer depends on how plausible a case we make out. Here we make a few wild stabs at further meaning.

The Many Faces of Criminal Justice

One obvious, striking fact about criminal justice in Alameda County, in our period, was how many faces it had. We can hardly talk about *a* system of criminal justice at all. There were many systems, different in form, function, and method, arranged in layers one on top of another. We made this point at the outset, many pages back. The chapters in between have driven home the point.

We spoke, essentially, of three layers. At the top were the "celebrated cases"—lurid murders, crimes with political overtones—cases that made "good copy." Here, to the naked eye at least, was the heartland of the adversary system, of due process. Juries were slowly and carefully chosen. Every technicality, every "right," was exploited to the hilt. The trial was a genuine contest, sometimes quite bitterly fought. It was at times a maze of motions and maneuvers, at times a piece of high theater.

Lawyers dominated these cases. They managed every detail, from start to finish, down to Percy Pembroke's hair and Clara Fallmer's veil. For the general law-abiding public, these were the cases that told what the law was about. These were also, by and large, the cases that went up on appeal (if the defendant lost). A few of them raised "nice" points of law, which made them interesting to legal scholars. But they were also expensive and rare.

Cases of ordinary, serious crime made up the second or middle layer—dozens and dozens of cases of burglary, theft, bad checks, assault with a deadly weapon. The system here did not look much like its textbook picture, or like the picture in the daily press. Basic property crimes were the workhorses of this middle layer. (Later, in the 1920s, these were joined by traffic felonies, and, after 1950, by drug offenses.) What is striking here is not the drama, but the profound sense of routine. Even in 1880—if we take felony cases as a whole—less than half the cases went to trial. The system on balance was more *administrative* than *adjudicative*. There were many guilty pleas, many dismissals. Over the years, these trends became more pronounced. Guilty pleas took on more and more importance. We drew, for comparative purposes, a sample of felony cases in 1950–74. About 75 percent of these ended with some sort of guilty plea. And of those people who went to trial, only one out of seven was acquitted— 2 percent of felony defendants as a whole.

From this, one might jump to a certain conclusion: that the system got harsher over time, that fewer defendants got off. But this would be somewhat misleading. The system became more routine, more administrative. The center of gravity shifted away from judge and jury. "Acquittals" took place on the streets, in station houses, in the file folders of prosecutors. Defendants who were not filtered out were pretty much foredoomed. And they knew it. Most defendants in the 1960s and 1970s pleaded not guilty; then they bargained, changing their plea to guilty of something less than the charge. Plea bargaining was around in 1880–1910, but it became, after 1950, a pervasive system. Besides, when probation entered the system, acquittal and dismissal were no longer the only ways out of court and into freedom. Antics in front of a jury had less to do with outcomes than with what went on elsewhere in the system. The judge in his black robe was only one of many judges. Was he even the most important one?

The bottom layer was the layer of the basement courts—justice and police courts—and of the police. Here the sheer volume of business was breathtaking. Hundreds were arrested for drunkenness, assaults, disturbing the peace, fighting, gambling, violating ordinances, raising hell. Countless incidents of course never made their way to court. They began and ended on the streets, or informally, in the station house. Statistically speaking, the main function of this layer was not crime control at all. The main function was order, not law; discipline, not punishment. Control was relatively mild; and it was exercised mostly over members of the working class. Police patrolled the normative surface of society. They roamed the street, in a "trawling" operation. They swept offenders into their nets, in gigantic numbers, like schools of fish. For some—drunks and vagrants—this trawling was a repeated experience, a "revolving door." For most people it was not. Their cases were dismissed, or they forfeited bail or paid their fines or (worst of all) spent a day or two in jail. And that was that. In some ways, such trawling seems cruel, and rather pointless. But the experience was so common that it must have meant something in the social order. We suspect that the point was this: to show that order and discipline were alive, were real—and to show this both to those who made the rules and to those who broke them. Whether in the long run it did any good is another question. In any case, this layer, the layer of police and petty courts, was worlds apart from the upper two.

Herbert Packer has made a most useful distinction between two models of criminal process. He calls these the *crime control* and *due process* models. People who favor crime control want an efficient system, one that catches criminals and punishes them. Due process people are strong for defendants' rights; they are willing to trade some efficiency to get more fairness. They are leery of the state, afraid that police power will be abused; and they worry about convicting the innocent.[1]

The due process people could take comfort, on the whole, from the top layer in Alameda County. Here the defendant had a full, fair fight. This was precisely one of the functions of this layer: it *defined* due process. It broadcast the standard, official rules. But curiously enough, these were also the carnival trials, the crowd pleasers. There was a connection between these two functions. The people who

1. Herbert L. Packer, *The Limits of the Criminal Sanction* (Stanford, 1968), chap. 8.

flowed into the courtroom, looking for thrills, who devoured crime news in the paper, were also learning something. They were learning about the official code of law, and about unwritten laws as well. Without the fun and excitement, they would have paid much less attention. The top layer displayed the law in action as it was supposed to be; it taught the citizens where moral boundaries stood. But it also showed some limits (moral and customary) of official law. This was clear enough in Clara Fallmer's case. And, as we pointed out, there was a real contradiction between the message and the medium. The great cases were justice, law, due process—and at the same time vaudeville shows. The same citizen who learned (or thought he learned) that the law was tender and solicitous of defendants' rights also learned that justice was a game, a farce, a bag of wind. Hence, it would not surprise us if people found criminal justice disgusting, not noble, if they lost as much faith as they gained. It would not surprise us, too, if this were still true today. What do we learn from our Patty Hearst trials? the Candy Mossler case? or from others of this sort?

The middle layer was the domain of crime control. Process here was brisker, more efficient. There was less concern for show. The defendant had fewer real rights. There was no room here for tricks and maneuvers, no room for juggling evidence and doctrines, little room for motions and appeals. This was rather the domain of bargaining, hustling, give-and-take. Here the wriggling and conniving were of a different sort. This domain was more concerned with crime control, with getting results: harsh, effective treatment of the criminal. But we cannot be sure it *got* results—a theme we will return to. And, of course, ideas of due process must have had a certain impact on this layer. Lawyers and judges absorbed these ideas in their training. We suspect that the two layers interacted subtly. A certain amount of cynicism in the ordinary felony cases infected due process in the great trials; on the other hand, ideals of fairness and justice percolated down to influence the process below.

The bottom layer, the police court layer, was, as we said, the domain of discipline. Here traffic rules of life were enforced. Here the police put flesh and blood on the bones of the normative order. This layer, too, played the role of a teacher of sorts. Practice here gave instruction, mainly to workingmen, about rules of behavior in public places.

Criminal justice in Alameda County was a complex system. Forms and functions shifted over time, like oil in water. The system, after all, was never self-contained. Its behavior always reflected demands streaming in from the outside world. Criminal justice tells us as much about general social life as it does about itself. We talked about three layers. Of course, there were never literally three. The boundaries between layers were always fuzzy. The line between petty cases in police court and felonies in Superior Court was legally fairly sharp; but a great deal of *behavior* could go either way. It was partly a matter of definition: whether a punch in the face was a simple assault, or assault with intent to kill; whether picking a pocket was robbery or petty theft. Felony cases themselves formed a kind of continuum, from dull routine to great courtroom battles. Even within layers there were wide variations. Affairs in police court went all the way from drunk cases tossed off in five minutes to tough and important legal battles, carried on in front of the jury. And, of course, the police ran a kind of fourth system (or layer) of their own. Its "trials" were on the streets and in the station houses. As for the middle layer, it really splits into two parts: adjudication and administration. One was the realm of trials, the other that of bargain justice (plea bargains and other deals), dominated by the district attorney and his decisions to compromise, fight, or dismiss. This vital, growing sublayer left its mark all over the records.

Class Justice and the Functions of Criminal Law

Anyone who studies criminal justice is likely to ask, at some point, whether the system deserves the word "justice" at all. Criminal justice is almost by nature repressive: and the question is, is it unduly so? Did the system we studied oppress the poor and the weak? Was this the dirty secret at the core of the system? These are questions, of course, that we cannot really answer from our data. Much depends on how one looks at the facts: it is like asking if a glass is half full or half empty. A word like "repressive" is hard to turn into testable propositions. But that does not mean we cannot, and should not, make some stab at assessing our findings.

Let us take one example: the beginnings of juvenile justice. This is a much vexed, much researched question. The conventional line was that the "child savers" wanted to humanize treatment of children in trouble. A strong, strident literature tries to burst this balloon. The movement, according to Anthony Platt, was far from "benign." It was "regressive and nostalgic." Its most "direct consequences" fell on "children of the urban poor." It deprived them of "freedoms they had previously shared with adults." The "invention" of delinquency "consolidated the inferior social status and dependency of lower-class youth."[2]

Others claim that the evidence does not support this conclusion. There is nothing to show that children were worse off than before, or that more of them were institutionalized.[3] If Platt were right, we would expect to find signs that the police (or others) *forced* juvenile justice on working people and immigrants. But as far as we can tell these people are the *users*, as much as the used. Children are often victims, to be sure, but victims of their parents, and their parents' moral standards. In some ultimate sense, juvenile justice may have victimized the working class, grown-ups and children alike. But the surface at least was quite different. In the late nineteenth century, the public was gaining broader access to social institutions; parks, schools, and museums had once served a much narrower class. Similarly, access opened up to professional services, including justice and police. What many (most?) members of the working class wanted was middle-class morality, law and order, conventional standards of behavior. If their children fell short of these standards, some at least were willing to turn them over to public enforcers.

Let us follow this line of thought a bit further. One way to look at the criminal justice system is as a tool to preserve class structure. This naturally benefits the haves, against the have nots. Rights, due process, fairness can be important, not only in themselves, but also as propaganda. They seem timeless and classless, socially neutral, in a word. The idea that this kind of justice exists may be a kind of soothing syrup for the masses. The big trials, we argued, were designed to show criminal justice at work, though in a misleading way. The real day-by-day work went on unobserved, underneath.

The big show trials were, we said, a kind of false advertising. But the middle level too was the bearer of a myth. These cases made no pretence of due process, in its most persnickety sense. But they did pretend to social control. Here, if anywhere, was the bite of the law, its deterrent teeth. Yet what did this part of the system accomplish? Of course, no one set out, deliberately, to bamboozle the public; the fraud, if there was such, afflicted judges, prosecutors, police, as much as the public. The myth was about the defendants, and who they

2. Anthony M. Platt, *The Child Savers: The Invention of Delinquency* (Chicago, 1969), pp. 176, 177; see also Steven Schlossman and Stephanie Wallach, "The Crime of Precocious Sexuality: Female Juvenile Delinquency in the Progressive Era," *Harv. Educ. Rev.* 48 (1978): 65.

3. See on this point John Hagan and Jeffrey Leon, "Rediscovering Delinquency: Social History, Political Ideology and the Sociology of Law," *Am. Soc. Rev.* 42 (1977): 587 (Canadian data).

really were. In theory, they were a good sample of people who killed, robbed, burned, stole, raped, forged, passed bad checks, and assaulted the innocent—and a rich sample, too: that is, most criminals were found out, arrested, and punished. But we do not know whether this was the case at all. Many cases, judging from newspaper accounts and the files, had a suspicious smell about them. It is hard to resist the impression (it cannot be called more than that) that defendants were a poor sample of the "real" criminals. They were the unlucky, the inept—we called them "losers." We have no idea how many "real" thieves, robbers, burglars, arsonists, and other malefactors were loose in the county. What we do know is that time and time again, when we dig into the data, we find a pathetic, cowering, luckless creature on whom the massive jaws of the system have closed—a mouse caught in a beartrap.

This fact, if it is one, does shed light on the functions of criminal justice. Now "function" is a slippery word. It has at least two quite different meanings. The "function" of a system is what it is supposed to do; it is also what it actually does, which is a horse of a different color. Was criminal justice designed to suppress and oppress, in the interests of the rich and powerful? Of course, our luckless defendants *were* lower class (most, though by no means all). Their trials and tribulations do show class bias, but the bias is not class bias in a crude economic sense. Some defendants were, as we said, unlucky; their "crimes" were acts that were almost never punished, like statutory rape. Often we wonder: why was this man arrested for passing a fifteen-dollar check, or for picking a dollar or two out of somebody's pockets? There must have been hundreds who did these things and never got caught. But sometimes a victim was hard-nosed and unyielding, or a policeman happened along at the wrong time, or some unlucky star was in its apogee. Beyond this element of bad luck, we thought we sniffed a special quality about some of our defendants. They were the unattached, the drifters, the transients, people without connections to family, job, church, or community. From this group, some people were selected, almost at random, like virgins thrown in a volcano to appease the gods. The drama of criminal justice was vital to society, its peace of mind, its self-conception; it hardly mattered whether or not the players were shanghaied for their roles. One should add, of course, that rootless people were the least likely or able to protest injustice; to process them did not put "undue strain" on the system.[4] These defendants, then, were from an oppressed

---

4. William J. Chambliss and Robert Seidman, *Law, Order and Power* (Reading, Mass., 1971), p. 266.

class, but a class defined as much by life-style and social position as by "class" in the economic sense.

This conclusion fits what we know, or think we know, about law and society. We expect the legal system to reflect the norms of the general society. County, state, and country were complex organisms. They were not just economic organisms; the social order took property seriously, but it also took life-style seriously. It took moral norms seriously, too. There was a ladder of moral hierarchy, in society, just as there was a ladder of economic and political power. There were moral haves as well as money haves. The two groups overlapped, but not completely. The people of Alameda County were not animals who only ate, slept, breathed, and produced; they had heads and hearts, moral lives and sex lives too.

Who Was the Criminal?

We mention two further points about criminal justice (at least as we see it in the mirror of our county). First, serious crime was declining in Alameda County, as far as we can tell—the figures, we must repeat, are very rough. Second, law reform and legal change proceeded in a definite pattern in our period. If we had to sum up trends in a single formula (covering such changes as probation and parole), it would be this: punishment must be cut to fit the defendant, the particular person. Two people who committed the same act (breaking into a store, picking a pocket) would not receive the same punishment. It would depend on who they were: their characters, their backgrounds, their family inheritances. The shift in emphasis—from offense to offender—*may* be related to the drop in the crime rate. If a society is truly hysterical about crime, it has less patience to sift among offenders. A crime epidemic is like an open rebellion: it has to be crushed, before society can get around to anything else. The crime rate today is dangerously high; violence and the fear of violence haunt our cities. The polls show that people are deeply disturbed about crime, as well they might be. No wonder that "reform" has changed its direction. California, for example, has repealed its indeterminate sentence law. Even parole is under a cloud. Voices everywhere call for tougher treatment. Emphasis shifts once more toward the crime itself, the offense, not the particular offender.

Our period was, as we saw, deeply concerned with *who* the criminal was. There were two classes of criminals. One consisted of the born criminal, the hardened criminal, the hereditary criminal; the other was made up of weak-willed, misguided people—lambs strayed from the flock. The two types called for different kinds of treatment. This was a period, we must remember, that was learning to take heredity seriously. It was the age of Lombroso, of the "science" of criminal anthropology. The criminal was even *physically* different—in the shape of his head, his ears, in his inability to blush.[5] It was widely believed that the stamp of crime, like the mark of Cain, branded some men and women from birth—indeed, even before birth: from conception; indeed, even before conception, that is, in the evil blood and seed of their ancestors. Lombroso felt these people were throwbacks left over from a primitive stage of evolution.

It was nothing new to divide criminals into two classes, the redeemable and the irredeemable. What was new in each period was how and where the line was drawn, and the theories about why people fell in one category or the other. No doubt, at one time, many people felt that the "hardened" criminal was possessed by devils. In our period, deep-down crime was not a matter of class, in the economic sense; not a matter of sins or of devils; not a matter of poverty, discrimination, squalor, or a twisted social structure. It was rather breeding and blood.

Of course, if we put it in such bald terms, we overstate the point. Few people took so extreme a view. People still said that bad companions, drink, sin, and so on led people into crime. Lombroso had his critics. But drink, sin, and bad company were more the mark of the redeemable (up to a point). There was a real change in emphasis in the late nineteenth century. Some of it came from the fascination with genetics, and the new science of heredity.[6] Books like Dugdale's study of the Jukes family, a study of bad seed, confirmed the popular view.[7] And all these ideas had their echo in the way criminal justice was run. Perhaps the most blatant was the law passed in California in 1909, which allowed "asexualization" of anyone convicted of a second sex offense, or any three-time loser who showed "moral and sexual depravity."[8] But the mark of Cain was everywhere: in probation, parole, sentencing practice, penology, juvenile justice.

5. Arthur MacDonald, in *Hearing on the Bill (H.R. 14798) to Establish a Laboratory for the Study of the Criminal, Pauper, and Defective Classes* (Washington, D.C., 1902), p. 43.

6. Marc Haller, *Eugenics* (New Brunswick, N.J., 1963); see also Charles E. Rosenberg, "The Bitter Fruit: Heredity, Disease and Social Thought in Nineteenth-Century America," in *Perspectives in Human History*, ed. Donald Fleming and Bernard Bailyn (Cambridge, Mass., 1974), 8:189.

7. R. L. Dugdale, *"The Jukes": A Study in Crime, Pauperism, Disease and Heredity*, 2nd ed. (New York, 1877); see, in general, Ysabel Rennie, *The Search for Criminal Man: A Conceptual History of the Dangerous Offender* (Lexington, Mass., 1978); Dr. Nathan Oppenheim, "The Stamping Out of Crime," *Popular Science Monthly* 48 (Feb. 1896), p. 527.

8. Laws Cal. 1909, ch. 729. Few prisoners were in fact sterilized. In 1918 the warden of San Quentin reported a rate of about one a year, "and all we have had in the past

Victimless Crime

If we look at criminal justice as a whole, another point strikes us forcibly. The base of the system, as we noted, was concerned with order, discipline, good behavior. It spent a great deal of effort on gambling, drink, and vice. From about 1870 on, we can detect a marked change in legal emphasis, not just in California, but elsewhere as well. The law paid more attention to offenses against the sexual code. Our period begins too late to provide us with data on the early nineteenth century; but there is good reason to suspect that American criminal justice in that period was not much concerned with enforcement of the sexual code. There were laws on the books, and a few flagrant offenders were prosecuted; but the main effort of criminal justice was directed against property crimes.

From about 1870 on, one can detect a revival of interest in victimless crime. First came the Comstock laws, and a crusade for "purity in print."[9] During our period, and in the decade afterwards, there were many more crusades: against cigarettes, drugs, prostitution, and liquor (ending with the Noble Experiment: Prohibition).[10] Most striking, perhaps, was what happened to the so-called age of consent. It rose in California from ten to eighteen, as we saw.[11] Sex with a woman below the age of consent was legally rape, a heavy crime indeed. And the probation system invited the law to peep into bedroom windows, even if the crime was as sexless as burglary or passing bad checks. Some burglars went to prison less for burglary than because they masturbated or patronized brothels, even because they drank and smoked. Many girls (and some boys) went to juvenile homes because they were (in modern jargon) "sexually active," and nothing more. Probation, we pointed out, was a step toward greater humanity, on the whole; some defendants avoided the horror of prison, and went conditionally free. What is interesting is *who* earned

---

five years have been made at the inmates' requests." Harry H. Laughlin, *Eugenical Sterilization in the United States* (Chicago, 1922), pp. 60–61.

9. Paul S. Boyer, *Purity in Print: The Vice-Society Movement and Book Censorship in America* (New York, 1968).

10. There is a large literature on this or that aspect of the outburst of late nineteenth-century and early twentieth-century moral regulation. See David J. Pivar, *Purity Crusade: Sexual Morality and Social Control, 1868–1900* (Westport, Conn., 1973). On the temperance movement, see Joseph Gusfield's seminal work, *Symbolic Crusade: Status Politics and the American Temperance Movement* (Urbana, Ill., 1963); on drugs, see Troy Duster, *The Legislation of Morality: Law, Drugs and Moral Judgment* (New York, 1970), chap. 1.

11. There was a general trend in this direction, by no means confined to California. In Indiana, for example, the age of consent rose in 1893 from twelve to fourteen (Laws Ind. 1893, ch. 23), and in 1907 to sixteen (Laws Ind. 1907, ch. 60).

a second chance, and why. The system had an almost morbid interest in what we call life-style, and in family, background, and habits.

Each generation brands criminal those acts it deems especially dangerous. Changes in the Penal Code, whatever else they mean, show shifts in social judgments about the danger or innocence of conduct. Our period, then, was convinced that teen-age sex was somehow dangerous. Society (or part of it) earnestly believed that gambling, vice, drink, and prostitution had to be wiped out—not winked at, not tolerated, not merely controlled, but destroyed. The question is, why?

We suggest tentatively, two answers, both in the realm of speculation. The first is this: in 1800, in the United States (even more so in England), a small elite group of men ran society. They were educated, cultured, respected. Political, social, and moral leaders came from their ranks. They differed among themselves in many ways, but they shared a common culture and tradition. They were men like Thomas Jefferson, or John Adams, or Washington. (Women, of course, had no political power, and small economic power; they had a certain amount of moral power.) The norms of this group of men were *the* norms of society. Their behavior set the tone for the whole community.

Even earlier, in (say) Massachusetts Bay in the seventeenth century, a single moral standard prevailed. Not that everybody adhered to it, by any means. But those who did not were, if possible, punished. In the court records of Massachusetts Bay, the "crime" we meet most often is fornication. The colony took moral behavior very, very seriously. By the early 1800s, this was no longer true, The modal crime had become theft.[12] The "neglect" of victimless crime, in the nineteenth century, was common to both England and the United States. One reason was lack of means and resources: fornication is no easy crime to ferret out, in growing cities with transient populations. Perhaps a more important reason was that people did not care as much as before. As cities grew and immigration increased, an attitude emerged somewhat like an attitude we attribute to the British upper class. Why expect morality from the common man? Why make a fuss if an apprentice, or a factory worker, sleeps with a servant girl? Only the churches cared; and they were losing their grip. To take an ex-

---

12. On this thesis in general, see William E. Nelson, "Emerging Notions of Modern Criminal Law in the Revolutionary Era: An Historical Perspective," *N.Y.U. L. Rev.* 42 (1967): 450; Lawrence M. Friedman, "Notes toward a History of American Justice," *Buffalo L. Rev.* 24 (1974): 111; Michael S. Hindus, "The Contours of Crime and Justice in Massachusetts and South Carolina, 1767–1878," *Am. J. Legal Hist.* 21 (1977): 212; Hendrik Hartog, "The Public Law of a County Court: Judicial Government in Eighteenth Century Massachusetts," *Am. J. Legal Hist.* 20 (1976): 282, 299–308.

treme case: certainly nobody cared if two black slaves made love. (Legal marriage was forbidden to them, anyway.) Boys will be boys; animals will be animals: useless to look for "higher" aspirations. Wallace, in his study of Rockdale, an industrial village in Pennsylvania, in the first half of the nineteenth century, tells us that the managerial class "definitely looked down on the members of other classes as inferior . . . not merely in education, power, and wealth, but also in moral strength and emotional sensibility." "Women of the lower class" were considered "deficient" in "inner feelings," and "lacking in moral strength." Exceptional individuals could rise above their base; but the classes themselves were "fixed and permanent institutions."[13]

By 1900, the situation was radically different. The old elite was only a memory. A huge, new, middle class had risen to power. There were people who took seriously the idea of one society, one community, one code of moral law, uniform and binding on all, high or low. In a curious way, the idea of a single moral community was a kind of triumph for democracy. *Everybody* ought to be held to one standard— rich and poor, young and old, immigrants and Yankees—everybody. Standards were universal. They were not narrow religious standards, but standards rooted in human nature, and in the needs of society. A community that did not obey moral laws would rot away like ancient Rome, or be laid waste like Sodom and Gomorrah. This led to an upsurge in moral laws, an outburst of legislation, creating new victimless crimes and sharpening old ones. If, in 1820, the system seemed anxious above all to guard a person's goods, in 1900, to put it baldly, it was concerned with souls as well, and with vital bodily fluids. Of course, in the end, the movement was a failure: Prohibition, its proudest achievement, was hooted into oblivion; it became the very symbol of the follies of enforcing an unbending moral code. Drug laws, too, did immense damage to society; their toxic side effects were worse, perhaps, than any chemical poisons. But all that lay in the future.

A second reason is even more fanciful and speculative. It has to do with the nature of individualism. The nineteenth century was obsessed (so runs the cliché) with individualism. The ruling idea was that people could and should get ahead through their own efforts. Government must stay out of their lives as much as possible. It is easy to exaggerate this attitude. It is also easy to misunderstand what people had in mind. The nineteenth century prattled endlessly about

13. Anthony F. C. Wallace, *Rockdale: The Growth of an American Village in the Early Industrial Revolution* (New York, 1978), p. 51.

the individual; but what individual did they have in mind? Certainly not a free spirit, someone who "did his own thing." Would anything horrify the solid citizen of 1880 or 1890 more than the modern counterculture—candle selling, guitar strumming, flame-colored vans, long hair? The Horatio Alger myth did not exalt the free-thinking rebel. The nineteenth-century "individual" was hardworking, moral, moderate in all things. The state did not control this individual, because he was in tight control of himself. Church, family, country, and custom guided him; he needed no external guides. The norms of right conduct were inside him, part of his being, part of his soul.[14]

But what if these inner controls began to crumble (or if people thought they were crumbling)? Then solid citizens might demand social means of keeping society in order. The nineteenth century did without certain restraints because they were not needed. The twentieth century turned to social controls, because people had become *more* genuinely individual, not less. Now there was no agreement on a single moral code, or on the right to prescribe that code. What we might call the moral minorities demanded, not tolerance, not the Victorian compromise, but open legitimation. This meant a culture clash, head on, with the majority. The old moral majority, at bay, turned to the state for help, without hesitation or qualm. They turned to the state and demanded use of that crude, blunt instrument: criminal justice. Hence the crusades to enforce morality through law. The crusades were, in the long run, a failure. But that, as we said, took place after our period was over.

A Last Word on Reform

Criminal justice, in theory *or* practice, has never satisfied everybody. One of the oldest clichés is how rotten it is, how badly it needs reform. Many, many times, waves of reform swept like winds across the face of the system. Our period was one of these times. Juvenile court, probation, parole were introduced into the system; later, the indeterminate sentence was added. Somehow, reforms rarely "worked" in the long run. Sometimes there was no clear idea of goals. Sometimes the theory was wrong: cockeyed ideas about the causes and cures of crime. More important, measures were always

14. Closely connected, of course, were ideas about sexuality. In this sphere, "Lack of control . . . was always seen as animal, as characteristic of a brutal, less highly organized being." Charles E. Rosenberg, *No Other Gods: On Science and American Social Thought* (Baltimore, 1976), p. 131.

very partial. On the whole, reform never really sank its teeth into the system. Reformers made few gains, a yard or two here and there; they never really transformed prisons, or revolutionized trials. Hardliners were no better off. They too could never grab hold, shake the system, forge the cold steel of their dreams. Problems seemed tough and resistant. The *system* was tough and resistant. This was, in a way, rather odd. A system is usually tough and tenacious when it is highly organized, has great strength of norms, and presents a thick hide to the exterior world. Criminal justice, on the other hand, was loose, bumbling, confused.

Yet this was, truth to tell, the source of its strength. "Strength" may not be the right word—"stubbornness," perhaps, or "intractability." The system was (and is) too complex, too disorganized for reform. There are too many little sovereignties, and no one in command. Legislatures grind out rules. Police and detectives find criminals and arrest them. Prosecutors prosecute. Defense lawyers defend. Judges, juries, probation officers, prison guards, the governor—all of these, and others, have parts to play; so too do defendants and their circle; so too do victims and *their* circle. Everybody had his own viewpoint and interests. No one is in control. Everybody can veto suggestions from everybody else. Everybody can make mincemeat out of the work of the others. The police can frustrate rules laid down by judges; judges can undo the work of the police, and can twist rules passed by the legislature. Prosecutors can use their discretion not to prosecute, despite what the other players want. Judge, jury, and police can stalemate prosecutors. Prison guards make nonsense of prison rules; the jury can laugh at principles of law. Some people scream for more iron and blood, some demand fairness or mercy. Both forget that the system is a leaky hose. You can turn the pressure up at one end; but this in itself does not pump out more water at the other. More pressure simply means more leaks. This does not mean that nothing can be changed. Changes take place constantly. But they seem merely to *happen*. They never come through cool and rational planning. Coordination is hopeless or impossible. The system is too gangly, too loose-jointed. It is terribly hard to change from above—or below.

When we look down at the system from our observation post, some ninety years later or so, what we see is a scene of enormous confusion—a great carnival, a circus, a kaleidoscope, a riot of colors and shapes. But this picture fits, theoretically. It is exactly what we should predict. Why should we find anything different? Nothing we know about law and society would lead us to expect the neatness and order of a formal garden. A square, single-purpose system of criminal justice would be as strange, as unforeseen, as a square, one-purpose society. The United States is huge, complex, interdependent; so is each of the states. Social forces are ragged and multiplex, tugging in different directions; the law is a mirror of this ragged multiplicity. In the United States—no doubt elsewhere, too—criminal justice resists deep structural reform. It is decentralized, fragmented, made up of bits and pieces. Such a system is like some huge and primitive beast, with primeval power to regenerate; snip off a leg, an arm, an organ here and there—"rationalize" it if you will—the missing part simply grows back. No brain is in control, no central nervous system. That was true in 1870 or 1910 in Alameda County, California, at the rim of the country, and no doubt true in the core as well. In this respect, at least, nothing has altered since then.

Index

length of, 185; final arguments, 185–86; sensational, 237–38, 237–60 passim; multiple, 255–56; as games, 256; functions of, 259–60. *See also* Jury; New trials; Superior Court
"Tricing," 294–95
Tristan da Cunha, 9

United States Constitution. *See* Constitution (United States)
Usury, constitutionality of, 283

Vagrancy, arrests for, 84, 88, 94n, 109
Vallejo, W. G., 289
Vallejo, 287
Verdicts, in Superior Court, 182, 189–90. *See also* Trials
Vice, war against, 93–95. *See also* Victimless crime
Victimless crime, 11, 143–44, 320–23
Voir dire, 184
Vollmer, August, 75, 77, 84, 92n, 219; and gambling in Berkeley, 93

Voting, illegal, 147

Wallace, Anthony F. C., 322
Waste, William H., 46, 143, 175
Wells, William S., 47, 227, 228n
Whidden, Myron, 53n, 63
White-collar crime, 143
Whitney, Charlotte Anita, 222
Whittier (state reform school), 219–21, 291
Wilkins, Mark, 304; trial of, 266; hanging of, 306–7
Wilson, James Q., 79
Women: lawyers, 57, 60; arrest rates, 107–9; defendants in Superior Court, 151; sentencing of, 217–18; appellants, 264; prisoners, 291, 294; in local jails, 302; and death penalty, 304n
Wong Loung, 280–81, 285

"Yellow journalism," 238
Young, John H., 267